Territorial Disputes in the Americas

Territorial disputes are intricate, shaped by historical, legal, geopolitical, social, cultural and other factors. This book uses a multidimensional approach to assess real case scenarios across the Americas, individually and collectively.

The work evaluates a selected sample of these disputes, tracing origins to colonial histories, unclear border demarcations or uncharted lands, and challenges enforcing legal boundaries. It then explores critical thematic areas, illustrated with compelling examples—disputes entangled with non-American agents like European nations; colonialism, neo-colonial interference and pervasive colonial mindsets; ongoing, regional differences between neighboring states; and the intricate, sometimes conflicting roles of indigenous communities and implanted populations asserting self-determination, often diverging from states' interests. The work reveals sovereignty and disputes intertwine, encompassing plural agents, roles, contexts, realms and modes of existence beyond traditional views. Cases like the Falkland/Malvinas Islands, Mexico-US border, Amazon region and Antarctica highlight how regional organizations and alliances could enhance peacebuilding, strengthen American states against external powers and challenge traditional unidimensional scholarly approaches with a nuanced, comprehensive perspective.

The book will appeal to researchers, academics and policymakers in the areas of Public International Law, Political Science and International Relations, Legal Philosophy, Political Philosophy and Jurisprudence.

Jorge Emilio Núñez is Reader/Associate Professor in Jurisprudence, Political Philosophy and International Relations at Manchester Law School, UK, and Visiting Professor at Facultad de Ciencias Jurídicas y Sociales, UNLP, Argentina.

Territorial Disputes in the Americas

International Law and Politics

Jorge Emilio Núñez

Routledge
Taylor & Francis Group
LONDON AND NEW YORK

First published 2026
by Routledge
4 Park Square, Milton Park, Abingdon, Oxon OX14 4RN

and by Routledge
605 Third Avenue, New York, NY 10158

Routledge is an imprint of the Taylor & Francis Group, an informa business

British Library Cataloguing-in-Publication Data
A catalogue record for this book is available from the British Library

Library of Congress Cataloging-in-Publication Data
Names: Núñez, Jorge E., author.
Title: Territorial disputes in the Americas:
international law and politics / Jorge Emilio Núñez.
Description: Abingdon, Oxon [UK]; New York, NY: Routledge, 2025. |
Includes bibliographical references and index.
Identifiers: LCCN 2025012572 | ISBN 9781032396705 (paperback) |
ISBN 9781032396699 (hardback) | ISBN 9781003350828 (ebook)
Subjects: LCSH: America–Boundaries. |
Territory, National–America. | Sovereignty.
Classification: LCC KZ3684.5.A45 N86 2025 |
DDC 341.4/2–dc23/eng/20250321
LC record available at https://lccn.loc.gov/2025012572

ISBN: 9781032396699 (hbk)
ISBN: 9781032396705 (pbk)
ISBN: 9781003350828 (ebk)

DOI: 10.4324/9781003350828

Typeset in Galliard
by Deanta Global Publishing Services, Chennai, India

A Maria da Graça Xuxa Meneghel,

A Fundação Angelica Goulart (ex Fundação Xuxa Meneghel),

A toda América, una América, más América que norte, sur, central,

A mi pueblo, a mi gente

Contents

Preface

Every book I write takes me on a journey. This one combined rigorous research that included several scholarly disciplines, many languages, jurisdictions, cultures and views as well as my own knowledge, understanding, evaluation and inspiration to be able to offer a new way to, I hope, more comprehensively deal with territorial disputes and sovereignty conflicts in a peaceful and permanent manner. More precisely, these pages combine my vision toward peacebuilding; my theoretical work that explains and articulates that vision; my professional experience in disciplines like law, political science and international relations, both in the academic world and as a practitioner, that have enabled me to bring that vision into reality by integrating otherwise fragmented knowledge, understandings and assessments; and, my personal life that has nurtured that vision since I was a child.

Although this monograph is one of a series of steps pertaining to sovereignty and territorial disputes in the hope of bringing together a body of theory and guidelines that favors cooperation over domination, I must be more precise. This is the first of its kind in the sense that it applies the theoretical framework, including theory and methodology—i.e. the multidimensional approach and the notion of pluralism of pluralisms, hermeneutical and conceptual means and real case scenarios data research, designed and brought together in Núñez (2017), Núñez (2020) and Núñez (2023), the three pillars upon which this and upcoming work are based. Following monographs will be dedicated to applying the frameworks in Núñez (2017), Núñez (2020) and Núñez (2023) in a similar manner and, in that sense, this monograph provides a blueprint for how to more comprehensively understand and assess territorial disputes and sovereignty conflicts encompassing other areas in the world and/or revisit already reviewed cases in more detail.

My gratitude is owed to the many Higher Education institutions, colleagues in disciplines like law, political science, international relations, anthropology, sociology, psychology and history, and the people at large that hosted and were present in the many talks, seminars, colloquiums, roundtables and other events I have delivered around the world. For example, I was blessed to be able to present Núñez (2023) to audiences in places like Greece, Colombia, Peru, Brazil, Argentina, the United Kingdom, Spain, Russia, France and South

Korea. In all cases, I am extremely thankful to those involved in the organization of these events, all attendees and, in particular, those whose comments and questions allow me to keep on learning and, in doing so, sharpen my work to better match my vision.

I am indebted to Gilbert A. Fajardo Torres (Universidad de los Andes, Bogotá, Colombia) and Fabio Fernández (Universidad San Ignacio de Loyola, Lima, Perú) for their research assistance on Chapters 4 and 7, respectively.

As I have done in my previous books, I must mention two collaborations that enrich my mind and soul and are a constant source of inspiration. Therefore, I give special thanks to the Juris North discussion group, of which I am a proud founding member and chair. My deepest gratitude goes to Fundação Angelica Goulart (formerly, Fundação Xuxa Meneghel). In their work, I see real meaning in mine.

I donated the royalties I received from the sales of Núñez (2017), Núñez (2020) and Núñez (2023) to Fundação Angelica Goulart in Pedra de Guaratiba, Rio de Janeiro, Brazil. Our Fundação works tirelessly to empower children, teenagers and adults, and we would appreciate any help you can offer. Many thanks to Vinicius, Barbara, Elaine, Fred, Milton, Simone and our entire team for their mutual and ever-growing collaboration.

For up-to-date details about my work, blog entries, social media contributions or our Fundação, visit my webpage https://drjorge.world

Jorge E. Núñez
La Plata, Argentina
Manchester, United Kingdom
March 2025

Part One

1 Territorial disputes in the Americas

Introduction

Territorial disputes[1] are more topical than ever, especially given the current crisis between Russia and Ukraine. Nevertheless, existing scholarship tends to carefully neglect the fact that these disputes are theorized and evaluated through unidimensional lenses, focusing invariably, for example, on scientific disciplines such as law or political science and neglecting the non-legal, non-political or non-disciplinary angles like rationality, emotion, nationalism, prejudice and other perspectives. This monograph argues that such unidimensional approaches need integration. More precisely, adopting only a disciplinary approach—e.g. only legal or only political—is not enough to fully capture the complexity of these disputes. There is a pressing need for a multidimensional approach that moves away from disciplinary unidimensionality, taking into consideration other elements and factors as they are hedged around issues that are cross-disciplinary or non-disciplinary.[2]

Any situation of crisis requires a coherent, cohesive and comprehensive legal and political response. Territorial disputes are but one example of domestic, regional and international crises. Leaders, organizations and academics around the world are failing to comprehend, assess and address crises in an efficient manner, as clearly shown by COVID-19 and its ramifications in terms of legal and socio-political inequalities; the economic prospect for recovery depending on places and social characteristics such as gender, ethnicity, age, skill levels and local government support; and the effects on the environment. COVID-19 has proved that the randomized approaches to comprehend, assess and address crises only result in ongoing legal and political limbo. Unsurprisingly,

1 A territorial dispute is a disagreement between states about the sovereignty over territory (land or water). For further details including their nature, categories of claims, issues at stake and context see Jorge E. Núñez, *Territorial Disputes and State Sovereignty: International Law and Politics* (London and New York, NY: Routledge, Taylor & Francis Group, 2020), Chapter 4.

2 For details about dimensional understanding including uni- and multidimensionality see Jorge E. Núñez, *Cosmopolitanism, State Sovereignty, International Law and Politics: A Theory* (London and New York, NY: Routledge, Taylor & Francis Group, 2023).

DOI: 10.4324/9781003350828-2

the same is true about other situations of crisis including territorial disputes; pandemics; arms, drug and human trafficking; terrorism; the flow of refugees; and war.

In the particular case of the Americas, there are several territorial disputes.[3] From ongoing cases, such as San Andrés and Providencia and the Falkland/Malvinas Islands, to already settled disputes that still bring controversy, such as the Amazon and the Mexico–United States border, knowledge, understanding and assessment of territorial disputes in the Americas are fragmented. This fragmentation includes different academic and non-academic views of individuals, communities and states on the historical background as well as pertaining to myriad issues such as legal, political and sociological elements and features. A multidimensional approach that incorporates interdisciplinary as well as non-disciplinary understandings is needed because of the multi-faceted and multi-layered nature of territorial disputes. These disputes include issues pertaining to law, politics, nationalism, national identity, natural resources, prestige and many other elements and issues with domestic, regional and international contexts. For example, while an important body of literature examines law and affect, issues of sovereignty are carefully overlooked. On the other hand, when sovereignty is examined it is usually in relation to statehood whereas the notion of affect gets sidestepped; i.e. ignoring the fact that these disputes are often highly emotional, with the participants taking the view that "victory for us is to see you suffer."[4] Directly linked with emotions and nationalism, an ongoing dispute guarantees a higher payoff to leaders' prestige, for example, by distracting from internal issues by identifying an external foe.[5] Indeed, there is a need for researchers and stakeholders to engage in understanding such territorial disputes, and consider how both rational and non-rational factors influence positions across these geopolitical divisions.

Territorial disputes are highly intricate because of their multi-subjective, multi-contextual, multi-faceted and multidimensional nature. Unsurprisingly, the differences in the Americas present that intricacy.[6] Historically, states in the region have been able to resolve their differences peacefully. There are still, however, some ongoing disputes such as the Falkland/Malvinas Islands and

3 For territorial disputes in the Americas see Jorge E. Núñez, *Territorial Disputes and State Sovereignty: International Law and Politics* (London and New York, NY: Routledge, Taylor & Francis Group, 2020), Chapter 6.

4 Philip C. Winslow, *Victory for Us Is To See You Suffer: In the West Bank with the Palestinians and the Israelis* (Boston, MA: Beacon Press, 2007).

5 Jorge E. Núñez, *Territorial Disputes and State Sovereignty: International Law and Politics* (London and New York, NY: Routledge, Taylor & Francis Group, 2020).

6 For a very brief notion of these differences by the author see Jorge E. Núñez, "Territorial Disputes," in Liliana Obregón Tarazona, Laura Betancur-Restrepo and Juan Manuel Amaya Castro, eds., *The Oxford Handbook of International Law and the Americas* (online edn., Oxford: Oxford Academic) available at https://doi.org/10.1093/oxfordhb/9780197661062.001.0001 accessed 5 July 2023.

the San Andrés and Providencia cases. Furthermore, there is actual and potential controversy with issues surrounding the Mexico–United States border, Guantanamo Bay, Antarctica and indigenous rights that share some resemblance to territorial disputes. While some territorial disputes have escalated into conflict, and regional and international elements may explain why there are still a few ongoing disputes, the continent has a tendency for peaceful and permanent resolution. Although the success or failure in peacebuilding depends on several factors, the presence of regional arbitrators and guarantors suggests a higher likelihood for peacebuilding in the Americas.

Different scholarly disciplines including legal and political sciences and international relations, and different regional and international organizations, present a vast array of rules to deal with territorial disputes. These include procedures at the United Nations (UN)[7] and the Organization of American States (OAS)[8] levels such as mediation and conciliation, and remedies like the United Nations trusteeship, the Antarctic Treaty formula, integration or free association of the claimant party and the claimed territory, and the granting of independence.[9] Although these procedures and remedies are useful in certain conflicts, they are futile in others. Noticeably, the research in legal and political sciences pertaining to territorial disputes in general and to territorial disputes in the Americas, in particular, is either outdated or fragmented. First, there is disciplinary fragmentation because of the lack of interdisciplinary studies on territorial disputes. Secondly, there is disciplinary fragmentation because, despite attempts to conduct interdisciplinary studies, they are circumscribed to an element or a feature of a particular dispute.

It is important to acknowledge that these differences, as the examples explored in this monograph will show, are often complex and include several legal as well as extra-legal elements and features. Therefore, to apply a single approach—e.g. only legal, only political—on a single element or feature—e.g. population, territory or government—concerning a single territorial dispute cannot offer a comprehensive understanding of the intricacy of the issue.

7 See for example Article 33 (1) UN Charter, which states: "The parties to any dispute, the continuance of which is likely to endanger the maintenance of international peace and security, shall, first of all, seek a solution by negotiation, enquiry, mediation, conciliation, arbitration, judicial settlement, resort to regional agencies or arrangements, or other peaceful means of their own choice;" and UN General Assembly Resolution 2625 (Declaration on Principles of International Law Concerning Friendly Relations and Cooperation among States, 1970) Article 1: "[…] States shall accordingly seek early and just settlement of their international disputes by negotiation, inquiry, mediation, conciliation, arbitration, judicial settlement, resort to regional agencies or arrangements or other peaceful means of their choice."

8 For details about the OAS see Chapter 2.

9 For a detailed account on dispute resolution procedures and remedies see Jorge E. Núñez, *Sovereignty Conflicts and International Law and Politics: A Distributive Justice Issue* (London and New York, NY: Routledge, Taylor & Francis Group, 2017), Chapter 5, and Jorge E. Núñez, *Territorial Disputes and State Sovereignty: International Law and Politics* (London and New York, NY: Routledge, Taylor & Francis Group, 2020), Chapter 5.

Consequently, this monograph introduces a common set of conceptual and hermeneutical tools to explore and evaluate territorial disputes in the continent. In Núñez (2017)[10] the author conducted a theoretical experiment in which challenger and challenged agents in a sovereignty conflict over a populated third territory were assumed to have certain characteristics. The author assumed certain elements related to the procedure they would follow and particular characteristics in defining the representatives of each population in presupposed negotiations. However, the author made clear the goal was only to come up with an ideal solution that no reasonable party could reject. The author's next step in Núñez (2020)[11] aimed to bring together some key conceptual elements and review them in the context of several ongoing real territorial disputes, including a dedicated chapter that explored territorial disputes in the Americas. In turn, Núñez (2023)[12] introduced a novel theory and methodology. Instead of applying a unidimensional analysis in the assessment of global situations of crisis such as territorial disputes, the author developed a multidimensional approach that acknowledges the pluralism of pluralisms that characterizes them. Therefore, any comprehensive analysis of territorial disputes should include different agents (e.g. individuals, communities and states) acting in their different roles (i.e. hosts, participants, attendees and viewers) and also consider their interrelations in the domestic, regional and international contexts. Moreover, these agents and players interrelating in different contexts should be examined simultaneously by the application of a set of conceptual and hermeneutical tools common to different disciplines such as law, political science and international relations. The ongoing territorial disputes in the Americas as well as other cases that, despite their resolution, still generate controversy are an example of crises that permeate domestic borders and have regional and international influences and ramifications. Following the author's previous work on territorial disputes and state sovereignty, this research monograph assembles the concepts agreed in Núñez (2020), and the approach developed in Núñez (2023), with a detailed focus on territorial disputes in the Americas and shows how the theoretical model created in Núñez (2017) could work in assessing and potentially solving them.

The overarching aim of this monograph, therefore, is to apply a multidimensional approach in order to assess and explain territorial disputes in the Americas. The hypothesis is that such an approach enables to think differently about conflict since all views and claims are considered through a lens of neutrality and context. This is key to regarding conflict as a mechanism

10 Jorge E. Núñez, *Sovereignty Conflicts and International Law and Politics: A Distributive Justice Issue* (London and New York, NY: Routledge, Taylor & Francis Group, 2017), Chapter 6.

11 Jorge E. Núñez, *Territorial Disputes and State Sovereignty: International Law and Politics* (London and New York, NY: Routledge, Taylor & Francis Group, 2020).

12 Jorge E. Núñez, *Cosmopolitanism, State Sovereignty, International Law and Politics: A Theory* (London and New York, NY: Routledge, Taylor & Francis Group, 2023).

for positive change. For instance, the approach helps in considering data and views regardless of their background of origin and the shifting of traditional role-playing within the dispute. Moreover, it may foster the development of tools for future dialogue and neutralize preconceived views about conflict. Furthermore, it promotes the inclusion of emotional intelligence by means of self-awareness of positioning in relation to the dispute arguably based on emotional (non-rational) factors that in time have found or created rationale in law and politics. Lastly, the multidimensional approach supports the "art of questioning" without preconceptions or assumptions.

General structure

The book opens in Part One with a top-down global and interdisciplinary study in order to bring together a common set of conceptual and hermeneutical tools about sovereignty, territorial disputes, the pluralism of pluralisms present in them and the multidimensional approach used in this monograph for their assessment. This is followed in Part Two with a bottom-up domestic and regional set of examples, enabling the application of these theoretical elements and features to real case territorial disputes in the Americas.

The first part of the book will briefly sketch sovereignty, territorial disputes, the notions of pluralism of pluralisms and multidimensionality. Sovereignty is limited in law and politics, and it is because of its limitations that sovereignty can accept pluralism. In a similar vein, territorial disputes assume a plurality of agents, with at least a challenger and a challenged party. Furthermore, the book refers not to pluralism but to the pluralism of pluralisms characteristic in both sovereignty and territorial disputes (whether it is explicitly recognized or not) and moves away from traditional unidimensional scholarly views that may focus only on, for example, either legal or political elements and features discarding, ignoring or simply neglecting others. The second part of the monograph will use territorial disputes in the Americas to illustrate how they embody the complexity of the different claims, issues at stake and other conceptual and hermeneutical elements introduced in the first section. The third and final part makes use of the theoretical elements from Part One and the partial conclusions from Part Two in regard to particular territorial disputes in the Americas and applies them to the case of Antarctica. Furthermore, it includes a set of guidelines and final overall conclusions. In brief, any conflict resolution procedure and remedy will fail to solve these disputes unless they acknowledge the pluralism of pluralisms present in these differences. In a similar vein, if existing understandings of sovereignty and territorial disputes continue, they will only perpetuate a *status quo* and therefore, legal and political uncertainty.

More precisely, this monograph has three parts that are outlined below with chapter synopses:

Part One refers to the current situation in legal and political sciences and international relations in regard to the relationship between sovereignty and territorial disputes, the wrong assumptions and preconceptions that cause bias in the relevant scientific analysis and its application, and a view that proposes a pluralism of pluralisms.

Chapter 1: Introduction

The introduction presents the overall aim of this work, its methodology and potential implications in order to deal more comprehensibly with territorial disputes. It defines the meaning of sovereignty and territorial disputes. It also introduces the notion of pluralism of pluralisms and multidimensionality. In short, the goal is to offer a common conceptual ground for discussion. There are many reasons for the origin and ongoing nature of local, regional and international pervasive negative issues: they are complex in nature (multi-faceted), and although several sciences address them, these sciences (and people at large and their representatives) do not follow a coherent and cohesive approach in assessing and solving them. This chapter, therein, exposes the biases in legal and political sciences and international relations with regard to the relationship between sovereignty and territorial disputes. The answer lies not in rejecting current concepts and creating new ones but in a change of perspective—i.e. from a unidimensional view that centers only on, for example, a particular agent or feature in the dispute, to a multidimensional view that acknowledges their complexity.

Chapter 2: Sovereignty and territorial disputes

Chapter 2 aims to show that sovereignty may be defined by reference to territory but it does not need to (it may refer to, for example, population). This is particularly important in cases in which there are indigenous peoples, implanted populations and differences of interest within the participant states in territorial disputes—i.e. sovereign states are often acknowledged in legal and political sciences and international relations as a single legal and political agent with a singular interest. Moreover, the chapter acknowledges that sovereignty is not absolute, and it is because of its limitations that individuals, communities and states are able to have interrelations in fact and in law with other agents in the form of domination or cooperation.

Thereafter, the chapter considers the reasons how and why territorial disputes start, and why some continue endlessly while others reach a solution. Although relevant, the usual causes for these differences, such as strategic location of territory, its economic value, homogeneity with bordering minorities or political unification, fail to provide a satisfactory and comprehensive explanation. The chapter examines how the domestic context influences the regional and international dimensions and vice versa. The chapter follows Núñez (2020) in arguing that while international elements may explain the escalation into conflict, they do not necessarily explain the reasons that originate the disputes in the first place. Conversely, local and regional elements that give birth to these disputes are not sufficient conditions for their escalation. Empirical data supports these claims.

Finally, at the crossroad between sovereignty and territorial disputes, the chapter introduces the legal and political regional organizations and available means for peacebuilding present in the Americas.

Chapter 3: Pluralism of pluralisms and the multidimensional approach

Both sovereignty and territorial disputes are complex. They involve different agents (for example, individuals, communities and states) that play a role in several contexts (local, regional and international). In addition to this, the complexity expands with the different possible facets of reference, whether purely logical or theoretical, factual or empirical and axiological. Finally, the dimensions where these players interact, coupled with the contexts in which they happen and the science of reference, may add, for example, a vertical or a horizontal angle, time and space to the whole intricacy. Sovereignty and territorial disputes are multi-subjective, multi-contextual and multi-faceted. In brief, they are multidimensional and, consequently, require a multidimensional analysis if the aim is to fully comprehend them and to tackle crisis. This chapter introduces the notion of pluralism of pluralisms present in territorial disputes; this notion includes agents and players, contexts, realms and modes of existence, dimensions, time and space. The multidimensional approach is proposed as a means to assess and explain more comprehensively these differences.

Part Two refers specifically to territorial disputes in the context of the Americas. With former colonial powers dividing the territory with little regard to, for example, the sociological and cultural components, these differences find their roots in a common past. Importantly, this section refers to the tension between the right of indigenous peoples versus the European "right-peopling."[13] A crucial lesson that stems from the region in solving territorial disputes is explored—i.e. the role of regional guarantors in enabling a permanent and peaceful understanding between the challenger and challenged agents.

Chapter 4: Common roots to the territorial disputes in America

There are common roots to the territorial disputes in America.[14] Colonial empires divided the territory with little regard to native communities and the

13 Oded Haklai and Nephytos Loizides, "Settlers and Conflict Over Contested Territories," in Oded Haklai and Neophytos Loizides, eds., *Settlers in Contested Lands. Territorial Disputes and Ethnic Conflicts* (Stanford, CA: Stanford University Press, 2015), 1–16.

14 David Downing, *An Atlas of Territorial and Border Disputes* (London: New English Library, 1980), 84; Peter Calvert, *Boundary Disputes in Latin America* (London: Institute for the Study of Conflict, 1983); Jack Child, *Geopolitics and Conflict in South America* (New York, NY: Praeger, 1985); Gordon Ireland, *Boundaries, Possessions, and Conflicts in South America* (Cambridge, MA: Harvard University Press, 1938); and many more.

environment. Consequently, domestic and regional conflict brought about other evils such as poverty, humanitarian crises, arms trafficking and guerrilla warfare.[15] The chapter classifies these common roots to dispute into three clearly defined historical periods and characterizes each of them: pre-Columbian times; post-Columbian but pre-independence times; and post-independence times.

In pre-Columbian times there was a large population, estimated to be up to 112 million, that included organized empires such as the Aztecs, Mayas and Incas as well as smaller tribes and nomads.[16] Territorial disputes existed mainly because of the expansion of empires.[17] However, it is only with the European presence in the continent that the native population was reduced dramatically.[18] In turn, the post-Columbian but pre-independence period comprised European colonizers invading the land and annihilating the local empires.[19] In time, European states applied their legal and political understanding to America. Examples of this practice are the Papal bulls of Alexander VI: *Inter caetera*, *Inter caetera II*, *Eximiae devotionis* and *Dudum siquidem*. Natives were not acknowledged rights. Finally, post-independence times see the arrival of newly established states in America and the adoption of the *uti possidetis juris* principle.[20] Consequently, these states claimed *de jure* sovereignty over territories in which they already had *de facto* presence.[21] Because the borders that were agreed or simply accepted in fact by the European empires were in

15 Paul R. Hensel, "One Thing Leads to Another: Recurrent Militarized Disputes in Latin America, 1816–1986," *Journal of Peace Research* 31:3 (1994): 281–297; Paul R. Hensel, "Contentious Issues and World Politics: The Management of Territorial Claims in the Americas, 1816–1992," *International Studies Quarterly* 45:1 (2001): 81–109.

16 William M. Denevan, *The Native Population of the Americas in 1492* (Madison, WI: University of Wisconsin Press, 1992); Henry F. Dobyns, "An Appraisal of Techniques with a New Hemispheric Estimate," *Current Anthropology* 7:4 (1966): 395–416.

17 Geoffrey W. Conrad and Arthur A. Demarset, *Religion and Empire: The Dynamics of Aztec and Inca Expansionism* (Cambridge: Cambridge University Press, 1984).

18 Noble David Cook, *Born to Die: Disease and the New World Conquest, 1492–1650* (Cambridge: Cambridge University Press, 1998).

19 Linda A. Newson, "The Demographic Collapse of Native Peoples of the Americas, 1492–1650," *Proceedings of the British Academy* 81 (1993): 247–288.

20 For the difference between *uti possidetis de facto* and *uti possidetis de jure* see Frederic William Ganzert, "The Boundary Controversy in the Upper Amazon between Brazil, Bolivia, and Peru, 1903–1909," *Hispanic American Historical Review* 14:4 (1934): 427–449, 430ff.; Jonathan I. Charney and Lewis M. Alexander, eds., *International Maritime Boundaries, Volume I* (Boston, MA: Martinus Nijhoff, 1996), 777–783.

21 Steven R. Ratner, "Drawing a Better Line: *Uti Possidetis* and the Borders of New States," *American Journal of International Law* 90:4 (1996): 590–624; Malcom N. Shaw, *International Law* (Cambridge: Cambridge University Press, 2003), 446–451; Ian Brownlie, *Principles of Public International Law* (Oxford: Oxford University Press, 2003), 129–130; and many others.

many cases either unclear or non-existent, territorial disputes between newly sovereign states in the continent followed.[22]

Chapter 5: Ongoing European influence in the Americas

The Falkland/Malvinas Islands dispute[23] between Argentina and the United Kingdom is probably the most noticeable example of the enduring European colonial legacy in America. There are, however, other cases related to ongoing European presence in the continent such as the Hans Island dispute[24] (Canada and Denmark) and the Marouini River tract dispute[25] (Suriname and French Guiana). Furthermore, the settled territorial dispute over the archipelago of San Andrés, Providencia and Santa Catalina provides examples of several issues involving domestic, regional and international contexts that include the tension between a local ethnic and racial minority (Raizal community) and the Colombian state's interests.[26] Similar in that respect to the Falklands/Malvinas case, the San Andrés, Providencia and Santa Catalina situation involves the presence of a population implanted by a former colonial power.

The chapter introduces these cases to demonstrate that, on the surface, the differences seem to center on very clearly defined claims and issues at stake

22 Alan J. Day, ed., *Border and Territorial Disputes* (Essex: Longman, 1982), 332–333.

23 See Jorge E. Núñez, *Territorial Disputes and State Sovereignty: International Law and Politics* (London and New York, NY: Routledge, Taylor & Francis Group, 2020), Chapter 6; Jorge E. Núñez, *Sovereignty Conflicts and International Law and Politics: A Distributive Justice Issue* (London and New York, NY: Routledge, Taylor & Francis Group, 2017), Chapter 7; Alan J. Day, ed., *Border and Territorial Disputes* (Essex: Longman, 1982), 340–345; Peter Beck, *The Falkland Islands as an International Problem* (London and New York, NY: Routledge, 1998); Peter Beck, "The Future of the Falkland Islands: A Solution Made in Hong Kong?" *International Affairs* 61 (1985): 643–660; Peter Beck, "Looking at the Falkland Islands from Antarctica: The Broader Regional Perspective," *Polar Record* 30 (1994): 167–180; Peter Beck, "Britain's Falkland Future—the Need to Look Back," *The Round Table* 73 (1984): 139–152; Peter Beck, "Cooperative Confrontation in the Falkland Island Dispute," *Journal of Inter-American Studies and World Affairs* 24 (1982): 37–57. For official historical accounts see http://www.falklands.gov.fk/our-people/our-history/ (UK) and https://www.cancilleria.gob.ar/es/politica-exterior/cuestion-malvinas/antecedentes/antecedentes-historicos (Argentina), both accessed 23 June 2023.

24 Christopher Stevenson, "Hans Off!: The Struggle for Hans Island and the Potential Ramifications for International Border Dispute Resolution," *Boston College International and Comparative Law Review* 30:1 (2007): 263–275; A. H. Kessel, "Canadian Arctic Sovereignty: Myths and Realities," in D. A. Berry, N. Bowles and H. Jones, eds., *Governing the North American Arctic* (London: Palgrave Macmillan, 2016), 242–246.

25 Thomas W. Donovan, "The Marouini River Tract and Its Colonial Legacy in South America," *Chicago-Kent Journal of International and Comparative Law* 4 (2004): 1–28.

26 Pablo Alonso González, Wilhelm Londoño and Eva Parga-Dans, "Equality and Hierarchy, Sovereignty and Multiculturalism: The Heritagisation of Raizals in Santa Catalina (Colombia)," *Journal of Ethnic and Migration Studies* 46:19 (2018): 4066–4085; James Ross, "Routes for Roots: Entering the 21st Century in San Andrés Island, Colombia," *Caribbean Studies* 35:1 (2007): 3–36.

between specific claiming agents. However, these territorial disputes include a myriad of actual and potential elements such as the historical and legal claims, the principle of territorial integrity, the economic value of natural resources and their exploration and exploitation, the geostrategic location and, in some cases, their importance as a link to claims in Antarctica. Moreover, the disputes include a combination of domestic, regional and international contexts fostering a stalemate. Domestically, although a stalemate may seem negative and governments are assumed to seek peaceful and permanent dispute settlements, the *status quo* serves other purposes to local politics because it guarantees an endless legal and political limbo that benefits a leader's position.[27] Finally, the international context plays a role in terms of prestige because great powers would opt to go to war to preserve their status even if the practical results seemed trivial.[28]

Chapter 6: Neo-colonialism and colonial mindset

This chapter explores past and ongoing influence pertaining to the origin, continuation and potential escalation into conflict of territorial disputes in the region, but with a focus on central sovereign states beyond European influence. For instance, in modern times, Latin America has been under the influence of either the United States or Russia. More currently, while the United States has had (and still does have) different degrees of interference in domestic and regional legal and political agendas of other states in the continent, there are other sovereign states such as China, India and Russia with a strong direct and indirect presence and ascendancy.

The chapter refers to the notion of domination applied to the interrelation between agents such as individuals, communities and sovereign states. Some territorial disputes in the Americas can be characterized as being intertwined with different forms of domination, namely colonialism, neo-colonialism and colonial mindset. By presenting several examples, the chapter discusses these different forms of domination that have resulted in territorial disputes. Broadly, domination implies the ability agents may have to pursue their own interests at the expense of others in an unrestrained and systematic way.[29] The

27 Huth explains how an ongoing dispute can benefit leaders. Paul K. Huth, *Standing Your Ground: Territorial Disputes and International Conflict* (Ann Arbor, MI: University of Michigan Press, 2001), 171–172 and 178–179.

28 Matthieu Grandpierron, "Preserving 'Great Power Status': The Complex Case of the British Intervention in the Falklands (1982)," *Croatian International Relations Review* 23:79 (2017): 127–156.

29 Cecile Laborde, "Republicanism and Global Justice: A Sketch," *European Journal of Political Theory* 9 (2010): 48–69. For a more detailed account about republican freedom and non-domination see Lena Halldenius, "Building Blocks of a Republican Cosmopolitanism: The Modality of Being Free," *European Journal of Political Theory* 9:1 (2010): 12–30; and Philip Pettit, "A Republican Law of Peoples," *European Journal of Political Theory* 9:1 (2010): 70–94. For the author's views on domination and non-domination see Jorge E. Núñez, *Sov-*

cases explored in the chapter are selected to show that central states like the United States, Russia, China and India use different mechanisms to either involve themselves directly in the region by means of the role they play in territorial disputes—i.e. neo-colonialism, or involve themselves indirectly, by manipulating the way in which they are perceived by regional agents in order to secure them regional standing—i.e. colonial mindset.

Chapter 7: Americans versus Americans

In contrast to the cases of the Mexico–United States border and Guantanamo Bay, other territorial disputes in the continent present agents with similar bargaining power. Nevertheless, in these cases the disputes are originated and fueled by other features such as historical roots, exploration and exploitation of natural resources and sociological, ethnic and cultural components.

Colonial legacies, the 1982 United Nations Convention on the Law of the Sea and redefinition of areas (for example, as exclusive economic zones), new technologies and the presence of natural resources have resulted in several differences arising in the Caribbean, in places such as Guatemala and Belize,[30] Guyana and Suriname,[31] Venezuela and Guyana,[32] Nicaragua and Costa Rica and El Salvador and Honduras.[33]

Most of the territorial disputes in the Amazon[34] and the Southern Cone are now resolved. They all had their roots in colonial times. There are, however, several hallmarks in relation to territorial disputes in these areas: a territory rich in natural resources attracts domestic, regional and international agents[35] such

ereignty Conflicts and International Law and Politics: A Distributive Justice Issue (London and New York, NY: Routledge, Taylor & Francis Group, 2017), Chapter 4.

30 Alma H. Young and Dennis H. Young, "The Impact of the Anglo-Guatemalan Dispute on the Internal Politics of Belize," *Latin American Perspectives* 15:2 (1988): 6–30; William Bianchi, *Belize: The Controversy between Guatemala and Great Britain over the Territory of British Honduras in Central America* (New York, NY: Las Americas, 1959).

31 Thomas W. Donovan, "Suriname-Guyana Maritime and Territorial Disputes: A Legal and Historical Analysis," *Journal of Transnational Law and Policy* 13:1 (2003): 41–98.

32 Thomas W. Donovan, "Challenges to the Territorial Integrity of Guyana: A Legal Analysis," *Georgia Journal of International and Comparative Law* 32 (2004): 661–724; Jacqueline Braveboy-Wagner, *The Venezuela-Guyana Border Dispute* (Boulder, CO: Westview Press, 1984).

33 L. H. Martin and Y. B. Parkhomenko, "The Territorial and Maritime Dispute (Nicaragua v. Colombia) and Its Implications for Future Maritime Delimitations in the Caribbean Sea and Elsewhere," in E. Sobenes Obregon and B. Samson, eds., *Nicaragua Before the International Court of Justice* (Cham: Springer, 2018), 113–141; Martin Pratt, "The Maritime Boundary Dispute between Honduras and Nicaragua in the Caribbean Sea," *Boundary and Security Bulletin* 9:2 (2001): 106–116.

34 Note the author uses the terms Amazonia or Amazon rainforest to refer to the geographical area in which many sovereign states in South America may have sovereignty claims.

35 Paul E. Little, *Amazonia: Territorial Struggles on Perennial Frontiers* (Baltimore, MD: Johns Hopkins University Press, 2001).

as sovereign states, indigenous peoples, non-governmental organizations, multinational private companies and scientists; and politicians and academics seem to agree that the internationalization[36] of the Amazon is not advisable. Other current issues[37] include illegal cross-border immigration and differences over resource extraction; border reconfiguration[38] can emerge as a social construction; indigenous communities[39] do not necessarily conform to legally defined borders and their claims to ethno-territorial rights are usually opposed to the interests of sovereign states and private companies; and the presence of external guarantors suggests an arguably more robust peaceful agreement. For example, the guarantors[40] were key in the final dispute resolution between Ecuador and Peru[41] achieved by the 1998 Brasilia Peace Agreement.[42]

Chapter 8: Indigenous rights and implanted populations

Chapter 8 exposes a puzzling issue in law and politics: in the context of international law and politics, settlers are considered "persons" and may be able to claim the territory they inhabit, while the legal and political status of indigenous populations is still unsettled.

36 See the speech by Cristovam Buarque, Professor at the University of Brasilia, former candidate for the Presidency of Brazil (2006), former District Governor and Senator, in *Revista Diálogo Educacional* 3:5 (2002): 107–108 available (in Portuguese) at https://periodicos.pucpr.br/index.php/dialogoeducacional/article/download/4753/4705 accessed 23 June 2023. There are many resources in Portuguese opposed to the internationalization of Amazonia that are not translated into English. See, for example, Pio Penna Filho, "Interações Regionais e Pressões Internacionais sobre a Pan-Amazônia: Perspectivas Brasileiras," in Gilberto F. Gheller, Selma L. M. Gonzales and Laerte P. Mello, eds., *Amazônia e Atlântico Sul: Desafios e Perspectivas para a Defesa no Brasil* (Brasilia: IPEA, 2015), 149–184; Arthur C. F. Reis, "A Amazônia e a Integridade do Brasil" (Brasilia: Senado Federal Conselho Editorial, 2001); and many more.

37 Ligia T. L. Simonian and Rubens da Silva Ferreira, "Brazilian Migrant Workers in French Guiana," in Ruben Gowricharn, ed., *Caribbean Transnationalism: Migration, Pluralization, and Social Cohesion* (Lanham, MD: Lexington Books, 2006), 99–116.

38 Laetitia Perrier Buslé, "Multi-Scalar Perspectives and Multi-Agent Process in a South American Borderland Region," *Geopolitics* 18:3 (2013): 584–611.

39 Markus Kröger and Rickard Lalander, "Ethno-Territorial Rights and the Resource Extraction Boom in Latin America: Do Constitutions Matter?" *Third World Quarterly* 37:4 (2016): 682–702.

40 Complete text of the 1942 Rio de Janeiro Protocol available at https://www.cia.gov/library/readingroom/docs/CIA-RDP08C01297R000700110015-9.pdf accessed 23 June 2023.

41 David Scott Palmer, "Peru-Ecuador Border Conflict: Missed Opportunities, Misplaced Nationalism, and Multilateral Peacekeeping," *Journal of Interamerican Studies and World Affairs* 39:3 (1997): 109–148.

42 Complete text of the 1998 Brasilia Peace Agreement (in Spanish) available at https://www.usip.org/sites/default/files/file/resources/collections/peace_agreements/ep_brasilia10261998.pdf accessed 23 June 2023; Monica Herz and João Pontes Nogueira, *Ecuador vs. Peru: Peacemaking Amid Rivalry* (London: Lynne Rienner, 2002), 97–100.

Colonial empires discarded claims to the territories by indigenous peoples.[43] Indigenous peoples were not legally "persons" or they were considered inferior.[44] Internationally, there seems to be a move toward supporting indigenous rights but in relation to issues other than territorial claims.[45] Regional states are reviewing[46] the way they interact with these populations.[47] Arguably, self-determination and consequent self-government could be the next steps in this legal evolution toward the recognition of indigenous rights in relation to territorial disputes.[48]

While the legal and political status of indigenous populations is in question in terms of territorial disputes,[49] the Americas also include populations that were at one time settlers and nowadays claim self-determination, such as the Falkland/Malvinas Islanders. "Right-peopling"[50] the territory with settlers was a way in which some former colonial powers (and, arguably, some modern states like Israel) secured their claim to sovereignty over new territories.

Part Three brings together the theoretical elements from Parts One and Two, showing how they can be used to assess and potentially solve territorial disputes and suggesting some guidelines for policymaking in regard to dealing with crisis.

43 M. F. Lindley, *The Acquisition and Government of Backward Territory in International Law: Being a Treatise on the Law and Practice Relating to Colonial Expansion* (New York, NY: Negro University Press, 1969), 11–12.

44 Jérémie Gilbert, *Indigenous Peoples' Land Rights under International Law: From Victors to Actors* (Ardsley, NY: Transnational, 2006), 1–2.

45 Jérémie Gilbert, "Indigenous Rights in the Making: The United Nations Declaration on the Rights of Indigenous Peoples," *International Journal on Minority and Group Rights* 14 (2007): 207–230.

46 Allen Gerlach, *Indians, Oil, and Politics: A Recent History of Ecuador* (Wilmington, NC: Scholarly Resources, 2003).

47 Austen L. Parrish, "Changing Territoriality, Fading Sovereignty, and the Development of Indigenous Rights," *American Indian Law Review* 31:2 (2006/2007): 291–313; Willem van Genugten and Camillo Perez-Bustillo, "The Emerging International Architecture of Indigenous Rights: The Interaction between Global, Regional, and National Dimensions," *International Journal on Minority and Group Rights* 11 (2004): 379–409; Gemma van der Haar, "The Zapatista Uprising and the Struggle for Indigenous Autonomy," *European Review of Latin American and Caribbean Studies* 76 (2004): 98–108; Donna Lee Van Cott, "Broadening Democracy: Latin America's Indigenous Peoples' Movements," *Current History* 103 (2004): 80–85; Shane Greene, "Getting Over the Andes: The Geo-Eco-Politics of Indigenous Movements in Peru's Twenty-First Century Inca Empire," *Journal of Latin American Studies* 38:2 (2006): 327–354.

48 See, for example, the United States and the case of Hawaii in Keri E. Iyall Smith, *The State and Indigenous Movements* (New York, NY: Routledge, 2006).

49 Rachel Sieder, "Indigenous Peoples' Rights and the Law in Latin America," in Corinne Lennox and Damien Short, eds., *Handbook of Indigenous Peoples' Rights* (London and New York, NY: Routledge, 2016), 414–423.

50 Brendan O'Leary, "The Elements of Right-Sizing and Right-Peopling the State," in Brendan O'Leary, Ian S. Lustick and Thomas Callaghy, eds., *Right-Sizing the State: The Politics of Moving Borders* (Oxford: Oxford University Press, 2001), 15–73.

Chapter 9: Territorial claims over Antarctica

The Antarctic Treaty[51] mostly refers to scientific exploration of Antarctica and, therefore, in terms of sovereignty the legal situation is a *status quo ante*.[52] Whether it is futile or not to refer to the question about sovereign rights in Antarctica in light of the Antarctic Treaty,[53] it is still a fact there are seven states with territorial claims—i.e. Argentina, Australia, Chile, France, New Zealand, Norway and the United Kingdom—with others such as the Russian Federation and the United States with research facilities in the area and many more interested agents like Brazil, China, India and other Indian Ocean states.[54]

Núñez (2020) included some basic guidelines for a permanent and peaceful understanding in Antarctica such as that sovereignty can be shared and that any arrangements should avoid domination, guarantee equal footing in the decision-making process and be independent from the United Nations system legally and politically. In the same vein, this chapter explores these guidelines in light of the multidimensional approach presented in Part One and the partial conclusions from the chapters in Part Two under the ideal circumstances designed in Núñez (2017).

51 For a complete version of the Antarctic Treaty see http://www.ats.aq/documents/ats/treaty_original.pdf accessed 23 June 2023.

52 Article IV of the Antarctic Treaty refers to territorial claims: "1. Nothing contained in the present Treaty shall be interpreted as: (a) a renunciation by any Contracting Party of previously asserted rights of or claims to territorial sovereignty in Antarctica; (b) a renunciation or diminution by any Contracting Party of any basis of claim to territorial sovereignty in Antarctica which it may have whether as a result of its activities or those of its nationals in Antarctica, or otherwise; (c) prejudicing the position of any Contracting Party as regards its recognition or non recognition of any other State's right of or claim or basis of claim to territorial sovereignty in Antarctica. 2. No acts or activities taking place while the present Treaty is in force shall constitute a basis for asserting, supporting or denying a claim to territorial sovereignty in Antarctica. No new claim, or enlargement of an existing claim, to territorial sovereignty shall be asserted while the present Treaty is in force." See J. Peter A. Bernhardt, "Sovereignty in Antarctica," *California Western International Journal* 5 (1975): 297–349.

53 Benedetto Conforti, "Territorial Claims in Antarctica: A Modern Way to Deal with an Old Problem," *Cornell International Law Journal* 19:2 (1986): 249–258.

54 For a very comprehensive study see Anne-Marie Brady, ed., *The Emerging Politics of Antarctica* (Oxford and New York, NY: Routledge, 2013). See also Klaus Dodds, Alan D. Hemmings and Peder Roberts, eds., *Handbook on the Politics of Antarctica* (Cheltenham: Edward Elgar Publishing, 2017); Wei-chin Lee, "China and Antarctica: So Far and Yet So Near," *Asian Survey* 30:6 (1990): 576–586; Anne-Marie Brady, "China's Rise in Antarctica?" *Asian Survey* 50:4 (2010): 759–785; Jonathan Harrington, "China in Antarctica: A History," *Southeast Review of Asian Studies* 37 (2015): 1–19; Anne-Marie Brady, *China as a Polar Great Power* (Cambridge: Cambridge University Press, 2017); Christopher C. Joyner, "Antarctica and the Indian Ocean States: The Interplay of Law, Interests, and Geopolitics," *Ocean Development and International Law* 21:1 (1990): 41–70; and many others.

Chapter 10: Conclusive remarks, limitations and implications

The last chapter brings together the main points of this monograph. It highlights the book's explanatory importance in legal and political sciences and international relations and shows further possible application of the conceptual and hermeneutical tools and multidimensional approach to other disputes.

Aims, rationale and objectives

Territorial disputes have at least two claiming parties arguing over the exclusive sovereignty of the same territory. The challenger and the challenged agents will have their own reasons to claim sovereignty. Moreover, there may be a myriad of issues at stake with links of different natures to the domestic, regional and international contexts. Although territorial disputes have been and are the object of study of many sciences—i.e. law, political science, international relations, only to name a few—these disciplines apply different methodological approaches, assumptions, views and conceptual bases resulting in incomplete perceptions of the same territorial dispute.

In order to demonstrate the fragmentation (either by science or by object of study) of current scholarly publications about territorial disputes in general, and of territorial disputes in the Americas in particular, three lists are presented below to provide a range of examples:[55]

1. Latest monographs on territorial disputes (in descending chronological order)

López-Flores, Pabel C. and Penelope Anthias, eds., *Neoextractivism and Territorial Disputes in Latin America: Social-ecological Conflict and Resistance on the Front Lines* (London and New York, NY: Routledge, Taylor & Francis Group, 2023).

Frettingham, Edmund and Yih-Jye Hwang, eds., *Maritime and Territorial Disputes in the South China Sea: Faces of Power and Law in the Age of China's Rise* (London and New York, NY: Routledge, Taylor & Francis Group, 2021).

Garcia, Zenel, *China's Military Modernization, Japan's Normalization and the South China Sea* (Cham: Palgrave Macmillan, 2019).

Kohen, Marcelo G. and Mamadou Hébié, eds., *Research Handbook on Territorial Disputes in International Law* (Cheltenham and Northampton: Edward Elgar Publishing Ltd., 2018).

Plant, Brendan, *International Law and the Adjudication of Territorial Disputes* (Oxford: Oxford University Press, 2018).

55 For a complete list of sources on territorial disputes related to the Americas and other regions in the world see Jorge E. Núñez, *Territorial Disputes and State Sovereignty: International Law and Politics* (London and New York, NY: Routledge, Taylor & Francis Group, 2020).

Murdoch, David, *Territorial Disputes* (CreateSpace Independent Publishing Platform, 2017).

Guo, Rongxing, *Territorial Disputes and Conflict Management* (New York, NY: Routledge, 2014).

Pinfari, Marco, *Peace Negotiations and Time: Deadline Diplomacy in Territorial Disputes* (New York, NY: Routledge, 2012).

Jeffrey, S. B., *Border Wars: Politics and Territorial Disputes* (Webster's Digital Services, 2011).

Kolers, Avery, *Land, Conflict, and Justice: A Political Theory of Territory* (Cambridge: Cambridge University Press, 2011).

Wiegand, Krista Eileen, *Enduring Territorial Disputes: Strategies of Bargaining, Coercive Diplomacy and Settlements* (Athens, GA: University of Georgia Press, 2011).

Guo, Rongxing, *Territorial Disputes and Resource Management: A Global Handbook* (London: Nova Science Pub. Inc., 2006).

Tir, Jaroslav, *Redrawing the Map to Promote Peace: Territorial Dispute Management Via Territorial Changes* (Lanham, MD: Lexington Books, 2006).

Calvert, Peter, *Border and Territorial Disputes* (London: John Harper Publishing, 2004).

2. Global sources (in alphabetical order)

Allock, John *et al.*, *Border and Territorial Disputes* (London: Longman, 1992).

Anderson, Ewan, *An Atlas of World Political Flashpoints* (London: Pinter Publishers, 1993).

Brecher, Michael *et al.*, *Crises in the Twentieth Century*, vol. 1 (New York, NY: Pergamon Press, 1988).

Brogan, Patrick, *The Fighting Never Stopped* (New York, NY: Vintage Books, 1990).

Butterworth, Robert, *Managing Interstate Conflict, 1945–74: Data with Synopses* (Pittsburgh, PA: University Center for International Studies, University of Pittsburgh, 1976).

Central Intelligence Agency, *The World Factbook* (Washington, DC: Government Printing Office, ongoing).

Day, Alan, ed., *Border and Territorial Disputes* (London: Longman, 1987).

Downing, David, *An Atlas of Territorial Border Disputes* (London: New English Library Limited, 1980).

Grundy-Warr, Carl, ed., *International Boundaries and Boundary Conflict Resolution* (Durham: International Boundaries Research Unit, University of Durham, 1990).

International Boundary Study (Washington, DC: The Geographer, Bureau of Intelligence and Research, Department of State, ongoing).

James, Alan, *Peacekeeping in International Politics* (London: International Institute for Strategic Studies, 1990).

Kacowicz, Arie, *Peaceful Territorial Change* (Columbia: University of South Carolina Press, 1994).

Kratochwil, Friederich *et al.*, *Peace and Disputes Sovereignty: Reflections on Conflict over Territory* (Lanham, MD: University Press of America, 1985).

Munro, David and Day, Alan, *A World Record of Major Conflict Areas* (London: Edward Arnold, 1990).

Prescott, J.R.V., *Political Frontiers and Boundaries* (Boston: Allen & Unwin, 1987).

Sharma, Surya, *International Boundary Disputes and International Law* (Bombay: N.M. Tripathi Private Limited, 1976).

Tillema, Herbert, *International Armed Conflict since 1945* (Boulder, CO: Westview Press, 1991).

Yearbook of the United Nations (New York, NY: United Nations, ongoing).

3. Sources pertaining to territorial disputes in Central and South America (in alphabetical order)

Beck, Peter, "Cooperative Confrontation in the Falkland Island Dispute," *Journal of Interamerican Studies and World Affairs* 24 (1982): 37–57.

Beck, Peter, "Britain's Falkland Future—the Need to Look Back," *The Round Table* 73 (1984): 139–152.

Beck, Peter, "The Future of the Falkland Islands: A Solution Made in Hong Kong?" *International Affairs, Royal Institute of International Affairs* 61 (1985): 643–660.

Beck, Peter, "Looking at the Falkland Islands from Antarctica: The Broader Regional Perspective," *Polar Record* 30 (1994): 167–180.

Beck, Peter, *The Falkland Islands as an International Problem* (London and New York, NY: Routledge, 1998).

Bender, Lynn, *Cuba vs. United States* (San Juan: Inter American University Press, 1981).

Bianchi, William, *Belize: The Controversy between Guatemala and Great Britain over the Territory of British Honduras in Central America* (New York, NY: Las Americas Publishing Co., 1959).

Braveboy-Wagner, Jacqueline, *The Venezuela-Guyana Border Dispute* (Boulder, CO: Westview Press, 1984).

Bustamante, Fernando, "Ecuador: Putting an End to Ghosts of the Past?" *Journal of Interamerican Studies and World Affairs* 34 (1992–93): 195–224.

Calvert, Peter, *Boundary Disputes in Latin America* (London: Institute for the Study of Conflict, 1983).

Charlton, Michael, *The Little Platoon: Diplomacy and the Falklands Dispute* (New York, NY: Blackwell, 1989).

Child, Jack, *Geopolitics and Conflict in South America* (New York, NY: Praeger, 1985).

DeSoto, Anthony, *Bolivia's Right to an Access to the Sea* (Pasadena, CA: Jensen Publishing Co., 1962).

Farnsworth, David and McKenney, James, *U.S.–Panama Relations 1903–1978* (Boulder, CO: Westview, 1983).

Ireland, Gordon, *Boundaries, Possessions, and Conflicts in South America* (Cambridge, MA: Harvard University Press, 1938).

Jessup, Philip, "El Chamizal," *American Journal of International Law* 67 (1973): 423–445.

Kinney, Douglas, *National Interest/National Honor: The Diplomacy of the Falklands Crisis* (New York, NY: Praeger, 1989).

Krieg, William, *Ecuadorean-Peruvian Rivalry in the Upper Amazon* (Bethesda, MD: William Krieg, 1986).

LaFeber, Walter, *The Panama Canal* (New York, NY: Oxford University Press, 1978).

Lamborn, Alan and Mumme, Stephen, *Statecraft, Domestic Politics, and Foreign Policy Making: The El Chamizal Dispute* (Boulder, CO: Westview Press, 1988).

Lanus, Juan, *De Chapultepec al Beagle: Política Exterior Argentina* (Buenos Aires: Emece Editores, 1984).

Liss, Sheldon, *A Century of Disagreement* (Washington, DC: The University Press, 1965).

Manfedo, Jr., Fernando, "The Future of the Panama Canal," *Journal of Interamerican Studies and World Affairs* 35 (1993): 103–128.

Moraga, Oscar, *El Precio de la Paz Chileno-Argentina* (Santiago: Editorial Nascimento, 1969).

Osborne, Alfred, "On the Economic Cost to Panama of Negotiating a Peaceful Solution to the Panama Canal Question," *Journal of Interamerican Studies and World Affairs* 19 (1977): 509–521.

Zammit, J. Ann, *The Belize Issue* (London: Latin American Bureau, 1978).

Zook, David, *Zarumilla y Marañón: The Ecuador-Peru Dispute* (New York, NY: Bookman Associates Inc., 1964).

By acknowledging the complex, multi-level and multi-faceted nature of territorial disputes, this monograph applies a multidimensional approach to assess certain real case scenarios in part and as a whole. In contrast to a unidimensional analysis that may relate to one science, refer to one territorial dispute or, more often, to one feature in a given territorial dispute, the multidimensional approach includes several aspects such as claims, issues at stake and different contexts.

This monograph aims to introduce and explore in depth a sample of some of the territorial disputes in the Americas by application of a multidimensional approach. First, it introduces the common roots in all cases: the historical component based on colonial times and the lack of clear border demarcation at the time or, in the cases in which the demarcation had taken place in law, the difficulty in applying the decision to the areas in question. Thereafter, three main thematic areas and some controversial examples in each area are reviewed, as follows: cases that include a participant in the dispute outside the

American continent; interference by central states such as the United States in other more permeable states; and ongoing territorial disputes between states in the region.

The sample introduced and explored in this analysis provides relevant indications of the origin of these disputes. Together with the historical background and the lack of clearly defined boundaries in colonial times, current international law such as the Law of the Sea, new technologies for exploration and exploitation of natural resources, the existence or absence of indigenous or implanted populations in the territories under question, and several other elements result in multi-faceted and multi-layered territorial disputes.

Some preliminary partial conclusions suggest that any population in a disputed territory, whether implanted for "right-peopling" reasons or indigenous, may present a different interest to the ones represented by the claimant sovereign states. Moreover, these differences have domestic, regional and international contexts that influence each other. For example, the existence of guarantors in a settlement arrangement may help maintain a permanent and peaceful understanding between conflicting parties.

Finally, in particular cases such as those arising in the Falkland/Malvinas Islands, the Mexico–United States border, the Amazon region and Antarctica, it is at least plausible to argue a regional approach in the form of a bloc, subcontinental or continental alliance could foster peacebuilding. Moreover, such an approach could strengthen the position of continental actors against external interests in the region by bettering the bargaining power of what could otherwise be individually weak international agents.

In light of the overall aims and rationale outlined above, the key objectives in this book are:

- To agree that there is a fragmentation in the study of territorial disputes in the Americas.
- To acknowledge some key concepts in the study of territorial disputes that go beyond disciplinary boundaries and can be used by different disciplinary traditions.
- To understand that territorial disputes in the Americas are complex, multisubjective, multi-contextual and multi-faceted.
- To accept that such a complexity requires a comprehensive and multidimensional analysis.
- To identify common theoretical and factual elements pertaining to different territorial disputes in the Americas.
- To identify legal and political practices in the continent that have proved to be effective in permanently and peacefully solving territorial disputes.
- To develop and consolidate a multidisciplinary and international basis for the exchange of knowledge, discussion and research of global and regional issues in order to deal with them locally in novel ways (i.e. in that sense, this work is multidisciplinary, and the main disciplines are law, political science and international studies).

- To identify, compare, contrast and evaluate relevant law and policy applicable to different states with regard to the same issue.
- To disseminate key findings with conclusive remarks in the form of guidelines for future research.
- The main long-term objective (local-to-global aspect) is to draw on the foundation knowledge gained across the theory and methodology applied in this monograph and to make recommendations about how to more comprehensively assess and explicate territorial disputes.

Methodology

While bringing together a common conceptual and hermeneutical set of tools and real case scenarios, this book applies two different approaches—a modified realist model and a case study. Used by the author in Núñez (2020) and Núñez (2023), the modified realist model enables a consideration of the simultaneous impact of both domestic- and international-level variables. The examination of case studies allows the testing of generated hypotheses. By integrating these approaches, the resultant theoretical framework should have a considerable explanatory power to better understand territorial disputes. At the same time, these theoretical models can be carefully subjected to empirical analysis.

The notions of sovereignty and territorial disputes in this monograph

Sovereignty and territorial disputes are intertwined.[56] Despite their particular characteristics, all territorial disputes, to different degrees, have something to do with sovereignty. It is simplistic to assume that territorial disputes only revolve around a single component of a sovereign state, whether it may be its population (minorities, ethnic conflicts, etc.), its territory (natural resources, borders, etc.) or its government (leaders' popularity, applicable law, etc.). In reality, territorial disputes are often complex and include several of these features.

Brevitatis causa, the definitions, views and conceptions about sovereignty are numerous.[57] They may differ because of their frame of reference. For instance, "sovereignty" may imply a normative or factual realm and mean power or authority depending on whether the scholar follows a legal or political sciences tradition.[58] They may differ because of the facet of reference and

56 For the author's views on sovereignty and territorial disputes see Jorge E. Núñez, *Territorial Disputes and State Sovereignty: International Law and Politics* (London and New York, NY: Routledge, Taylor & Francis Group, 2020).

57 For an extensive analysis on the different views, conceptions and historical evaluations of "sovereignty" see Jorge E. Núñez, *Sovereignty Conflicts and International Law and Politics: A Distributive Justice Issue* (London and New York, NY: Routledge, Taylor & Francis Group, 2017), Chapter 2.

58 For the author's views on sovereignty and its different realms see Jorge E. Núñez, *Cosmopolitanism, State Sovereignty, International Law and Politics: A Theory* (London and New York, NY: Routledge, Taylor & Francis Group, 2023), Chapter 5.

can be understood as internal or external. They may also differ because of the subject which is being related to, such as in references to an attribute of a person, a body, a state or a supranational entity. This monograph acknowledges that sovereignty at the level of the state is normatively and factually limited and it is because of these limitations that sovereign states may enter into relationships with other agents by means of cooperation and domination.[59] In addition to state sovereignty, the book will incorporate other agents in the analyses of territorial disputes such as sovereignty at the level of individuals and sovereignty at the level of communities.

Territorial disputes have to do with a conflict of interest[60] and may be understood in a narrow and in a broad sense. In a narrow sense, they refer to a disagreement between states about the sovereignty over territory, e.g. land or water.[61] In a broad sense, they refer to a disagreement between any kind of agent—e.g. individuals, communities and states—about the sovereignty over any kind of space.[62] In any territorial dispute, depending on the role that individuals, communities and states play, there will be many elements and features.[63] In that vein, for example, a narrow account might consider only sovereign states as a type of legal and legitimate agent while a broad account might incorporate collective groups such as indigenous peoples.

The notions of pluralism of pluralisms and multidimensional analysis in this monograph

Territorial disputes have their own elements and features.[64] Despite these differences, traditional scholarly approaches are characterized by their unidimensionality in assessing and explaining territorial disputes. For example, a unidimensional view on a sovereign state's role may focus only on particular

59 For cooperation, domination and the axiological choice with regard to sovereignty see Jorge E. Núñez, *Cosmopolitanism, State Sovereignty, International Law and Politics: A Theory* (London and New York, NY: Routledge, Taylor & Francis Group, 2023).

60 For the notions of identity and conflict of interest the author follows Rawls. See Jorge E. Núñez, *Territorial Disputes and State Sovereignty: International Law and Politics* (London and New York, NY: Routledge, Taylor & Francis Group, 2020), Chapter 4; and John Rawls, *A Theory of Justice*, Revised Edition (Oxford: Oxford University Press, 1999), 4.

61 See Jorge E. Núñez, *Territorial Disputes and State Sovereignty: International Law and Politics* (London and New York, NY: Routledge, Taylor & Francis Group, 2020), Chapter 4.

62 For the different notions pertaining to space see Jorge E. Núñez, *Cosmopolitanism, State Sovereignty, International Law and Politics: A Theory* (London and New York, NY: Routledge, Taylor & Francis Group, 2023), Chapter 6.

63 For the different roles that agents such as individuals, communities and states may play in territorial disputes see Jorge E. Núñez, *Cosmopolitanism, State Sovereignty, International Law and Politics: A Theory* (London and New York, NY: Routledge, Taylor & Francis Group, 2023), Chapter 4.

64 See Jorge E. Núñez, *Territorial Disputes and State Sovereignty: International Law and Politics* (London and New York, NY: Routledge, Taylor & Francis Group, 2020), Chapters 6, 7 and 8 for individual territorial disputes in more detail.

existing claims, issues at stake or contexts.[65] In order to more comprehensively understand the intricate nature of territorial disputes, this monograph makes use of the notions of "pluralism of pluralisms" and a multidimensional approach.[66]

Pluralism of pluralisms means the acknowledgment that territorial disputes encompass a variety of agents (individuals, communities and states) and players (host, participant, attendees and viewers), and, hence, there is recognition of the plurality of subjects at play and the different roles they may play. Furthermore, these agents and players act in several contexts (local, regional and international) and their actions, omissions and interrelations exist simultaneously in three realms (rational, empirical and axiological). To add to the intricacy, the many views (law, politics, philosophy and non-scientific ones) about agents, players, contexts and realms have a horizontal and vertical dimension that should take into account two variables: time and space.

Traditional scholarly studies in legal and political sciences and international relations have adopted a unidimensional exploration of territorial disputes that result in fragmented views about them. They may, for example, focus on the challenger or the challenged agents; legal, historical, political or sociological claims; a particular issue at stake; etc. Conversely, a multidimensional analysis accepts that territorial disputes are complex, multi-agent, multi-contextual and multi-faceted. Indeed, they encompass a pluralism of pluralisms. Clearly, territorial disputes involve more agents than only states; have more contexts than the domestic one; contain a combination of factual, normative and axiological realms; and also include a myriad of ideal, natural, cultural and metaphysical elements and features. Without a dimensional framework, unidimensionality is the *a priori* way in which current scholarly research operates. Therein, a multidimensional analysis proposes a comprehensive assessment of phenomena.

Choice of examples

This monograph, consistent with its predecessors, Núñez (2017), Núñez (2020) and Núñez (2023), is concerned with territorial disputes pertaining to two or more fully sovereign states (both *de jure* and *de facto*). That is not to say the study will exclude other agents such as individuals and communities and their respective interests or that it may not apply more generally to other problems. Pragmatically, it would be impossible to include every territorial dispute in the Americas in the analysis. Consequently, the examples incorporated in this study consist of current (still ongoing) issues based on the criteria

65 Paul F. Diehl, "What Are They Fighting For? The Importance of Issues in International Conflict Research," *Journal of Peace Research* 29:3 (1992): 333–344.

66 For a detailed account of the notions of pluralism of pluralisms and multidimensionality see Jorge E. Núñez, *Cosmopolitanism, State Sovereignty, International Law and Politics: A Theory* (London and New York, NY: Routledge, Taylor & Francis Group, 2023).

detailed above (i.e. two or more sovereign states). In all cases, however, the monograph explores the potential to find commonalities in the different territorial disputes, in the ways in which they may be assessed and explained. These commonalities in the form of partial conclusions may translate into guidelines for the future assessments and explanations, by means of analogy, of cases not included in these pages.

Conclusion

Current events such as COVID-19, the ongoing Israel–Palestine difference, terrorism, the socio-political crisis in Venezuela, Russia's relationship with neighboring states and Brexit are a few examples of domestic, regional and international multi-layered crises.

Territorial disputes, as an example of crises, have at least two claiming parties with a conflict of interest concerning the exclusive sovereignty of the same territory.

This chapter introduced the monograph's overarching aim, its structure and methodology. This monograph seeks to apply a multidimensional approach in order to assess and explain territorial disputes in the Americas. *Brevitatis causa*, any study on territorial disputes should acknowledge their intrinsic pluralism of pluralisms if the intention is to have a robust and in-depth understanding of their complexity. Firstly, involved agents such as individuals, communities and states have different claims, assumptions, perceptions, subgroups, interests and views they represent. Secondly, there are several issues at stake. Finally, any evaluation should contextualize the dispute locally, regionally and internationally for a more accurate comprehension.

It is in this comprehensive understanding of the multi-layered and multi-contextual nature of territorial disputes that a path toward a better explanation of their complexity can be built. For instance, civil societies may include internal divisions based on history, ethnicity, religion, etc. that can have an impact on the way these different groups perceive the dispute and their role as a political community in them. It is also possible that governments and leaders may opt to maintain the difference in a political and legal *status quo* because of the higher payoff to their prestige and power (rather than a definitive and peaceful solution). Furthermore, together with local and regional actors, there are other international agents (not necessarily regional ones) that have a direct interest in these areas and, consequently, the way in which the dispute develops depending on their own interests and their alliances with any of the original local and regional claimants. Therein, the monograph as a whole argues for a reconceived, more robust, exhaustive and accurate understanding of their intricacy.

The recognition of sovereignty as a bounded legal norm is not static; the transferable notion of national sovereignty remains a major subject in law, politics and international relations. Events such as the crisis in Ukraine and Russia's annexation of Crimea demonstrate that sovereignty is increasingly becoming dynamic and fluid, flowing at times from one country to another because of some event of political restructuring within the international community or the shifting sands of geopolitics.

The scholarly literature in the fields of legal and political sciences and international relations offer a plethora of views on sovereignty and territorial disputes, both nationally and internationally. Many scholars of legal and political sciences and international relations use terms such as "sovereignty," "territorial dispute" and similar terminology to refer to various different realities. However, for the numerous reasons briefly presented in this chapter and that will be explored in detail in the following pages, such conceptions fall short in offering common grounds for debate.

In the first part of this book, the following chapters will bring together a set of common hermeneutical tools applicable to legal and political sciences and international relations and their studies on territorial disputes. Ultimately, any national, regional or international scholarly assessment and explanation that intends to tackle territorial disputes must acknowledge the pluralism of pluralisms present in fact and in law. In a similar vein, if existing analyses and understandings in terms of territorial disputes continue with their unidimensional approaches, they will only guarantee views too narrow or too partial to fully comprehend their intricacy or to offer viable ways to deal with them peacefully and permanently.

Bibliography

Alonso González, Wilhelm Pablo Londoño and Eva Parga-Dans. "Equality and Hierarchy, Sovereignty and Multiculturalism: The Heritagisation of Raizals in Santa Catalina (Colombia)." *Journal of Ethnic and Migration Studies* 46:19 (2018): 4066–4085.

Beck, Peter. "Britain's Falkland Future—the Need to Look Back." *The Round Table* 73 (1984): 139–152.

Beck, Peter. "Cooperative Confrontation in the Falkland Island Dispute." *Journal of Interamerican Studies and World Affairs* 24 (1982): 37–57.

Beck, Peter. "Looking at the Falkland Islands from Antarctica: The Broader Regional Perspective" *Polar Record* 30 (1994): 167–180.

Beck, Peter. *The Falkland Islands as an International Problem.* London and New York, NY: Routledge, 1998.

Beck, Peter. "The Future of the Falkland Islands: A Solution Made in Hong Kong?" *International Affairs* 61 (1985): 643–660.

Bender, Lynn. *Cuba vs. United States.* San Juan: Inter American University Press, 1981.

Bernhardt, J. Peter A. "Sovereignty in Antarctica." *California Western International Journal* 5 (1975): 297–349.

Bianchi, William. *Belize: The Controversy between Guatemala and Great Britain over the Territory of British Honduras in Central America.* New York, NY: Las Americas, 1959.

Brady, Anne-Marie. *China as a Polar Great Power.* Cambridge: Cambridge University Press, 2017.

Brady, Anne-Marie. "China's Rise in Antarctica?" *Asian Survey* 50:4 (2010): 759–785.
Brady, Anne-Marie, ed. *The Emerging Politics of* Antarctica. Oxford and New York, NY: Routledge, 2013.
Braveboy-Wagner, Jacqueline. *The Venezuela-Guyana Border Dispute.* Boulder, CO: Westview Press, 1984.
Brownlie, Ian. *Principles of Public International Law.* Oxford: Oxford University Press, 2003.
Buarque, Cristovam. "A internacionalização do mundo." *Revista Diálogo Educacional* 3:5 (2002): 107–108.
Calvert, Peter. *Boundary Disputes in Latin America.* London: Institute for the Study of Conflict, 1983.
Charney, Jonathan I. and Lewis M Alexander, eds. *International Maritime Boundaries, Volume I.* Boston, MA: Martinus Nijhoff, 1996.
Child, Jack. *Geopolitics and Conflict in South America.* New York, NY: Praeger, 1985.
Conforti, Benedetto. "Territorial Claims in Antarctica: A Modern Way to Deal with an Old Problem." *Cornell International Law Journal* 19:2 (1986): 249–258.
Conrad, Geoffrey W. and Arthur A Demarset. *Religion and Empire: The Dynamics of Aztec and Inca Expansionism.* Cambridge: Cambridge University Press, 1984.
Cook, Noble David. *Born to Die: Disease and the New World Conquest, 1492–1650.* Cambridge: Cambridge University Press, 1998.
Day, Alan J., ed. *Border and Territorial Disputes.* Essex: Longman, 1982.
Denevan, William M. *The Native Population of the Americas in 1492.* Madison, WI: University of Wisconsin Press, 1992.
Diehl, Paul F. "What Are They Fighting For? The Importance of Issues in International Conflict Research." *Journal of Peace Research* 29:3 (1992): 333–344.
Dobyns, Henry F. "An Appraisal of Techniques with a New Hemispheric Estimate." *Current Anthropology* 7:4 (1966): 395–416.
Dodds, Klaus, Alan D. Hemmings and Peder Roberts, eds. *Handbook on the Politics of Antarctica.* Cheltenham: Edward Elgar Publishing, 2017.
Donovan, Thomas W. "Challenges to the Territorial Integrity of Guyana: A Legal Analysis." *Georgia Journal of International and Comparative Law* 32 (2004): 661–724.
Donovan, Thomas W. "Suriname-Guyana Maritime and Territorial Disputes: A Legal and Historical Analysis." *Journal of Transnational Law and Policy* 13:1 (2003): 41–98.
Donovan, Thomas W. "The Marouini River Tract and Its Colonial Legacy in South America." *Chicago-Kent Journal of International and Comparative Law* 4 (2004): 1–28.
Downing, David. *An Atlas of Territorial and Border Disputes.* London: New English Library, 1980.
Ganzert, Frederic William. "The Boundary Controversy in the Upper Amazon between Brazil, Bolivia, and Peru, 1903–1909." *Hispanic American Historical Review* 14:4 (1934): 427–449.
Gerlach, Allen. *Indians, Oil, and Politics: A Recent History of Ecuador.* Wilmington, NC: Scholarly Resources, 2003.
Gilbert, Jérémie. *Indigenous Peoples' Land Rights under International Law: From Victors to Actors.* Ardsley, NY: Transnational, 2006.

Gilbert, Jérémie. "Indigenous Rights in the Making: The United Nations Declaration on the Rights of Indigenous Peoples." *International Journal on Minority and Group Rights* 14 (2007): 207–230.

Grandpierron, Matthieu. "Preserving 'Great Power Status': The Complex Case of the British Intervention in the Falklands (1982)." *Croatian International Relations Review* 23:79 (2017): 127–156.

Greene, Shane. "Getting Over the Andes: The Geo-Eco-Politics of Indigenous Movements in Peru's Twenty-First Century Inca Empire." *Journal of Latin American Studies* 38:2 (2006): 327–354.

Haklai, Oded and Nephytos Loizides. "Settlers and Conflict Over Contested Territories." In *Settlers in Contested Lands. Territorial Disputes and Ethnic Conflicts*, Haklai, Oded and Loizides, Nephytos, eds. 1–16. Stanford, CA: Stanford University Press, 2015.

Halldenius, Lena. "Building Blocks of a Republican Cosmopolitanism: The Modality of Being Free." *European Journal of Political Theory* 9:1 (2010): 12–30.

Harrington, Jonathan. "China in Antarctica: A History." *Southeast Review of Asian Studies* 37 (2015): 1–19.

Hensel, Paul R. "Contentious Issues and World Politics: The Management of Territorial Claims in the Americas, 1816–1992." *International Studies Quarterly* 45:1 (2001): 81–109.

Hensel, Paul R. "One Thing Leads to Another: Recurrent Militarized Disputes in Latin America, 1816–1986." *Journal of Peace Research* 31:3 (1994): 281–297.

Herz, Monica and João Pontes Nogueira. *Ecuador vs. Peru: Peacemaking Amid Rivalry*. London: Lynne Rienner, 2002.

Huth, Paul K. *Standing Your Ground: Territorial Disputes and International Conflict*. Ann Arbor, MI: University of Michigan Press, 2001.

Ireland, Gordon. *Boundaries, Possessions, and Conflicts in South America*. Cambridge, MA: Harvard University Press, 1938.

Iyall Smith, Keri E. *The State and Indigenous Movements*. New York, NY: Routledge, 2006.

Joyner, Christopher C. "Antarctica and the Indian Ocean States: The Interplay of Law, Interests, and Geopolitics." *Ocean Development and International Law* 21:1 (1990): 41–70.

Kessel, A. H. "Canadian Arctic Sovereignty: Myths and Realities." In *Governing the North American Arctic*, Berry, D. A., Bowles, N. and Jones, H., eds. 242–246. London: Palgrave Macmillan, 2016.

Kröger, Markus and Rickard Lalander. "Ethno-Territorial Rights and the Resource Extraction Boom in Latin America: Do Constitutions Matter?" *Third World Quarterly* 37:4 (2016): 682–702.

Laborde, Cecile. "Republicanism and Global Justice: A Sketch." *European Journal of Political Theory* 9 (2010): 48–69.

Lee, Wei-chin. "China and Antarctica: So Far and Yet So Near." *Asian Survey* 30:6 (1990): 576–586.

Lindley, M. F. *The Acquisition and Government of Backward Territory in International Law: Being a Treatise on the Law and Practice Relating to Colonial Expansion*. New York, NY: Negro University Press, 1969.

Little, Paul E. *Amazonia: Territorial Struggles on Perennial Frontiers*. Baltimore, MD: Johns Hopkins University Press, 2001.

Martin, L. H. and Y. B. Parkhomenko. "The Territorial and Maritime Dispute (Nicaragua v. Colombia) and Its Implications for Future Maritime Delimitations in the Caribbean Sea and Elsewhere." In *Nicaragua Before the International Court of Justice*, Sobenes Obregon, E. and Samson, B., eds. 113–141. Cham: Springer, 2018.

Newson, Linda A. "The Demographic Collapse of Native Peoples of the Americas, 1492–1650." *Proceedings of the British Academy* 81 (1993): 247–288.

Núñez, Jorge E. *Cosmopolitanism, State Sovereignty, International Law and Politics: A Theory.* London and New York, NY: Routledge, Taylor & Francis Group, 2023.

Núñez, Jorge E. *Sovereignty Conflicts and International Law and Politics: A Distributive Justice Issue.* London and New York, NY: Routledge, Taylor & Francis Group, 2017.

Núñez, Jorge E. *Territorial Disputes and State Sovereignty: International Law and Politics.* London and New York, NY: Routledge, Taylor & Francis Group, 2020.

Núñez, Jorge E. "Territorial Disputes." In *The Oxford Handbook of International Law and the Americas*, Obregón Tarazona, Liliana, Betancur-Restrepo, Laura and Amaya Castro, Juan Manuel, eds. Online edn. Oxford: Oxford Academic, 2024.

O'Leary, Brendan. "The Elements of Right-Sizing and Right-Peopling the State." In *Right-Sizing the State: The Politics of Moving Borders*, O'Leary, Brendan, Lustick, Ian S. and Callaghy, Thomas, eds. 15–73. Oxford: Oxford University Press, 2001.

Palmer, David Scott. "Peru-Ecuador Border Conflict: Missed Opportunities, Misplaced Nationalism, and Multilateral Peacekeeping." *Journal of Interamerican Studies and World Affairs* 39:3 (1997): 109–148.

Parrish, Austen L. "Changing Territoriality, Fading Sovereignty, and the Development of Indigenous Rights." *American Indian Law Review* 31:2 (2006/2007): 291–313.

Penna Filho, Pio. "Interações Regionais e Pressões Internacionais sobre a Pan-Amazônia: Perspectivas Brasileiras." In *Amazônia e Atlântico Sul: Desafios e Perspectivas para a Defesa no Brasil*, Gheller, Gilberto F., Gonzales, Selma, L. M. and Mello, Laerte P., eds. 149–184. Brasilia: IPEA, 2015.

Perrier Buslé, Laetitia. "Multi-Scalar Perspectives and Multi-Agent Process in a South American Borderland Region." *Geopolitics* 18:3 (2013): 584–611.

Pettit, Philip. "A Republican Law of Peoples." *European Journal of Political Theory* 9:1 (2010): 70–94.

Pratt, Martin. "The Maritime Boundary Dispute between Honduras and Nicaragua in the Caribbean Sea." *Boundary and Security Bulletin* 9:2 (2001): 106–116.

Ratner, Steven R. "Drawing a Better Line: *Uti Possidetis* and the Borders of New States." *American Journal of International Law* 90:4 (1996): 590–624.

Rawls, John. *A Theory of Justice.* Revised Edition. Oxford: Oxford University Press, 1999.

Reis, Arthur C. F. "A Amazônia e a Integridade do Brasil." Brasilia: Senado Federal Conselho Editorial, 2001.

Ross, James. "Routes for Roots: Entering the 21st Century in San Andrés Island, Colombia." *Caribbean Studies* 35:1 (2007): 3–36.

Shaw, Malcom N. *International Law.* Cambridge: Cambridge University Press, 2003.

Sieder, Rachel. "Indigenous Peoples' Rights and the Law in Latin America." In *Handbook of Indigenous Peoples' Rights*, Lennox, Corinne and Short, Damien, eds. 414–423. London and New York, NY: Routledge, 2016.

Simonian, Ligia T. L. and Rubens da Silva Ferreira. "Brazilian Migrant Workers in French Guiana." In *Caribbean Transnationalism: Migration, Pluralization, and*

Social Cohesion, Gowricharn, Ruben, ed. 99–116. Lanham, MD: Lexington Books, 2006.

Stevenson, Christopher. "Hans Off!: The Struggle for Hans Island and the Potential Ramifications for International Border Dispute Resolution." *Boston College International and Comparative Law Review* 30:1 (2007): 263–275.

Van Cott, Donna Lee. "Broadening Democracy: Latin America's Indigenous Peoples' Movements." *Current History* 103 (2004): 80–85.

van der Haar, Gemma. "The Zapatista Uprising and the Struggle for Indigenous Autonomy." *European Review of Latin American and Caribbean Studies* 76 (2004): 98–108.

van Genugten, Willem and Camillo Perez-Bustillo. "The Emerging International Architecture of Indigenous Rights: The Interaction between Global, Regional, and National Dimensions." *International Journal on Minority and Group Rights* 11:4 (2004): 379–409.

Winslow, Philip C. *Victory for Us Is To See You Suffer: In the West Bank with the Palestinians and the Israelis.* Boston, MA: Beacon Press, 2007.

Young, Alma H. and Dennis H. Young. "The Impact of the Anglo-Guatemalan Dispute on the Internal Politics of Belize." *Latin American Perspectives* 15:2 (1988): 6–30.

2 Sovereignty and territorial disputes

Introduction

Sovereignty and territorial disputes are two notions, pertaining to scholarly disciplines such as legal and political sciences and international relations, that are intertwined in domestic, regional and international contexts. Sovereignty is often perceived as referring to one kind of agent, that is states and, more particularly, one of state's necessary elements, its territory. Territorial disputes may center on state's territorial elements and features such as borders, geo-strategic location and natural resources but may incorporate issues concerning other agents, such as individuals and communities, and other aspects that go beyond territorially defined constructs like those related to population and government. Therefore, in order to gain a comprehensive understanding of territorial disputes in the Americas, their origin, continuation and potential escalation into conflict, and to discuss means for their potential peaceful and permanent solution, this chapter conceptualizes and characterizes the notions of sovereignty and territorial disputes in ways that capture their multidimensional nature. Moreover, and because of their multidimensional nature, this monograph argues there are domestic, regional and international contextual influences—actual and potential—in the interrelation between sovereignty and territorial disputes. Therein, in addition to the acknowledgment of other global means for their potential peaceful and permanent solution, the chapter will refer to regional organizations and their role in peacebuilding.

In order to conceptualize and characterize the notions of sovereignty and territorial disputes, the starting point will be the acknowledgment of different disciplinary methodological approaches, assumptions, views and conceptual bases already existing in legal and political sciences and international relations. From these current unidimensional starting points, a more sophisticated way of understanding, knowing and assessing sovereignty and territorial disputes is possible by means of an integrated approach. Therein, the chapter is divided into three main sections.

In the first section, the chapter aims to show that sovereignty may be defined by reference to territory, but it does not need to be (it may refer to, for example, population). This is particularly important in cases in which

DOI: 10.4324/9781003350828-3

there are indigenous peoples, implanted populations and differences of interest within the participant states in territorial disputes—i.e. a sovereign state is often acknowledged in legal and political sciences and international relations as a single legal and political agent with a singular interest. Moreover, the chapter acknowledges that sovereignty is not absolute, and it is because of its limitations that individuals, communities and states are able to have interrelations in fact and in law with other agents in the form of domination or cooperation. In that vein, this section will present factual or *de facto* sovereignty, normative or *de jure* sovereignty and axiological or value sovereignty.

Sovereignty, or to adopt a more adequate term, state sovereignty, can be defined and characterized in several ways.[1] Starting with a widely accepted definition of sovereignty, the first part of the section shows how conceptually and substantially complex this notion is. Despite its complexity, there is arguably an agreement in scholarly literature about its relevance in law and politics. Indeed, sovereignty encompasses legal and not necessarily political issues, i.e. normative sovereignty, and extra-legal and not necessarily legal aspects, i.e. factual sovereignty. In a similar fashion, there are several definitions and characterizations of the state. While public international law recognizes that a state's necessary elements include population, territory and government,[2] some political science scholars include aspects such as force and morality.[3]

The second section considers the reasons how and why territorial disputes start, and why some continue endlessly while others reach a solution. Although relevant, the usual causes for these differences, such as strategic location of territory, its economic value, homogeneity with bordering minorities or political unification, fail to provide a satisfactory and comprehensive explanation. The chapter examines how the domestic context influences the regional and international dimensions and vice versa. The chapter follows Núñez (2020) in arguing that while international elements may explain the escalation into

1 For an extensive analysis on different views, conceptions and historical evaluations of "sovereignty" see Jorge E. Núñez, "State Sovereignty: Concept and Conceptions," *International Journal for the Semiotics of Law* 37 (2024): 2131–2150; Jorge E. Núñez, *Territorial Disputes and State Sovereignty: International Law and Politics* (London and New York, NY: Routledge, Taylor & Francis Group, 2020), Chapter 3; and Jorge E. Núñez, *Sovereignty Conflicts and International Law and Politics: A Distributive Justice Issue* (London and New York, NY: Routledge, Taylor & Francis Group, 2017), Chapter 2. For the latest on "sovereignty" see Christian Volk, "The Problem of Sovereignty in Globalized Times," *Law, Culture and the Humanities* 18:3 (2022): 716–738; Neil Walker, ed., *Relocating Sovereignty* (London and New York, NY: Routledge, Taylor & Francis Group, 2018); Kirby Brown, "Sovereignty," *Western American Literature* 53:1 (2018): 81–89; Giovanni Picker, "Sovereignty Beyond the State: Exception and Informality in a Western European City," *International Journal of Urban and Regional Research* 43:3 (2019): 576–581; and others.

2 Complete text available from the United Nations Treaty Collection at https://treaties.un.org/pages/showDetails.aspx?objid=0800000280166aef accessed 5 July 2023.

3 For a more detailed understanding of these views see John Hoffman and Paul Graham, *Introduction to Political Theory* (Oxford and New York, NY: Routledge, 2015), Chapter 1.

conflict, they do not necessarily explain the reasons that originate the disputes in the first place. Conversely, local and regional elements that give birth to these disputes are not sufficient conditions for their escalation. Indeed, territorial disputes encompass several pluralisms including the domestic, regional and international contexts that may influence their dynamics.

Finally, at the intersection between sovereignty and territorial disputes, the third section introduces the legal and political regional organizations present in the Americas with particular focus on their direct and indirect influence with regard to conflict resolution. The chapter refers to available regional dispute settlement means, their viability in dealing with these kinds of differences and highlights the role of regional organizations and guarantors in peacebuilding.

Sovereignty

Different disciplines such as legal and political sciences and international relations define and characterize sovereignty using different assumptions and justifications.[4] The concept of "sovereignty" may refer to, for example, supreme authority or power; a body, a person or an institution; its inward or outward views; and several other issues.[5]

In a similar way, different disciplines refer to the concept of the "state" and its characterization in different ways. For instance, public international law stipulates that: "The state as a person of international law should possess the following qualifications: a) a permanent population; b) a defined territory; c) government; and d) capacity to enter into relations with the other states."[6] In turn, political science includes some notions that incorporate the use of force, others that consider that the state is the realization of morality

4 For a detailed account on "sovereignty" see Jorge E. Núñez, *Territorial Disputes and State Sovereignty: International Law and Politics* (London and New York, NY: Routledge, Taylor & Francis Group, 2020), Chapter 3; and Jorge E. Núñez, *Sovereignty Conflicts and International Law and Politics: A Distributive Justice Issue* (London and New York, NY: Routledge, Taylor & Francis Group, 2017), Chapter 2. See also Robert Jackson, ed., *Sovereignty at the Millennium* (Oxford: Blackwell Publishers, 1999), in partic. 148, fn. 10; Christian Volk, "The Problem of Sovereignty in Globalized Times," *Law, Culture and the Humanities* 18:3 (2022): 716–738; Neil Walker, ed., *Relocating Sovereignty* (London and New York, NY: Routledge, Taylor & Francis Group, 2018); Kirby Brown, "Sovereignty," *Western American Literature* 53:1 (2018): 81–89; Giovanni Picker, "Sovereignty Beyond the State: Exception and Informality in a Western European City," *International Journal of Urban and Regional Research* 43:3 (2019): 576–581; and others.

5 For a more detailed analysis of each of these issues see Jorge E. Núñez, *Sovereignty Conflicts and International Law and Politics: A Distributive Justice Issue* (London and New York, NY: Routledge, Taylor & Francis Group, 2017), Chapter 2.

6 Article 1 of the Montevideo Convention on Rights and Duties of States (1933). Complete text available from the United Nations Treaty Collection at https://treaties.un.org/pages/showDetails.aspx?objid=0800000280166aef accessed 5 July 2023.

and hybrid understandings that combine both force and morality.[7] From the legal and political standpoints, therefore, it is possible to identify that a state requires three necessary elements in order to exist: territory, population and government (or government and law).[8] Bringing together the concepts and characterizations from legal and political sciences and international relations concerning "state" and "sovereignty," a sovereign state involves people (population) living in a space of land, water, etc. (territory) who have a common government that can exclusively create and apply the highest law for them in that territory.

A multidimensional view on "state" and "sovereignty" acknowledges the different ways in which disciplines such as legal and political sciences and international relations apply these notions and their consequent use in issues pertaining to law and politics. The Organization of American States (OAS) is one example that illustrates this point. The OAS Charter clearly refers to legal and political constructs such as "sovereignty," "political independence" and the principles of non-intervention and territorial integrity.[9] Politically, there is clearly a move toward continental cooperation. However, the OAS legal framework—unlike the European Union (EU) and the principle of conferral (art. 5.2 Treaty on EU) that has enabled a combination of supremacy and intergovernmental relations[10]—still accepts its Member States, i.e. sovereign states in the terms of this monograph, as having complete exclusive sovereignty over their affairs.

7 For a more detailed understanding of these views see John Hoffman and Paul Graham, *Introduction to Political Theory* (Oxford and New York, NY: Routledge, 2015), Chapter 1.

8 For a view of state as composed by population, territory, government and law see Alan James, *Sovereign Statehood: The Basis of International Society* (London: Allen & Unwin, 1986), in particular Chapter 2; John A. Hall and G. John Ikenberry, *The State* (Milton Keynes: Open University Press, 1989); Patrick Dunleavy and Brendan O'Leary, *Theories of the State: The Politics of Liberal Democracy* (Basingstoke and London: MacMillan, 1987); Malcom D. Evans, *International Law* (Oxford: Oxford University Press, 2010); Antonio Cassese, *International Law* (Oxford: Oxford University Press, 2001); Ian Brownlie, *Principles of Public International Law* (Oxford: Oxford University Press, 2008); and many others.

9 See, for example, Article 1 OAS, which refers to the organization's objectives: "The American States establish by this Charter the international organization [...] to defend their sovereignty, their territorial integrity, and their independence [while] none of whose provisions authorizes it to intervene in matters that are within the internal jurisdiction of the Member States;" and Article 28 OAS concerning collective security: "Every act of aggression by a State against the territorial integrity or the inviolability of the territory or against the sovereignty or political independence of an American State shall be considered an act of aggression against the other American States." Complete OAS Charter text available on http://www.oas.org/dil/1948%20charter%20of%20the%20organization%20of%20american%20states.pdf accessed 5 July 2023.

10 For details about intergovernmentalism and supranationalism in relation to the European Union (EU) see Jorge E. Núñez, *Cosmopolitanism, State Sovereignty, International Law and Politics: A Theory* (London and New York, NY: Routledge, Taylor & Francis Group, 2023), Chapter 5.

Brevitatis causa, scholarly disciplines such as legal and political sciences and international relations differentiate between *de facto* sovereignty and *de jure* sovereignty (factual and normative sovereignty). Although in most cases a state has *de facto* sovereignty as well as *de jure* sovereignty over a territory, there are several examples of territorial disputes that clearly show exceptions. For example, in the particular cases concerning the Americas, there are several situations that show a tension between *de facto* sovereignty and *de jure* sovereignty. Such cases include the Falkland/Malvinas Islands, where the United Kingdom has *de facto* sovereignty while *de jure* sovereignty is in question; the archipelago of San Andrés, Providencia and Santa Catalina, where although the International Court of Justice (ICJ) answered the sovereignty question between Nicaragua and Colombia, arguments between both states remain common;[11] and Guantanamo,[12] where sovereignty is not split into two, between Cuba and the United States,[13] because Guantanamo is legally leased by Cuba to the United States.[14]

The way in which each agent—e.g. individuals, communities and states—considers sovereignty in law and politics has to do with the notion itself, its nature and the way it is perceived or valued. This has direct implications in situations where sovereignty issues have a central role, such as how each population and government understand their role with regard to their membership in regional and international organizations or their positioning as the challenger or challenged parties in territorial disputes. To characterize sovereignty in law and politics as either absolute or limited, closed or open, exclusive or inclusive depends on the choice each agent makes, e.g. the choice of individuals, communities and states, and that choice affects the way in which they interact. The author has explained elsewhere that if these agents opt to acknowledge sovereignty—i.e. axiological sovereignty—as an absolute and closed concept in fact and/or in law—i.e. factual or normative sovereignty—the choice implies, for example, exclusionary power and it follows that all other agents have a duty not to interfere.[15] Therein, in order to advance any comprehensive study on territorial disputes, it is important, first, to bring a common hermeneutical understanding to their assessment that is applicable by different scholarly disciplines when referring to sovereignty and, secondly, for scholars to use this understanding in their analyses. In doing so, and to offer a coherent and

11 Mariano V. Ospina, "Nicaragua v. Colombia: A Stalemate in the Caribbean," *Global Security Studies* 4:4 (2013): 31–40.

12 Amy Kaplan, "Where is Guantánamo?" *American Quarterly* 57:3 (2005): 831–858.

13 For a view on why the sovereignty over Guantanamo is split between Cuba and the United States, see Steven Press, "Sovereignty at Guantánamo: New Evidence and a Comparative Historical Interpretation," *The Journal of Modern History* 85:3 (2013): 592–631.

14 Michael J. Strauss, "Guantanamo Bay and the Evolution of International Leases and Servitudes," *City University of New York Law Review* 10:2 (2007): 479–509.

15 Jorge E. Núñez, *Cosmopolitanism, State Sovereignty, International Law and Politics: A Theory* (London and New York, NY: Routledge, Taylor & Francis Group, 2023), Chapter 2.

cohesive way to assess and explain territorial disputes in the Americas throughout this monograph, the following subsections will briefly reintroduce different views on sovereignty in order to clearly distinguish what may be legal and not necessarily political, i.e. normative sovereignty, from what may be extra-legal and include political elements, i.e. factual sovereignty, and to discern what constitutes an axiological decision in terms of its absoluteness or limitedness in law and politics.[16]

Factual or de facto *sovereignty*

A factual understanding refers to how sovereignty is. More precisely, *de facto* sovereignty pertains to the actual control a population or their representatives have over a territory.[17] This factual understanding accepts that sovereignty encompasses elements and sub-elements with an empirical presence. This empirical presence may be most obvious when considering the sociological element in a sovereign state, that is their population. A factual comprehension about sovereignty enables the discernment between unidimensional current understandings in law and political science that perceive a population within a state as a uniform mass of people and the fact that, conversely, there are individual and group characteristics that result in several differences including gender diversity, age group, social class and caste. Moreover, as part of the multidimensional approach, a factual understanding on sovereignty enables an acceptance that, in addition to population, the other necessary requisites that define and characterize a sovereign state according to law and political science—i.e. territory and government—also encompass empirical elements and sub-elements such as territorial extension, the presence or not or natural resources and the dynamics behind political parties and pressure groups as collective agents. Arguably, the factual realm helps explain the rationale behind sovereignty's legal and political makings. To illustrate what *de facto* sovereignty may encompass, the following paragraphs refer to each necessary element that defines and characterizes a sovereign state according to legal and political sciences and international relations—i.e. population, territory and government—in the context of territorial disputes in the Americas.[18]

16 For a detailed account on factual, normative and axiological sovereignty see Jorge E. Núñez, *Cosmopolitanism, State Sovereignty, International Law and Politics: A Theory* (London and New York, NY: Routledge, Taylor & Francis Group, 2023), Chapters 2 and 5.

17 For an understanding about the distinction between *de facto* sovereignty and *de jure* sovereignty see Nina Caspersen, "Collective Non-Recognition of States," in G. Visoka, J. Doyle and E. Newman, eds., *Routledge Handbook of State Recognition* (Oxford and New York, NY: Routledge, 2020), 231–241; Kostas A. Lavdas, Spyridon N. Litsas and Dimitrios V. Skiadas, *Stateness and Sovereign Debt: Greece in the European Conundrum* (Lanham, MD: Lexington Books, 2013), 66–70; R. K. Pruthi, *The Political Theory* (New Delhi: Sarup and Sons, 2005), 72.

18 Note the illustrations concerning normative, factual and axiological sovereignty are incorporated here solely to provide greater precision about their meaning and do not include particu-

Population in territorial disputes in the Americas includes native and implanted people; bordering minorities; discussions about time of settlements and the origin of settlements (willed or forced); rural or urban residence; and additional societal elements and features such as forced migrations.

In terms of territory, disputes in the Americas encompass large, medium or small extension spaces in land and water; fertile or barren areas; richness or scarcity of natural resources; access to the sea or landlocked zones; and terrains that make it difficult to apply legal constructs pertaining to conflict resolution procedures and remedies.

Governments in territorial disputes in the Americas, in fact, comprise groups of people, communities or one individual—e.g. a dictatorship. They involve representatives that may or may not follow the wishes of the populations or groups they represent; may or may not follow the rule of law; may or may not share the same ethnicity, religious beliefs, language, etc. of those whom they represent.

Normative or de jure *sovereignty*

A normative understanding refers to how sovereignty ought to be. More accurately, *de jure* sovereignty concerns two main facets: (a) internal, that implies the existence of a set of law-making and law-applying authorities (government) within a territory and in respect of a population, and (b) external, that includes, for example, peers' recognition as sole lawmakers and law interpreters with regard to a defined population and territory. Although legal and political sciences and international relations assume *de jure* sovereignty as a territorially defined concept, an actual exercise of power over the territory is not necessary. For example, despite the lack of actual control over the islands, Argentina claims to have *de jure* sovereignty against the United Kingdom over the Falklands/Malvinas.

A normative understanding of sovereignty makes it possible to appreciate why scholarly disciplines like the legal and political sciences appear to have disagreements in the way they perceive, assess and explicate territorial disputes. For example, in several cases in the Americas there are tensions that include the interests of settlers or implanted populations and indigenous peoples and the legal and political constructs of "sovereignty" and "self-determination." While a unidimensional normative view may assume territorial disputes centered on the element "territory," a multidimensional normative view acknowledges that (a) "territory" is important; and (b) it is crucial to discern that, normatively, "sovereignty" centers on the state while "self-determination"

lar real case examples. Actual territorial disputes in the Americas and their respective elements and features are assessed in detail in following chapters.

focuses on people.[19] Therein, it should be unsurprising that in cases such as the Falkland/Malvinas Islands and San Andrés, Providencia and Santa Catalina, populations wish to exercise self-determination while sovereign states deny them that right. The disagreement between the challenger and the challenged agents has to do with (a) the focusing of the bases of their respective arguments on a different element relating to the territorial dispute—i.e. either territory or population; and (b) the normative way in which they perceive such element.

Traditionally, a normative view on sovereignty allows scholars of legal and political sciences and international relations to incorporate in their analyses an understanding that includes territorially defined notions such as jurisdiction, borders and boundaries and extraterritoriality. This is not enough to fully comprehend normatively territorial disputes in the Americas. By incorporating the multidimensional approach, a normative understanding of sovereignty encompasses population and government because it acknowledges their *de jure* elements and sub-elements. In the same fashion as applied to the previous discussion of *de facto* sovereignty, population, territory and government are briefly outlined below following normative reasoning.

Population in territorial disputes in the Americas refers to, normatively, the legal principles of nationality, i.e. bloodline, birthplace and residence, that are the requisites to be or to become nationals of the state in question; and several distinctions, such as the difference between citizens and foreigners and legally abled and legally disabled individuals, that result in different legal rights and obligations.

Territory with reference to *de jure* sovereignty in territorial disputes in the Americas may refer to states, provinces and departments; land, water, outer space and cyberspace; and legal constructs like the exclusive economic zone.

Normatively, governments distribute and allocate power and authority in different ways that comprise constitutionalism, democracy and dictatorship; national and supranational institutions; division of powers, checks and balances systems, federal states with central law-making and law-applying organs and unipersonal summation of power that override checks and balances.

Axiological or value sovereignty

Sovereignty plays a major role in territorial disputes both factually and normatively. However, this does not exhaust its influence. More precisely, it is how the agent in question—e.g. individuals, communities and states—understands and assesses, on an axiological level, the factual and normative facets of sovereignty that may result in closed and exclusionary as well as open and inclusive views. While a factual understanding refers to how sovereignty is and a

19 P. H. Kooijmans, "Tolerance, Sovereignty and Self-Determination," *Netherlands International Law Review* 43:2 (1996): 211–217.

normative understanding refers to how sovereignty ought to be, an axiological or value understanding refers to how sovereignty should or could be.

Historically, there are several cases in the Americas that clearly illustrate how axiological choices shape agents' understandings about sovereignty, both in fact and in law, and determine the way in which these agents perceive self and others. Consider the cases of the empires in colonial times. Among other Papal bulls, the *Inter caetera* granted Spanish and Portuguese sovereignty over the Americas and ignored native American populations.[20] Therein, these colonial empires could claim exclusive sovereignty over their respective granted domains. In their interrelations, they had equal footing in the sense that they accepted each other's sovereignties and consequent spheres of influences in fact and in law. Conversely, these same empires acknowledged other agents as lacking sovereignty or, at best, if they accepted other agents had some degree of sovereignty, they were conditioned according to different levels. For instance, these times are characterized by the lack of normative acknowledgment of indigenous peoples as "persons" in law. If they were minimally recognized in law as "persons," their territorial claims were ignored, neglected or overridden.[21]

The axiological choice has had lasting consequences in the Americas. For example, the ongoing interference of former colonial powers in the region because of the way they perceived self and others resulted in the Monroe, Calvo and Drago doctrines.[22] Basic principles of public international law stem from them: (a) no colonization, (b) non-intervention of European states in the affairs of America and (c) reciprocal non-intervention in European affairs. Despite the apparent moves in fact and in law since these times, the axiological choice of how to understand sovereignty factually and normatively continues nowadays. Indeed, there are several international legal norms such as the Universal Declaration of Human Rights (1948)[23] and the United Nations Declaration on the Rights of Indigenous Peoples (2007)[24] and,

20 H. Vander Linden, "Alexander VI and the Demarcation of the Maritime and Colonial Domains of Spain and Portugal, 1493–1494," *The American Historical Review* 22:1 (1916): 1–20.

21 Jérémie Gilbert, *Indigenous Peoples' Land Rights under International Law: From Victors to Actors* (Ardsley, NY: Transnational, 2006), 1–2.

22 See Elihu Root, "The Real Monroe Doctrine," *American Society of International Law* 8 (1914): 6–22; Mark T. Gilderhus, "The Monroe Doctrine: Meanings and Implications," *Presidential Studies Quarterly* 36 (2006): 5–16; Amos S. Hershey, "The Calvo and Drago Doctrines," *The American Journal of International Law* 1 (1907): 26–45; Luis M. Drago and H. Edward Nettles, "The Drago Doctrine in International Law and Politics," *The Hispanic American Historical Review* 8 (1928): 204–223; Crammond Kennedy, "The Drago Doctrine," *The North American Review* 185 (1907): 614–622; and many others.

23 Complete text available at https://www.un.org/en/universal-declaration-human-rights/index.html accessed 5 July 2023.

24 Overview and complete text available at https://www.un.org/development/desa/indigenouspeoples/declaration-on-the-rights-of-indigenous-peoples.html accessed 5 July 2023.

regionally, concerning the Americas, the American Declaration on the Rights of Indigenous Peoples (2016).[25] However, indigenous communities claiming ethno-territorial rights still find it difficult to challenge legally defined borders against sovereign states and private companies.[26]

Territorial disputes

Territorial disputes may be defined and characterized in a narrow and in a broad sense. Narrowly, a territorial dispute is a disagreement between states about the sovereignty over territory—e.g. land or water.[27] More broadly, a territorial dispute refers to a disagreement between agents—e.g. individuals, communities and states—about the sovereignty over space[28]—i.e. land, water, space and cyberspace. The narrow and the broad accounts both characterize territorial disputes as a conflict of interests.[29]

Territorial disputes encompass several pluralisms.[30] They include different agents—e.g. individuals, communities and states—that may play different roles in their interrelations—i.e. hosts, participants, attendees and viewers. Moreover, these agents and their interrelations may be influenced by different contexts—i.e. domestic, regional and international. Finally, territorial disputes can be comprehended in several ways—i.e. factually, normatively and axiologically—and comprise elements and features with various modes of existence—i.e. ideal, natural, cultural and metaphysical. Therein, the main difference between the narrow and broad account with regard to territorial disputes is related to the pluralisms—and consequent elements and features—that characterize the given case at hand.

A narrow account may consider, for example, a territorial dispute in a unidimensional form in respect to its normative realm and a particular kind of agent

25 Complete text available at https://www.oas.org/en/sare/documents/DecAmIND.pdf accessed 5 July 2023.

26 Markus Kröger and Rickard Lalander, "Ethno-Territorial Rights and the Resource Extraction Boom in Latin America: Do Constitutions Matter?" *Third World Quarterly* 37:4 (2016): 682–702.

27 See Jorge E. Núñez, *Cosmopolitanism, State Sovereignty, International Law and Politics: A Theory* (London and New York, NY: Routledge, Taylor & Francis Group, 2023), Chapter 7; and Jorge E. Núñez, *Territorial Disputes and State Sovereignty: International Law and Politics* (London and New York, NY: Routledge, Taylor & Francis Group, 2020), Chapter 4.

28 For different notions of space see Jorge E. Núñez, *Cosmopolitanism, State Sovereignty, International Law and Politics: A Theory* (London and New York, NY: Routledge, Taylor & Francis Group, 2023), Chapter 6.

29 For the notions of identity and conflict of interest the author follows Rawls. See Jorge E. Núñez, *Territorial Disputes and State Sovereignty: International Law and Politics* (London and New York, NY: Routledge, Taylor & Francis Group, 2020), Chapter 4; and John Rawls, *A Theory of Justice*, Revised Edition (Oxford: Oxford University Press, 1999), 4.

30 For the notion of pluralism of pluralisms see Jorge E. Núñez, *Cosmopolitanism, State Sovereignty, International Law and Politics: A Theory* (London and New York, NY: Routledge, Taylor & Francis Group, 2023).

such as the sovereign state. In that sense, "dispute" can be differentiated from "situation" and "conflict." While a "situation" refers to a chain of events and issues giving rise to not one but several disputes that are interrelated to each other, e.g. the situation in the Caribbean Sea, a "conflict" refers to a general state of hostility between states and other subjects of international law, e.g. the 1982 Falklands/Malvinas conflict. This is a scenario which mostly involves use of force by states. In public international law, for instance, a "dispute" has a specific meaning. Normally, the term covers disagreement between sovereign states with respect to issues such as determination of their legal rights, duties, obligations, interests, or interpretation of treaties and delineation of boundaries. Even if there is a "dispute" between states, at times it may be difficult for states to agree on the fact that there is a dispute between them. In such cases, international courts or tribunals have to determine the existence of a dispute.[31]

Legal and political sciences and international relations understand, explain and assess territorial disputes unidimensionally. For example, state behavior concerning territorial disputes is often characterized by reference to one or a few of the existing claims, issues at stake or contexts.[32] In that sense, a unidimensional approach may enable an understanding of a specific element or feature pertaining to a territorial dispute. However, this fragmented understanding is neither useful in capturing the intricate nature of a territorial dispute nor can it benefit from cutting across seemingly different disputes in order to find commonalities. Conversely, a multidimensional view enables both an understanding of an individual territorial dispute and its intricate nature and the possibility to integrate the knowledge, understanding and assessment of different cases. For instance, a multidimensional approach acknowledges that any territorial dispute encompasses many pluralisms and traits that are

31 See, for example, Greece v. UK (1924) (the Mavrommatis Palestine Concessions) where the Permanent Court of International Justice (PCIJ) adopted the definition of the term as follows: "a dispute is a disagreement on a point of law or fact, a conflict of legal views or of interests between two parties."

Another example is Belgium v Senegal [2002] ICJ Rep 1 [Question Relating to the Obligation to Prosecute or Extradite], where it was stated that "in order to establish whether a dispute exists, it must be shown that the claim of one party is positively opposed by the other, and that, whether there exists an international dispute is a matter for objective determination." Belgium argued that Senegal had an obligation to prosecute Mr. Habre, the former President of Chad, who was in asylum in Senegal. Failing to prosecute him, Belgium argued that Senegal should extradite him to Belgium for trial. Belgium argued Senegal having failed to prosecute or extradite was in breach of Articles 5 and 6 of the Torture Convention 1984. Senegal argued that there was no dispute between them on the interpretation of the convention and as such, the ICJ had no jurisdiction to hear the case. See also Georgia v Russian Federation [Case Concerning Application of the International Convention on the Elimination of All Forms of Racial Discrimination] (Preliminary Objections Judgement) (2011) where the ICJ stated that "the existence of a dispute may be inferred from the failure of a state to respond to a claim in circumstances where a response is called for."

32 Paul F. Diehl, "What Are They Fighting For? The Importance of Issues in International Conflict Research," *Journal of Peace Research* 29:3 (1992): 333–344.

constant regardless of the peculiarities present in individual cases. Such a multidimensional approach recognizes that: (a) claims are not mutually exclusive or collectively exhaustive; (b) issues at stake are not mutually exclusive or collectively exhaustive; and (c) to gain a more comprehensive understanding of a territorial dispute all three contexts should be considered: domestic, regional and international.[33]

There are several examples in the Americas that are clearly complex and require integrated and multidimensional analyses. Consider what was at a time an area mostly free of disputes, the Caribbean Sea, and the several differences that include many regional agents such as Guatemala, Belize, Suriname, Venezuela, Guyana, Nicaragua, Costa Rica, El Salvador and Honduras.[34] Despite some colonial roots, from a more modern perspective, these differences include the normative realm—e.g. the 1982 UN Convention on the Law of the Sea brought concepts such as exclusive economic zones that resulted in, for example, overlapping areas; and the factual realm—e.g. new technologies to explore and exploit natural resources that were considered inaccessible or their existence was simply ignored. These normative and factual issues have resulted in several "new" territorial disputes.

Despite sovereign states' jurisdictions, the presence of indigenous peoples in the Americas cuts across legally and politically defined boundaries and combines elements and features that include normative, factual and axiological realms. Since colonial times, their territorial claims have been systematically ignored or discarded.[35] The reasons for this outcome can be distinguished between those that considered these populations as not being legally "persons" or, if they were considered "persons" in law, those that considered they were inferior.[36] Several states in Latin America are acknowledging this different treatment based on norms, facts or value judgments, and, consequently, there is a move toward reviewing the way in which they interact with these populations to include notions such as self-determination, protected areas, nationalism and plurinationalism.[37]

33 For more details about claims, issues at stake and contexts relevant to territorial disputes refer to Jorge E. Núñez, *Territorial Disputes and State Sovereignty: International Law and Politics* (London and New York, NY: Routledge, Taylor & Francis Group, 2020), Chapter 4.

34 For an account of territorial disputes in the Americas see Jorge E. Núñez, *Territorial Disputes and State Sovereignty: International Law and Politics* (London and New York, NY: Routledge, Taylor & Francis Group, 2020), Chapter 6; and Jorge E. Núñez, "Territorial Disputes," in Liliana Obregón, Juan Amaya-Castro and Laura Betancur-Restrepo, eds., *The Oxford Handbook of International Law and the Americas* (online edn., Oxford: Oxford Academic, 2024).

35 M. F. Lindley, *The Acquisition and Government of Backward Territory in International Law: Being a Treatise on the Law and Practice Relating to Colonial Expansion* (New York, NY: Negro University Press, 1969), 11–12.

36 Jérémie Gilbert, *Indigenous Peoples' Land Rights under International Law: From Victors to Actors* (Ardsley, NY: Transnational, 2006), 1–2.

37 Roger Merino, "Conflicting Sovereignties: Global Conservation, Protected Areas, and Indigenous Nations in the Peruvian Amazon," *Global Environmental Politics* 22:2 (2022): 95–116;

Interestingly, while there is a move toward questioning the way in which sovereign states interact legally and politically with indigenous populations in terms of territorial disputes, the Americas present another layer concerning people, sovereignty and territorial disputes. For example, the Falkland/Malvinas Islanders[38] and the Raizal community,[39] who were both settlers at one time, claim self-determination. Despite their differences, these cases include elements and features pertaining to the domestic, regional and international contexts. For instance, the transition from factual settlement to legal

Roger Merino, "Reimagining the Nation-State: Indigenous Peoples and the Making of Plurinationalism in Latin America," *Leiden Journal of International Law* 31:4 (2018): 773–792; Anna F. Laing, "Re-Producing Territory: Between Resource Nationalism and Indigenous Self-Determination in Bolivia," *Geoforum* 108 (2020): 28–38; Austen L. Parrish, "Changing Territoriality, Fading Sovereignty, and the Development of Indigenous Rights," *American Indian Law Review* 31:2 (2006/2007): 291–313; Rachel Sieder, "Indigenous Peoples' Rights and the Law in Latin America," in Corinne Lennox and Damien Short, eds., *Handbook of Indigenous Peoples' Rights* (New York, NY: Routledge, 2016), 414–423; Willem van Genugten and Camillo Perez-Bustillo, "The Emerging International Architecture of Indigenous Rights: The Interaction between Global, Regional, and National Dimensions," *International Journal on Minority and Group Rights* 11:4 (2004): 379–409; Gemma van der Haar, "The Zapatista Uprising and the Struggle for Indigenous Autonomy," *European Review of Latin American and Caribbean Studies* 76 (2004): 98–108; Donna Lee Van Cott, "Broadening Democracy: Latin America's Indigenous Peoples' Movements," *Current History* 103:670 (2004) 80–85; Shane Greene, "Getting Over the Andes: The Geo-Eco-Politics of Indigenous Movements in Peru's Twenty-First Century Inca Empire," *Journal of Latin American Studies* 38:2 (2006): 327–354.

38 Refer to the author's previous works for further reading. In particular, Jorge E. Núñez, *Territorial Disputes and State Sovereignty: International Law and Politics* (London and New York, NY: Routledge, Taylor & Francis Group, 2020), Chapter 6. See also Alan J. Day, ed., *Border and Territorial Disputes* (Essex: Longman, 1982), 340–345; Peter Beck, *The Falkland Islands as an International Problem* (London and New York, NY: Routledge, 1998); Peter Beck, "The Future of the Falkland Islands: A Solution Made in Hong Kong?" *International Affairs* 61 (1985): 643–660; Peter Beck, "Looking at the Falkland Islands from Antarctica: The Broader Regional Perspective," *Polar Record* 30 (1994): 167–180; Peter Beck, "Britain's Falkland Future—the Need to Look Back," *The Round Table* 73 (1984): 139–152; Peter Beck, "Cooperative Confrontation in the Falkland Island Dispute," *Journal of Inter-American Studies and World Affairs* 24 (1982): 37–57. For official historical accounts see the UK and Argentina's governmental websites. Argentina's official position at the UN is available at https://www.cancilleria.gob.ar/es/politica-exterior/cuestion-malvinas/malvinas-en-naciones-unidas accessed 9 August 2023. UK Parliament files, The House of Lords (27 March 2017), are available at http://researchbriefings.files.parliament.uk/documents/LIF-2017-0028/LIF-2017-0028.pdf accessed 9 August 2023. The official Falkland/Malvinas Islands position is available at https://www.falklands.gov.fk/assembly/un-commitee-of-24 accessed 9 August 2023.

39 Pablo Alonso González, Wilhelm Londoño and Eva Parga-Dans, "Equality and Hierarchy, Sovereignty and Multiculturalism: The Heritagisation of Raizals in Santa Catalina (Colombia)," *Journal of Ethnic and Migration Studies* 46:19 (2020): 4066–4085; James Ross, "Routes for Roots: Entering the 21st Century in San Andrés Island, Colombia," *Caribbean Studies* 35:1 (2007): 3–36.

claim of sovereignty by means of the "right-peopling"[40] of the territory with settlers was a way in which some former colonial powers alien to the region secured their claim to sovereignty over new territories. Moreover, states in the Americas and those former colonial powers with ongoing presence in the region such as the United Kingdom are members of organizations like the OAS, the North Atlantic Treaty Organization (NATO) and the United Nations (UN). Notably, this results in a combination of an intra- and inter-state dynamic. Part of the intra-state dynamic behind territorial disputes in the Americas can be explained because of socioeconomic and political interests from subgroups such as the Revolutionary Armed Forces of Colombia (FARC).[41]

Each territorial dispute has its own characteristics.[42] Indeed, territorial disputes may be defined and characterized unidimensionally in several ways: (a) according to the elements of a sovereign state they may be based on, e.g. population (minorities, ethnic conflicts, etc.), territory (natural resources, borders, etc.) and government (leaders' popularity, applicable law, etc.); (b) according to the claims introduced by the challenger and challenged party, based on effective control, territorial integrity, historical, cultural, economic, elitist, ideological or colorable claim; (c) according to the issues at stake, centered on strategic location of the territory, ties to bordering minority, political unification or economic value of the territory; (d) according to the many elements and features related to the context in question, e.g. international, regional and domestic. However, territorial disputes are often more intricate and require a multidimensional approach to fully understand, explain and assess them. Consequently, without discarding unidimensional views, the same territorial dispute could be understood, explained and assessed more comprehensively by taking a multidimensional approach that considers, for instance, agents other than solely sovereign states. For example, a multidimensional approach may also consider communities such as indigenous peoples, whether normatively they constitute a state or not, the different categories of claims and issues that are at stake and the contexts that may influence their dynamics.

40 Brendan O'Leary, "The Elements of Right-Sizing and Right-Peopling the State" in Brendan O'Leary, Ian S. Lustick and Thomas Callaghy, eds., *Right-Sizing the State: The Politics of Moving Borders* (Oxford: Oxford University Press, 2001), 15–73.

41 Luis Gabriel Salas Salazar, Jonas Wolff and Fabián Eduardo Camelo, "Towards Violent Peace? Territorial Dynamics of Violence in Tumaco (Colombia) before and after the Demobilisation of the FARC-EP," *Conflict, Security & Development* 19:5 (2019): 497–520.

42 See Jorge E. Núñez, *Territorial Disputes and State Sovereignty: International Law and Politics* (London and New York, NY: Routledge, Taylor & Francis Group, 2020), Chapters 6, 7 and 8 for individual territorial disputes in more detail.

Categories of claims

Claims over disputed territories may have legal and/or non-legal or extra-legal bases.[43] These include effective control, history, culture, territorial integrity, economy, elitism and ideology. Effective control implies the display of power and authority over a territory and its population. For example, effective control is displayed by newly formed states, like the post-colonial Latin American states, claiming control over territories once under colonial rule. A historical claim is based on past facts related to the disputed territory whether there is current actual occupation and effective control or not. For example, these are typified by former colonial powers and their claims on discovery and settlement. A cultural claim refers to a population or subgroup of people who identify themselves as part of a group because of common bonds such as ethnicity, language and religion—this may result in self-determination. A territorial integrity claim is based on the geographical location of the territory in question, as for example in the Falkland/Malvinas Islands and the Argentine view. An economic claim is linked to the importance of the disputed territory in relation to the welfare of the state in question—i.e. arguably, it is necessary for their development. An elitist claim refers to a particular minority understanding they have the right or duty to control the disputed territory. An ideological claim has to do with purely ideological arguments, for example, with reference to spreading faith or particular idiosyncratic principles such as communism. Regardless of their peculiarities, all categories of claims can be characterized as a colorable claim.[44] A claim includes any valid legal and/or non-legal or extra-legal reason to support an argument over the sovereignty of the disputed territory. That reason should be "colorable" enough to demonstrate that intended rights are at least sufficiently plausible to be acknowledged and that they can be based on reasonable circumstances, such as political, historical, legal or geographical arguments.

43 See Jorge E. Núñez, *Cosmopolitanism, State Sovereignty, International Law and Politics: A Theory* (London and New York, NY: Routledge, Taylor & Francis Group, 2023), Chapter 7; Jorge E. Núñez, *Territorial Disputes and State Sovereignty: International Law and Politics* (London and New York, NY: Routledge, Taylor & Francis Group, 2020), Chapter 4; and Jorge E. Núñez, *Sovereignty Conflicts and International Law and Politics: A Distributive Justice Issue* (London and New York, NY: Routledge, Taylor & Francis Group, 2017), Chapter 6.

44 See Jorge E. Núñez, *Cosmopolitanism, State Sovereignty, International Law and Politics: A Theory* (London and New York, NY: Routledge, Taylor & Francis Group, 2023), Chapter 7; Jorge E. Núñez, *Territorial Disputes and State Sovereignty: International Law and Politics* (London and New York, NY: Routledge, Taylor & Francis Group, 2020), Chapter 4; and Jorge E. Núñez, *Sovereignty Conflicts and International Law and Politics: A Distributive Justice Issue* (London and New York, NY: Routledge, Taylor & Francis Group, 2017), Chapter 6.

Constant issues at stake

Issues at stake in territorial disputes refer to features that could help explain why they may originate, continue or escalate into conflict. They are closely related to claims and may have different characteristics including legal and non-legal or extra-legal considerations. There are several issues at stake present in different cases that concern (a) territory—e.g. strategic location and its economic value; (b) population—e.g. ties with bordering minorities; and (c) government—e.g. political unification. For instance, the geostrategic location and/or the presence of natural resources in or around the disputed territory can define its relevance in the domestic, regional and international context. Example cases include original claims to Antarctica, which were intertwined with claims to the closest islands such as the Falklands/Malvinas where those states with overlapping claims either disagreed or refused to recognize them,[45] and the exploration and exploitation of natural resources in the Caribbean Sea and the Falkland/Malvinas Islands pertaining to the exclusive economic zone on areas where claimed jurisdictions overlap. Ties with bordering minorities refer to homogeneity in terms of culture, ethnicity, etc. between a state's population and people living close by in another state and they can contribute to the origin and ongoing nature of territorial disputes. The borders of modern Latin American states, created by European authorities, had little regard for socio-cultural characteristics. Consequently, a current legally and politically defined typical boundary may bring together different ethnic groups. Political unification in the Americas include several historical cases with failed attempts—e.g. the Republic of Great Colombia (1822–1830), the Federal Republic of the United Provinces of Central America (1823–1838) and the Peruvian–Bolivian Confederation (1836–1839) in which states intended to incorporate another territory.[46]

Context in territorial disputes

The domestic or local, regional and international or global contexts may influence the origin, continuation and potential escalation into conflict of territorial disputes. The international context presents elements and features such as

45 See Discovering Antarctica available at https://discoveringantarctica.org.uk/how-is-antarctica-governed/the-antarctic-treaty/making-claims/ accessed 24 July 2023. Note how research published before the Antarctic Treaty was signed (01/12/1959, entered into force 23/06/1961) referred to this point. See C. H. M. Waldock, "Disputed Sovereignty in the Falklands Islands Dependencies," *British Yearbook of International Law* 25 (1948): 311–353.

46 Gordon Mace, "Regional Integration in Latin America: A Long and Winding Road," *International Journal* 43:3 (1988): 404–427.

balance of military forces,[47] prior gain of territory,[48] common alliance[49] and previous settlement. For example, by the end of the 1980s most of the South American states had peacefully resolved their differences.[50] The geopolitical term of "shatterbelt" refers to a region where conflict may escalate.[51] The regional context[52] encompasses other factors such as common past, geographical location,[53] development and natural resources. Resource-rich areas and defense influence the regional dynamics. For instance, warfare only requires a few select bases,[54] and cases like the Falkland/Malvinas Islands show that their location is key in relation to (a) the resources of Antarctica,[55] and (b) transport and sea lanes in the South Atlantic.[56] Finally, the domestic context includes matters such as prior unresolved disputes,[57] prior loss of territory[58] and decolonization.[59] Political leaders may use justifications such as the restoration of

47 For an in-depth analysis of the relationship between territorial disputes and the military see David B. Carter, "The Strategy of Territorial Conflict," *American Journal of Political Science* 54:4 (2010): 969–987.

48 Paul K. Huth, *Standing Your Ground: Territorial Disputes and International Conflict* (Ann Arbor, MI: University of Michigan Press, 2001), 88.

49 Paul K. Huth, *Standing Your Ground: Territorial Disputes and International Conflict* (Ann Arbor, MI: University of Michigan Press, 2001), 118–119, 160.

50 Jorge Mario Battaglino, "The Coexistence of Peace and Conflict in South America: Toward a New Conceptualization of Types of Peace," *Revista Brasileira de Política Internacional* 55:2 (2012): 131–151.

51 Philip L. Kelly, "Escalation of Regional Conflict: Testing the Shatterbelt Concept," *Political Geography Quarterly* 5:2 (1986): 161–180.

52 For this monograph, regions are territorially characterized. For a more detailed understanding of the term "region" see Alexander B. Murphy, "Regions as Social Construct: The Gap between Theory and Practice," *Progress in Human Geography* 15:1 (1991): 22–35.

53 Kentaro Sakuwa, "The Regional Consequences of Territorial Disputes: An Empirical Analysis of the South China Sea Disputes," *Journal of Asian Security and International Affairs* 4:3 (2017): 316–336; David A. Lake and Patrick M. Morgan, "Regional Security Complexes: A Systems Approach," in David A. Lake and Patrick M. Morgan, eds., *Regional Orders: Building Security in the New World* (University Park, PA: Pennsylvania State University, 1997), 45–67; David A. Lake, "Regional Hierarchy: Authority and Local International Order," *Review of International Studies* 35:1 (2009): 35–58.

54 Philip L. Kelly, "Escalation of Regional Conflict: Testing the Shatterbelt Concept," *Political Geography Quarterly* 5:2 (1986): 161–180, 174.

55 Klaus Dodds and Alan D. Hemmings, "Britain and the British Antarctic Territory in the Wider Geopolitics of the Antarctic and the Southern Ocean," *International Affairs* 89:6 (2013): 1429–1444.

56 Detlef Nolte and Leslie E. Wehner, "Geopolitics in Latin America, Old and New," in David R. Mares and Arie M. Kacowicz, eds., *Routledge Handbook of Latin American Security* (Abingdon: Routledge, 2015), 33–43.

57 Paul K. Huth, *Standing Your Ground: Territorial Disputes and International Conflict* (Ann Arbor, MI: University of Michigan Press, 2001), 93.

58 Paul K. Huth, *Standing Your Ground: Territorial Disputes and International Conflict* (Ann Arbor, MI: University of Michigan Press, 2001), 98.

59 Paul K. Huth, *Standing Your Ground: Territorial Disputes and International Conflict* (Ann Arbor, MI: University of Michigan Press, 2001), 99. See the UN Charter Chapter XII (system

national honor. For example, in the Falkland/Malvinas Islands, Argentina's governments continuously denounce the United Kingdom for the "usurpation" of the archipelago.[60]

Legal and political regional organizations

There are several regional organizations in the Americas.[61] The list below includes their acronyms, full denomination and foundation year.[62]

ACS	Association of Caribbean States 1994
ACTO	Amazon Cooperation Treaty Organization 1995
ALADI	Latin American Integration Association 1960
ALBA	Bolivarian Alliance for the Peoples of Our America 2004
ANDEAN	Andean Community 1969
CACM	Central American Common Market 1960
CALC	Latin American and Caribbean Summit on Integration and Development 2008
CARICOM	Caribbean Community 1965
CELAC	Community of Latin American and Caribbean States 2011
MERCOSUR	Southern Common Market 1994
NAFTA	North American Free Trade Organization 1994
OAS	Organization of American States 1948
ODECA	Organization of Central American States 1951
OECS	Organization of Eastern Caribbean States 1981
PA	Pacific Alliance 2012
SELA	Latin American Economic System 1975
SICA	Central American Integration System 1991
UNASUR	Union of South American Nations 2008

Despite their particularities, regional organizations in the Americas focus on economic integration and relevant law and policies. This is different from the most developed legal and political process of integration followed by the EU, which has evolved from the primary aim of the European Economic

of Mandates), the UN Charter Chapter XI (non-self-governing territories) and UN General Assembly resolution 1514 (XV).

60 Argentina's official position (Ministry of Foreign Affairs and Worship, Argentine Republic): "The Question of the Malvinas Islands," available at https://www.mrecic.gov.ar/en/question-malvinas-islands-0 accessed 9 August 2023.

61 From 1945 to 2015, 18 regional organizations were created in the Americas and only two dissolved. For an extensive analysis see Diana Panke, Sören Stapel and Anna Starkmann, "Regional Organizations in the Americas," in Diana Panke, Sören Stapel and Anna Starkmann, eds., *Comparing Regional Organizations: Global Dynamics and Regional Particularities* (Bristol: Bristol University Press, 2020), 65–82.

62 List based on Diana Panke and Anna Starkmann, "Trajectories of Regional Cooperation: A Comparative Analysis," *Comparative European Politics* 19 (2021): 1–25.

Community in creating a common market (art. 3.3 Treaty on EU) and currently acknowledges the four fundamental freedoms of movement of goods, services, persons and capital (art. 6.2, 6.3 and 21 Treaty on EU and art. 26.2 Treaty on the Functioning of the EU).[63] Regional organizations in the Americas tend to have a limited number of policy competencies—e.g. the Association of Caribbean States (ACS) has 12. However, there are exceptions such as in the case of the Central American Integration System (SICA) with 125 different policy competencies.[64]

In the particular case of territorial disputes, regional organizations have direct and indirect influence. Indirectly, regional integration fosters the chances of settlement because peaceful interrelation between agents otherwise in conflict is necessary to participate in regional organizations.[65] Directly, regionalism and conflict management are interweaved.[66]

Regional dispute settlement means

Regionally, public international law has some legal norms related to international dispute settlement. The OAS has played a major role in conflict resolution.[67] In this regard, the OAS Charter includes—among its applicable norms concerning amicable relationships between Member States and, in particular, dispute resolution—Chapter V that stipulates:[68]

> Article 24: International disputes between Member States shall be submitted to the peaceful procedures set forth in this Charter. This provision shall not be interpreted as an impairment of the rights and obligations of the Member States under Articles 34 and 35 of the Charter of the United Nations.
>
> Article 25: The following are peaceful procedures: direct negotiation, good offices, mediation, investigation and conciliation, judicial

63 For a detailed comparison between the EU and MERCOSUR by the author, see Jorge E. Núñez and Verónica Ichniowski, "Movilidad Internacional de Personas: MERCOSUR y Unión Europea," *Universidad Nacional de La Plata* (2014) available at http://sedici.unlp.edu.ar/handle/10915/44666 accessed 26 July 2023.

64 Diana Panke and Anna Starkmann, "Trajectories of Regional Cooperation: A Comparative Analysis," *Comparative European Politics* 19 (2021): 1–25.

65 Beth A. Simmons, "Capacity, and Compliance: International Institutions and Territorial Disputes," *The Journal of Conflict Resolution* 46:6 (2002): 829–856.

66 Muthiah Alagappa, "Regionalism and Conflict Management: A Framework for Analysis," *Review of International Studies* 21 (1995): 359–387.

67 Jorge I. Domínguez, "Boundary Disputes in Latin America," *United States Institute of Peace* 50 (2003): 3–45 available at https://www.usip.org/sites/default/files/pwks50.pdf accessed 9 August 2023.

68 Charter of the Organization of American States available at http://www.oas.org/dil/1948%20charter%20of%20the%20organization%20of%20american%20states.pdf accessed 27 July 2023.

settlement, arbitration, and those which the parties to the dispute may especially agree upon at any time.

Article 26: In the event that a dispute arises between two or more American States which, in the opinion of one of them, cannot be settled through the usual diplomatic channels, the parties shall agree on some other peaceful procedure that will enable them to reach a solution.

Article 27: A special treaty will establish adequate means for the settlement of disputes and will determine pertinent procedures for each peaceful means such that no dispute between American States may remain without definitive settlement within a reasonable period of time.

Brevitatis causa, this section introduces broadly each of the main means to settle international disputes according to the OAS—negotiation, mediation, inquiry, conciliation, arbitration, judicial settlement—and highlights some limitations in dealing with them.[69]

Negotiation is a dispute settlement method by which states themselves may put an end to their differences.[70] Unsurprisingly, the main issue in relation to negotiations is the parties' consent. The lack of consent can vary from a simple refusal to deal with a counterpart, as with Argentina and the United Kingdom after the 1982 Falklands/Malvinas war, or a complete denial of standing to any other party. Moreover, the representatives in the negotiation may not actually be acting on behalf of those who are meant to be represented. Finally, unequal power between the participants may raise several negative issues. For instance, although only directly involved states may take part in the negotiations, the fact of any of these states being part of a coalition may have an effect on the process and the outcome.[71]

Mediation implies the intervention of a third party.[72] In contrast to arbitration and adjudication, the third party only aims to persuade the challenger and

69 Due to this monograph's object of study, territorial disputes, other organizations will not be discussed. For further details about each dispute settlement procedure see Jorge E. Núñez, *Territorial Disputes and State Sovereignty: International Law and Politics* (London and New York, NY: Routledge, Taylor & Francis Group, 2020), Chapter 5.

70 Barry O'Neill, "International Negotiation: Some Conceptual Developments," *Annual Review of Political Science* 21:1 (2018): 515–533; Brigid Starkey, Mark A. Boyer and Jonathan Wilkenfeld, *International Negotiation in a Complex World* (Lanham, MD: New Millennium Books in International Studies, Rowman and Littlefield, 2005); and Brigid Starkey, Mark A. Boyer and Jonathan Wilkenfeld, *Negotiating a Complex World: An Introduction to International Negotiation* (Lanham, MD: New Millennium Books in International Studies, Rowman and Littlefield, 2005).

71 Christophe Dupont, "Coalition Theory: Using Power to Build Cooperation," in Ira William Zartman, ed., *International Multilateral Negotiation: Approaches to the Management of Complexity* (San Francisco, CA: Jossey-Bass, 1994), 148–177.

72 J. Bercovitch and J. Z. Rubin, *Mediation in International Relations: Multiple Approaches to Conflict Management* (London: Palgrave Macmillan, 1992); Saadia Touval and I. William Zartman, eds., *International Mediation in Theory and* Practice (Boulder, CO: Westview Press,

the challenged agents to agree on a peaceful settlement by offering non-binding suggestions.[73] Similar to the case of negotiation, the success of the process of mediation and its outcome depends on the willingness of the participants to compromise. Furthermore, even if an agreement is achieved, its actual implementation may not be. There are some circumstances that may decide the success or failure in mediation, including identification, cohesiveness, type of regime, motivation, previous and ongoing relationships, and distribution of power.[74]

Inquiry is the process performed by a court or another body to resolve an issue of fact.[75] States may choose to have their disagreement on some issues independently investigated.[76] It requires the agreement of the parties in conflict, and the final report is limited to stating the facts and, therefore, is not binding. The procedure has several issues. First, the facts are usually open to different interpretations and can be dealt with through negotiation between the claiming parties. Second, there are other means for dispute settlement that are less cumbersome. Third, in general, few attempts to settle disputes by third parties are popular: states are more interested in advancing their views than in settling the dispute.

Conciliation includes elements of both inquiry and mediation and implies a third party dealing with the dispute by investigating its basis and submitting a report with suggestions for settlement.[77] The parties may agree to some-

---

1985); Jacob Bercovitch, "Mediation at the Interstate Level: Engagement or Neutrality as the Key to Success," in N. Ropers, ed., *Peaceful Conflict Management on the Interstate Level* (Bonn: International Peace Foundation, 1995), 89–112; Jacob Bercovitch, *Theory and Practice of International Mediation* (London and New York, NY: Routledge, Taylor & Francis Group, 2011); and many others.

73 For a distinction between "pure mediation," in which the parties retain control over the outcome, and "mediation with muscle," in which the third party may deploy positive and negative inducements see Peter Wallensteen and Isak Svensoon, "Talking Peace: International Mediation in Armed Conflicts," *Journal of Peace Research* 51:2 (2014): 315–327.

74 Marieke Kleiboer, "Understanding Success and Failure of International Mediation," *Journal of Conflict Resolution* 40:2 (1996): 360–389. See also J. Bercovitch, "International Mediation and Dispute Settlement: Evaluating the Conditions for Successful Mediation," *Negotiation Journal* 7:1 (1991): 17–30.

75 Inquiry as a specific procedure is distinguished from the general fact-finding process used as part of other means to settle a dispute. Richard B. Lillich, ed., *Fact-Finding Before International Tribunals: Eleventh Sokol Colloquium* (Ardsley-on-Hudson, NY: Transnational Public Inc., 1991); J. Collier and V. Lowe, *The Settlement of Disputes in International Law: Institutions and Procedures* (Oxford: Oxford University Press, 1999), 24; N. Bar-Yaacov, *The Handling of International Disputes by Means of Inquiry* (London: Oxford University Press, 1975).

76 J. G. Merrills, *International Dispute Settlement* (Cambridge: Cambridge University Press, 2017), 43.

77 Conciliation means: "a method for the settlement of international disputes of any nature according to which a Commission set up by the Parties, either on a permanent basis or on an ad hoc basis to deal with a dispute, proceeds to the impartial examination of the dispute and attempts to define the terms of a settlement susceptible of being accepted by them, or of affording the Parties, with a view to its settlement, such aid as they may have requested."

thing different.[78] Few international disputes have been dealt with through conciliation,[79] despite the fact many international instruments include conciliation. First, some treaties restrict its application to certain classes of disputes or include several reservations for its application. Second, there are many other means to deal with an international difference, such as arbitration, that may be more practical and cost-effective approaches.[80]

Arbitration refers to legal issues and implies a binding decision.[81] States settle their differences by judges of their own choice based on law.[82] As with the previously mentioned dispute settlement procedures, arbitration has some limitations.[83] First, there is the reluctance of claimant states to commit to a judicial decision.[84] Second, there is the lack of means in public international

---

See art. 1 Regulations on the Procedure of International Conciliation by the Institute of International Law (1961) available at http://www.idi-iil.org/app/uploads/2017/06/1961_salz_02_en.pdf accessed 9 August 2023. See also J. Collier and V. Lowe, *The Settlement of Disputes in International Law: Institutions and Procedures* (Oxford: Oxford University Press, 1999), 29; N. Bar-Yaacov, *The Handling of International Disputes by Means of Inquiry* (London: Oxford University Press, 1975), Chapters 5 and 7; J. G. Merrills, *International Dispute Settlement* (Cambridge: Cambridge University Press, 2017), Chapter 4; Malcolm N. Shaw, *International Law* (Cambridge: Cambridge University Press, 2003), 925–928; and many others.

78 See, for example, art. 14 (3) of the Treaty Establishing the Organization of Eastern Caribbean States (1981), which states that "Member States undertake to accept the conciliation procedure referred to in the preceding paragraph as compulsory. Any decisions or recommendations of the Conciliation Commission in resolution of the dispute shall be final and binding on the Member States."

79 J. G. Merrills, *International Dispute Settlement* (Cambridge: Cambridge University Press, 2017), 84–87.

80 Ian Sinclair, *The Vienna Convention on the Law of Treaties* (Manchester: Manchester University Press, 1984) available at https://www.escholar.manchester.ac.uk/api/datastream?publicationPid=uk-ac-man-scw:265335&datastreamId=FULL-TEXT.PDF accessed 9 August 2023. See in particular p. 235 which states: "No State is anxious to indulge in lengthy and expensive international conciliation or litigation. This imposes a very heavy burden upon Foreign Offices and upon their legal advisers, with the outcome far from certain."

81 J. G. Merrills, *International Dispute Settlement* (Cambridge: Cambridge University Press, 2017), Chapter 5; Malcolm N. Shaw, *International Law* (Cambridge: Cambridge University Press, 2003), 951–958. See also L. Simpson and H. Fox, *International Arbitration: Law and Practice* (London: Stevens and Sons Limited, 1959); S. Schwebel, *International Arbitration: Three Salient Problems* (Cambridge: Grotius Publications Limited, 1987); Henry T. King and James D. Graham, "Origins of Modern International Arbitration," *Dispute Resolution Journal* 51:1 (1996): 42; Carla S. Copeland, "The Use of Arbitration to Settle Territorial Disputes," *Fordham Law Review* 67:6 (1999): 3073–3108; Todd L. Allee and Paul K. Huth, "The Pursuit of Legal Settlements to Territorial Disputes," *Conflict Management and Peace Science* 23:4 (2006): 285–307; and many others.

82 Articles 15 (1899) 37 (1907), Hague Conventions for the Pacific Settlement of Disputes.

83 Stephen E. Gent, "The Politics of International Arbitration and Adjudication," *Penn State Journal of Law and International Affairs* 2:1 (2013): 66–77.

84 Stephen E. Gent and Megan Shannon, "Decision Control and the Pursuit of Binding Conflict Management: Choosing the Ties that Bind," *Journal of Conflict Resolution* 55:5 (2011): 710–734.

law to enforce the awards. Finally, and arguably, there is the lack of real neutrality of the third party acting as arbitrator and, therefore, the risk of a biased decision.[85]

The OAS's structure includes organs such as the General Assembly, the Meeting of Consultation of Ministers of Foreign Affairs, the Permanent Council, the Inter-American Council for Integral Development, the Inter-American Judicial Committee, the Inter-American Commission on Human Rights and the General Secretariat, and it also coordinates specialized conferences and organizations.[86] Regardless of these organs and activities, the OAS has no court of general jurisdiction. Therefore, if there is a territorial dispute between Member States, they have an obligation to use the aforementioned pacific means of settlement or submit the dispute to the ICJ or the UN Security Council. Any peaceful method of dispute settlement on which the parties agree may be used despite the priorities of the Organization. The details concerning the OAS dispute settlement process, Member States' obligation to use pacific means and the different available procedures—i.e. good offices, mediation, investigation, conciliation, the *ipso facto* recognition of the ICJ jurisdiction and relevant judicial procedure, arbitration, fulfillment of decisions and advisory opinions—are included in the American Treaty on Pacific Settlement "Pact of Bogotá" (A-42) signed on 30 April 1948 and in force for 15 out of 35 states.[87]

Judicial settlement by the ICJ can play an important role.[88] Following contentious[89] or advisory[90] procedures and with decisions based on international law,[91] the Court only interprets existing law and does not legislate.[92] The main issue with the ICJ in settling territorial disputes is the fact that these

85 Stephen E. Gent and Megan Shannon, "The Effectiveness of International Arbitration and Adjudication: Getting into a Bind," *The Journal of Politics* 72:2 (2010): 366–380.

86 For details about the OAS structure and each organ refer to their website available at https://www.oas.org/en/about/our_structure.asp accessed 27 July 2023.

87 Complete text of the American Treaty on Pacific Settlement "Pact of Bogotá" (A-42), including details about signatories and ratifications available at https://www.oas.org/en/sla/dil/inter_american_treaties_A-42_pacific_settlement_pact_bogota.asp accessed 27 July 2023.

88 J. G. Merrills, *International Dispute Settlement* (Cambridge: Cambridge University Press, 2017), Chapter 6; Malcolm N. Shaw, *International Law* (Cambridge: Cambridge University Press, 2003), 959–1005; Malcolm N. Shaw, ed., *Rosenne's Law and Practice of the International Court: 1920–2015* (Leiden: Brill, 2016); Arthur Eyffinger and Arthur Witteveen, *The International Court of Justice 1946–1996* (The Hague, London and Boston, MA: Kluwer Law International, 1996); and many others.

89 Renata Szafarz, *The Compulsory Jurisdiction of the International Court of Justice* (Dordrecht: Kluwer Academic Publishers, 1993).

90 Kenneth James Keith, *The Extent of the Advisory Jurisdiction of the International Court of Justice* (Leiden: A. W. Sijthoff, 1971).

91 *The Haya de la Torre Case* (ICJ Reports, 1951); *The Northern Cameroons Case* (ICJ Reports, 1963).

92 *Legality of the Threat or Use of Nuclear Weapons* (ICJ Reports, 1966).

differences are not limited to legal issues but also include political realities.[93] Moreover, the Court is not concerned with compliance with its decisions,[94] so its enforcement relies on the goodwill of the parties.[95] Finally, regardless of its potential advantages, only a very small number of contentious cases have appeared before the Court since 1945.[96]

In addition to these rules and means concerning dispute settlement, the OAS General Assembly by Resolution 1756 (XXX-O/00) established in 2000 the OAS Peace Fund as a mechanism to provide financial resources to OAS Member States in order to enable the organization to manage territorial disputes.[97] As part of their peaceful settlement of territorial disputes means, according to the OAS General Assembly Resolution 2858 (XLIV-O/14), the General Secretariat continues to strengthen its knowledge and experience in the area of peaceful settlement of territorial disputes.[98] The OAS Peace Fund has been instrumental in dealing with the cases between Honduras and Nicaragua related to maritime boundaries, El Salvador and Honduras pertaining to the demarcation of their border and, more recently, the territorial dispute between Belize and Guatemala.[99]

The role of regional organizations and guarantors

Clearly, states in the Americas have access to several procedures in order to deal with a dispute, and they have a legal obligation to use them. In addition to these regional means, there are other procedures pertaining to the international legal order.[100] Notwithstanding these regional and international menus

93 See J. G. Merrills, *International Dispute Settlement* (Cambridge: Cambridge University Press, 2017), 162–166.
94 The Nuclear Test case, ICJ Report, 1974, 477.
95 Examples of non-compliance are Albania in the Corfu Channel Case (ICJ Reports, 1949), Iceland in the Fisheries Jurisdiction case (ICJ Reports, 1974) and Iran in the Iranian Hostages case (ICJ Reports, 1980).
96 See J. G. Merrills, *International Dispute Settlement* (Cambridge: Cambridge University Press, 2017), 171–176.
97 The OAS Peace Fund website is available at https://www.oas.org/sap/peacefund/peacefund/ accessed 27 July 2023.
98 For the OAS General Assembly Resolutions concerning the Peace Fund see their dedicated webpage available at https://www.oas.org/sap/peacefund/resolutions/ accessed 27 July 2023.
99 For details about these three cases see the OAS Peace Fund website, General information, available at https://www.oas.org/sap/peacefund/peacefund/ accessed 27 July 2023.
100 For an extensive analysis on different dispute settlement procedures and remedies see Jorge E. Núñez, *Territorial Disputes and State Sovereignty: International Law and Politics* (London and New York, NY: Routledge, Taylor & Francis Group, 2020), Chapter 5; and Jorge E. Núñez, *Sovereignty Conflicts and International Law and Politics: A Distributive Justice Issue* (London and New York, NY: Routledge, Taylor & Francis Group, 2017), Chapter 5. For the most comprehensive and up-to-date list of resources about dispute settlement (including handbooks, leading articles, bibliographies, periodicals, serial publications and documents

of procedures and resultant remedies to deal with territorial disputes, they all present a degree of uncertainty that, arguably, may make the challenger and the challenged parties doubt the viability of their application. Yet, in precise terms, if the agents in question accept them and these procedures result in a peaceful settlement, there is no question about their viability. However, all existing procedures and resultant remedies, whether unilateral, bilateral or multilateral,[101] may be reasonably rejected by one or more involved parties. The reasons for their rejection include solutions that imply ignoring claims, unfair policies, use of force or any action that may go against an otherwise peaceful situation. Therefore, there is a case to argue for the need for a peaceful solution that current international procedures and remedies cannot offer, a solution that no party may reasonably reject.[102]

Despite the desirability of achieving a peaceful settlement, the viability of regional organizations such as the OAS[103] in attaining a solution in cases concerning territorial disputes is limited in various ways.[104] Geographically, the international context that exacerbates the differences may be overlooked—i.e. the direct and indirect influence of agents alien to the region.[105] In that vein, current territorial disputes in the Americas include parties alien to the

of interest) see the Peace Palace Library available at https://www.peacepalacelibrary.nl/research-guides/settlement-of-international-disputes/settlement-of-international-disputes/ accessed 27 July 2023.

101 For the classification of unilateral, bilateral and multilateral solutions see Jorge E. Núñez, *Territorial Disputes and State Sovereignty: International Law and Politics* (London and New York, NY: Routledge, Taylor & Francis Group, 2020), Chapter 5; and Jorge E. Núñez, *Sovereignty Conflicts and International Law and Politics: A Distributive Justice Issue* (London and New York, NY: Routledge, Taylor & Francis Group, 2017), Chapter 5.

102 For the difference between principles "which no one could reasonably reject" and principles "which everyone could reasonably accept" see T. M. Scanlon, "Contractualism and Utilitarianism," in Amartya Sen and Bernard Williams, eds., *Utilitarianism and Beyond* (Cambridge: Cambridge University Press; Paris: Editions de la Maison des Sciences de l'Homme, 1982), 103–128.

103 For an account of territorial dispute cases in which the OAS has been involved see V. Jeifets and L. Khadorich, "OAS and Interstate Dispute Resolution at the Beginning of the 21st Century: General Pattern and Peculiarities," *International Journal of Cognitive and Language Sciences* 9:4 (2015): 1148–1155.

104 R. Allison, "Regionalism, Regional Structures and Security Management in Central Asia," *International Affairs* 80:3 (2004): 463–483; B. Buzan and O. Wæver, *Regions and Powers: The Structure of International Security* (Cambridge: Cambridge University Press, 2003); L. Cliffe, "Regional Dimensions of Conflict in the Horn of Africa," *Third World Quarterly* 20:1 (1999): 89–111; M. Leifer, *ASEAN and the Security of South-East Asia* (London: Routledge, 1989); J. Mearsheimer, "The False Promise of International Institutions," *International Security* 19:3 (1994): 5–49; Tullio Treves, "International Organizations as Parties to Contentious Cases: Selected Aspects," in Laurence Boisson de Chazournes, Cesare Romano and Ruth Mackenzie, eds., *International Organizations and International Dispute Settlement: Trends and Prospects* (New York, NY: Transnational Publishers, 2002), 37–48; and many others.

105 See Chapters 5 and 6.

region or that are not part of the regional organization in question, such as the Falkland/Malvinas Islands case and the United Kingdom. Additionally, not all regional organizations have jurisdiction over internal affairs. Finally, a common problem to any international organization, including the OAS, is the question about enforcement of the decision once there is a settlement.

The viability of dispute settlement procedures in peacefully and permanently solving these differences may be questionable. However, when these procedures are combined with regional agents and institutions, there is arguably a stronger likelihood for their success. It cannot be questioned that in the Americas regional institutions such as the OAS and neighboring states acting as guarantors have facilitated peaceful permanent understandings after conflict. For example, regional arbitrators and guarantors defined peacebuilding in the continent such as in the South American cases of: (1) the 1932–1933 Colombia–Peru War (or the Leticia Incident) that, despite the Salomón–Lozano Treaty (1922),[106] finished with the 1934 Rio Protocol;[107] (2) the 1932–1938 Chaco War between Bolivia and Paraguay[108] that was settled by the Peace, Friendship and Boundary Treaty[109] and had as its guarantors Argentina, Brazil, Chile and Uruguay; and (3) the 1941–1942 Ecuadorian–Peruvian War that, despite the 1942 Rio de Janeiro Protocol,[110] was finalized by means of the 1998 Brasilia Peace Agreement[111] and required Argentina, Brazil, Chile and the United States to play a central role as guarantors.

Although the success or failure in peacebuilding depends on several issues, the previous examples suggest that the presence of regional arbitrators and guarantors may result in a higher likelihood for peacebuilding. Therefore, in the Americas, successful resolution of conflict and the fostering of regional

106 A. Curtis Wilgus, "The Leticia Incident," *World Affairs* 95:3 (1932): 179–181; Carlos Camacho Arango, *El Conflicto de Leticia (1932–1933) y los Ejércitos de Perú y Colombia* (Bogotá: Universidad Externado de Colombia, 2016).

107 Protocol of Friendship and Co-operation, and Additional Act Between the Republic of Colombia and the Republic of Peru, signed in Rio de Janeiro on 24 May 1934 available at https://archives.ungeneva.org/no-3786-colombie-et-perou-protocole-damitie-et-de-cooperation-et-acte-additionnel-signes-a-rio-de-janeiro-le-24-mai-1934-et-echange-de-notes-y-relatif-bogota-les-2-et-5-mars-1935-enregistres-le-4-decembre-1935-a-la-demande-du-delegue-p/download accessed 7 August 2023.

108 Bruce Farcau, *The Chaco War: Bolivia and Paraguay, 1932–35* (Westport, CT: Praeger, 1996).

109 Bolivia–Paraguay: Treaty of Peace, Friendship and Boundaries, *The American Journal of International Law* 32:4 (1938): 139–141 available at http://www.jstor.org/stable/2213730 accessed 6 November 2024.

110 Complete text of the 1942 Rio Protocol available at https://peacemaker.un.org/sites/peacemaker.un.org/files/Rio%20Protocol%20English%201942.pdf accessed 7 August 2023.

111 Complete text of the 1998 Brasilia Peace Agreement available at https://www.peaceagreements.org/viewmasterdocument/212 accessed 7 August 2023; Monica Herz and João Pontes Nogueira, *Ecuador vs. Peru: Peacemaking Amid Rivalry* (Boulder, CO: Lynne Rienner 2002), 97–100.

peacemaking and peacekeeping may be due to several of these issues and, in particular, to the exclusion of exogenous legal, political and geographical influence and the role of regional arbitrators and guarantors.[112]

Conclusion

In order to introduce key notions and institutions pertaining to legal and political sciences and international relations concerned with territorial disputes in the Americas that will be used in the rest of the monograph, the chapter referred to sovereignty, territorial disputes and regional organizations. Clearly, sovereignty and territorial disputes are intertwined. Historically, the Americas have witnessed disputes between agents such as individuals, communities and states related to sovereignty claims over territories based on several issues such as geostrategic location, colonial roots, public international law and new technologies. At the intersection between sovereignty and territorial disputes, among other means for conflict resolution, states around the world have created or joined organizations to attain or maintain a peaceful understanding with other agents despite potential or actual differences. Like other regions around the world, the Americas have several regional organizations of different natures that incorporate conflict resolution means, including those referring to territorial disputes.

The first part of the chapter centered on the notion of "sovereignty." By accepting that different disciplines such as legal and political sciences and international relations comprehend, explain and assess "sovereignty" in their own ways and apply these understandings to law and politics under these bases, it was possible to discern that they have unidimensional views about the same object of study. Coupled with the notion of "state" and its necessary elements—i.e. population, territory and government—the first section incorporated the idea of realms to characterize factual, normative and axiological sovereignty. The section did not argue against these unidimensional views on state sovereignty. The argument was for the acknowledgment of their incompleteness because of their fragmentation in order to demonstrate that only a multidimensional view on state sovereignty can enable a robust comprehension, explanation and analysis of cases in which the notion is important. Several examples relevant to the Americas, including historical, legal and political elements and features, were very briefly offered to illustrate this point.

In turn, the second part focused on territorial disputes and started by presenting narrow and broad accounts of the notions that characterize them as conflict of interests. In any case, territorial disputes encompass several

112 For a more detailed account of the reasons behind peacemaking and peacekeeping in the Americas see Jorge I. Domínguez, "Boundary Disputes in Latin America," *United States Institute of Peace* 50 (2003): 3–45 available at https://www.usip.org/sites/default/files/pwks50.pdf accessed 9 August 2023.

pluralisms—e.g. agents, contexts, realms. Accordingly, the chapter advanced the idea that a narrow or broad account of a territorial dispute will depend on the way in which scholarly disciplines such as legal and political sciences and international relations understand, explain and assess them, whether unidimensionally or multidimensionally. To bring evidence for this argument, several examples in the Americas were briefly referred to. These cases demonstrated that territorial disputes are constituted by a variety of categories of claims, constant issues at stake and contexts. It followed from this discussion that the scholarly choice to understand, explain and assess territorial disputes might be to focus, for example, on only legal or only political issues, and only be concerned with a particular element or feature such as population, territory or government. However relevant and valuable this kind of unidimensional approach might be, the section suggested the outcome would be incomplete because of its fragmentation.

The chapter finished with the third section on legal and political regional organizations in the Americas. All existing organizations were listed because, as explained, they might have direct and indirect influence on situations pertaining to sovereignty and territorial disputes. Thereafter, the focus moved to the OAS because it is the only organization that, regionally, deals directly with territorial disputes. Relevant legal norms and regional dispute settlements were introduced and a subsection explained why the challenger and the challenged parties in a territorial dispute might doubt the viability of their application. By referring to some historical examples in the Americas, the final subsection highlighted the fact that the role of regional organizations and guarantors suggests a higher likelihood for peacemaking and peacekeeping.

Clearly, to gain a more robust understanding of territorial disputes in the Americas, their intricacy must be accepted. It follows from this statement that any scholarly exploration of these disputes should first acknowledge their complexity and, secondly, be able to offer a way to explain and assess the many elements and features that are involved. Consequently, the next chapter will introduce two notions: pluralism of pluralisms, as a way to characterize territorial disputes and their intricate nature, and the multidimensional approach, as a means to assess and explain them more comprehensively.

Bibliography

Alagappa, Muthiah. "Regionalism and Conflict Management: A Framework for Analysis." *Review of International Studies* 21 (1995): 359–387.

Allee, Todd L. and Paul K. Huth. "The Pursuit of Legal Settlements to Territorial Disputes." *Conflict Management and Peace Science* 23:4 (2006): 285–307.

Allison, R. "Regionalism, Regional Structures and Security Management in Central Asia." *International Affairs* 80:3 (2004): 463–483.

Bar-Yaacov, N. *The Handling of International Disputes by Means of Inquiry*. London: Oxford University Press, 1975.

Battaglino, Jorge Mario. "The Coexistence of Peace and Conflict in South America: Toward a New Conceptualization of Types of Peace." *Revista Brasileira de Política Internacional* 55:2 (2012): 131–151.

Beck, Peter. "Britain's Falkland Future—the Need to Look Back." *The Round Table* 73 (1984): 139–152.

Beck, Peter. "Cooperative Confrontation in the Falkland Island Dispute." *Journal of Interamerican Studies and World Affairs* 24 (1982): 37–57.

Beck, Peter. "Looking at the Falkland Islands from Antarctica: The Broader Regional Perspective." *Polar Record* 30 (1994): 167–180.

Beck, Peter. *The Falkland Islands as an International Problem*. London and New York, NY: Routledge, 1998.

Beck, Peter. "The Future of the Falkland Islands: A Solution Made in Hong Kong?" *International Affairs, Royal Institute of International Affairs* 61 (1985): 643–660.

Bercovitch, Jacob. "International Mediation and Dispute Settlement: Evaluating the Conditions for Successful Mediation." *Negotiation Journal* 7:1 (1991): 17–30.

Bercovitch, Jacob. "Mediation at the Interstate Level: Engagement or Neutrality as the Key to Success." In *Peaceful Conflict Management on the Interstate Level*, Ropers, N., ed. 89–112. Bonn: International Peace Foundation, 1995.

Bercovitch, Jacob. *Theory and Practice of International Mediation*. London and New York, NY: Routledge, Taylor & Francis Group, 2011.

Bercovitch, Jacob and Jeffrey Z. Rubin. *Mediation in International Relations: Multiple Approaches to Conflict Management*. London: Palgrave Macmillan, 1992.

Brown, Kirby. "Sovereignty." *Western American Literature* 53:1 (2018): 81–89.

Brownlie, Ian. *Principles of Public International Law*. Oxford: Oxford University Press, 2008.

Buzan, B. and O. Wæver. *Regions and Powers: The Structure of International Security*. Cambridge: Cambridge University Press, 2003.

Camacho Arango, Carlos. *El Conflicto de Leticia (1932–1933) y los Ejércitos de Perú y Colombia*. Bogotá: Universidad Externado de Colombia, 2016.

Carter, David B. "The Strategy of Territorial Conflict." *American Journal of Political Science* 54:4 (2010): 969–987.

Caspersen, Nina. "Collective Non-Recognition of States." In *Routledge Handbook of State Recognition*, Visoka, G., Doyle, J. and Newman, E., eds. 231–241. Oxford and New York, NY: Routledge, 2020.

Cassese, Antonio. *International Law*. Oxford: Oxford University Press, 2001.

Cliffe, L. "Regional Dimensions of Conflict in the Horn of Africa." *Third World Quarterly* 20:1 (1999): 89–111.

Collier, J. and V. Lowe. *The Settlement of Disputes in International Law: Institutions and Procedures*. Oxford: Oxford University Press, 1999.

Copeland, Carla S. "The Use of Arbitration to Settle Territorial Disputes." *Fordham Law Review* 67:6 (1999): 3073–3108.

Curtis Wilgus, A. "The Leticia Incident." *World Affairs* 95:3 (1932): 179–181.

Day, Alan J., ed. *Border and Territorial Disputes*. Essex: Longman, 1982.

Diehl, Paul F. "What Are They Fighting For? The Importance of Issues in International Conflict Research." *Journal of Peace Research* 29:3 (1992): 333–344.

Dodds, Klaus and Alan D. Hemmings. "Britain and the British Antarctic Territory in the Wider Geopolitics of the Antarctic and the Southern Ocean." *International Affairs* 89:6 (2013): 1429–1444.

Domínguez, Jorge I. "Boundary Disputes in Latin America." *United States Institute of Peace* 50 (2003): 3–45.

Drago, Luis M. and H. Edward Nettles. "The Drago Doctrine in International Law and Politics." *The Hispanic American Historical Review* 8 (1928): 204–223.

Dunleavy, Patrick and Brendan O'Leary. *Theories of the State: The Politics of Liberal Democracy*. Basingstoke and London: MacMillan, 1987.

Dupont, Christophe. "Coalition Theory: Using Power to Build Cooperation." In *International Multilateral Negotiation: Approaches to the Management of Complexity*, Zartman, Ira William, ed. 148–177. San Francisco, CA: Jossey-Bass Publishers, 1994.

Evans, Malcom D. *International Law*. Oxford: Oxford University Press, 2010.

Eyffinger, Arthur and Arthur Witteveen. *The International Court of Justice 1946–1996*. The Hague, London and Boston, MA: Kluwer Law International, 1996.

Farcau, Bruce. *The Chaco War: Bolivia and Paraguay, 1932–35*. Westport, CT: Praeger, 1996.

Gent, Stephen E. "The Politics of International Arbitration and Adjudication." *Penn State Journal of Law and International Affairs* 2:1 (2013): 66–77.

Gent, Stephen E. and Megan Shannon. "Decision Control and the Pursuit of Binding Conflict Management: Choosing the Ties that Bind." *Journal of Conflict Resolution* 55:5 (2011): 710–734.

Gent, Stephen E. and Megan Shannon. "The Effectiveness of International Arbitration and Adjudication: Getting into a Bind." *The Journal of Politics* 72:2 (2010): 366–380.

Gilbert, Jérémie. *Indigenous Peoples' Land Rights under International Law: From Victors to Actors*. Ardsley, NY: Transnational, 2006.

Gilderhus, Mark T. "The Monroe Doctrine: Meanings and Implications." *Presidential Studies Quarterly* 36 (2006): 5–16.

González, Pablo Alonso, Wilhelm Londoño and Eva Parga-Dans. "Equality and Hierarchy, Sovereignty and Multiculturalism: The Heritagisation of Raizals in Santa Catalina (Colombia)." *Journal of Ethnic and Migration Studies* 46:19 (2020): 4066–4085.

Greene, Shane. "Getting Over the Andes: The Geo-Eco-Politics of Indigenous Movements in Peru's Twenty-First Century Inca Empire." *Journal of Latin American Studies* 38:2 (2006): 327–354.

Hall, John A. and G. John Ikenberry. *The State*. Milton Keynes: Open University Press, 1989.

Hershey, Amos S. "The Calvo and Drago Doctrines." *The American Journal of International Law* 1 (1907): 26–45.

Herz, Monica and João Pontes Nogueira. *Ecuador vs. Peru: Peacemaking Amid Rivalry*. Boulder, CO: Lynne Rienner, 2002.

Hoffman, John and Paul Graham. *Introduction to Political Theory*. Oxford and New York, NY: Routledge, 2015.

Huth, Paul K. *Standing Your Ground: Territorial Disputes and International Conflict*. Ann Arbor, MI: University of Michigan Press, 2001.

Jackson, Robert, ed. *Sovereignty at the Millennium*. Oxford: Blackwell Publishers, 1999.

James, Alan. *Sovereign Statehood: The Basis of International Society*. London: Allen & Unwin, 1986.

Jeifets, V. and L. Khadorich. "OAS and Interstate Dispute Resolution at the Beginning of the 21st Century: General Pattern and Peculiarities." *International Journal of Cognitive and Language Sciences* 9:4 (2015): 1148–1155.

Kaplan, Amy. "Where is Guantánamo?" *American Quarterly* 57:3 (2005): 831–858.

Keith, Kenneth James. *The Extent of the Advisory Jurisdiction of the International Court of Justice*. Leiden: A. W. Sijthoff, 1971.

Kelly, Philip L. "Escalation of Regional Conflict: Testing the Shatterbelt Concept." *Political Geography Quarterly* 5:2 (1986): 161–180.

Kennedy, Crammond. "The Drago Doctrine." *The North American Review* 185 (1907): 614–622.

King, Henry T. and James D. Graham. "Origins of Modern International Arbitration." *Dispute Resolution Journal* 51:1 (1996): 42.

Kleiboer, Marieke. "Understanding Success and Failure of International Mediation." *Journal of Conflict Resolution* 40:2 (1996): 360–389.

Kooijmans, P.H. "Tolerance, Sovereignty and Self-Determination." *Netherlands International Law Review* 43:2 (1996): 211–217.

Kröger, Markus and Rickard Lalander. "Ethno-Territorial Rights and the Resource Extraction Boom in Latin America: Do Constitutions Matter?" *Third World Quarterly* 37:4 (2016): 682–702.

Laing, Anna F. "Re-Producing Territory: Between Resource Nationalism and Indigenous Self-Determination in Bolivia." *Geoforum* 108 (2020): 28–38.

Lake, David A. "Regional Hierarchy: Authority and Local International Order." *Review of International Studies* 35:1 (2009): 35–58.

Lake, David A. and Patrick M. Morgan. "Regional Security Complexes: A Systems Approach." In *Regional Orders: Building Security in the New World*, Lake, David A. and Morgan, Patrick M., eds. 45–67. University Park, PA: Pennsylvania State University, 1997.

Lavdas, Kostas A., Spyridon N. Litsas and Dimitrios V Skiadas. *Stateness and Sovereign Debt: Greece in the European Conundrum*. Lanham, MD: Lexington Books, 2013.

Leifer, M. *ASEAN and the Security of South-East Asia*. London: Routledge, 1989.

Lillich, Richard B., ed. *Fact-Finding Before International Tribunals: Eleventh Sokol Colloquium*. Ardsley-on-Hudson, NY: Transnational Public Inc., 1991.

Linden, H. Vander. "Alexander VI and the Demarcation of the Maritime and Colonial Domains of Spain and Portugal, 1493–1494." *The American Historical Review* 22:1 (1916): 1–20.

Lindley, M. F. *The Acquisition and Government of Backward Territory in International Law: Being a Treatise on the Law and Practice Relating to Colonial Expansion*. New York, NY: Negro University Press, 1969.

Mace, Gordon. "Regional Integration in Latin America: A Long and Winding Road." *International Journal* 43:3 (1988): 404–427.

Mearsheimer, J. "The False Promise of International Institutions." *International Security* 19:3 (1994): 5–49.

Merino, Roger. "Conflicting Sovereignties: Global Conservation, Protected Areas, and Indigenous Nations in the Peruvian Amazon." *Global Environmental Politics* 22:2 (2022): 95–116.

Merino, Roger. "Reimagining the Nation-State: Indigenous Peoples and the Making of Plurinationalism in Latin America." *Leiden Journal of International Law* 31:4 (2018): 773–792.

Merrills, J. G. *International Dispute Settlement*. Cambridge: Cambridge University Press, 2017.

Murphy, Alexander B. "Regions as Social Construct: The Gap between Theory and Practice." *Progress in Human Geography* 15:1 (1991): 22–35.

Nolte, Detlef and Leslie E. Wehner. "Geopolitics in Latin America, Old and New." In *Routledge Handbook of Latin American Security*, Mares, David R. and Kacowicz, Arie M., eds. 33–43. Abingdon: Routledge, 2015.

Núñez, Jorge E. *Cosmopolitanism, State Sovereignty, International Law and Politics: A Theory*. London and New York, NY: Routledge, Taylor & Francis Group, 2023.

Núñez, Jorge E. *Sovereignty Conflicts and International Law and Politics: A Distributive Justice Issue*. London and New York, NY: Routledge, Taylor & Francis Group, 2017.

Núñez, Jorge E. "State Sovereignty: Concept and Conceptions." *International Journal for the Semiotics of Law* 37 (2024): 2131–2150.

Núñez, Jorge E. *Territorial Disputes and State Sovereignty: International Law and Politics*. London and New York, NY: Routledge, Taylor & Francis Group, 2020.

Núñez, Jorge E. "Territorial Disputes." In *The Oxford Handbook of International Law and the Americas*, Obregón Tarazona, Liliana, Betancur-Restrepo, Laura and Amaya Castro, Juan Manuel, eds. Online edn. Oxford: Oxford Academic, 2023: 1–27.

Núñez, Jorge E. and Verónica Ichniowski. "Movilidad Internacional de Personas: MERCOSUR y Unión Europea." *Universidad Nacional de La Plata* (2014) available at http://sedici.unlp.edu.ar/handle/10915/44666 accessed 26 July 2023.

O'Leary, Brendan. "The Elements of Right-Sizing and Right-Peopling the State." In *Right-Sizing the State: The Politics of Moving Borders*, O'Leary, Brendan, Lustick, Ian S. and Callaghy, Thomas, eds. 15–73. Oxford: Oxford University Press, 2001.

O'Neill, Barry. "International Negotiation: Some Conceptual Developments." *Annual Review of Political Science* 21:1 (2018): 515–533.

Ospina, Mariano V. "Nicaragua v. Colombia: A Stalemate in the Caribbean." *Global Security Studies* 4:4 (2013): 31–40.

Panke, Diana, Sören Stapel and Anna Starkmann. "Regional Organizations in the Americas." In *Comparing Regional Organizations: Global Dynamics and Regional Particularities*, Panke, Diana, Stapel, Sören and Starkmann, Anna, eds. 65–82. Bristol: Bristol University Press, 2020.

Panke, Diana, and Anna Starkmann. "Trajectories of Regional Cooperation: A Comparative Analysis." *Comparative European Politics* 19 (2021): 1–25.

Parrish, Austen L. "Changing Territoriality, Fading Sovereignty, and the Development of Indigenous Rights." *American Indian Law Review* 31:2 (2006/2007): 291–313.

Picker, Giovanni. "Sovereignty Beyond the State: Exception and Informality in a Western European City." *International Journal of Urban and Regional Research* 43:3 (2019): 576–581.

Press, Steven. "Sovereignty at Guantánamo: New Evidence and a Comparative Historical Interpretation." *The Journal of Modern History* 85:3 (2013): 592–631.

Pruthi, R. K. *The Political Theory*. New Delhi: Sarup and Sons, 2005.

Rawls, John. *A Theory of Justice*. Revised Edition. Oxford: Oxford University Press, 1999.

Root, Elihu. "The Real Monroe Doctrine." *American Society of International Law* 8 (1914): 6–22.

Ross, James. "Routes for Roots: Entering the 21st Century in San Andrés Island, Colombia." *Caribbean Studies* 35:1 (2007): 3–36.

Sakuwa, Kentaro. "The Regional Consequences of Territorial disputes: An Empirical Analysis of the South China Sea Disputes." *Journal of Asian Security and International Affairs* 4:3 (2017): 316–336.

Salas Salazar, Luis Gabriel, Jonas Wolff and Fabián Eduardo Camelo. "Towards Violent Peace? Territorial Dynamics of Violence in Tumaco (Colombia) before and after the Demobilisation of the FARC-EP." *Conflict, Security & Development* 19:5 (2019): 497–520.

Scanlon, T. M. "Contractualism and Utilitarianism." In *Utilitarianism and Beyond*, Sen, Amartya and Williams, Bernard, eds. 103–128. Cambridge: Cambridge University Press; Paris: Editions de la Maison des Sciences de l'Homme, 1982.

Schwebel, S. *International Arbitration: Three Salient Problems.* Cambridge: Grotius Publications Limited, 1987.

Shaw, Malcolm N. *International Law.* Cambridge: Cambridge University Press, 2003.

Shaw, Malcolm N., ed. *Rosenne's Law and Practice of the International Court: 1920–2015.* Leiden: Brill, 2016.

Sieder, Rachel. "Indigenous Peoples' Rights and the Law in Latin America." In *Handbook of Indigenous Peoples' Rights*, Lennox, Corinne and Short, Damien, eds. 414–423. New York, NY: Routledge, 2016.

Simmons, Beth A. "Capacity, and Compliance: International Institutions and Territorial Disputes." *The Journal of Conflict Resolution* 46:6 (2002): 829–856.

Simpson, L. and H. Fox. *International Arbitration: Law and Practice.* London: Stevens and Sons Limited, 1959.

Sinclair, Ian. *The Vienna Convention on the Law of Treaties.* Manchester: Manchester University Press, 1984.

Starkey, Brigid, Mark A. Boyer and Jonathan Wilkenfeld. *International Negotiation in a Complex World.* Lanham, MD: New Millennium Books in International Studies, Rowman and Littlefield, 2016.

Starkey, Brigid, Mark A. Boyer and Jonathan Wilkenfeld. *Negotiating a Complex World: An Introduction to International Negotiation.* Lanham, MD: New Millennium Books in International Studies, Rowman and Littlefield, 2005.

Strauss, Michael J. "Guantanamo Bay and the Evolution of International Leases and Servitudes." *City University of New York Law Review* 10:2 (2007): 479–509.

Szafarz, Renata. *The Compulsory Jurisdiction of the International Court of Justice.* Dordrecht: Kluwer Academic Publishers, 1993.

Touval, Saadia and I. William Zartman, eds. *International Mediation in Theory and Practice.* Boulder, CO: Westview Press, 1985.

Treves, Tullio. "International Organizations as Parties to Contentious Cases: Selected Aspects." In *International Organizations and International Dispute Settlement: Trends and Prospects*, Boisson de Chazournes, Laurence, Romano, Cesare and Mackenzie, Ruth, eds. 37–48. New York, NY: Transnational Publishers, 2002.

Van Cott, Donna Lee. "Broadening Democracy: Latin America's Indigenous Peoples' Movements." *Current History* 103:670 (2004): 80–85.

van der Haar, Gemma. "The Zapatista Uprising and the Struggle for Indigenous Autonomy." *European Review of Latin American and Caribbean Studies* 76 (2004): 98–108.

van Genugten, Willem and Camillo Perez-Bustillo. "The Emerging International Architecture of Indigenous Rights: The Interaction between Global, Regional, and National Dimensions." *International Journal on Minority and Group Rights* 11:4 (2004): 379–409.

Volk, Christian. "The Problem of Sovereignty in Globalized Times." *Law, Culture and the Humanities* 18:3 (2022): 716–738.

Waldock, C. H. M. "Disputed Sovereignty in the Falklands Islands Dependencies." *British Yearbook of International Law* 25 (1948): 311–353.
Walker, Neil, ed. *Relocating Sovereignty*. London and New York, NY: Routledge, Taylor & Francis Group, 2018.
Wallensteen, Peter and Isak Svensoon. "Talking Peace: International Mediation in Armed Conflicts." *Journal of Peace Research* 51:2 (2014): 315–327.

3 Pluralism of pluralisms and the multidimensional approach

Introduction

This chapter delineates the notion of pluralism of pluralisms present in territorial disputes. This notion encompasses several pluralisms including agents and players, contexts, realms and modes of existence and variables such as time and space. Moreover, this chapter proposes the multidimensional approach as a means to assess and explain these differences more comprehensively. This way of understanding territorial disputes and this approach to assess and explain them will be applied in the following chapters when exploring case studies concerning the Americas.

Both sovereignty and territorial disputes are complex. They involve different agents (for example, individuals, communities and states) that play a role in several contexts (local, regional and international). In addition to this, the complexity expands with the different possible facets of reference, whether purely logical or theoretical, factual or empirical and axiological. Finally, the dimensions in which these players interrelate, coupled with the contexts where the interactions happen and the science of reference, may add, for example, a vertical or a horizontal angle, time and space to the whole intricacy. This pluralism of pluralisms that characterizes sovereignty and territorial disputes means they are multi-subjective, multi-contextual and multi-faceted. In brief, they are multidimensional and, consequently, require a multidimensional analysis if the aim is to fully comprehend them and, ultimately, find peaceful and permanent ways to solve them.

Núñez (2023) introduced this new way to comprehend phenomena.[1] In the same vein, this book understands sovereignty, territorial disputes and their interrelations as a pluralism of pluralisms, a view applicable to any phenomena, including territorial disputes in the Americas.

1 Jorge E. Núñez, *Cosmopolitanism, State Sovereignty, International Law and Politics: A Theory* (London and New York, NY: Routledge, Taylor & Francis Group, 2023).

DOI: 10.4324/9781003350828-4

The first part of the chapter will refer to and characterize the notion of "pluralism of pluralisms."[2] Firstly, it will be acknowledged that human interrelations may encompass a variety of agents such as individuals, communities and states and each of them may play different roles and, therefore, act or omit to act in their individuality or in relation to any other agent. These are two different pluralisms that have to do with both the variety of "agents" at play and the different roles each of them may have as "players." For example, agents such as individuals, communities and states may interrelate with themselves, with other individuals, their own communities or outlying ones and their state as well as other states. In these different interrelations, depending on several factors, they may act in various roles as players: acting as hosts, participants, attendees and viewers. Secondly, another pluralism that characterizes sovereignty and territorial disputes relates to the context in which these agents operate. They may exist, interrelate in and be influenced by the domestic, regional and international contexts. Thirdly, the aforementioned pluralisms, i.e. agents, players and contexts, may be associated with plural realms and, consequently, be understood, known and assessed as they ought to be (normative realm), as they are (factual realm) and as they could/should be (axiological realm). Finally, yet another pluralism encompasses the many elements and features pertaining to phenomena by accepting that they may have several modes of existence and be ideal, natural, cultural and metaphysical.

The second part of the chapter briefly reintroduces the author's multidimensional approach to understanding, knowing and assessing phenomena. Traditional scientific approaches used in disciplines such as legal and political sciences and international relations to explain and evaluate phenomena are unidimensional because they start with assumptions, beliefs and justifications that are fragmented. Existing scholarship tends to carefully neglect the fact that these disputes are theorized and evaluated through unidimensional lenses, focusing invariably, for example, on scientific disciplines such as law or political science and neglecting the non-legal, non-political or non-disciplinary angles like rationality, emotion, nationalism, prejudice and perspectives. From there, while a unidimensional understanding is interested in the way in which a particular scholarly discipline "thinks" about an object or the structure of that "thinking," a multidimensional analysis is guided by the way in which the object or subject exists. In order to bring more precision, the section will explain that the several pluralisms encompassing sovereignty and territorial

2 As in Núñez (2023), the monograph will refer to "plurality" and "pluralism" without distinction. As in that case, the choice of the expression "pluralism of pluralisms" is pragmatic in order to maintain a coherent, cohesive and simplified style. For more detail see Jorge E. Núñez, *Cosmopolitanism, State Sovereignty, International Law and Politics: A Theory* (London and New York, NY: Routledge, Taylor & Francis Group, 2023), Chapter 1.

disputes and their interrelations may become, i.e. emerge or manifest, in different dimensions, i.e. linear and nonlinear. In turn, each dimension offers several possibilities for the understanding, knowing and assessing of phenomena that will be explored.

The third part of the chapter will refer to variables that may influence sovereignty, territorial disputes and their assessments. More precisely, this monograph acknowledges that despite the peculiarities that actual and assumed situations encompassing sovereignty and territorial disputes might present and the different ways they could be understood, known and assessed—i.e. in unidimensional, multidimensional, linear and nonlinear ways—they are somewhat conditioned by variables including time and space.

Finally, all the aforementioned pluralisms are brought together in a blueprint that will be used in the following chapters in order to assess and explain territorial disputes in the Americas. Overall, the chapter does not suggest that the current scholarly understanding about territorial disputes in the Americas may be intrinsically wrong or biased. In order to make such a claim, each individual academic investigation would need a thorough review. However, instrumentally, it is possible to claim they are incomplete and not accurate because of their limited analyses and consequent fragmented appreciations of the issues.

Pluralism of pluralisms

This monograph explores territorial disputes in the Americas by acknowledging them in a reconceived and more comprehensive way. Rather than explaining and exploring these cases in their individuality or focusing on a single element or feature, this book understands territorial disputes in the Americas as a pluralism of pluralisms.

In doing so, this section will refer to several agents that may influence the origin, ongoing nature, potential escalation into conflict and possible peaceful resolution of territorial disputes (individuals, communities and states). By applying game theory and depending on several factors, the roles these agents play in their individuality and in their interrelations with other agents will be classified into hosts, participants, attendees and viewers.

The next step distinguishes the domestic, local or national, regional, and global or international contexts in which these agents may interrelate in their different roles. Indeed, it may be the case that a particular context is more relevant or more influential in relation to a particular agent or role. However, all these contexts should be clearly differentiated and carefully considered when explaining and assessing cases pertaining to sovereignty, and in particular territorial disputes, because they may influence or be influenced by agents and their roles to a different degree.

The introduction of the next pluralism, realms, explains why different scholarly disciplines, policymakers and people at large may have controversial understandings related to a territorial dispute. This is because they have preconceptions, assumptions and beliefs that are either based on factual, normative or axiological bases. Coupled with these different realms, the last pluralism, i.e. modes of existence, shows that part of the challenge in understanding the intricacy that territorial disputes present has to do with the many elements and features that integrate them—i.e. ideal, natural, cultural and metaphysical.

In a simplistic way, territorial disputes can be characterized as having at least two claiming parties arguing over the exclusive sovereignty of the same territory.[3] However, territorial disputes are more intricate and require a more comprehensive view that accepts their many pluralisms. Broadly, the territorial disputes in the Americas have common roots in all cases, either because of the historical component based on colonial times and the lack of clear border demarcation at the time or, in the cases in which the demarcation had taken place in law, the difficulty in applying the decision to the areas in question. Together with the historical background and the lack of clearly defined boundaries in colonial times, current international law—such as the Law of the Sea, new technologies for exploration and exploitation of natural resources, the existence or absence of indigenous or implanted populations in the territories under question, and several other elements—result in multi-faceted and multi-layered territorial disputes. Therein, a study solely concerned with a territorial dispute and its historical roots (factual realm) would be fragmented because it might not consider later normative or axiological developments, e.g. indigenous peoples might have not been considered as "persons" according to the law of the time and, therefore, their right to claim sovereignty was ignored, neglected or completely rejected; and principles of justice and fairness might have changed over time and what was considered as a "just acquisition" might be challenged by later decolonial views. Similarly, a study focused solely on the roles of sovereign states as the only agents interested in a territorial dispute and their claims based on their legal titles (normative realm) would omit other relevant agents such as individuals and communities, e.g. indigenous peoples and implanted populations. Consequently, any robust study on territorial disputes should acknowledge their intrinsic pluralism of pluralisms.

Agents and players

Scholarly literature has a tendency to narrow the focus on sovereignty and territorial disputes to one kind of agent, i.e. states. As the previous chapter shows, remedies and organizations dealing with territorial disputes only center on

3 See Chapter 2.

sovereign states, disregarding all other agents.[4] This kind of focus disregards the internal differences within states when there is a territorial dispute, as for example with competing individual and community interests, because states are considered, legally and politically, as a single agent.

Following Núñez (2023),[5] the analyses and explications of territorial disputes in this monograph will consider that there are at least three types of agents, i.e. individuals, communities and states. Indeed, there are several other agents or subcategories of them. For instance, the Amazon[6] is a clear example of a region containing several subgroups of agents, such as minorities within a community (e.g. indigenous peoples), non-governmental organizations, multinational private companies and scientists. The choice to focus this monograph on three types of agents, i.e. individuals, communities and states, is a pragmatic one because it would not be feasible for a single research study on several differences to be comprehensive enough when the goal is to showcase the many pluralisms at hand. In that respect, the crucial point that this monograph highlights is that sovereignty and territorial disputes may be concerned with sovereign states, but they are not limited to them, and, therein, any comprehensive study should somchow incorporate this variety of agents.

Politically, a state is a community with a certain degree of power or authority.[7] Legally, public international law stipulates that: "The state as a person of international law should possess the following qualifications: a) a permanent population; b) a defined territory; c) government; and d) capacity to enter into relations with the other states."[8] Therein, legally and politically, the state has in principle three key elements related to power or authority: territory, population and government (or government and law).[9] Similarly, individuals and communities can be characterized in several

4 See Chapter 2.

5 For a detailed account on agents and players see Jorge E. Núñez, *Cosmopolitanism, State Sovereignty, International Law and Politics: A Theory* (London and New York, NY: Routledge, Taylor & Francis Group, 2023), Chapter 4.

6 Paul E. Little, *Amazonia: Territorial Struggles on Perennial Frontiers* (Baltimore, MD: Johns Hopkins University Press, 2001).

7 For sovereignty as a form of authority or power or both see Jorge E. Núñez, *Sovereignty Conflicts and International Law and Politics: A Distributive Justice Issue* (London and New York, NY: Routledge, Taylor & Francis Group, 2017), Chapter 2.

8 Complete text available from the United Nations Treaty Collection at https://treaties.un.org/pages/showDetails.aspx?objid=0800000280166aef accessed 17 August 2023.

9 For a view of state as composed by population, territory, government and law see Alan James, *Sovereign Statehood: The Basis of International Society* (London: Allen and Unwin, 1986), in particular Chapter 2; John A. Hall and G. John Ikenberry, *The State* (Milton Keynes: Open University Press, 1989); Patrick Dunleavy and Brendan O'Leary, *Theories of the State: The Politics of Liberal Democracy* (Basingstoke and London: Macmillan, 1987); Malcom D. Evans, *International Law* (Oxford: Oxford University Press, 2010); Antonio Cassese, *International*

ways. According to law, the individuals constituting a state's population are defined by different principles, i.e. *jus sanguinis* or right of blood, *jus soli* or birthplace or residence.[10] Political science may refer to individuals as any inhabitant of a particular territory regardless of their legal status as nationals or foreigners and a community as their resultant aggregations.[11] Despite the way in which these agents—e.g. individuals, communities and states—are defined and characterized by reference, for example, to legal or non-legal features, the acknowledgment is that they may have similar or different interests. Importantly, this includes different assumptions, views and conceptual bases relevant to territorial disputes. Cases such as the Falkland/Malvinas Islands, the archipelago of San Andrés, Providencia and Santa Catalina and the Amazon region clearly show there should be a higher level of precision when referring to notions such as "peoples"—i.e. the distinction between native and implanted populations.[12]

These agents may act (or omit to act) in different ways in their interrelations with self, others and the environment. Depending on the roles these agents play in a territorial dispute, this monograph classifies them into four different kinds of players: hosts, participants, attendees and viewers. "Hosts" are necessary players because without them there is no dispute; i.e. they have a colorable claim[13] and can take part in the dispute. "Participants" are not necessary players because, regardless of their colorable claim, their ability to participate is conditional upon the hosts' acceptance. "Attendees" are not necessary players because, regardless of their colorable claim, hosts could not accept them or simply ignore or reject them. "Viewers" are not necessary players and are not part of the dispute because they do not have any colorable claim. Ideal theory may assume the rationality of these players, their choices in terms of strategies and the information available to them. Real territorial disputes, however, are more intricate. The following quotation illustrates the point:

Law (Oxford: Oxford University Press, 2001); Ian Brownlie, *Principles of Public International Law* (Oxford: Oxford University Press, 2008); and many others.

10 T. Alexander Aleinkoff and Douglas Klusmeyer, eds., *Citizenship Today. Global Perspectives and Practices* (Washington, DC: Carnegie Endowment for International Peace, 2001), in particular Chapter 1 in which the author compares several national legal orders.

11 Robert Nozick, *Anarchy, State and Utopia* (New York, NY: Basic Books, 1974), in particular Part I, Chapter 2.

12 See Chapter 8.

13 For the notion of colorable claim see Jorge E. Núñez, *Cosmopolitanism, State Sovereignty, International Law and Politics: A Theory* (London and New York, NY: Routledge, Taylor & Francis Group, 2023), Chapter 7; Jorge E. Núñez, *Territorial Disputes and State Sovereignty: International Law and Politics* (London and New York, NY: Routledge, Taylor & Francis Group, 2020), Chapter 4; and Jorge E. Núñez, *Sovereignty Conflicts and International Law and Politics: A Distributive Justice Issue* (London and New York, NY: Routledge, Taylor & Francis Group, 2017), Chapter 6.

> The Falklands conflict serves as an example [...] Argentina may have assumed that the United Kingdom had payoffs more in-line with expected utility and the traditional game of chicken, and would avoid conflict. However, if the United Kingdom was also in a domain of losses and their payoffs mirrored the Argentineans, conflict is obviously on the horizon.[14]

Theoretically, it may be possible to reduce to a two-person, non-zero-sum game, a case like the Falkland/Malvinas Islands. Evidently, any other agent (individuals, communities and other states and their interests) and their different roles in the dispute as players (hosts, participants, attendees and viewers) would be omitted. Therein, the analyses and explanations of case studies included in this monograph will use the aforementioned terms so characterized solely to discern the different agents involved and their different roles as players without intending to foresee any theoretical outcome.

Contexts

As in Núñez (2023),[15] "context" is defined in this monograph as the conditions or factors that influence the different pluralisms and their interrelations. This notion includes legal and political understandings such as the distinction between "boundary" and "border"[16] and the definitions stemming from international legal instruments—e.g. the Law of the Sea. Furthermore, the notion includes non-legal elements and features—e.g. bordering minorities may be defined according to sociological and ethnic elements. Therein, this monograph considers three contexts: (1) domestic, local or national; (2) regional; and (3) international or global.

As the following chapters pertaining to real case scenarios in the Americas will demonstrate in more detail, it may be the case that a particular context may be more relevant than the others with regard to a particular territorial dispute. However, a multidimensional approach suggests the incorporation of all contexts in the explication and exploration of these differences. For example, cases such as the Falkland/Malvinas Islands, the Caribbean Sea—e.g. the archipelago of San Andrés, Providencia and Santa Catalina—and the Mexico–United States border have influences from the domestic, regional and international

14 Brett A. DeAngelis, *A Line in the Sand: Prospect Theory and Nash Arbitration in Resolving Territorial Disputes* (Monterey, CA: Dudley Knox Library, Naval Postgraduate School, 2012), 43.

15 Jorge E. Núñez, *Cosmopolitanism, State Sovereignty, International Law and Politics: A Theory* (London and New York, NY: Routledge, Taylor & Francis Group, 2023), Chapter 5.

16 Jorge E. Núñez, *Territorial Disputes and State Sovereignty: International Law and Politics* (London and New York, NY: Routledge, Taylor & Francis Group, 2020), Chapter 8.

contexts. On the surface, the Falkland/Malvinas Islands territorial dispute appears to be about clearly defined issues at stake including the historical claim and the principle of territorial integrity. However, any comprehensive study should incorporate their geostrategic location and the direct and indirect ramifications such as the economic value of the territory's natural resources, its relevance as a route for maritime commercial traffic and the impact any decision regarding the sovereignty over the islands might have over Antarctica. Similarly, despite the settlement between Nicaragua and Colombia, the case of the archipelago of San Andrés, Providencia and Santa Catalina is still a matter of controversy between these states, has negative impact at the regional level and presents social minority tensions affecting the Raizal community. Finally, the seemingly resolved Mexico–United States border case clearly involves the domestic, regional and international contexts in the form of, for example, nationalism, leaders' domestic consensus, migration and human rights violations.

The aforementioned briefly introduced examples do not intend to suggest that any of these contexts and their combinations could necessarily result in an outcome that may foster a territorial dispute. Any of these contexts and their combinations may affect these differences in a positive and/or negative way. Each of these contexts has their own legally and non-legally defined characteristics that may help in understanding the origin, continuation and potential escalation of territorial disputes as well as their peaceful and permanent settlement. While in legal and political sciences and international relations, sovereignty in the domestic context refers to single states and their organization of public authority within that state and the level of effective control exercised by those holding authority,[17] territorial disputes characterize themselves because of the different agents at play—e.g. individual and community interests that may be similar or different to those of the ruling party. This may result in the leaders' prestige being directly linked to issues such as nationalism and the rationale behind the ongoing nature of a dispute or its resolution. In turn, the regional context permeates the sovereignty's exclusiveness that is characteristic of the domestic context and allows for plurality—e.g. legally and politically, in the form of regional organizations such as the Organization of American States (OAS). As in the case of the domestic context, the ruling party and the leaders' prestige, regional organizations and neighbor states can have direct and indirect influence on territorial dispute resolution.[18] Internationally, despite sovereign states' central role, actual and potential territorial disputes have found several alternatives such as integration and

17 See Chapter 2 for further details. See also Stephen D. Krasner, *Sovereignty: Organized Hypocrisy* (Princeton, NJ: Princeton University Press, 1999).

18 See Chapter 2.

free association, trusteeship, the Antarctic Treaty formula, international condominiums, leaseback with guarantees or the Hong Kong model of "one country, two systems" and the case of the Åland Islands.

Evidently, different agents play different roles in territorial disputes and are influenced by the domestic, regional and international contexts. Accordingly, if the aim is to more accurately understand, explicate and assess any territorial dispute, scholarly studies should acknowledge their multi-contextual nature and incorporate a multidimensional approach.

Realms

There are different ways in which an object or subject of study can be grasped. This monograph refers to them as "realms" and distinguishes three of them: normative, factual and axiological.[19] While a normative comprehension allows the scholar to understand, know and assess the object as it ought to be, a factual understanding accepts the scholar's psychophysical experience in relation to the object as it is. Finally, every object or subject of study can be understood, known and assessed in a positive or negative way—i.e. "X is good" or "X is bad," in which "X" can be any fact, omission, situation, norm, etc. and "good" or "bad" can be any positive or negative value.

The factual realm acknowledges that sovereignty and territorial disputes include elements and sub-elements with empirical presence. Traditionally, in the domestic, regional and international contexts, law and politics fail to accommodate factual differences because current understandings in legal and political sciences characterize a state's necessary elements pertaining to population, territory and government broadly. For example, domestic, regional and international law may define and characterize "population" as a uniform mass of people regardless of their individual and group peculiarities. Furthermore, if there seems to be a departure from this kind of uniform treatment by way of exceptions to a general rule, these special cases primarily have to do with groups rather than individuals (e.g. the way in which children should be treated rather than a particular child, or how the principle of non-discrimination may affect the LGBTQ+ community).

The normative realm refers to sovereignty and territorial disputes and their relevant elements and sub-elements pertaining to population, territory and government according to determined criteria based on abstract, conceptual or normative presuppositions. Importantly, these criteria may be legal and extra- or non-legal because there are other normative systems that may influence cases concerning sovereignty and territorial disputes, such as morality and religion.

19 Jorge E. Núñez, *Cosmopolitanism, State Sovereignty, International Law and Politics: A Theory* (London and New York, NY: Routledge, Taylor & Francis Group, 2023), Chapter 5.

The axiological realm acknowledges that sovereignty and territorial disputes can be valued differently—broadly, in a positive and negative way—by different agents. For instance, different agents in a territorial dispute will play different roles and have common interests and conflicts of interest. Regardless of the factual and normative realms related to that dispute, these agents have an axiological choice between conflict and peacemaking by means of, for example, cooperation.

An example relevant to sovereignty and territorial disputes that demonstrates clearly how the acknowledgment of the three aforementioned realms helps discern different views on the same object is the principle of equality of the states—e.g. art. 2, paragraph 1 of the United Nations Charter. This legal principle (normative realm) recognizes sovereign equality, but this recognition may not result in empirical equality (factual realm). Therein, weak states may favor the application of the legal principle in states' bilateral and multilateral relationships while strong states may intervene as they wish in the internal and external affairs of their weaker peers (axiological realm).[20] Arguably, realpolitik shows that some states are more equal than others despite this legal principle in public international law.[21]

Discerning these realms is important, as it avoids unnecessary discrepancies over the apparent differences in the way scholarly studies understand, know and assess cases concerning sovereignty and territorial disputes. More clearly, if the scholar departs from factual assumptions, beliefs and justifications, the resultant explanations and explorations will be different from those that have normative or axiological bases. Consequently, abstract, conceptual or normative questions such as "What ought sovereignty to be?" or "How ought this territorial dispute be addressed?" cannot be answered by empirical data or a value judgment; empirical questions of the form "What is sovereignty?" or "Which of these populations were chronologically the first settlers over this disputed territory?" cannot be responded to with conceptual or normative definitions or axiological choices; and situations in which a territory in an ongoing dispute had been part of other conflicts in the past, and the involved agents had to decide whether these disputes were just or not and whether the just side won, cannot be solely understood, known and assessed by reference

20 Examples in the following chapters will show how former colonial powers in the Americas treated themselves reciprocally as equals in law and politics while they discarded native populations. Arguably, there are still ongoing interferences by central, strong or advantaged agents in the domestic, regional and international legal and political agendas of other states in the continent. See Chapters 4, 5 and 6.

21 R. P. Anand, "Sovereign Equality of States in International Law," *International Studies* 8:3 (1966): 213–224; Hans Kelsen, "The Principle of Sovereign Equality of States as a Basis for International Organization," *Yale Law Journal* 53:2 (1944): 207–220; R. Hjorth, "Equality in the Theory of International Society: Kelsen, Rawls and the English School," *Review of International Studies* 37:5 (2011): 2585–2602.

to facts or norms. Ergo, in order to more fully comprehend sovereignty and territorial disputes the consideration of any of these realms should not be at the expense of sacrificing the others.

Modes of existence

Sovereignty and territorial disputes include a vast variety of elements and features that different disciplines explicate and evaluate as objects or subjects of study—i.e. any living or inanimate "thing" or "entity," action or omission capable of being studied by any scholarly discipline. According to their modes of existence, these objects or subjects of study may be classified as ideal, natural, cultural and metaphysical. Because of the particularities of these objects or subjects of study, scientific disciplines apply a relevant method to understand and assess them. Similarly, different scientific disciplines use relevant epistemological acts to interpret them in a way they can be transferred as knowledge. The following paragraphs will briefly refer to and characterize each mode of existence and the suitable method and epistemological act in each case.[22]

Ideal objects are unreal—i.e. they simply are but do not properly exist. They are not in the experience (not apprehensible through the senses), they are timeless and they are neutral to value judgments (they do not imply any axiological qualification). Among them are the objects that refer to logic and mathematics (for example, the triangle). Truths concerning ideal objects are obtained by a deductive rational method, and by deducing from one or more general truths, disciplines such as logic and mathematics draw from them a particular truth. The epistemological act with which the deductive rational method is constituted is called intellectual intuition or intuitive intellection—i.e. different from sensible intuition that encompass senses, intellectual intuition pertains to the intellect.

The natural objects studied by the various sciences of nature are real, they have existence, are in the experience, are in time and are neutral to value judgments—i.e. they are not per se good or bad, just or unjust, beautiful or ugly or useful or useless. Natural objects, as studied by the various sciences of nature, have to do with truths obtained by the inductive empirical method. The epistemological act with which the medium of the inductive empirical method is constituted is called explanation.

Cultural objects are created by humans acting according to their volition. They are real, in the experience, in time and they are valuable positively or negatively—e.g. fair or unfair, beautiful or ugly, useful or useless. Their properties can qualify their being, and they must always have at least one class

22 For a detailed account of each mode of existence see Jorge E. Núñez, *Cosmopolitanism, State Sovereignty, International Law and Politics: A Theory* (London and New York, NY: Routledge, Taylor & Francis Group, 2023), Chapter 5.

qualification. It is possible to distinguish between substrate and sense in the case of cultural objects. Substrate is related to the material underneath human activity, and that raw material has meaning (sense) depending on the psychological intention of the attributed author. The intuition of the cultural object is based on a double intuition: the sensitive intuition of the substrate and the emotional/rational intuition of the value. Therefore, the epistemological act in cultural objects implies taking a position by the knowing subject and is called understanding. To understand is to know the meaning of something in its "being" when it is being. The suitable method to know a cultural object is the dialectical empirical method, moving from the materiality of the substrate to the experience of its meaning and vice versa.

Finally, metaphysical objects are real, they exist, are not in the experience and are valuable positively and negatively. For example, God, who is conceived as a reality and the highest goodness, is not in the experience, as He cannot be seen anywhere nor be accessed through any other of the senses. However, at least for believers, He is a reality, accessible through faith and therefore exists.

Consider a case encompassing agents such as sovereign states having a territorial dispute. The same case may be characterized as a hawk-dove game as follows: "to H, (V-C)/2 against H, and V against D; to D. 0 against H, and V/2 against D" (ideal objects).[23] A different scholar may choose to focus the study of the same territorial dispute on the territory's changes over time—e.g. a river that was once agreed to be the boundary between two sovereign states and has changed its original course (natural objects).[24] Yet, another scholar may intend to discuss whether the public international law principle of territorial integrity is applicable (cultural object).[25] Finally, another view may consider that, in addition to public international law, religion as a normative system should be taken into account and, therefore, include in the analysis God as owner of the land and states as their administrator (metaphysical object).[26] Indeed, as with the aforementioned pluralisms, it is of utmost importance to accept that, regardless of the particular focus a study may have, the intricacy present in cases referred to sovereignty and territorial disputes involve different modes of existence.[27]

23 Alan Grafen, "The Logic of Divisively Asymmetric Contests: Respect for Ownership and the Desperado Effect," *Animal Behaviour* 35:2 (1987): 462–467.

24 L. J. Bouchez, "The Fixing of Boundaries in International Boundary Rivers," *International and Comparative Law Quarterly* 12:3 (1963): 789–817.

25 Jure Vidmar, "Territorial Integrity and the Law of Statehood," *George Washington International Law Review* 44:4 (2012): 697–748.

26 E. Powell, "Islamic States and Peaceful Resolution of Territorial Disputes," *International Organization* 69:4 (2015): 777–807.

27 See Chapters 4, 5, 6 and 7 for examples.

Multidimensional approach

A dimensional understanding applied to sovereignty and territorial disputes is the acknowledgment that the aforementioned pluralisms that characterize them are somehow related to the others and, therefore, may have reciprocal influence to an extent. There are different ways to apply the proposed dimensional view. A unidimensional approach focuses on how a particular scholarly discipline "thinks" about an object or the structure of that "thinking." A multidimensional approach centers on the object or subject of study itself, its respective pluralisms and interrelations. For example, when these approaches are applied to sovereignty and territorial disputes by disciplines such as legal and political sciences and international relations, a unidimensional view may refer to an act of scholarly intellectual understanding with regard to a legal norm, a legal system or a policy, while a multidimensional view may be interested in the legal norm, legal system or policy and their interrelations with other pluralities—instead of the way the scholar or the scholarly discipline thinks about them.

Because a unidimensional view is related to the way a particular scholar or a particular scholarly discipline "thinks" about the relevant object or subject of study, this way of thinking conditions, for example, the applicable methodology. Conversely, by accepting the many pluralities and interrelations pertaining to an object or subject of study, a multidimensional understanding enables the avoidance of *a priori* conditioning and fragmentation in, for example, the methodology choice and, therefore, allows for non-traditional outcomes. By accepting that these pluralisms may interrelate in traditionally accepted ways as well as unconventional ones, a dimensional understanding, in turn, encompasses linear and nonlinear dimensional models. The former accepts traditional understandings pertaining to disciplines such as legal and political sciences and international relations in relation to how different pluralisms may interrelate and, consequently, results in fixed effects. The latter embraces non-traditional interrelations of the same pluralities and permits analyses that may bring other possible outcomes.

Linear dimensions

The linear dimensional model interprets the pluralisms that characterize sovereignty and territorial disputes and their interrelations in a fixed and more traditional manner. This fixed and more traditional manner is in part determined by the object or subject of study and, mainly, by the way in which a particular discipline such as the legal and political sciences "thinks" that object or subject should be assessed. For example, a unidimensional linear vertical approach in legal science traditionally understands sovereign states as the ultimate lawmaker and law interpreter in a territory and for a particular population. In turn, a multidimensional linear vertical approach encompasses the aforementioned view and includes extra-legal elements and features pertaining to other disciplines such as political science and international relations. Therein, a multidimensional linear vertical approach would include in the discussion issues pertaining to, for example, the legitimate or illegitimate relationship between government and population as two different layers in the same sovereign state.[28] Regardless of their peculiarities, for these ways of thinking, the difference between supreme and subordinate refers "to a relative place on a scale."[29] In relation to sovereignty, clearly, it has to do with a vertical view—i.e. one that has a superior cannot be a sovereign as sovereignty means supreme, the highest authority on a scale.[30] In that sense, when dealing with international agents, a state is sovereign as long as it has supreme authority over its territory and population. If it does not, it may be something else, e.g. a colony, member of a federal state, etc., but not a sovereign state. However, sovereign states encompass several pluralisms and, therefore, a vertical view cannot capture its complexity. Accordingly, the linear dimensional approach may comprise several views including vertical, horizontal, diagonal and curved or spiral.

a) Vertical

For this kind of dimensional understanding, pluralisms are part of a hierarchy. As a result, agents may be subclassified into inferiors and superiors according to different criteria—e.g. relevant to realms, normative criteria would define roles and responsibilities in an organization; relevant to contexts, normative criteria determine the relation of inferiority or superiority with regard to domestic and international law. The following chapters will show how this understanding has been applied historically, politically, sociologically and legally in the Americas—e.g. in consideration of lord and servant, central and non-central states—and, consequently, the interrelation between free individual and slave, and sovereign state and colony, respectively.

28 For a detailed analysis of the concept of "state," its elements and relevant theories in legal and political sciences see Jorge E. Núñez, *Territorial Disputes and State Sovereignty: International Law and Politics* (London and New York, NY: Routledge, Taylor & Francis Group, 2020), Chapter 2.

29 Herbert L. A. Hart, *The Concept of Law* (Oxford: Oxford University Press, 1994), 105–106; and Jorge E. Núñez, *Sovereignty Conflicts and International Law and Politics: A Distributive Justice Issue* (London and New York, NY: Routledge, Taylor & Francis Group, 2017), Chapter 2.

30 See Chapter 2.

b) Horizontal

By accepting that pluralisms can interrelate at the same level, this type of dimensional understanding explores these interrelations. For instance, considering agents and the roles they may play in a territorial dispute, the challenger may perceive another agent as a mere attendee or viewer while the challenged party may recognize them as participants—e.g. as in the Falkland/Malvinas Islands case, where the islanders are mere attendees for Argentina because the Argentine government has systematically neglected their right to participate in any negotiation about the sovereignty over the territory in question, while the United Kingdom accepts them as participants.

c) Diagonal or transversal, curved or spiral and other linear relationships

These approaches integrate vertical and horizontal views by cutting across them in different ways. A diagonal or transversal linear understanding, for example, enables the exploration of how a sovereign state that plays an apparent viewer's role in a territorial dispute based in another geographical region may influence directly and indirectly a territorial dispute elsewhere—e.g. the case of Antarctica in which states like the United States and the United Kingdom have been heavily invested.[31] A curved or spiral linear view permits, for example, a different exploration of cases in which the affected agents may seem not to be related to the origin of the territorial dispute in question.

Nonlinear dimensions

Scientific disciplines such as legal and political sciences and international relations have their own assumptions, beliefs and understandings that determine the way they assess and explain issues pertaining to sovereignty and territorial disputes. Therein, despite their peculiarities, they all follow linear dimensional approaches. Introduced in Núñez (2023),[32] without discarding the value of these linear approaches, the nonlinear dimensional views accept unexpected interrelations and results in the explanation and evaluation of phenomena. This way of dealing with issues relevant to sovereignty and territorial disputes enables the use of interdisciplinary analyses as well as elements and features that may go beyond scholarly disciplinary fixed boundaries—e.g. extra- or

31 See Jorge E. Núñez, *Territorial Disputes and State Sovereignty: International Law and Politics* (London and New York, NY: Routledge, Taylor & Francis Group, 2020), Chapters 6, 7 and 8 for details about territorial disputes in the Americas, Europe and Asia and Africa and the Middle East, respectively.

32 Jorge E. Núñez, *Cosmopolitanism, State Sovereignty, International Law and Politics: A Theory* (London and New York, NY: Routledge, Taylor & Francis Group, 2023), Chapter 6.

non-legal or political influences such as emotion, passion and perception. Therefore, the nonlinear approaches allow for the consideration of otherwise unexpected, ignored or neglected results. The list below includes a sample of different nonlinear approaches.

a) Self-referred

Each, a few and/or all of the pluralisms and their interrelations may be self-confined and self-interactive. For instance, a unidimensional nonlinear self-referred view of an agent such as a military government in a non-democratic state might not acknowledge any other sovereign over a particular territory and that might be the only rationale behind the origin or maintenance of a territorial dispute—i.e. the sole cause for this territorial dispute would be an ideological claim. A multidimensional nonlinear self-referred view of the same situation might acknowledge that the military government is using the dispute and an external foe to feed domestic support in order to keep their standing in power by manipulating popular emotion, passion and, ultimately, nationalism.

b) Regressive

Circumstances encompassing sovereignty and territorial disputes might follow traditional linear paths such as origin-settlement, origin-escalation or origin-ongoing/never-ending. However, these are not the only ways in which these situations could unfold. Any difference might see the challenger and challenged agents move from a state of evolution to one of involution or entanglement in their interrelations—e.g. what in principle might have appeared to be a final understanding between the challenger and challenged agents over a disputed territory could move very quickly to a war situation because of the domestic situation of any or all of the involved parties, and the regional and international contexts. Therein, what might have seemed at the time by experts in legal and political sciences and international relations as an unexpected escalation into conflict of an otherwise peaceful bilateral relationship between sovereign states could be explained and studied as an intentional "relapse" of the state of affairs. A unidimensional nonlinear regressive view might consider, for example, the legal and political fragile situation of a particular agent such as the challenger's ruling party while a multidimensional nonlinear regressive approach would incorporate in the assessment the counterpart's domestic situation as well as the influences brought by the regional and international contexts.

c) Chaotic and random

Both chaotic and random nonlinear approaches imply that non-traditional journeys will be followed. While a chaotic view is characterized by a system that complies with defined criteria, a random understanding is not determined by any preconceived notion. Therein, a nonlinear chaotic view on a territorial dispute could apply, for example, notions that in principle are alien to disciplines that traditionally study them such as legal and political sciences and international relations. For example, legal or political sciences or international relations scholars might choose to use methodologies concerning natural sciences or game theory to explain and foresee individual and group behavior—i.e. the concepts and methods applied by the legal or political sciences or international relations scholars might be novel to them, but they are already stipulated and widely accepted by experts in natural sciences and game theory. Differently, the same scholars might choose to depart from traditional and deterministic *a priori* assumptions, beliefs and understandings by, for example, altering any, a few or all these concepts and methods by going beyond actual or assumed ontological or epistemological limitations—i.e. arguably, much of humanity's scientific evolution has had to do with this approach.

Variables

The previous sections showed how situations encompassing sovereignty and territorial disputes could be understood, known and assessed in different manners—i.e. in unidimensional, multidimensional, linear and nonlinear ways. In several respects, these situations and the way in which they are studied can be influenced by several variables. *Brevitatis causa*, the following subsections will characterize two of these variables: time and space.[33]

Time

Broadly, "time" can be distinguished between existential time and cosmological time depending on whether there is a physical or metaphysical understanding. The former refers to successive totalities and is a physical and factual conception. The latter is the abstract notion that refers to a succession of instants that exclude themselves reciprocally and are equally empty—e.g. the time indicated by clocks with their equal hours, minutes and seconds. More precisely, different understandings regarding "time" may be classified into different groups: eternalists and non-eternalists; finitists and infinitists; chance originationists; speculators about the past, the future and both; and annihilationist.

33 For a detailed account on time and space see Jorge E. Núñez, *Cosmopolitanism, State Sovereignty, International Law and Politics: A Theory* (London and New York, NY: Routledge, Taylor & Francis Group, 2023), Chapter 6.

Eternalists favor conceptions that are abstract and metaphysical allowing them to claim their permanent, imperishable and unchangeable nature. Conversely, non-eternalists accept conceptions may not be permanent in nature and, therefore, that they are subject to change over time. For example, a territorial claim may be based on a God-given assumed right and, therefore, the relevant agents may consider their sovereignty unquestionable, imprescriptible and not open to discussion. Yet, the claim may be also based on the actual first settlement of an originally uninhabited territory—i.e. right to claim sovereignty is based on empirical facts, whether they can be demonstrated or not at a later stage.

In turn, the distinction between finitists' and infinitists' understandings regarding time has to do with claiming bound and limited conceptions or universal and general conceptions. For example, despite their non-eternal character, a ruling party, clan or elite group may claim to have no limits in their authority and power because of their ancestry, blood lineage or cast—i.e. they condition their infinite standing to their own existence as a continuous family or group whether they may or may not base their right to uncontested sovereignty on a superempirical normative authority such as God. In contrast, they may acknowledge both their own temporality and the finitude in their standing because they may accept sovereign claims are only relevant for those who can actually exercise the resultant rights and obligations—i.e. they condition their finite standing to their own particular temporal existence whether they may or may not base their right to uncontested sovereignty on a superempirical normative authority such as God.

The rest of the understandings concerned with time—i.e. chance originationists; speculators about the past, the future and both; and annihilationists—have to do with the way in which a conception may be understood as either necessary or contingent depending on criteria that include actual or assumed historical coincidences; transcendental and representational explanations, whether empirically demonstrable or not; and their complete lack of temporal conditioning.

Whether the view related to a notion and its existence in time is characterized as an eternal or non-eternal, finite or infinite, chance originationist, annihilationist or speculative view about time, the important point is to appreciate that it is a variable that conditions assumptions, beliefs and understandings. By "temporalizing"[34] the object or subject of study and relevant notions, the scholar contextualizes explanations and assessments and, as a result, avoids the application of unaccounted later assumptions, beliefs and understandings to past evidence.[35]

34 Marcelo Finger and Dov M. Gabbat, "Adding a Temporal Dimension to a Logic System," *Journal of Logic, Language and Information* 1 (1992): 203–233.

35 Stroud Francis Charles Milsom, *A Natural History of the Common Law* (New York, NY: Columbia University Press, 2003), xvi.

Space

"Space" is the actual or virtual area where pluralisms and their interrelations happen, such as land, water, outer space and cyberspace. The notion encompasses material (natural) as well as abstract (cultural) elements and features and can be classified: (a) according to its scope; and (b) according to the way it is perceived. In turn, space according to its scope can be subclassified in the narrow, integral and representational sense while space according to the way it is perceived may be subdivided into physical, social and mental space.

a) According to its scope:

Space in the narrow sense is a synonym of territory. At the level of the state, it implies notions like "borders" and "boundaries." For example, a state is currently characterized in law by reference to territorial sovereignty.[36] At the level of the individual and the community, it is related to notions like "property" or "possession," as for example in the notions of self-ownership or property in the person.[37]

Space in the integral sense includes territorially and non-territorially characterized elements and features such as social and economic relations that are historically specific. For example, at the level of the state, it implies institutional practices, and at the level of the individual and the community, it has to do with the way in which societal interactions change over time.

Space in the representational sense refers to the way in which it is conceived or conceptualized as a figment of intellectual analysis, as for example in the way in which different disciplines use the notion.

b) According to the way it is perceived:

Physical space is material or a natural area where interrelations between agents happen.

Social space refers to artificial (abstract) constructions created by human convention such as the hierarchy in an institution or in a family group.

Mental space is intellectual abstraction not necessarily based on social interrelations that refer to purely conceptual representations.

The aforementioned classifications are important when explaining and assessing issues encompassing sovereignty such as territorial disputes. For instance, in territorial disputes such as the Falkland/Malvinas Islands and the archipelago of San Andrés, Providencia and Santa Catalina, clearly, there are

36 See Malcom N. Shaw, *International Law* (Cambridge: Cambridge University Press, 2017). See in particular Chapter 9.

37 See Jorge E. Núñez, *Sovereignty Conflicts and International Law and Politics: A Distributive Justice Issue* (London and New York, NY: Routledge, Taylor & Francis Group, 2017), Chapter 4.

some evident similarities and differences in terms of physical space—e.g. they are all islands or groups located in different parts of the world. In terms of their territorial sovereignty, i.e. space in the narrow sense, they are part of a sovereign state or their sovereignty is still being discussed. Depending on whether they are a *de jure* and *de facto* part of another state or their sovereignty is still under discussion, their respective socioeconomic and political changes—i.e. space in the integral sense—are dependent on extra-territorial factors such as blockades.[38] Finally, they are in law classed as "islands" and the Law of the Sea Convention is applicable.[39]

Depending on the understanding of "space," agents may not have a physical space or even a space in the narrow sense, yet they are part of territorial disputes. The question "who counts?"[40] as a claiming party is open to interpretation. This is because, arguably, legal and political sciences and international relations currently understand "states" as requiring "territorial sovereignty," and, in turn, they understand "territorial sovereignty" as space in the narrow and physical senses only.

Deploying the multidimensional approach

Before advancing in the assessment and explication of territorial disputes in the Americas, and in order to provide a blueprint that better illustrates how this monograph will apply the multidimensional approach to these differences, the following tables bring together the aforementioned pluralisms (see Tables 3.1, 3.2, 3.3, 3.4, 3.5 and 3.6).

Although the tables have been introduced separately for the purpose of this monograph and in order to offer a more visual structure, the comprehension, exploration and explanation of any real case scenario will aim to embrace all of them in multidimensional ways and in relation to variables such as time and space.

38 For example, Argentina has threatened an economic blockade, an idea supported by other Latin-American States with visible immediate negative results for the islanders. For further details, see Jorge E. Núñez, *Sovereignty Conflicts and International Law and Politics: A Distributive Justice Issue* (London and New York, NY: Routledge, Taylor & Francis Group, 2017), Chapter 7; and Jorge E. Núñez, *Territorial Disputes and State Sovereignty: International Law and Politics* (London and New York, NY: Routledge, Taylor & Francis Group, 2020), Chapter 6.

39 Clive R. Symmons, "Some Problems Relating to the Definition of Insular Formations in International Law: Islands and Low-Tide Elevations," Clive Schofield and Peter Hocknell, eds., *Maritime Briefing* 1:5 (1995) https://www.durham.ac.uk/media/durham-university/research-/research-centres/ibru-centre-for-borders-research/maps-and-databases/publications-database/maritime-briefings/mb_1-5.pdf accessed 31 August 2023.

40 See the author's view about this point in Jorge E. Núñez, *Sovereignty Conflicts and International Law and Politics: A Distributive Justice Issue* (London and New York, NY: Routledge, Taylor & Francis Group, 2017), Chapter 6.

Table 3.1 Overview: Pluralism of pluralisms[a]

	Sovereign state A	*Sovereign state B*	*Disputed territory C*	*Any other agent/s D/E/etc.*	*Regional organization/s*	*International organization/s*
Agents	State Communities Individuals	State Communities Individuals	State Communities Individuals	States Communities Individuals	States	States
Roles	Host	Host	Participant or Attendee	Viewer?	Viewer?	Viewer?
Contexts	Domestic Regional International	Domestic Regional International	Domestic Regional International	Regional? International	Regional	International
Realms (e.g. bases for the colorable claim[b])	Factual Normative Axiological	Factual Normative Axiological	Factual Normative Axiological	Factual Normative Axiological	Factual Normative Axiological	Factual Normative Axiological
Modes of existence (e.g. based on issues at stake[c])	Ideal Natural Cultural Metaphysical	Ideal Natural Cultural Metaphysical	Ideal Natural Cultural Metaphysical	Ideal Natural Cultural Metaphysical	Ideal Natural Cultural Metaphysical	Ideal Natural Cultural Metaphysical

[a] For complete details about these tables refer to Jorge E. Núñez, *Cosmopolitanism, State Sovereignty, International Law and Politics: A Theory* (London and New York, NY: Routledge, Taylor & Francis Group, 2023), Chapters 7 and 8.

[b] For colorable claim see Jorge E. Núñez, *Sovereignty Conflicts and International Law and Politics: A Distributive Justice Issue* (London and New York, NY: Routledge, Taylor & Francis Group, 2017); and, in particular, Jorge E. Núñez, *Territorial Disputes and State Sovereignty: International Law and Politics* (London and New York, NY: Routledge, Taylor & Francis Group, 2020), Chapter 4.

[c] For issues at stake see Jorge E. Núñez, *Territorial Disputes and State Sovereignty: International Law and Politics* (London and New York, NY: Routledge, Taylor & Francis Group, 2020), Chapter 4.

Table 3.2 Pluralisms 1: Agents, features and elements[a]

	Sovereign state A	*Sovereign state B*	*Disputed territory C*
Territory			
Religion			
Territorial size			
Population size			
Wealth			
Defense			
Natural resources			
Geographical proximity			

[a] Based on the definition of "state" that refers to its necessary elements, i.e. population, territory and government. For this definition and relevant sub-elements, see Jorge E. Núñez, *Sovereignty Conflicts and International Law and Politics: A Distributive Justice Issue* (London and New York, NY: Routledge, Taylor & Francis Group, 2017); and Jorge E. Núñez, *Territorial Disputes and State Sovereignty: International Law and Politics* (London and New York, NY: Routledge, Taylor & Francis Group, 2020).

Table 3.3 Pluralisms 2: Players

	Sovereign state A	*Sovereign state B*	*Disputed territory C*
Role			
Rationality			
Strategy			
Information			

Table 3.4 Pluralisms 3: Contexts[a]

	Sovereign state A	*Sovereign state B*	*Disputed territory C*
Domestic			
Regional			
International			

[a] Elements related to each context from Jorge E. Núñez, *Territorial Disputes and State Sovereignty: International Law and Politics* (London and New York, NY: Routledge, Taylor & Francis Group, 2020), Chapter 4.

Table 3.5 Pluralisms 4: Realms[a]

	Sovereign state A	*Sovereign state B*	*Disputed territory C*
Factual			
Normative			
Axiological			

[a] The "realms" table uses here, as an example, bases for a colorable claim each agent may have. For details about the colorable claim see Jorge E. Núñez, *Sovereignty Conflicts and International Law and Politics: A Distributive Justice Issue* (London and New York, NY: Routledge, Taylor & Francis Group, 2017); and, in particular, Jorge E. Núñez, *Territorial Disputes and State Sovereignty: International Law and Politics* (London and New York, NY: Routledge, Taylor & Francis Group, 2020), Chapter 4.

Table 3.6 Pluralisms 5: Modes of existence[a]

	Sovereign state A	*Sovereign state B*	*Disputed territory C*
Ideal			
Natural			
Cultural			
Metaphysical			

Conclusion

This chapter introduced the notion of pluralism of pluralisms that characterizes sovereignty and territorial disputes—i.e. agents, players, contexts, realms and modes of existence—in order to present an alternative way to explain and assess them. Thereafter, and in order to tackle the complexity that sovereignty and territorial disputes encompass, the chapter referred to the multidimensional approach.

The first pluralisms referred to agents and their roles as players in their interrelations. It was explained that a state may be a single agent according to scientific disciplinary understanding. However, there are other agents concerned with issues pertaining to sovereignty and territorial disputes, such as individuals and communities. Because disciplines such as legal and political sciences and international relations understand, know and value these agents differently, their analyses exclude different methodological approaches, assumptions and conceptual bases that are often overlooked and the results, unsurprisingly, present fragmented views. Moreover, it was argued that, in addition to distinguishing these different agents, it is important to accept that they might play several roles in their interrelations. These different roles deserve further study in order to avoid the aforementioned fragmentation in understanding and knowledge, and to extend analysis further.

Other pluralisms were introduced to show the intricacy present in sovereignty and territorial disputes—i.e. contexts, realms and modes of existence. Whether or not a particular context might be more relevant to an agent and their role, they all might influence their interrelations and, therefore, should be taken into account when explaining and assessing issues concerning them. Moreover, it was highlighted that these agents, their roles, interrelations and contexts might encompass factual, normative or axiological angles. Finally, the need for more precision in the explanation and assessment of issues related to sovereignty and territorial disputes was suggested by maintaining that they can be characterized by reference to ideal, natural, cultural or metaphysical elements and features.

Having established that sovereignty and territorial disputes encompass several pluralisms, the rest of the chapter explained why traditional scholarly approaches used in disciplines such as the legal and political sciences and international relations are limited because of their tunnel visions and argued for a move away from these unidimensional views toward multidimensionality. More precisely, the argument was not intended to make a case against these disciplines and their current concepts, assumptions, beliefs, understandings and methodologies but to advocate for their enhancement. Originally introduced in Núñez (2023), two dimensional approaches were briefly characterized. While the unidimensional approach seeks to explore and understand a fragment of the object or subject of study in question and the way a scholarly discipline conceives it, the multidimensional approach is more interested in the object or subject of study itself, its elements, features and interrelations. Furthermore, it was briefly reiterated that these approaches may choose to assess the object or subject of study in linear and nonlinear ways either by applying the more conventional understanding found in scholarly literature or by accepting non-traditionally considered interrelations of the same pluralities and, therefore, other possible outcomes. Thereafter, two variables that might influence the object or subject of study and their comprehension were incorporated, i.e. time and space.

The chapter finished by bringing together all the aforesaid pluralisms in the form of a blueprint. The following chapters will make use of this blueprint in order to explain and assess real case scenarios of territorial disputes in the Americas.

Bibliography

Aleinkoff, T. Alexander and Douglas Klusmeyer, eds. *Citizenship Today. Global Perspectives and Practices.* Washington, DC: Carnegie Endowment for International Peace, 2001.

Anand, R. P. "Sovereign Equality of States in International Law." *International Studies* 8:3 (1966): 213–224.

Bouchez, L. J. "The Fixing of Boundaries in International Boundary Rivers." *International and Comparative Law Quarterly* 12:3 (1963): 789–817.

Brownlie, Ian. *Principles of Public International Law.* Oxford: Oxford University Press, 2008.

Cassese, Antonio. *International Law.* Oxford: Oxford University Press, 2001.

DeAngelis, Brett A. *A Line in the Sand: Prospect Theory and Nash Arbitration in Resolving Territorial Disputes.* Monterey, CA: Dudley Knox Library, Naval Postgraduate School, 2012.

Dunleavy, Patrick and Brendan O'Leary. *Theories of the State: The Politics of Liberal Democracy.* Basingstoke and London: Macmillan, 1987.

Evans, Malcom D. *International Law.* Oxford: Oxford University Press, 2010.

Finger, Marcelo and Dov M. Gabbat. "Adding a Temporal Dimension to a Logic System." *Journal of Logic, Language and Information* 1 (1992): 203–233.

Grafen, Alan. "The Logic of Divisively Asymmetric Contests: Respect for Ownership and the Desperado Effect." *Animal Behaviour* 35:2 (1987): 462–467.

Hall, John A. and G. John Ikenberry. *The State.* Milton Keynes: Open University Press, 1989.

Hart, Herbert L. A. *The Concept of Law*. Oxford: Oxford University Press, 1994.
Hjorth, R. "Equality in the Theory of International Society: Kelsen, Rawls and the English School." *Review of International Studies* 37:5 (2011): 2585–2602.
James, Alan. *Sovereign Statehood: The Basis of International Society*. London: Allen and Unwin, 1986.
Kelsen, Hans. "The Principle of Sovereign Equality of States as a Basis for International Organization." *Yale Law Journal* 53:2 (1944): 207–220.
Krasner, Stephen D. *Sovereignty: Organized Hypocrisy*. Princeton, NJ: Princeton University Press, 1999.
Little, Paul E. *Amazonia: Territorial Struggles on Perennial Frontiers*. Baltimore, MD: Johns Hopkins University Press, 2001.
Milsom, Stroud Francis Charles. *A Natural History of the Common Law*. New York, NY: Columbia University Press, 2003.
Nozick, Robert. *Anarchy, State and Utopia*. New York, NY: Basic Books, 1974.
Núñez, Jorge E. *Cosmopolitanism, State Sovereignty, International Law and Politics: A Theory*. London and New York, NY: Routledge, Taylor & Francis Group, 2023.
Núñez, Jorge E. *Sovereignty Conflicts and International Law and Politics: A Distributive Justice Issue*. London and New York, NY: Routledge, Taylor & Francis Group, 2017.
Núñez, Jorge E. *Territorial Disputes and State Sovereignty: International Law and Politics*. London and New York, NY: Routledge, Taylor & Francis Group, 2020.
Powell, E. "Islamic States and Peaceful Resolution of Territorial Disputes." *International Organization* 69:4 (2015): 777–807.
Shaw, Malcom N. *International Law*. Cambridge: Cambridge University Press, 2017.
Symmons, Clive R. "Some Problems Relating to the Definition of Insular Formations in International Law: Islands and Low-Tide Elevations." Schofield, Clive and Hocknell, Peter, eds. *Maritime Briefing* 1:5 (1995) https://www.durham.ac.uk/media/durham-university/research-/research-centres/ibru-centre-for-borders-research/maps-and-databases/publications-database/maritime-briefings/mb_1-5.pdf accessed 31 August 2023.
Vidmar, Jure. "Territorial Integrity and the Law of Statehood." *George Washington International Law Review* 44:4 (2012): 697–748.

Part Two

4 Common roots to the territorial disputes in the Americas

Introduction

There are common roots to the territorial disputes in the Americas.[1] Colonial empires divided the territory with little regard to native communities and the environment. Consequently, domestic and regional conflict brought about evils such as poverty, humanitarian crises, arms trafficking and guerrilla warfare.[2] First, this chapter classifies the common roots to the disputes into three clearly defined historical periods and characterizes each of them: the three eras are pre-Columbian times; post-Columbian but pre-independence times; and post-independence times. Indeed, despite their particularities, these different historical periods share common roots that include a pluralism of elements and features, such as legal, political and sociological factors.

In pre-Columbian times there was a large population estimated to be up to 112 million that included organized empires such as the Aztecs, Mayas and Incas as well as smaller tribes and nomads.[3] Territorial disputes existed mainly because of the expansion of empires.[4] However, it was only with the arrival of a European presence on the continent that the native population was reduced dramatically.[5] In turn, post-Columbian but pre-independence times witnessed

1 David Downing, *An Atlas of Territorial and Border Disputes* (London: New English Library, 1980), 84; Peter Calvert, *Boundary Disputes in Latin America* (London: Institute for the Study of Conflict, 1983); Jack Child, *Geopolitics and Conflict in South America* (New York, NY: Praeger, 1985); Gordon Ireland, *Boundaries, Possessions, and Conflicts in South America* (Cambridge, MA: Harvard University Press, 1938); and many more.

2 Paul R. Hensel, "One Thing Leads to Another: Recurrent Militarized Disputes in Latin America, 1816–1986," *Journal of Peace Research* 31:3 (1994): 281–297; Paul R. Hensel, "Contentious Issues and World Politics: The Management of Territorial Claims in the Americas, 1816–1992," *International Studies Quarterly* 45:1 (2001): 81–109.

3 William M. Denevan, *The Native Population of the Americas in 1492* (Madison, WI: University of Wisconsin Press, 1992); Henry F. Dobyns, "An Appraisal of Techniques with a New Hemispheric Estimate," *Current Anthropology* 7:4 (1966): 395–416.

4 Geoffrey W. Conrad and Arthur A. Demarset, *Religion and Empire: The Dynamics of Aztec and Inca Expansionism* (Cambridge: Cambridge University Press, 1984).

5 Noble David Cook, *Born to Die: Disease and the New World Conquest, 1492–1650* (Cambridge: Cambridge University Press, 1998).

DOI: 10.4324/9781003350828-6

European colonizers invading the land and annihilating the local empires.[6] In time, European states applied their legal and political understanding to America. Examples of this practice are the Papal bulls of Alexander VI: *Inter caetera*, *Inter caetera II*, *Eximiae devotionis* and *Dudum siquidem*. Natives were not acknowledged rights. Finally, post-independence times see newly established states in America and the adoption of the *uti possidetis juris* principle.[7] Consequently, these states claimed *de jure* sovereignty over territories in which they already had *de facto* presence.[8] Because the borders that were agreed or simply accepted in fact by the European empires were in many cases either unclear or non-existent, territorial disputes followed between the now sovereign states in the continent.[9]

Territorial disputes in the Americas, as elsewhere, are highly intricate because of their multidimensional nature. While some territorial disputes have escalated into conflict and international and regional elements may explain why there are still a few ongoing differences, the continent has a tendency for peaceful and permanent resolution. Therefore, by acknowledging the pluralism of pluralisms that characterizes these differences, this chapter moves to expose the reasons behind their origin, continuation and potential escalation into conflict as well as their permanent and peaceful settlement. By applying the multidimensional approach, the second part of the chapter focuses on post-independence differences in the Americas that are now resolved. Stemming from separatist movements in the continent and being either against former colonial powers or between former colonies trying to ascertain or extend their territorial sovereignty, these territorial disputes bring together the several pluralisms introduced in the previous chapter—i.e. agents, players, contexts, realms and modes of existence. Importantly, the final section shows that, although the claiming parties may achieve a settlement, domestic, regional and international issues at stake may still turn the situation volatile, and regional guarantors are key in peacekeeping.

6 Linda A. Newson, "The Demographic Collapse of Native Peoples of the Americas, 1492–1650," *Proceedings of the British Academy* 81 (1993): 247–288.

7 For the difference between *uti possidetis de facto* and *uti possidetis de jure* see Frederic William Ganzert, "The Boundary Controversy in the Upper Amazon between Brazil, Bolivia, and Peru, 1903–1909," *Hispanic American Historical Review* 14:4 (1934): 427–449, 430ff.; Jonathan I. Charney and Lewis M. Alexander, eds., *International Maritime Boundaries, Volume I* (Boston, MA: Martinus Nijhoff, 1996), 777–783.

8 Steven R. Ratner, "Drawing a Better Line: *Uti Possidetis* and the Borders of New States," *American Journal of International Law* 90:4 (1996): 590–624; Malcom N. Shaw, *International Law* (Cambridge: Cambridge University Press, 2003), 446–451; Ian Brownlie, *Principles of Public International Law* (Oxford: Oxford University Press, 2003), 129–130; and many others.

9 Alan J. Day, ed., *Border and Territorial Disputes* (Essex: Longman, 1982), 332–333.

Historical division of territory

In order to more clearly present, explain and assess the common roots to territorial disputes in the Americas, this monograph distinguishes three historical periods: pre-Columbian times; post-Columbian but pre-independence times; and post-independence times.

Pre-Columbian times

The population in the Americas is calculated to have been between 54 and 112 million in pre-Columbian times.[10] These peoples were organized into empires such as those of the Aztecs, Mayas and Incas as well as into smaller tribes and nomadic groups.[11] Regardless of their differences, in all cases, their geographical location was influenced by religious components and basic needs such as the provision of water, food and shelter. There is clear evidence that some of these populations were highly advanced.[12] Territorial disputes were mainly because of the expansion of empires.[13]

Post-Columbian but pre-independence times

With European conquest, the native population was dramatically reduced—i.e. fewer than 10 million indigenous peoples survived.[14] The former Aztec, Mayan and Incan empires were dismantled and many tribes simply became extinct.[15] Similar to cases in Africa, Asia and the Middle East, European colonization had little regard for the original occupants of the land and caused profound socio-political changes across the Americas.[16] Moreover, European

10 William M. Denevan, *The Native Population of the Americas in 1492* (Madison, WI: University of Wisconsin Press, 1992); Henry F. Dobyns, "An Appraisal of Techniques with a New Hemispheric Estimate," *Current Anthropology* 7:4 (1966): 395–416.

11 William M. Denevan, *The Native Population of the Americas in 1492* (Madison, WI: University of Wisconsin Press, 1992); Henry F. Dobyns, "An Appraisal of Techniques with a New Hemispheric Estimate," *Current Anthropology* 7:4 (1966): 395–416.

12 Hector Diaz Polanco, *Indigenous Peoples in Latin America: The Quest for Self-Determination* (New York, NY: Routledge: 2018); Susana Lobo, Steve Talbot and Traci. L. Morris, eds., *Native American Voices: A Reader* (London and New York, NY: Routledge, 2010); Michael P. Closs, ed., *Native American Mathematics* (Austin, TX: University of Texas Press, 1997); and many more.

13 Geoffrey W. Conrad and Arthur A. Demarset, *Religion and Empire: The Dynamics of Aztec and Inca Expansionism* (Cambridge: Cambridge University Press, 1984).

14 Noble David Cook, *Born to Die: Disease and the New World Conquest, 1492–1650* (Cambridge: Cambridge University Press, 1998).

15 Linda A. Newson, "The Demographic Collapse of Native Peoples of the Americas, 1492–1650," *Proceedings of the British Academy* 81 (1993): 247–288.

16 See Jorge E. Núñez, *Territorial Disputes and State Sovereignty: International Law and Politics* (London and New York, NY: Routledge, Taylor & Francis Group, 2020), Chapters 6, 7 and 8 for individual territorial disputes in more detail.

colonizers brought their legal and political understanding of territorial sovereignty, such as through the Papal bulls of Alexander VI: *Inter caetera*, *Inter caetera II* (*Eximiae devotionis*), *Inter caetera III* and *Dudum siquidem*. For example, the *Inter caetera* bulls granted sovereignty to the Spanish and Portuguese monarchs *erga omnes* over territories in the Americas, established a line of demarcation and, unsurprisingly, the indigenous populations were not acknowledged.[17] The 1494 Treaty of Tordesillas between Spain and Portugal would cement these bases.[18]

Post-independence times

The states that formed after colonial times applied the principle of *uti possidetis juris* by which they assumed to have sovereignty over their formerly colonized areas—i.e. they claimed *de jure* sovereignty over territories in which they already had *de facto* presence.[19] The borders were "settled" in such a way that proved to be unclear or non-existent and generated competing claims that resulted in territorial disputes.[20]

Former colonial powers interfered directly and indirectly in the Americas. As a response to these interferences, the newly formed states brought forward the Monroe, Calvo and Drago doctrines.[21] The Monroe Doctrine can be summarized into the following basic principles of public international law: (a) no colonization; (b) non-intervention of European states in the affairs of America; and (c) reciprocal non-intervention in European affairs. The Calvo and Drago doctrines prohibit the intervention of a sovereign state if the purpose of that intervention is solely to oblige the target state to fulfill its international financial

17 H. Vander Linden, "Alexander VI and the Demarcation of the Maritime and Colonial Domains of Spain and Portugal, 1493–1494," *The American Historical Review* 22:1 (1916): 1–20.

18 Complete text of the Treaty of Tordesillas available at https://avalon.law.yale.edu/15th_century/mod001.asp accessed 13 September 2023.

19 Steven R. Ratner, "Drawing a Better Line: *Uti Possidetis* and the Borders of New States," *American Journal of International Law* 90:4 (1996): 590–624; Malcom N. Shaw, *International Law* (Cambridge: Cambridge University Press, 2003), 446–451; Ian Brownlie, *Principles of Public International Law* (Oxford: Oxford University Press, 2003), 129–130; and many others.

20 Alan J. Day, ed., *Border and Territorial Disputes* (Essex: Longman, 1982), 332–333.

21 See Elihu Root, "The Real Monroe Doctrine," *American Society of International Law* 8 (1914): 6–22; Mark T. Gilderhus, "The Monroe Doctrine: Meanings and Implications," *Presidential Studies Quarterly* 36 (2006): 5–16; Amos S. Hershey, "The Calvo and Drago Doctrines," *The American Journal of International Law* 1 (1907): 26–45; Luis M. Drago and H. Edward Nettles, "The Drago Doctrine in International Law and Politics," *The Hispanic American Historical Review* 8 (1928): 204–223; Crammond Kennedy, "The Drago Doctrine," *The North American Review* 185 (1907): 614–622; and many others.

obligations—e.g. Venezuela's international public debt in 1901 later resulted in the naval blockade by Great Britain, Germany and Italy.[22]

Claims to territory by indigenous peoples continue to be systematically discarded in this period,[23] based on two reasons: the natives were not legally "persons" or they were considered inferior.[24] However, Latin American states are currently reviewing the way in which they interact with these populations.[25]

The table below includes a list of post-independence territorial disputes.[26]

22 Juan Flores Zendejas and Felipe Ford Cole, "Sovereignty and Debt in Nineteenth-Century Latin America," in Pierre Pénet and Juan Flores Zendejas, eds., *Sovereign Debt Diplomacies: Rethinking Sovereign Debt from Colonial Empires to Hegemony* (Oxford: Oxford University Press, 2021), 49–72.

23 M. F. Lindley, *The Acquisition and Government of Backward Territory in International Law: Being a Treatise on the Law and Practice Relating to Colonial Expansion* (New York, NY: Negro Universities Press, 1969), 11–12.

24 Jérémie Gilbert, *Indigenous Peoples' Land Rights under International Law: From Victors to Actors* (Ardsley, NY: Transnational 2006), 1–2. This is a complex issue that will be addressed extensively in Chapter 8.

25 Roger Merino, "Conflicting Sovereignties: Global Conservation, Protected Areas, and Indigenous Nations in the Peruvian Amazon," *Global Environmental Politics* 22:2 (2022): 95–116; Roger Merino, "Reimagining the Nation-State: Indigenous Peoples and the Making of Plurinationalism in Latin America," *Leiden Journal of International Law* 31:4 (2018): 773–792; Anna F. Laing, "Re-producing Territory: Between Resource Nationalism and Indigenous Self-determination in Bolivia," *Geoforum* 108 (2020): 28–38; Austen L. Parrish, "Changing Territoriality, Fading Sovereignty, and the Development of Indigenous Rights," *American Indian Law Review* 31:2 (2006/2007): 291–313; Rachel Sieder, "Indigenous Peoples' Rights and the Law in Latin America," in Corinne Lennox and Damien Short, eds., *Handbook of Indigenous Peoples' Rights* (New York, NY: Routledge 2016), 414–423; Willem Van Genugten and Camillo Perez-Bustillo, "The Emerging International Architecture of Indigenous Rights: The Interaction between Global, Regional, and National Dimensions," *International Journal on Minority and Group Rights* 11:4 (2004): 379–409; Gemma van der Haar, "The Zapatista Uprising and the Struggle for Indigenous Autonomy," *European Review of Latin American and Caribbean Studies* 76 (2004): 98–108; Donna Lee Van Cott, "Broadening Democracy: Latin America's Indigenous Peoples' Movements," *Current History* 103:670 (2004): 80–85; Shane Greene, "Getting Over the Andes: The Geo-Eco-Politics of Indigenous Movements in Peru's Twenty-First Century Inca Empire," *Journal of Latin American Studies* 38:2 (2006): 327–354.

26 This section focuses only on the post-independence period. For more details, see, among others, David Downing, *An Atlas of Territorial and Border Disputes* (London: New English Library, 1980), 84; Peter Calvert, *Boundary Disputes in Latin America* (London: Institute for the Study of Conflict, 1983); Jack Child, *Geopolitics and Conflict in South America* (New York, NY: Praeger, 1985); Gordon Ireland, *Boundaries, Possessions, and Conflicts in South America* (Cambridge, MA: Harvard University Press, 1938); Paul R. Hensel, "One Thing Leads to Another: Recurrent Militarized Disputes in Latin America, 1816–1986," *Journal of Peace Research* 31:3 (1994): 281–297; Paul R. Hensel, "Contentious Issues and World Politics: The Management of Territorial Claims in the Americas, 1816–1992," *International Studies Quarterly* 45:1 (2001): 81–109.

Post-Independence Times							
North America							
States	*Issue*	*Years*		*Territorial Disputes*			
		Beginning–Ending		*(Intent of) Peaceful Resolutions*	*Militarized Confrontations*	*Guarantees*	*Agreements/Ruling Cases*
Great Britain v. United States	Oregon Dispute[a]	1818	1846	2	1	0	Convention of 1818,[b] Oregon Treaty (1846)[c]
Great Britain v. United States	Battle of Caribou	1838	1842	1	1	0	Webster-Ashburton Treaty (1842)[d]
Great Britain v. United States	Sugar Island Dispute	±1827	1842	1	0	0	Webster-Ashburton Treaty (1842)[e]
Great Britain v. United States	Alaska Boundary[f]	1871	1903	1	0	Court of Arbitration (1903)[g]	Hay-Harbert Treaty (1903)
Canada v. United States	The Grey Zone[h]	1977	Ongoing	0	0	0	0
Canada v. United States	Dixon Entrance[i]	±1897–Ongoing		2	0	Court of Arbitration (1903)[j]	Pacific Salmon Treaty (1985)[k]
Canada v. Denmark	Hans Island Dispute	1970	2022	1	2	0	Canada-Denmark/ Greenland Agreement on Hans Island (2022)[l]

Canada v. Russia	The Canada Basin/Alpha Rise[m]	1980s	Ongoing	0	0	0	0
Mexico v. United States	Texas Dispute[n]	1829	1848	1	1	0	Treaty of Guadalupe Hidalgo (1848)[o]
Mexico v. United States	Chamizal Dispute[p]	1848	1964	4	0[q]	International Boundary and Water Commission (1910)	Chamizal Convention Act (1964)[r]
United States v. Cuba	Guantanamo Bay[s]	1898	Ongoing	1	0	0	1903 Lease agreement (1903),[t] Cuban American Treaty of Relations (1934)[u]
Mexico v. France	Clipperton Island	±1897	1931	1	0	Italy (King of Italy Victor Emmanuel III)[v]	Clipperton Island Case (1931)
United States v. Great Britain	Pig War[w]	±1845	1874	1	1	0	Treaty of Washington (1871)[x]
United States v. Russia	The Northeast Passage[y]	1980s		0	0	0	0

(*Continued*)

Post-Independence Times							
Caribbean and Central America							
States	*Issue*	*Years*		*Territorial Disputes*			
		Beginning–Ending		*(Intent of) Peaceful Resolutions*	*Militarized Confrontations*	*Guarantees*	*Agreements, Arbitral Awards or Ruling Cases*
Belize (United Kingdom until 1981) v. Guatemala	Belize-Guatemala territorial dispute	1940	Ongoing	3	0	OAS (2000–2002),[z] ICJ (2019)	Head of Agreements (1981). Case Pending in the ICJ (2019)[aa]
Belize v. Honduras v. Guatemala	Sapodilla Cayes Dispute[bb]	1980	Ongoing	0	0	0	0
Costa Rica v. Nicaragua	Annexation of Nicoya Jurisdiction[cc]	1824	1858/1888	12	0	0	1. **Treaties without Parties' ratification:** Oreamuno-Buitrago Treaty (1838), Madriz-Zavala Treaty (1846), Molina-Juárez Treaty (1848), Molina-Marcoleta Treaty (1854), Cañas-Juárez Treaty (1857) and Cañas-Martínez Treaty (1857).

							2. Failed negotiations: Webster-Crampton Proposals (1852). Herrera-Zavala Negotiations (1872) and Víquez-Pasos Negotiations (1886). **3. Signed treaties without success:** Zambrana-Álvarez Treaty (1883) and Castro-Navas (1884) Treaty. **4. Ratified treaty:** Caña-Jerez Treaty (1858). **5. Arbitral Award:** Cleveland Arbitral Award (1888)[dd]
Costa Rica v. Nicaragua	Portillo Island Dispute[ee]	2010	2017	1	0	International Court of Justice	ICJ Case Concerning Land Boundary in the Northern Part of Isla Portillos (2017)[ff]

(*Continued*)

Cuba v. USA	Isla de Pinos Disputes[gg]	1902	1925	1	0	0	Hay-Quesada Treaty (1925)
Dominican Republic v. USA	Samaná Bay[hh]	1894	1904	0	0	0	0
El Salvador v. Honduras	Bolsones Meanguera, Meanguerita, El Tigre in the Gulf of Fonseca Dispute[ii]	1854	1992	1	1	International Court of Justice	ICJ Case Concerning Land, Island and Maritime Frontier Dispute (1992)[jj]
El Salvador v. Honduras	Portillo de Teotecacinte Dispute	1894–1906; 1906–1961		3	0	King of Spain, OAS, International Court of Justice	Bonilla-Gamez Treaty (1894),[kk] Arbitral Award of King of Spain (1906)[ll]
Haiti v. USA	Navassa Island[mm]	1857–1914, 1935–ongoing		0	1	0	0
Haiti v. USA	Môle Saint-Nicolas Affair[nn]	1889	1915	1	2 (protest of citizens)	0	0
Colombia, Honduras and the United States	The Bajo Nuevo and Serranilla Banks[oo]	1870s	2011 (ongoing?)	1	0	International Court of Justice	ICJ Cases Concerning Territorial and Maritime Dispute (Nicaragua v. Colombia)[pp]

Nicaragua v. Colombia	San Andrés and Providencia Archipelago Banco Quitasueño, Serrana Dispute[qq]	2001	2012–2022 (ongoing?)[rr]	1	0	International Court of Justice	ICJ Cases Concerning Territorial and Maritime Dispute (Nicaragua v. Colombia)[ss]
Post-Independence Times							
South America							
States	*Issue*	*Years*		*Territorial disputes*			
		Beginning–Ending		*(Intent of) Peaceful Resolutions*	*Militarized Confrontations*	*Guarantees*	*Agreements/Ruling Cases*
Argentina v. Brazil	Misiones Dispute[tt]	1841	1895	3	0	President Cleveland (USA)	Boundary Differences Treaty (1885), Arbitral Award of President Cleveland (1895)[uu]
Argentina v. Chile	Boundary Dispute of La Cordillera de los Andes[vv]	1883	1902	1	0	Great Britain	International Arbitral Award by King Edward VII (1902)[ww]

(*Continued*)

Argentina v. Chile	Beagle Channel Dispute (Picton, Nueva and Lennox Islands)[xx]	1904	1985	4	0	The Pope (The Vatican)	International Arbitral Award (1977),[yy] Agreement of Puerto Montt (1978),[zz] Act of Montevideo (1979),[aaa] Papal Mediation (1980),[bbb] Treaty of Peace and Friendship between Argentina and Chile (1984)[ccc]
Argentina v. Chile	Laguna del Desierto Dispute[ddd]	1810	1994	0	0	0	1994 Laguna del Desierto Arbitral Award[eee]
Argentina, Bolivia v. Chile	Puna de Atacama dispute[fff]	1879	1898	3	1	Mister William Buchachan (USA)	Quirno-Vaca Treaty (1889), Matta-Reyes Protocol (1891), Puna de Atacama Arbitral Award (1898)[ggg]
Argentina v. United Kingdom	Falklands/ Malvinas Islands[hhh]	1830s	Ongoing	2	2	United Nations Security Council[iii]	Arana-Southern Treaty (1850),[jjj] Communications Agreement of 1971 (1971),[kkk] United Nations General Assembly (several resolutions)[lll]

Bolivia, Peru v. Chile	Atacama Border Dispute[mmm]	1825	Ongoing	5	1	OAS, International Court of Justice	Boundary Treaty of 1866 (1886),[nnn] Treaty of Defensive Alliance (1873), Treaty of Sucre (1874), ICJ Case Concerning Obligation to Negotiate Access to the Pacific Ocean (2018)[ooo]
Bolivia v. Paraguay	Chaco War[ppp]	1932	1938	2	±8	Argentina, Brazil, Chile, Uruguay and USA	Paraguayan Referendum (1938), Peace, Friendship and Boundary Treaty (1938)[qqq]
Brazil v. Bolivia	Acre War[rrr]	1899	1903	1	5	0	Treaty of Petrópolis (1903)[sss]
Colombia v. Peru	Leticia Incident[ttt]	1932	1933	1	4	Brazil, League of Nations	Salomón-Lozano Treaty (1922)
Colombia v. Venezuela	Los Monjes Island[uuu]	1833–1951; 1951–Ongoing		1	0	0	Colombian unilateral declaration affirming the Venezuelan sovereignty over Los Monjes Island (1951)[vvv]

(*Continued*)

Colombia v. Venezuela	Colombian-Venezuelan Boundary[www]	±1886–1941		2	0	Spain	Arbitration Award of Queen Maria Cristina of 1891 (1891), Treaty of Limits and River Navigation of 1941 (1941)
Ecuador v. Peru	Ecuadorian-Peruvian War	1858	1860	1	2	Spain	Mapasingue Treaty (1860)
Ecuador v. Peru	Ecuadorian-Peruvian War	1941	1942	2	±7	Brazil	Ceasefire agreement (1941), Rio de Janeiro Protocol (1942)[xxx]
Ecuador v. Peru	Paquisha Incident	1981		1	1	Argentina, Brazil, Chile and USA	Sorrosa-Du Bois Act (1981)
Ecuador v. Peru	Cenepa War[yyy]	1995		1	1	Argentina, Brazil, Chile, and USA	Presidential Act of Brasilia (1998)[zzz]
Guyana v. Suriname	New River Triangle or Tigri Area Dispute[aaaa]	1975–ongoing		1	0	0	0

Guyana v. Venezuela	Esquibo (or Essequibo) Dispute[bbbb]	1830s–ongoing		2	0	0	1899 Paris Arbitral Award, 1966 Geneva Agreement,[cccc] ICJ on Arbitral Award of 3 October 1899 (Guyana v. Venezuela)[dddd]
Suriname v. French Guiana	Marouini (or Maroni) River Tract Dispute[eeee]	1700s	2021	1	0	0	2021 Protocol[ffff]

a Patrick James, Johann Park and Seung-Whan Choi, "Democracy and Conflict Management: Territorial Claims in the Western Hemisphere Revisited," *International Studies Quarterly* 50:4 (2006): 803–817 available at https://doi.org/10.1111/j.1468-2478.2006.00426.x accessed 24 July 2024.
b The complete British–American Diplomacy Convention of 1818 between the United States and Great Britain is available at https://avalon.law.yale.edu/19th_century/conv1818.asp#art2 accessed 24 July 2024.
c See Henry Commager, "England and Oregon Treaty of 1846," *Oregon Historical Quarterly* 28:1 (1927): 18–38 available at http://www.jstor.org/stable/20610369 accessed 24 July 2024; Walter N. Sage, "The Oregon Treaty of 1846," *Canadian Historical Review* 27:4 (1946): 349–367 available at https://utpjournals.press/doi/10.3138/chr-027-04-01 accessed 24 July 2024.
d The complete Webster-Ashburton Treaty is available at https://avalon.law.yale.edu/19th_century/br-1842.asp accessed 24 July 2024.
e The complete Webster-Ashburton Treaty is available at https://avalon.law.yale.edu/19th_century/br-1842.asp accessed 24 July 2024.
f Edward P. Kohn, *This Kindred People: Canadian-American Relations and the Anglo-Saxon Idea, 1895–1903* (Montreal: McGill-Queen's University Press, 2004).
g The Alaska Boundary Case (Great Britain, United States), Final Award, *Reports of International Awards*, 20 October 1903, Vol. XV, 481–540 available at https://legal.un.org/riaa/cases/vol_XV/481-540.pdf accessed 24 July 2024.
h Beverly Cook, "Lobster Boat Diplomacy: The Canada–US Grey Zone," *Marine Policy* 29:5 (2005): 385–390 available at https://www.sciencedirect.com/science/article/pii/S0308597X04000582 accessed 24 July 2024.
i Paul R. Hensel, "Contentious Issues and World Politics: The Management of Territorial Claims in the Americas, 1816–1992," *International Studies Quarterly* 45:1 (2001): 81–109 available at https://www.jstor.org/stable/3096102 accessed 24 July 2024.
j The Alaska Boundary Case (Great Britain, United States), Final Award, *Reports of International Awards*, 20 October 1903, Vol. XV, 481–540 available at https://legal.un.org/riaa/cases/vol_XV/481-540.pdf accessed 24 July 2024.
k The complete Treaty between the Government of Canada and the Government of the United States of America Concerning Pacific Salmon (The 1985 Pacific Salmon Treaty) is available at https://www.psc.org/about-us/history-purpose/pacific-salmon-treaty/#:~:text=The%20Treaty%20embodies%20the

(*Continued*)

%20commitment,salmon%20originating%20in%20their%20waters accessed 24 July 2024; Thomas C. Jensen, "The United States-Canada Pacific Salmon Interception Treaty: An Historical and Legal Overview," *Environmental Law* 16:3 (1986): 363–422 available at https://www.jstor.org/stable/43265761 accessed 24 July 2024.

l Complete agreement between Canada and Denmark available at https://www.ft.dk/ripdf/samling/20231/beslutningsforslag/b14/20231_b14_som_fremsat.pdf accessed 24 July 2024.

m Viatcheslav Gavrilov, Ted L. McDorman and Clive Schofield, "Canada and the Russian Federation," *Arctic Review on Law and Politics* 13 (2022): 219–231.

n Paul R. Hensel, "Territorial Claims and Armed Conflict between Neighbors," paper presented to the *Lineae Terrarum International Borders Conference*, El Paso, Texas, 2006 available at https://www.paulhensel.org/Research/lineae.pdf accessed 24 July 2024.

o Byron Calkins, Lance Aspaas, Charles Nettleman, Amanda Ramirez, Kyle Spolar and Ty Tramell, "The Boundary Survey of the United States and Mexico 'Hidalgo de Guadalupe Medir'—Treaty of Guadalupe Hidalgo (1848)," *Surveying and Land Information Science* 68:4 (2008): 221–237 available at https://www.ingentaconnect.com/content/aags/salis/2008/00000068/00000004/art00004 accessed 24 July 2024.

p A. C. Lamborn and Stephen P. Mumme, *Statecraft, Domestic Politics, and Foreign Policy Making: The El Chamizal Dispute* (New York, NY: Routledge, 2019).

q Luis L. Schenoni, Gary Goertz, Andrew P. Owsiak and Paul F. Diehl, "Settling Resistant Territorial Disputes: The Territorial Boundary Peace in Latin America," *International Studies Quarterly* 64:1 (2020): 57–70 available at https://academic.oup.com/isq/article/64/1/57/5701080 accessed 24 July 2024.

r American–Mexican Chamizal Convention Act (Adopted in April 1964) available at https://www.congress.gov/88/statute/STATUTE-78/STATUTE-78-Pg184.pdf accessed 24 July 2024.

s Paul R. Hensel, "Contentious Issues and World Politics: The Management of Territorial Claims in the Americas, 1816–1992," *International Studies Quarterly* 45:1 (2001): 81–109 available at https://www.jstor.org/stable/3096102 accessed 24 July 2024.

t The complete 1903 Agreement Between the United States and Cuba for the Lease of Coaling and Naval Stations is available at https://avalon.law.yale.edu/20th_century/dip_cuba002.asp accessed 24 July 2024.

u Lester H. Woolsey, "The New Cuban Treaty," *The American Journal of International Law* 28:3 (1934): 530–534 available at https://www.jstor.org/stable/2190379 accessed 24 July 2024.

v Clipperton Island Case (Mexico v. France), 1931, Report of International Arbitral Awards, vol. II, 1105 abstract available at https://legal.un.org/ilc/documentation/english/a_cn4_151.pdf and complete text available at https://jusmundi.com/en/document/decision/fr-ile-de-clipperton-mexique-contre-france-sentence-wednesday-28th-january-1931 accessed 31 July 2024; "Arbitral Award on the Subject of the Difference Relative to the Sovereignty over Clipperton Island," *The American Journal of International Law* 26:2 (1932): 390–394 available at https://www.jstor.org/stable/2189369 accessed 31 July 2024.

w Scott Kaufman, *The Pig War: The United States, Britain, and the Balance of Power in the Pacific Northwest, 1846–72* (Lanham, MD: Lexington, 2004).

x 1871 Amity Treaty of Washington complete text available at https://maint.loc.gov/law/help/us-treaties/bevans/b-gb-ust000012-0170.pdf accessed 31 July 2024.

y Andrey Todorov, "Dire Straits of the Russian Arctic: Options and Challenges for a Potential US FONOP in the Northern Sea Route," *Marine Policy* 139 (2022): 105020 available at https://www.sciencedirect.com/science/article/pii/S0308597X22000677 accessed 31 July 2024; Andrey A. Todorov, "The Russia-USA Legal Dispute over the Straits of the Northern Sea Route and Similar Case of the Northwest Passage," *Arctic and North* 29:1 (2017): 62–75 available at file:///C:/Users/55112704/Downloads/The_Russia-USA_legal_dispute_over_the_straits_of_t.pdf accessed 31 July 2024.

z See the Organization of American States (OAS), "The Fund for Peace: Peaceful Settlement of Territorial Disputes and the Role of the OAS in Mediating the Belize-Guatemala Territorial Dispute," available at https://www.oas.org/es/sap/dsdme/pubs/role_of_the_oas_belize_guatemala.pdf accessed 31 July 2024.

aa Guatemala's Territorial, Insular and Maritime Claim (Guatemala v. Belize), Extension of the Time-limits for the Filing of the Initial Pleadings, 2020 International Court of Justice, Press Release available at https://www.icj-cij.org/public/files/case-related/177/177-20200424-PRE-01-00-EN.pdf accessed 31 July 2024.

bb Arlenie Perez, "Fisheries Management at the Tri-national Border between Belize, Guatemala and Honduras," *Marine Policy* 33:2 (2009): 195–200 available at https://www.sciencedirect.com/science/article/pii/S0308597X08000997 accessed 31 July 2024.

cc Jesús Estacio Ferro, "El Rio San Juan: Dos Siglos de Conflicto entre Costa Rica y Nicaragua," *Revista Electrónica Iberoamericana* 12:1 (2018): 1–32 available at https://www.urjc.es/images/ceib/revista_electronica/vol_12_2018_1/REIB_12_01_Art3.pdf accessed 31 July 2024; Hugo Murillo Jiménez, "La Controversia de Límites entre Costa Rica y Nicaragua. El Laudo Cleveland y los Derechos Canaleros 1821–1903," *Anuario de Estudios Centroamericanos* 12:2 (1986): 45–58 available at https://www.jstor.org/stable/25661897 accessed 31 July 2024.

dd *Award in regard to the Validity of the Treaty of Limits between Costa Rica and Nicaragua of 15 July 1858* (Costa Rica v. Nicaragua), 1888 Reports of International Awards, Vol. XXVIII, 189–236 available at https://legal.un.org/riaa/cases/vol_XXVIII/189-213.pdf accessed 31 July 2024.

ee Eric Tremolada Alvarez, "The Recent Land and Maritime Delimitation of the Court of the Hague in the Affairs of Costa Rica v. Nicaragua, in Light of Their Proposals," *Paix et Securite Internationales – Journal of International Law and International Relations* 7 (2019): 47–84 available at https://heinonline.org/HOL/Page?handle=hein.journals/paixsi7&div=6&g_sent=1&casa_token=&collection=journals accessed 31 July 2024.

ff Maritime Delimitation in the Caribbean Sea and the Pacific Ocean and Land Boundary in the Northern Part of Isla Portillos (Costa Rica v. Nicaragua), International Court of Justice (2018) available at https://www.icj-cij.org/case/157 accessed 1 August 2024.

gg Paul R. Hensel, "Contentious Issues and World Politics: The Management of Territorial Claims in the Americas, 1816–1992," *International Studies Quarterly* 45:1 (2001): 81–109 available at https://www.jstor.org/stable/3096102 accessed 24 July 2024; Paul R. Hensel, "Territorial Claims and Armed Conflict between Neighbors," paper presented to the *Lineae Terrarum International Borders Conference*, El Paso, Texas, 2006 available at https://www.paulhensel.org/Research/lineae.pdf accessed 24 July 2024.

hh G. Pope Atkins, *The Dominican Republic and the United States: From Imperialism to Transnationalism* (Athens, GA: University of Georgia Press, 1998).

ii Paul R. Hensel, "Contentious Issues and World Politics: The Management of Territorial Claims in the Americas, 1816–1992," *International Studies Quarterly* 45:1 (2001): 81–109 available at https://www.jstor.org/stable/3096102 accessed 24 July 2024; Paul R. Hensel, "Territorial Claims and Armed Conflict between Neighbors," paper presented to the *Lineae Terrarum International Borders Conference*, El Paso, Texas, 2006 available at https://www.paulhensel.org/Research/lineae.pdf accessed 24 July 2024.

jj Land, Island and Maritime Frontier Dispute (El Salvador v. Honduras), International Court of Justice (1990) available at https://www.icj-cij.org/case/75 accessed 1 August 2024.

kk Convención de Límites entre Nicaragua y Honduras (1894) available at https://sajurin.enriquebolanos.org/docs/1894%20Convenci%C3%B3n%20de%20L%C3%ADmites%20Gamez%20Bonilla.pdf accessed 1 August 2024.

ll Arbitral Award made on 23 December 1906 by H.M. Alfonso XIII, King of Spain, in the Border Dispute between the Republics of Honduras and Nicaragua from the Atlantic to the Portillo de Teotecacinte (Honduras v. Nicaragua), United Nations Reports of International Awards Vol. XI, 111–117 available at https://legal.un.org/riaa/volumes/riaa_XI.pdf accessed 1 August 2024.

mm Joseph Blocher and Mitu Gulati, "Navassa: Property, Sovereignty, and the Law of the Territories," *Yale Law Journal* 131:8 (2021): 2390–2448; Paul R. Hensel, "Contentious Issues and World Politics: The Management of Territorial Claims in the Americas, 1816–1992," *International Studies Quarterly* 45:1 (2001): 81–109 available at https://www.jstor.org/stable/3096102 accessed 24 July 2024; Paul R. Hensel, "Territorial Claims and Armed Conflict between

(*Continued*)

Neighbors," paper presented to the *Lineae Terrarum International Borders Conference*, El Paso, Texas, 2006 available at https://www.paulhensel.org/Research/lineae.pdf accessed 24 July 2024.

nn Frederick Douglass, "Haïti and the United States. Inside History of the Negotiations for the Môle St. Nicolas. II," *The North American Review* 153:419 (1891): 450–459; Paul R. Hensel, "Contentious Issues and World Politics: The Management of Territorial Claims in the Americas, 1816–1992," *International Studies Quarterly* 45:1 (2001): 81–109 available at https://www.jstor.org/stable/3096102 accessed 24 July 2024; Paul R. Hensel, "Territorial Claims and Armed Conflict between Neighbors," paper presented to the *Lineae Terrarum International Borders Conference*, El Paso, Texas, 2006 available at https://www.paulhensel.org/Research/lineae.pdf accessed 24 July 2024.

oo US Department of the Interior, Acquisition Process of Insular Areas available at https://www.doi.gov/oia/islands/acquisitionprocess accessed 27 March 2024. For an account see Kacper Grass, "Geopolitics in the Western Hemisphere after Trump: Has the United States Abandoned Hegemony in Latin America?" *Revista Internacional de Pensamiento Politico* 16 (2021): 473–492.

pp International Court of Justice Judgments concerning Territorial and Maritime Dispute (Nicaragua v. Colombia) available at https://www.icj-cij.org/case/124/judgments; and International Court of Justice Judgments on Alleged Violations of Sovereign Rights and Maritime Spaces in the Caribbean Sea (Nicaragua v. Colombia) available https://www.icj-cij.org/case/155/judgments all accessed 1 August 2024.

qq See Chapters 5 and 8. See also Paul R. Hensel, "Contentious Issues and World Politics: The Management of Territorial Claims in the Americas, 1816–1992," *International Studies Quarterly* 45:1 (2001): 81–109 available at https://www.jstor.org/stable/3096102 accessed 24 July 2024; Paul R. Hensel, "Territorial Claims and Armed Conflict between Neighbors," paper presented to the *Lineae Terrarum International Borders Conference*, El Paso, Texas, 2006 available at https://www.paulhensel.org/Research/lineae.pdf accessed 24 July 2024.

rr See Chapters 5 and 8. See also International Court of Justice Judgment on Alleged Violations of Sovereign Rights and Maritime Spaces in the Caribbean Sea (Nicaragua v. Colombia), 21 April 2022 available at https://www.icj-cij.org/public/files/case-related/155/155-20220421-JUD-01-00-EN.pdf accessed 1 August 2024.

ss See Chapters 5 and 8. See also International Court of Justice Judgments concerning Territorial and Maritime Dispute (Nicaragua v. Colombia) available at https://www.icj-cij.org/case/124/judgments; and International Court of Justice Judgments on Alleged Violations of Sovereign Rights and Maritime Spaces in the Caribbean Sea (Nicaragua v. Colombia) available https://www.icj-cij.org/case/155/judgments all accessed 1 August 2024.

tt Paul R. Hensel, "Contentious Issues and World Politics: The Management of Territorial Claims in the Americas, 1816–1992," *International Studies Quarterly* 45:1 (2001): 81–109 available at https://www.jstor.org/stable/3096102 accessed 24 July 2024; Paul R. Hensel, "Territorial Claims and Armed Conflict between Neighbors," paper presented to the *Lineae Terrarum International Borders Conference*, El Paso, Texas, 2006 available at https://www.paulhensel.org/Research/lineae.pdf accessed 24 July 2024.

uu Award for the Settlement of the Disputed Boundary between Argentina and Brazil at Uruguay and Yguazu Rivers (Argentina v. Brazil), 5 February 1895, Reports of International Arbitral Awards, Vol. XXVIII, 277–282 available at https://legal.un.org/riaa/cases/vol_XXVIII/277-282.pdf accessed 6 August 2024.

vv Emilio Lamarca, *Boundary Agreements in Force between the Argentine Republic and Chile* (Buenos Aires: M. Biedma e Hijo, 1898).

ww The Cordillera of the Andes Boundary Case (Argentina v, Chile), 20 November 1902, Reports of International Arbitral Awards, Vol. IX, 37–49 available at https://legal.un.org/riaa/cases/vol_IX/37-49.pdf accessed 6 August 2024.

xx Paul R. Hensel, "Contentious Issues and World Politics: The Management of Territorial Claims in the Americas, 1816–1992," *International Studies Quarterly* 45:1 (2001): 81–109 available at https://www.jstor.org/stable/3096102 accessed 24 July 2024; Paul R. Hensel, "Territorial Claims and Armed Conflict between Neighbors," paper presented to the *Lineae Terrarum International Borders Conference*, El Paso, Texas, 2006 available at https://www.paulhensel.org/Research/lineae.pdf accessed 24 July 2024; Andrés Villar Gertner, "The Beagle Channel Frontier Dispute between Argentina and Chile:

Converging Domestic and International Conflicts," *International Relations* 28:2 (2014): 207–227.
yy Dispute between Argentina and Chile Concerning the Beagle Channel (Argentina v. Chile), 18 February 1977, Reports of International Arbitral Awards, Vol. XXI, 53–264 available at https://legal.un.org/riaa/cases/vol_XXI/53-264.pdf accessed 6 August 2024.
zz Act of Puerto Montt Establishing a System of Negotiation Between the Republic of Argentina and the Republic of Chile, 20 February 1978 available at https://www.dipublico.org/doc/instrumentos/168.pdf accessed 6 August 2024.
aaa Act of Montevideo by which Chile and Argentina request the Holy See to act as a mediator with regard to their dispute over the Southern region and undertake not to resort to force in their mutual relations (with supplementary declaration), 8 January 1979 available at https://treaties.un.org/doc/Publication/UNTS/Volume%201137/volume-1137-I-17838-English.pdf accessed 6 August 2024.
bbb Lisa Lindsley, "The Beagle Channel Settlement: Vatican Mediation Resolves a Century-Old Dispute," *Journal of Church and State* 29:3 (1987): 435–456 available at https://heinonline.org/HOL/Page?handle=hein.journals/jchs29&div=39&g_sent=1&casa_token=&collection=journals accessed 6 August 2024.
ccc Chile and Argentina, Treaty of Peace and Friendship (with annexes and maps), Signed at Vatican City, 29 November 1984 available at https://treaties.un.org/doc/Publication/UNTS/Volume%201399/volume-1399-I-23392-English.pdf accessed 6 August 2024.
ddd Maria del Rosario de la Fuente, "Argentina–Chile Laguna del Desierto Arbitration," in K. W. Gray, ed., *Global Encyclopedia of Territorial Rights* (Cham: Springer International Publishing, 2022), 1–6.
eee 1994 Laguna del Desierto Arbitral Award available at https://jusmundi.com/en/document/decision/en-boundary-dispute-between-argentina-and-chile-concerning-the-frontier-line-between-boundary-post-62-and-mount-fitzroy-decision-friday-21st-october-1994 accessed 29 August 2024.
fff Paul R. Hensel, "Contentious Issues and World Politics: The Management of Territorial Claims in the Americas, 1816–1992," *International Studies Quarterly* 45:1 (2001): 81–109 available at https://www.jstor.org/stable/3096102 accessed 24 July 2024; Paul R. Hensel, "Territorial Claims and Armed Conflict between Neighbors," paper presented to the *Lineae Terrarum International Borders Conference*, El Paso, Texas, 2006 available at https://www.paulhensel.org/Research/lineae.pdf accessed 24 July 2024.
ggg Award Relating to the Demarcation of the Puna de Atacama Boundary between the Argentine Republic and Chile (Argentina v. Chile), Reports of International Awards, 24 March 1899, Vol. XXVIII, 323–330 available at https://legal.un.org/riaa/cases/vol_XXVIII/323-330.pdf accessed 6 August 2024.
hhh See Chapter 5.
iii UN Security Council resolution 505 (1982), Question Concerning the Situation in the Region of the Falkland Islands (Islas Malvinas), 26 May 1982 available at https://documents.un.org/doc/resolution/gen/nr0/435/29/pdf/nr043529.pdf accessed 6 August 2024.
jjj Graham Pascoe, *Falklands Facts and Fallacies: The Falkland Islands in History and International Law* (Surrey: Grosvenor House Publishing, 2022).
kkk "Anglo-Argentine Agreement about Communications with the Falkland Islands, 1971," *Polar Record* 16:100 (1972): 100–104 available at https://doi.org/10.1017/S0032247400062665 accessed 6 August 2024.
lll Refer to the UN, The UN and Decolonization, Falkland Islands (Malvinas) available at https://www.un.org/dppa/decolonization/en/content/falkland-islands-malvinas accessed 6 August 2024.
mmm Ronald Bruce St. John, *The Bolivia-Chile-Peru Dispute in the Atacama Desert* (Durham: International Boundaries Research Unit, Department of Geography, University of Durham, 1994).
nnn Boundary Treaty between Bolivia and Chile, August 1866 available at https://jusmundi.com/en/document/pdf/treaty/en-boundary-treaty-of-1866-between-chile-and-bolivia-treaty-of-territorial-limits-1866-friday-10th-august-1866 accessed 6 August 2024.
ooo Obligation to Negotiate Access to the Pacific Ocean (Bolivia v. Chile), ICJ Judgments, 24 September 2015 and 1 October 2018 available at https://www.icj-cij.org/case/153 accessed 6 August 2024.

(*Continued*)

ppp Bruce W. Farcau, *The Chaco War: Bolivia and Paraguay, 1932–1935* (Westport, CT: Praeger, 1996).
qqq "Bolivia-Paraguay: Treaty of Peace, Friendship and Boundaries," *The American Journal of International Law* 32:4 (1938): 139–141 available at https://doi.org/10.2307/2213730 accessed 6 August 2024.
rrr Frederic William Ganzert, "The Boundary Controversy in the Upper Amazon between Brazil, Bolivia, and Peru, 1903–1909," *The Hispanic American Historical Review* 14:4 (1934): 427–449 available at https://doi.org/10.2307/2506316 accessed 6 August 2024.
sss Brazil and Bolivia, Treaty of Petrópolis. 17 November 1903 available at https://treaties.un.org/doc/Publication/UNTS/Volume%20888/volume-888-II-698-English.pdf accessed 6 August 2024.
ttt A. Curtis Wilgus, "The Leticia Incident," *World Affairs* 95:3 (1932): 179–181; Lourdes Hurtado, "El Conflicto de Leticia (1932–1933) y los Ejércitos de Perú y Colombia (Universidad Externado de Colombia, 2016)," *Journal of Latin American Studies* 51:4 (2019): 950–952.
uuu Germán Cavelier, *Memoria Histórico-Jurídica sobre el Asunto de Los Monjes* (Bogotá: Editorial Kelly, 1977).
vvv Unilateral Acts of States, Eighth Report on Unilateral Acts of States, by Mr Víctor Rodríguez Cedeño, Special Rapporteur, A/CN.4/557 available at https://legal.un.org/ilc/documentation/english/a_cn4_557.pdf accessed 6 August 2024.
www L. D. M. Nelson, "The Arbitration of Boundary Disputes in Latin America," *Netherlands International Law Review* 20:3 (1973): 267–294.
xxx The Rio Protocol, Peace, Friendship, and Boundaries between Peru and Ecuador, Protocol between Peru and Ecuador (The 1942 Rio Protocol) available at https://peacemaker.un.org/sites/peacemaker.un.org/files/Rio%20Protocol%20English%201942.pdf accessed 6 August 2024.
yyy Paula Lekanda Laban, "El Conflicto Territorial entre Ecuador y Perú por el Río del Cenepa (1995): Entre una Mediación Fallida y otra Exitosa," *Pléyade* 4 (2010): 186–211.
zzz Acta Presidencial de Brasilia, (1998 Presidential Act of Brasilia) available at https://www.peaceagreements.org/viewmasterdocument/212 accessed 6 August 2024.
aaaa Patricia Marín Luján, "Geopolítica, Conflictos Fronterizos en América Latina," *Revista Geopolítica Transfronteiriça* 1:1 (2017): 1–14.
bbbb Leslie Bethell, "Notes on the History of the Venezuela/Guyana Boundary Dispute," *CEBRI-Revista: Brazilian Journal of International Affairs* 9 (2024): 156–175.
cccc M. Loader, "Essequibo," *Encyclopedia Britannica*, 9 January 2024 available at https://www.britannica.com/place/Essequibo accessed 6 August 2024.
dddd International Court of Judgment, Arbitral Award 3 October 1899 (Guyana v. Venezuela), Judgment of 18 December 2020 and Judgment of 6 April 2023 available at https://www.icj-cij.org/case/171/judgments accessed 6 August 2024.
eeee See Chapter 5. See also Thomas W. Donovan, "The Marouini River Tract and Its Colonial Legacy in South America," *Chicago-Kent Journal of International and Comparative Law* 4 (2004): 1–28.
ffff 2021 Protocol available at https://www.dna.sr/media/330804/21_1437__Pres._Ch._Santokhi__aanb._overeenkomst_protocol_tussen_Rep._Suriname_en_Franse_Rep._op_de_regeling_van_de_Grens_tussen_Suriname_en_Frans_Guyana_verdrag_parijs_30sept.1915_tot_vaststellen_van_de_Grens.pdf accessed 12 January 2024.

Common roots to territorial disputes and peacebuilding

Regardless of the particular characteristics of the three aforementioned historical periods, territorial disputes in the Americas have similar hallmarks. These hallmarks feature common roots that can help in understanding and explicating the ongoing differences on the continent. Importantly, by comprehending these common roots in a more integrated and robust way, it is possible to discern more clearly appropriate means for peacebuilding. In order to bring evidence of these claims, this section focuses in particular on now resolved differences, ongoing disputes and the several pluralisms at play. More precisely, stemming from separatist movements on the continent, post-independence differences can be broadly distinguished into two groups: (a) disputes against former colonial powers or (b) disputes between former colonies trying to ascertain or extend their territorial sovereignty. Interestingly, all these territorial disputes bring together the several pluralisms introduced in the previous chapter—i.e. agents, players, contexts, realms and modes of existence. Therefore, they will be reviewed in light of the multidimensional approach.

Agents and players

The territorial disputes in the post-independence period in the Americas are not limited to states but include individuals and communities playing defining roles. Acting as "hosts" of these disputes are either the former colonies (with individuals, communities or states playing this role in the Americas), former colonial powers (notably, the direct and indirect influence of the United Kingdom) or both. Other individuals, communities or states act as "participants" or "attendees" depending mainly on realpolitik issues, such as the bargaining power of acting as a bloc. Largely, indigenous communities are passive "viewers."

Particular individuals played a central part in disputes in their role as the "caudillo" figure. For example, relevant cases include: the War of the Peru–Bolivian Confederation, a short-lived state that unified Peru and Bolivia (1836–1839), a project of caudillo Andrés de Santa Cruz;[27] the Bolivian caudillo General Quevedo and the offer of support made by the Chilean government to help Bolivia obtain the Peruvian coast of Arica and Iquique at the expense of Peru in exchange for the cession of the Bolivian coast to Chile.[28] Furthermore, the somewhat slow territorial consolidation and state-building of Argentina and Chile due to their ongoing territorial disputes was in part

27 Natalia Sobrevilla Perea, *The Caudillo of the Andes: Andrés de Santa Cruz* (New York, NY: Cambridge University Press, 2011), 114.

28 Victor Andres Belaunde, "Peru's Attitude on the Tacna-Arica Issue," *Current History* 16:1 (1922): 17–21.

because of caudillos like Urquiza exercising their influence over the locals.[29] Interestingly, as the following chapters will show when reviewing current differences, internal political prestige can still be a strong reason to start a territorial dispute and keep it unresolved—i.e. the domestic political needs of state leaders can heavily influence their foreign policy agenda.[30]

Communities and subgroups in the Americas are socioeconomically and ethnically defined in this historical period, and, therefore, it is possible to distinguish between those of European descent, natives and mixed. Among these groups, for example, are those stemming from the immigration process, in which subgroups are clearly differentiated, such as rich landowners and implanted populations. Furthermore, implanted populations could be characterized more precisely as it is possible to distinguish between at least two cases, that of people brought to the region because of slavery and of others brought for the "right-peopling"[31] of the territory—e.g. as in the cases of San Andrés, Catalina and Providencia and the Falkland/Malvinas Islands, respectively.

Depending on the community, group or subgroup under consideration, their central or peripheral role in territorial disputes varies. Rich landowners—either competing with each other to gain power or because they shared ideology, identity as a collective and had common interests—were in part responsible for these differences, which resulted in a slow state-building process and weak states.[32] In turn, indigenous groups find themselves in territorial disputes with "civilized" states over what had been classed as "non-civilized" territories.[33] Based on European colonial understanding, indigenous peoples were not legally "persons"; or, if there was any degree of acknowledgment of their legal status, they were deemed inferior. Therefore, the legal and political justification in colonial times that continues in the post-independence period discards indigenous peoples' claims to territories either based on acquisition or extinguishment.[34] Conversely, implanted populations play a different role. By

29 Cameron G. Thies, "Territorial Nationalism in Spatial Rivalries: An Institutionalist Account of the Argentine-Chilean Rivalry," *International Interactions* 27:4 (2001): 399–431.

30 Paul K. Huth, *Standing Your Ground: Territorial Disputes and International Conflict* (Ann Arbor, MI: University of Michigan Press, 2001), 102.

31 Oded Haklai and Nephytos Loizides, "Settlers and Conflict Over Contested Territories," in Oded Haklai and Neophytos Loizides, eds., *Settlers in Contested Lands. Territorial Disputes and Ethnic Conflicts* (Stanford, CA: Stanford University Press, 2015), 1–16.

32 D. Barnaby Carter, "Los Terratenientes de Cautín: Actores Claves de la Contrarreforma," *Anales de la Universidad de Chile* 12 (2017): 233–253; Chiara Villani, "Regional Peace in Latin America: A Multifaceted Explanation," *Revista da Escola de Guerra Naval* 23:3 (2017): 721–754.

33 M. F. Lindley, *The Acquisition and Government of Backward Territory in International Law: Being a Treatise on the Law and Practice Relating to Colonial Expansion* (New York, NY: Negro Universities Press, 1969), 11–12.

34 Jérémie Gilbert, *Indigenous Peoples' Land Rights under International Law: From Victors to Actors* (Ardsley, NY: Transnational, 2006), 1–2.

application of the notion of "right-peopling"[35] of the territory, settlers argue for their right to self-determination; later, slavery resulted in tension between a local ethnic and racial minority.[36] Finally, other groups that are characteristic of Latin America and should be considered because of their influence in disputes and conflicts are that of the guerrilla movements and narcotraffickers.[37]

Contexts

The territorial disputes in the Americas in the post-independence period influence and are influenced by the domestic, regional and international contexts.

Domestically, former colonies bring together very different individual and community interests, ethnicities, socioeconomic levels, large territorial extensions and slim populations. The domestic context shows another angle. Some of the most notable issues involve prior unresolved disputes, prior loss of territory and domestic leaders. For instance, the strategic location of bordering territories may explain the reasons behind disputed islands in the Beagle Channel between Argentina and Chile.[38] The domestic political needs of state leaders to remain in power, such as in the case of military governments in Latin America, can heavily influence their foreign policy agenda.[39] Although authoritarian regimes may be willing to compromise,[40] arguably, the move from military governments to liberal democracies may explain the peacebuilding process in the region. Moreover, the United States domestic context may help

35 Brendan O'Leary, "The Elements of Right-Sizing and Right-Peopling the State," in Brendan O'Leary, Ian S. Lustick and Thomas Callaghy, eds., *Right-Sizing the State: The Politics of Moving Borders* (Oxford: Oxford University Press, 2001), 15–73.

36 Pablo Alonso González, Wilhelm Londoño and Eva Parga-Dans, "Equality and Hierarchy, Sovereignty and Multiculturalism: The Heritagisation of Raizals in Santa Catalina (Colombia)," *Journal of Ethnic and Migration Studies* 26:19 (2020): 4066–4085.

37 Luis L. Schenoni, Gary Goertz, Andrew P. Owsiak and Paul F. Diehl, "Settling Resistant Territorial Disputes: The Territorial Boundary Peace in Latin America," International Studies Quarterly 64:1 (2020): 57–70; Boris F. Martynov, "International Relations in Latin America (1945–1991)," in Anatoly V. Turkunov, William C. Wohlforth and Boris F. Martynov, eds., *History of International Relations and Russian Foreign Policy in the 20th Century: Volume II* (Newcastle upon Tyne: Cambridge Scholars Publishing, 2020), 291–313; Bernardo Mançano Fernandes and Cliff Welch, "Movements and Territorial Conflicts in Latin America," in Federico M. Rossi, ed., *The Oxford Handbook of Latin American Social Movements* (Oxford: Oxford University Press, 2023), 266–282.

38 Andrés Villar Gertner, "The Beagle Channel Frontier Dispute between Argentina and Chile: Converging Domestic and International Conflicts," *International Relations* 28:2 (2014): 207–227; Paul K. Huth, *Standing Your Ground: Territorial Disputes and International Conflict* (Ann Arbor, MI: University of Michigan Press, 2001), Chapter 4; Paul K. Huth, "Enduring Rivalries and Territorial Disputes, 1950–1990," *Conflict Management and Peace Science* 15:1 (1996): 7–41.

39 Paul K. Huth, *Standing Your Ground: Territorial Disputes and International Conflict* (Ann Arbor, MI: University of Michigan Press, 2001), 102.

40 Krista E. Wiegand, "Peaceful Dispute Resolution by Authoritarian Regimes," *Foreign Policy Analysis* 15:3 (2019): 303–321.

in understanding both the lack of support for military aid to Latin America at times[41] and the implementation of Operation Condor affecting directly and indirectly several other states by means of ideology, nationalism and geopolitical situations.[42]

Regionally, these newly formed states and their governments encountered unclear or non-existent borders and competing claims.[43] Coupled with these issues stemming from a common historical past, geographic proximity makes it more likely that intra-state issues may involve interaction between states[44] related to politics, law, natural resources, defense and bordering minorities (e.g. peasants, indigenous population). For example, Bolivia has territorial disputes that combine resource nationalism and indigenous self-determination;[45] Colombia and Nicaragua have an ongoing controversy surrounding the San Andrés Archipelago encompassing the Raizal community and the exploitation of natural resources by means of fishing rights;[46] in Argentina and Chile there is the Mapuche conflict;[47] and there is land occupation by groups of landless families due to inequality, economic crisis and political turmoil involving peasants, indigenous groups and implanted populations (descendants of former slaves) throughout Latin America.[48] Geographically, the Falkland/Malvinas Islands location between Latin America and Africa has implications for the control of maritime transport and sea lanes in the South Atlantic,[49] and the location of some American states in relation to Antarctica has resulted in their

41 John Child, *Unequal Alliance: The Inter-American Military System, 1938–1978* (Boulder, CO: Westview Press, 1980), 197.

42 Sebastián Hurtado-Torres and Joaquín Fermandois, "The War that Didn't Break Out: Military Rule and Regional Tensions in the Andes in the 1970s," *The International History Review* 42:5 (2020): 967–986.

43 Alan J. Day, ed., *Border and Territorial Disputes* (Essex: Longman, 1982), 332–333.

44 Kentaro Sakuwa, "The Regional Consequences of Territorial Disputes: An Empirical Analysis of the South China Sea Disputes," *Journal of Asian Security and International Affairs* 4:3 (2017): 316–336.

45 Anna F. Laing, "Re-Producing Territory: Between Resource Nationalism and Indigenous Self-Determination in Bolivia," *Geoforum* 108 (2020): 28–38.

46 Jingyao Wang and Qi Xu, "Reflections on the Nicaragua v. Colombia Case (2022): From the Perspective of Traditional Fishing Rights," *Frontiers in Marine Science* 10 (2023) available at https://www.frontiersin.org/articles/10.3389/fmars.2023.1126708/full accessed 10 October 2023.

47 Pablo Arturo Mansilla Quiñones and Miguel Melin Pehuen, "A Struggle for Territory, a Struggle Against Borders," *NACLA Report on the Americas* 51:1 (2019): 41–48.

48 Bernardo Mançano Fernandes and Cliff Welch, "Movements and Territorial Conflicts in Latin America," in Federico M. Rossi, ed., *The Oxford Handbook of Latin American Social Movements* (Oxford: Oxford University Press, 2023), 266–282.

49 See Chapter 5. See also Detlef Nolte and Leslie E. Wehner, "Geopolitics in Latin America, Old and New," in David R. Mares and Arie M. Kacowicz, eds., *Routledge Handbook of Latin American Security* (Abingdon: Routledge, 2015), 33–43.

influence in the creation of the Antarctic regime to deal with the territorial dispute.[50]

Internationally, there is the direct and indirect influence of states such as the United Kingdom, the United States and Russia, and financial institutions like the World Bank and the International Monetary Fund (IMF). For instance, the issue pertaining to the Falkland/Malvinas Islands involves naval rivalry between Argentina and the United Kingdom. In the case of the United States and Russia (formerly USSR), their naval rivalry is evident in the Caribbean, including the geostrategic location of the Panama Canal. British influence on the Venezuela–Guyana border and the Texas issue in British–American relations are two further examples that clearly show the influence of international agents in territorial disputes on the continent.[51] Additionally, international institutions in the past like the Baring Brothers, and current organizations such as the IMF and World Bank, have played an important part in the way disputes and conflicts have panned out by means of ideology, targeted aid and embargoes.[52]

Realms

Similar to the cases of multiple agents and contexts, territorial disputes in the Americas bring together issues pertaining to different realms, such as the factual, normative and axiological.

Factually, the Americas present several states with large territorial extensions. These states often share borders that include jungles, mountains and rivers making it difficult to (a) select in law a clear principle to discern the international border; (b) apply a chosen legal principle even when there is

50 See Chapter 9. See also Ignacio Javier Cardone and Pablo Gabriel Fontana, "Latin-American Contributions to the Creation of the Antarctic Regime," *The Polar Journal* 9:2 (2019): 300–323; Klaus Dodds and Alan D. Hemmings, "Britain and the British Antarctic Territory in the Wider Geopolitics of the Antarctic and the Southern Ocean," *International Affairs* 89:6 (2013): 1429–1444.

51 Michael A. Morris, "Maritime Geopolitics in Latin America," *Political Geography Quarterly* 5:1 (1986): 43–55; Jaqueline Anne Braveboy-Wagner, *The Venezuela-Guyana Border Dispute: Britain's Colonial Legacy in Latin America* (New York, NY and Oxford: Routledge, Taylor & Francis 1984); Nguyen Van Sang, Le Thanh Nam and Luu Trang, "Independent or Annexation: The Texas Issue in the British-American Relations (1836–1846)," *Academic Journal of Interdisciplinary Studies* 10:5 (2021): 201–215; and many more.

52 Juan H. Flores Zendejas, "The Entanglements of Domestic Polities: Public Debt and European Interventions in Latin America," in N. Barreyre and N. Delalande, eds., *A World of Public Debts* (Cham: Palgrave Macmillan, 2020), 111–133; Erik Voeten, *Ideology and International Institutions* (Princeton, NJ: Princeton University Press, 2021); Italo Beltrão Sposito and Fernando José Ludwig, "Mapping Inter-American Struggle (1946–2001): An Overview on Military Conflict and Economic Embargoes," *Revista de Paz y Conflictos* 14:1 (2021): 35–59; Jennie K. Lincoln and Elizabeth G. Ferris, eds., *The Dynamics Of Latin American Foreign Policies: Challenges For The 1980s* (New York, NY and Oxford: Routledge, Taylor & Francis, 2019).

agreement or settlement, because of the terrain in question that includes towering mountains, dense jungles, great rivers, ground water and swamps.[53] Moreover, these factual characteristics make immigration control problematic and, therefore, the influx of people for different reasons including social crisis and the flow of bordering minorities is constant.[54] In addition to this influx of people, it is important to note that other agents take advantage of these conditions—e.g. multinationals, guerrilla movements and narcotraffickers.[55]

The normative realm adds another layer to territorial disputes on the continent. Regardless of the many organizations, procedures and remedies at the international and regional level, there are domestic rules that need to be considered. For example, the concept of "territory" is included in all 35 American national constitutions.[56] This is a particularly important point because even when a territorial dispute is settled by means of a peaceful and permanent agreement—including an international award by the International Court of Justice (ICJ)—it is the exclusive prerogative of each sovereign state involved to comply with the decision. Clearly, the way in which each sovereign state complies with such settlements will largely depend on how their authorities interpret central concepts, such as their understanding of "territory."

53 Edgardo Manero, "A Retrospective Look at the Nature of National Borders in Latin America," in Doris Wastl-Walter, ed., *The Ashgate Research Companion to Border Studies* (Surrey: Ashgate Publishing Limited, 2011), 301–333; Todd Jarvis, Mark Giordano, Shammy Puri, Kyoko Matsumoto and Aaron Wolf, "International Borders, Ground Water Flow, and Hydroschizophrenia," *Groundwater* 43:5 (2005): 764–770; C. Freeman, "Borders," in M. Domosh, M. Heffernan and C. W. J. Withers, eds., *The SAGE Handbook of Historical Geography* (London: SAGE Publications, 2020), 537–558.

54 Mauricia John, "Venezuelan Economic Crisis: Crossing Latin American and Caribbean Borders," *Migration and Development* 8:3 (2019): 437–447; Gerardo Otero and Heidi A. Jugenitz, "Challenging National Borders from Within: The Political-Class Formation of Indigenous Peasants in Latin America," *Canadian Review of Sociology/Revue Canadienne de Sociologie* 40:5 (2003): 503–524; Fangbin Zou, Miraj Ahmed Bhuiyan, Tiziana Crovella and Annarita Paiano, "Analyzing the Borderlands: A Regional Report on the Colombia–Ecuador Border on Political, Economic, Social, Legal, and Environment Aspects," *International Migration Review* (2023) available at https://doi.org/10.1177/01979183221149019 accessed 27 September 2023; Douglas S. Massey, "The Real Crisis at the Mexico-US Border: A Humanitarian and Not an Immigration Emergency," *Sociological Forum* 35:3 (2020): 787–805.

55 Ivan Briscoe, "Trouble on the Borders: Latin America's New Conflict Zones," *FRIDE* (2008): 1–9 available at https://www.researchgate.net/profile/Ivan-Briscoe/publication/265029389_Trouble_on_the_borders_Latin_America's_new_conflict_zones/links/56b45f0308ae636a540da06b/Trouble-on-the-borders-Latin-Americas-new-conflict-zones.pdf accessed 27 September 2023; John P. Sullivan, "How Illicit Networks Impact Sovereignty," in Michael Miklaucic and Jacqueline Brewer, eds., *Convergence: Illicit Networks and National Security in the Age of Globalization* (Washington, DC: National Defense University Press, 2013), 171–188; Arie M. Kacowicz, Exequiel Lacovsky and Daniel F. Wajner, "Peaceful Borders and Illicit Transnational Flows in the Americas," *Latin American Research Review* 55:4 (2020): 727–741.

56 Walter Arévalo-Ramírez, "Constitutions Challenging the International Court of Justice's Jurisdiction to Adjudicate Territorial Disputes in Latin America," *Heidelberg Journal of International Law* 82:2 (2022): 425–448.

In addition to what the territorial dispute is or ought to be according to the factual and normative realms, undoubtedly, it can be valued differently by different agents. As mentioned in previous sections, in the colonial era the Papal bulls only acknowledged Spanish and Portuguese sovereignty over the Americas while the natives were completely ignored.[57] Clearly, sovereignty, legal personhood and the right to claim were absolute or not depending solely on an axiological choice—i.e. those who had power could act as they wished. Currently, there are several legal norms that offer a certain degree of recognition and protection to indigenous peoples such as, indirectly, the Universal Declaration of Human Rights (1948);[58] globally, the United Nations Declaration on the Rights of Indigenous Peoples (2007);[59] and, regionally, directly related to the Americas, the American Declaration on the Rights of Indigenous Peoples (2016).[60] However, these communities do not necessarily conform to legally defined borders and their claims to ethno-territorial rights are usually opposed to the interests of sovereign states and private companies.[61] Moreover, comparatively strong states in fact—e.g. financially, militarily—like the United States apply the notion of sovereignty interchangeably as limited and as absolute in law as they see fit and they excuse themselves from their domestic, regional and international behavior toward other agents, as the cases of Guantanamo Bay and the border with Mexico clearly demonstrate.[62]

Modes of existence

From the previous subsections relating to agents, players, contexts and realms, it is clear that territorial disputes in the Americas comprise a variety of modes of existence that are in tension. Ideal and metaphysical features in the form of ideologies and religious beliefs, and natural and cultural characteristics in relation to geostrategic location and people's perception, are a few of the elements that lie behind the intricate nature of these disputes.

Ideal objects such as concepts may appear similar on the surface but their meanings and uses may be different depending on, for example, the agent

57 H. Vander Linden, "Alexander VI and the Demarcation of the Maritime and Colonial Domains of Spain and Portugal, 1493–1494," *The American Historical Review* 22:1 (1916): 1–20.

58 Complete text available at https://www.un.org/en/universal-declaration-human-rights accessed 4 October 2023.

59 Overview and complete text available at https://www.un.org/development/desa/indigenouspeoples/declaration-on-the-rights-of-indigenous-peoples.html accessed 4 October 2023.

60 Complete text available at https://www.oas.org/en/sare/documents/DecAmIND.pdf accessed 4 October 2023.

61 Markus Kröger and Rickard Lalander, "Ethno-Territorial Rights and the Resource Extraction Boom in Latin America: Do Constitutions Matter?" *Third World Quarterly* 37:4 (2016): 682–702.

62 See Chapter 6.

considered. For instance, the noun "Mapuche" can be divided into the two smaller expressions "Mapu" and "che." "Mapu" refers to space in the narrow sense as a synonym of territory (space according to its scope) or physical space (space according to the way it is perceived)[63] and "che" means person, ontologically speaking. Therein, the term "Mapuche" indicates a close relationship between people and the land. One of the consequences of this for the Mapuche is that, for their understanding, the notions of borders or boundaries do not exist.[64] Clearly, any claim to ethno-territorial rights based on this way of understanding ideal objects, such as concepts pertaining to a territorial dispute, are usually opposed to the interests of sovereign states and private companies that apply the nation-state notion.[65]

Natural objects may change over time and, therefore, bring controversy to already settled cases. For example, in the case of the Marouini River tract dispute between Suriname and French Guiana, the river's tendency to change course has made it difficult to determine a permanent line, in particular with reference to the exclusive ownership of the islands in the area.[66]

In turn, cultural objects may introduce different elements to ongoing disputes and controversy to those differences that are already settled. For example, technological innovation and the presence of natural resources in these areas,[67] and border walls,[68] have fostered disagreements.

Metaphysical objects such as common faith and beliefs have had an impact too in territorial disputes on the continent. For example, while attempts made by the United Kingdom almost succeeded in bringing about a war because

63 For details about "space" see Chapter 3.

64 Pablo Arturo Mansilla Quiñones and Miguel Melin Pehuen, "A Struggle for Territory, a Struggle Against Borders," *NACLA Report on the Americas* 51:1 (2019): 41–48.

65 Markus Kröger and Rickard Lalander, "Ethno-Territorial Rights and the Resource Extraction Boom in Latin America: Do Constitutions Matter?" *Third World Quarterly* 37:4 (2016): 682–702.

66 Thomas W. Donovan, "The Marouini River Tract and Its Colonial Legacy in South America," *Chicago-Kent Journal of International and Comparative Law* 4 (2004): 1–28.

67 Leandro Bolzan De Rezende, Paul Blackwell and Marcos Degaut, "Brazilian National Defence Policy: Foreign Policy, National Security, Economic Growth, and Technological Innovation," *Defense and Security Analysis* 34:4 (2018): 385–409; Rodrigo Milindre Gonzalez and Sergio Gabriel Caplan, "The Expansion of Argentine Limits in the Continental Shelf: Implications in the International Scope," eds., *Érico Duarte and Manuel Correia de Barros:* In *Navies and Maritime Policies in the South Atlantic.* (2019), 69–95; Andreas Østhagen, "Maritime Boundary Disputes: What Are They and Why Do They Matter?" *Marine Policy* 120 (2020): 1–9.

68 Tony Payan and Pamela Lizette Cruz, "Redefining and Governing the Border as a Binational Commons," Policy Brief: Recommendations for the New Administration (Houston, TX: Baker Institute for Public Policy, 2021) available at https://repository.rice.edu/server/api/core/bitstreams/998fc807-b72b-4177-b3d0-a43a0764f69f/content accessed 17 January 2025; Élisabeth Vallet, "State of Border Walls in a Globalized World," in Andréanne Bissonnette and Élisabeth Vallet, eds., *Borders and Border Walls: In-Security, Symbolism, Vulnerabilities* (Oxford and New York, NY: Routledge, 2021), 7–24; Paulina Ochoa Espejo, *On Borders: Territories, Legitimacy and the Rights of Place* (Oxford: Oxford University Press, 2020), 273.

of the Beagle Channel Dispute, common faith by means of the Papal mediation—as Argentina and Chile are largely Catholic populations—was instrumental in the final peaceful settlement.[69]

Reasons for peacebuilding

Núñez (2020) explained why the aforementioned pluralisms that encompass different claims, issues at stake and contexts may work together in negative synergy and, therefore, result in the origin and continuation of territorial disputes and their potential escalation into conflict.[70] However, these pluralisms may also work together in positive synergy and foster peacebuilding. For instance, largely, territorial disputes in the Americas are now resolved.[71] For example, by the end of the 1980s most of the states in South America had peacefully ended their differences.[72] The success or failure in peacebuilding depends on several issues, including identification, cohesiveness, type of regime, motivation, previous and ongoing relationships and distribution of power.[73] In the Americas, successful resolution of conflict and the fostering of regional peacemaking and peacekeeping are due to several of these issues and, in particular,

69 James L. Garrett, "The Beagle Channel Dispute: Confrontation and Negotiation in the Southern Cone," *Journal of Interamerican Studies and World Affairs* 27:3 (1985): 81–109; Lisa Lindsley, "The Beagle Channel Settlement: Vatican Mediation Resolves a Century-Old Dispute," *Journal of Church and State* 29:3 (1987): 435–454. See related official documents: International Arbitral Award (1977), Dispute between Argentina and Chile concerning the Beagle Channel (Arg. v. Chile), 1977 RIAA Vol XXI, at 53; Agreement of Puerto Montt (1978), Act of Puerto Montt Establishing a System of Negotiation Between the Republic of Argentina and The Republic of Chile (signed 20 February 1978), UNTS Vol. 1088, No. 16668 (Agreement of Puerto Montt); Act of Montevideo (1979), Act of Montevideo by which Chile and Argentina request the Holy See to act as a mediator with regard to their dispute over the Southern region and undertake not to resort to force in their mutual relations (with supplementary declaration) (adopted 8 January 1979) UNTS Vol. 1088, 135 (Act of Montevideo); Treaty of Peace and Friendship between Argentina and Chile (1984), Treaty of Peace and Friendship (with annexes and maps) (adopted 29 November 1984) UNTS Vol. 1399, 1-23392, 103.

70 Jorge E. Núñez, *Territorial Disputes and State Sovereignty: International Law and Politics* (London and New York, NY: Routledge, Taylor & Francis Group, 2020), in particular Chapter 9.

71 Peacebuilding in the Americas will be addressed extensively in Chapter 10.

72 Jorge Mario Battaglino, "The Coexistence of Peace and Conflict in South America: Toward a New Conceptualization of Types of Peace," *Revista Brasileira de Política Internacional* 55:2 (2012): 131–151.

73 Marieke Kleiboer, "Understanding Success and Failure of International Mediation," *The Journal of Conflict Resolution* 40:2 (1996): 360–389; J. Bercovitch, "International Mediation and Dispute Settlement: Evaluating the Conditions for Successful Mediation," *Negotiation Journal* 7:1 (1991): 17–30.

to the exclusion of exogenous legal, political and geographical influence and the role of regional arbitrators and guarantors.[74]

Regional institutions and agents such as the Organization of American States (OAS) and neighboring states have facilitated peaceful permanent understandings after conflict.[75] Regional arbitrators and guarantors defined peacebuilding on the continent such as the Peace, Friendship and Boundary Treaty[76] that put an end to the Chaco war between Bolivia and Paraguay. Argentina, Brazil, Chile and the United States played a central role in the final dispute resolution between Ecuador and Peru[77] achieved in the 1998 Brasilia Peace Agreement.[78]

Conclusion

The chapter started by distinguishing three clearly defined historical periods concerning territorial disputes in the Americas and then characterized each of them: pre-Columbian times; post-Columbian but pre-independence times; and post-independence times. Regardless of their individual peculiarities, all these territorial disputes have at least two claiming parties arguing over the exclusive sovereignty of the same territory. The challenger and challenged agents have their own reasons to claim sovereignty. Moreover, there may be a myriad of issues at stake with links of different natures to the domestic, regional and international contexts. Therefore, the chapter acknowledged the pluralism of pluralisms that characterizes these differences by presenting a sample of some of the territorial disputes in the Americas with a particular focus on post-independence times.

Clearly, these differences have common roots in all cases: they include a historical component based on colonial times and the lack of clear border demarcation at the time or, in the cases in which the demarcation had taken place in law, the difficulty in applying the decision to the areas in question. The brief outline provided some indications of the origin of these disputes. Together

74 For a more detailed account of the reasons behind peacemaking and peacekeeping in the Americas see Chapter 7. See also Jorge I. Domínguez, *Boundary Disputes in Latin America* (Washington, DC: United States Institute of Peace, September 2003) available at https://www.usip.org/sites/default/files/pwks50.pdf accessed 4 October 2023.

75 For further details about legal and political regional organizations see Chapter 2.

76 Bolivia–Paraguay: Treaty of Peace, Friendship and Boundaries, *The American Journal of International Law* 32:4 (1938): 139–141 available at http://www.jstor.org/stable/2213730 accessed 6 November 2024.

77 David Scott Palmer, "Peru-Ecuador Border Conflict: Missed Opportunities, Misplaced Nationalism, and Multilateral Peacekeeping," *Journal of Interamerican Studies and World Affairs* 39:3 (1997): 109–148.

78 Complete text of the 1998 Brasilia Peace Agreement (in Spanish) available at https://www.usip.org/sites/default/files/file/resources/collections/peace_agreements/ep_brasilia10261998.pdf accessed 4 October 2023; Monica Herz and João Pontes Nogueira, *Ecuador vs. Peru: Peacemaking Amid Rivalry* (London: Lynne Rienner, 2002), 97–100.

with the historical background and the lack of clearly defined boundaries in the colonial era, current international law such as the Law of the Sea, new technologies for exploration and exploitation of natural resources, the existence or absence of indigenous or implanted populations in the territories under question, and several other elements result in multi-faceted and multi-layered territorial disputes.

Any study on territorial disputes should acknowledge the intrinsic pluralism of pluralisms. In doing so, this chapter concisely applied the multidimensional approach to demonstrate how and why this way of explaining and assessing territorial disputes can help gain a more robust understanding about them. Firstly, agents have different claims, evaluations, subgroups, interests and views they represent. Secondly, there are several issues at stake. Finally, any evaluation should contextualize the dispute locally, regionally and internationally for a more accurate comprehension. It is in this comprehensive understanding of the multi-layered and multi-contextual nature of territorial disputes that a path toward a better explanation of their complexity can be built. For instance, civil societies may include internal divisions based on history, ethnicity, religion, etc. that can have an impact on the way these different groups perceive the dispute and their role as a political community in them. Secondly, governments and leaders may opt to maintain the difference in a political and legal *status quo* because of the higher payoff to their prestige and power (rather than a definitive and peaceful solution). Furthermore, together with local and regional actors, there are other international agents (not necessarily regional ones) that have a direct interest in these areas and, consequently, the way in which the dispute develops depends on their own agendas and their alliances with any of the original local and regional claimants. By gaining a better, more robust, exhaustive and accurate understanding of the intricacy of these disputes, it may be possible to reimagine in theory, and hopefully in reality, a way toward solving them peacefully and permanently. For instance, the last section showed that, although the claiming parties may achieve a settlement, if there are any domestic, regional and international issues at stake, the situation may still turn volatile, and regional guarantors are key in peacekeeping.

The cases discussed in the following chapters have many of the hallmarks briefly outlined here. These cases include the ongoing European presence in the Americas (Chapter 5) as in the Falkland/Malvinas Islands dispute between Argentina and the UK; practices that suggest neo-colonialism (Chapter 6) as in the Mexico–United States border and Guantanamo; other territorial disputes between American states such as those in the Caribbean Sea and the Amazon region (Chapter 7); and disputes between different groups of "peoples" such as natives and implanted populations (Chapter 8). Therein, in order to assess and explain their intricacy, the following chapters will apply the multidimensional approach in more detail to ongoing territorial disputes in the Americas and to situations that, despite their settlement, remain controversial.

Bibliography

Alonso González, Pablo, Wilhelm Londoño and Eva Parga-Dans. "Equality and Hierarchy, Sovereignty and Multiculturalism: The Heritagisation of Raizals in Santa Catalina (Colombia)." *Journal of Ethnic and Migration Studies* 26:19 (2020): 4066–4085.

Arévalo-Ramírez, Walter. "Constitutions Challenging the International Court of Justice's Jurisdiction to Adjudicate Territorial Disputes in Latin America." *Heidelberg Journal of International Law* 82:2 (2022): 425–448.

Atkins, G. Pope. *The Dominican Republic and the United States: From Imperialism to Transnationalism*. Athens, GA: University of Georgia Press, 1998.

Battaglino, Jorge Mario. "The Coexistence of Peace and Conflict in South America: Toward a New Conceptualization of Types of Peace." Revista *Revista Brasileira de Política Internacional* 55:2 (2012): 131–151.

Belaunde, Victor Andres. "Peru's Attitude on the Tacna-Arica Issue." *Current History* 16:1 (1922): 17–21.

Beltrão Sposito, Italo and Fernando José Ludwig. "Mapping Inter-American Struggle (1946–2001): An Overview on Military Conflict and Economic Embargoes." *Revista de Paz y Conflictos* 14:1 (2021): 35–59.

Bercovitch, J. "International Mediation and Dispute Settlement: Evaluating the Conditions for Successful Mediation." *Negotiation Journal* 7:1 (1991): 17–30.

Bethell, Leslie. "Notes on the History of the Venezuela/Guyana Boundary Dispute." *CEBRI-Revista: Brazilian Journal of International Affairs* 9 (2024): 156–175.

Blocher, Joseph and Mitu Gulati. "Navassa: Property, Sovereignty, and the Law of the Territories." *Yale Law Journal* 131:8 (2021): 2390–2448.

Bolzan De Rezende, Leandro, Paul Blackwell and Marcos Degaut. "Brazilian National Defence Policy: Foreign Policy, National Security, Economic Growth, and Technological Innovation." *Defense and Security Analysis* 34:4 (2018): 385–409.

Braveboy-Wagner, Jaqueline Anne. *The Venezuela-Guyana Border Dispute: Britain's Colonial Legacy in Latin America*. New York, NY and Oxford: Routledge, Taylor & Francis, 1984.

Briscoe, Ivan. "Trouble on the Borders: Latin America's New Conflict Zones." *FRIDE* (2008): 1–9 available at https://www.researchgate.net/profile/Ivan-Briscoe/publication/265029389_Trouble_on_the_borders_Latin_America's_new_conflict_zones/links/56b45f0308ae636a540da06b/Trouble-on-the-borders-Latin-Americas-new-conflict-zones.pdf accessed 27 September 2023.

Brownlie, Ian. *Principles of Public International Law*. Oxford: Oxford University Press, 2003.

Calkins, Byron, Lance Aspaas, Charles Nettleman, Amanda Ramirez, Kyle Spolar and Ty Tramell. "The Boundary Survey of the United States and Mexico 'Hidalgo de Guadalupe Medir'—Treaty of Guadalupe Hidalgo (1848)." *Surveying and Land Information Science* 68:4 (2008): 221–237.

Calvert, Peter. *Boundary Disputes in Latin America*. London: Institute for the Study of Conflict, 1983.

Cardone, Ignacio Javier and Pablo Gabriel Fontana. "Latin-American Contributions to the Creation of the Antarctic Regime." *The Polar Journal* 9:2 (2019): 300–323.

Carter, D. Barnaby. "Los Terratenientes de Cautín: Actores Claves de la Contrarreforma." *Anales de la Universidad de Chile* 12 (2017): 233–253.

Cavelier, Germán. *Memoria Histórico-Jurídica sobre el Asunto de Los Monjes*. Bogotá: Editorial Kelly, 1977.

Charney, Jonathan I. and Lewis M. Alexander, eds. *International Maritime Boundaries, Volume I.* Boston, MA: Martinus Nijhoff, 1996.

Child, Jack. *Geopolitics and Conflict in South America.* New York, NY: Praeger, 1985.

Child, John. *Unequal Alliance: The Inter-American Military System, 1938–1978.* Boulder, CO: Westview Press, 1980.

Closs, Michael P., ed. *Native American Mathematics.* Austin, TX: University of Texas, 1997.

Commager, Henry. "England and Oregon Treaty of 1846." *Oregon Historical Quarterly* 28:1 (1927): 18–38.

Conrad, Geoffrey W. and Arthur A. Demarset. *Religion and Empire: The Dynamics of Aztec and Inca Expansionism.* Cambridge: Cambridge University Press, 1984.

Cook, Beverly. "Lobster Boat Diplomacy: The Canada–US Grey Zone." *Marine Policy* 29:5 (2005): 385–390.

Cook, Noble David. *Born to Die: Disease and the New World Conquest, 1492–1650.* Cambridge: Cambridge University Press, 1998.

Day, Alan J., ed. *Border and Territorial Disputes.* Essex: Longman, 1982.

de la Fuente, Maria del Rosario. "Argentina–Chile Laguna del Desierto Arbitration." In *Global Encyclopedia of Territorial Rights*, Gray, K. W., ed., 1–6. Cham: Springer International Publishing, 2022.

Denevan, William M. *The Native Population of the Americas in 1492.* Madison, WI: University of Wisconsin Press, 1992.

Dobyns, Henry F. "An Appraisal of Techniques with a New Hemispheric Estimate." *Current Anthropology* 7:4 (1966): 395–416.

Dodds, Klaus and Alan D. Hemmings. "Britain and the British Antarctic Territory in the Wider Geopolitics of the Antarctic and the Southern Ocean." *International Affairs* 89:6 (2013): 1429–1444.

Domínguez, Jorge I. *Boundary Disputes in Latin America.* Washington, DC: United States Institute of Peace, 2003.

Donovan, Thomas W. "The Marouini River Tract and its Colonial Legacy in South America." *Chicago-Kent Journal of International and Comparative Law* 4 (2004): 1–28.

Douglass, Frederick. "Haïti and the United States. Inside History of the Negotiations for the Môle St. Nicolas. II." *The North American Review* 153:419 (1891): 450–459.

Downing, David. *An Atlas of Territorial and Border Disputes.* London: New English Library, 1980.

Drago, Luis M. and H. Edward Nettles. "The Drago Doctrine in International Law and Politics." *The Hispanic American Historical Review* 8 (1928): 204–223.

Estacio Ferro, Jesús. "El Rio San Juan: Dos Siglos de Conflicto entre Costa Rica y Nicaragua." *Revista Electrónica Iberoamericana* 12:1 (2018): 1–32.

Farcau, Bruce W. *The Chaco War: Bolivia and Paraguay, 1932–1935.* Westport, CT: Praeger, 1996.

Freeman, C. "Borders." In *The SAGE Handbook of Historical Geography*, Domosh, M., Heffernan, M. and Withers, C. W. J., eds. 537–558. London: SAGE Publications, 2020.

Ganzert, Frederic William. "The Boundary Controversy in the Upper Amazon between Brazil, Bolivia, and Peru, 1903–1909." *Hispanic American Historical Review* 14:4 (1934): 427–449.

Garrett, James L. "The Beagle Channel Dispute: Confrontation and Negotiation in the Southern Cone." *Journal of Interamerican Studies and World Affairs* 27:3 (1985): 81–109.

Gavrilov, Viatcheslav, Ted L. McDorman and Clive Schofield. "Canada and the Russian Federation." *Arctic Review on Law and Politics* 13 (2022): 219–231.
Gilbert, Jérémie. *Indigenous Peoples' Land Rights under International Law: From Victors to Actors.* Ardsley, NY: Transnational, 2006.
Gilderhus, Mark T. "The Monroe Doctrine: Meanings and Implications." *Presidential Studies Quarterly* 36 (2006): 5–16.
Grass, Kacper. "Geopolitics in the Western Hemisphere after Trump: Has the United States Abandoned Hegemony in Latin America?" *Revista Internacional de Pensamiento Politico* 16 (2021): 473–492.
Greene, Shane. "Getting Over the Andes: The Geo-Eco-Politics of Indigenous Movements in Peru's Twenty-First Century Inca Empire." *Journal of Latin American Studies* 38:2 (2006): 327–354.
Haklai, Oded and Nephytos Loizides. "Settlers and Conflict Over Contested Territories." In *Settlers in Contested Lands. Territorial Disputes and Ethnic Conflicts*, Haklai, Oded and Loizides, Neophytos, eds. 1–16. Stanford, CA: Stanford University Press, 2015.
Hensel, Paul R. "Contentious Issues and World Politics: The Management of Territorial Claims in the Americas, 1816–1992." *International Studies Quarterly* 45:1 (2001): 81–109.
Hensel, Paul R. "One Thing Leads to Another: Recurrent Militarized Disputes in Latin America, 1816–1986." *Journal of Peace Research* 31:3 (1994): 281–297.
Hensel, Paul R. "Territorial Claims and Armed Conflict between Neighbors." Paper presented to the *Lineae Terrarum International Borders Conference*, El Paso, TX, 2006 available at https://www.paulhensel.org/Research/lineae.pdf accessed 24 July 2024.
Hershey, Amos S. "The Calvo and Drago Doctrines." *The American Journal of International Law* 1 (1907): 26–45.
Herz, Monica and João Pontes Nogueira. *Ecuador vs. Peru: Peacemaking Amid Rivalry.* London: Lynne Rienner, 2002.
Hurtado, Lourdes. "El Conflicto de Leticia (1932–1933) y los Ejércitos de Perú y Colombia (Universidad Externado de Colombia, 2016)." *Journal of Latin American Studies* 51:4 (2019): 950–952.
Hurtado-Torres, Sebastián and Joaquín Fermandois. "The War that Didn't Break Out: Military Rule and Regional Tensions in the Andes in the 1970s." *The International History Review* 42:5 (2020): 967–986.
Huth, Paul K. "Enduring Rivalries and Territorial Disputes, 1950–1990." *Conflict Management and Peace Science* 15:1 (1996): 7–41.
Huth, Paul K. *Standing Your Ground: Territorial Disputes and International Conflict.* Ann Arbor, MI: University of Michigan Press, 2001.
Ireland, Gordon. *Boundaries, Possessions, and Conflicts in South America.* Cambridge, MA: Harvard University Press, 1938.
James, Patrick, Johann Park and Seung-Whan Choi. "Democracy and Conflict Management: Territorial Claims in the Western Hemisphere Revisited." *International Studies Quarterly* 50:4 (2006): 803–817.
Jarvis, Todd, Mark Giordano, Shammy Puri, Kyoko Matsumoto and Aaron Wolf. "International Borders, Ground Water Flow, and Hydroschizophrenia." *Groundwater* 43:5 (2005): 764–770.
Jensen, Thomas C. "The United States-Canada Pacific Salmon Interception Treaty: An Historical and Legal Overview." *Environmental Law* 16:3 (1986): 363–422.

John, Mauricia. "Venezuelan Economic Crisis: Crossing Latin American and Caribbean Borders." *Migration and Development* 8:3 (2019): 437–447.

Kacowicz, Arie M., Exequiel Lacovsky and Daniel F. Wajner. "Peaceful Borders and Illicit Transnational Flows in the Americas." *Latin American Research Review* 55:4 (2020): 727–741.

Kaufman, Scott. *The Pig War: The United States, Britain, and the Balance of Power in the Pacific Northwest, 1846–72.* Lanham, MD: Lexington Books, 2004.

Kennedy, Crammond. "The Drago Doctrine." *The North American Review* 185 (1907): 614–622.

Kleiboer, Marieke. "Understanding Success and Failure of International Mediation." *The Journal of Conflict Resolution* 40:2 (1996): 360–389.

Kohn, Edward P. *This Kindred People: Canadian-American Relations and the Anglo-Saxon Idea, 1895*–1903. Montreal: McGill-Queen's University Press, 2004.

Kröger, Markus and Rickard Lalander. "Ethno-Territorial Rights and the Resource Extraction Boom in Latin America: Do Constitutions Matter?" *Third World Quarterly* 37:4 (2016): 682–702.

Laing, Anna F. "Re-Producing Territory: Between Resource Nationalism and Indigenous Self-Determination in Bolivia." *Geoforum* 108 (2020): 28–38.

Lamarca, Emilio. *Boundary Agreements in Force between the Argentine Republic and Chile.* Buenos Aires: M. Biedma e Hijo, 1898.

Lamborn, A. C. and Stephen P. Mumme. *Statecraft, Domestic Politics, and Foreign Policy Making: The El Chamizal Dispute.* New York, NY: Routledge, 2019.

Lekanda Laban, Paula. "El Conflicto Territorial entre Ecuador y Perú por el Río del Cenepa (1995): Entre una Mediación Fallida y otra Exitosa." *Pléyade* 4 (2010): 186–211.

Lincoln, Jennie K. and Elizabeth G. Ferris, eds. *The Dynamics Of Latin American Foreign Policies: Challenges For The 1980s.* New York, NY and Oxford: Routledge, Taylor & Francis, 2019.

Linden, H. Vander. "Alexander VI and the Demarcation of the Maritime and Colonial Domains of Spain and Portugal, 1493–1494." *The American Historical Review* 22:1 (1916): 1–20.

Lindley, M. F. *The Acquisition and Government of Backward Territory in International Law: Being a Treatise on the Law and Practice Relating to Colonial Expansion.* New York, NY: Negro Universities Press, 1969.

Lindsley, Lisa. "The Beagle Channel Settlement: Vatican Mediation Resolves a Century-Old Dispute." *Journal of Church and State* 29:3 (1987): 435–454.

Loader, M. "Essequibo." *Encyclopedia Britannica*, 9 January 2024 available at https://www.britannica.com/place/Essequibo accessed 6 August 2024.

Lobo, Susana, Steve Talbot, and Traci. L. Morris, eds. *Native American Voices: A Reader.* London and New York, NY: Routledge, 2010.

Luján, Patricia Marín. "Geopolítica, Conflictos Fronterizos en América Latina." *Revista Geopolítica Transfronteiriça* 1:1 (2017): 1–14.

Mançano Fernandes, Bernardo and Cliff Welch. "Movements and Territorial Conflicts in Latin America." In *The Oxford Handbook of Latin American Social Movements*, Rossi, Federico M., ed. 266–282. Oxford: Oxford University Press, 2023.

Manero, Edgardo. "A Retrospective Look at the Nature of National Borders in Latin America." In *The Ashgate Research Companion to Border Studies*, Wastl-Walter, Doris, ed., 301–333. Surrey: Ashgate Publishing Limited.

Mansilla Quiñones, Pablo Arturo and Miguel Melin Pehuen. "A Struggle for Territory, a Struggle Against Borders." *NACLA Report on the Americas* 51:1 (2019): 41–48.

Martynov, Boris F. "International Relations in Latin America (1945–1991)." In *History of International Relations and Russian Foreign Policy in the 20th Century: Volume II*, Turkunov, Anatoly V., Wohlforth, William C. and Martynov, Boris F., eds. 291–313. Newcastle upon Tyne: Cambridge Scholars Publishing, 2020.

Massey, Douglas S. "The Real Crisis at the Mexico-US Border: A Humanitarian and Not an Immigration Emergency." *Sociological Forum* 35:3 (2020): 787–805.

Merino, Roger. "Conflicting Sovereignties: Global Conservation, Protected Areas, and Indigenous Nations in the Peruvian Amazon." *Global Environmental Politics* 22:2 (2022): 95–116.

Merino, Roger. "Reimagining the Nation-State: Indigenous Peoples and the Making of Plurinationalism in Latin America." *Leiden Journal of International Law* 31:4 (2018): 773–792.

Milindre Gonzalez, Rodrigo and Sergio Gabriel Caplan. "The Expansion of Argentine Limits in the Continental Shelf: Implications in the International Scope." eds., *Érico Duarte and Manuel Correia de Barros:* In *Navies and Maritime Policies in the South Atlantic*, 69–95 (2019).

Morris, Michael A. "Maritime geopolitics in Latin America." *Political Geography Quarterly* 5:1 (1986): 43–55.

Murillo Jiménez, Hugo. "La Controversia de Límites entre Costa Rica y Nicaragua. El Laudo Cleveland y los Derechos Canaleros 1821–1903." *Anuario de Estudios Centroamericanos* 12:2 (1986): 45–58.

Nelson, L. D. M. "The Arbitration of Boundary Disputes in Latin America." *Netherlands International Law Review* 20:3 (1973): 267–294.

Newson, Linda A. "The Demographic Collapse of Native Peoples of the Americas, 1492–1650." *Proceedings of the British Academy* 81 (1993): 247–288.

Nolte, Detlef and Leslie E. Wehner. "Geopolitics in Latin America, Old and New." In *Routledge Handbook of Latin American Security*, Mares, David R. and Kacowicz, Arie M., eds. 33–43. Abingdon: Routledge, 2016.

Núñez, Jorge E. *Territorial Disputes and State Sovereignty: International Law and Politics.* London and New York, NY: Routledge, Taylor & Francis Group, 2020.

O'Leary, Brendan. "The Elements of Right-Sizing and Right-Peopling the State." In *Right-Sizing the State: The Politics of Moving Borders*, O'Leary, Brendan, Lustick, Ian S. and Callaghy, Thomas. eds., 15–73. Oxford: Oxford University Press, 2001.

Ochoa Espejo, Paulina. *On Borders: Territories, Legitimacy and the Rights of Place.* Oxford: Oxford University Press, 2020.

Østhagen, Andreas. "Maritime Boundary Disputes: What Are They and Why Do They Matter?" *Marine Policy* 120 (2020): 1–9.

Otero, Gerardo and Heidi A. Jugenitz. "Challenging National Borders from Within: The Political-Class Formation of Indigenous Peasants in Latin America." *Canadian Review of Sociology/Revue Canadienne de Sociologie* 40:5 (2003): 503–524.

Parrish, Austen L. "Changing Territoriality, Fading Sovereignty, and the Development of Indigenous Rights." *American Indian Law Review* 31:2 (2006/2007): 291–313.

Pascoe, Graham. *Falklands Facts and Fallacies: The Falkland Islands in History and International Law.* Surrey: Grosvenor House Publishing, 2022.

Payan, Tony and Pamela Lizette Cruz. "Redefining and Governing the Border as a Binational Commons." Policy Brief: Recommendations for the New Administration. Houston, TX: Baker Institute for Public Policy, 2021.

Perez, Arlenie. "Fisheries Management at the Tri-National Border between Belize, Guatemala and Honduras." *Marine Policy* 33:2 (2009): 195–200.
Polanco, Hector Díaz. *Indigenous Peoples in Latin America: The Quest for Self-Determination.* New York, NY: Routledge: 2018.
Ratner, Steven R. "Drawing a Better Line: *Uti Possidetis* and the Borders of New States." *American Journal of International Law* 90:4 (1996): 590–624.
Root, Elihu. "The Real Monroe Doctrine." *American Society of International Law* 8 (1914): 6–22.
Sage, Walter N. "The Oregon Treaty of 1846." *Canadian Historical Review* 27:4 (1946): 349–367.
Sakuwa, Kentaro. "The Regional Consequences of Territorial Disputes: An Empirical Analysis of the South China Sea Disputes." *Journal of Asian Security and International Affairs* 4:3 (2017): 316–336.
Schenoni, Luis L., Gary Goertz, Andrew P. Owsiak and Paul F Diehl. "Settling Resistant Territorial Disputes: The Territorial Boundary Peace in Latin America." *International Studies Quarterly* 64:1 (2020): 57–70.
Scott Palmer, David. "Peru-Ecuador Border Conflict: Missed Opportunities, Misplaced Nationalism, and Multilateral Peacekeeping." *Journal of Interamerican Studies and World Affairs* 39:3 (1997): 109–148.
Shaw, Malcom N. *International Law.* Cambridge: Cambridge University Press, 2003.
Sieder, Rachel. "Indigenous Peoples' Rights and the Law in Latin America." In *Handbook of Indigenous Peoples' Rights*, Lennox, Corinne and Short, Damien, eds., 414–423. New York, NY: Routledge, 2016.
Sobrevilla Perea, Natalia. *The Caudillo of the Andes: Andrés de Santa Cruz.* New York, NY: Cambridge University Press, 2011.
St. John, Ronald Bruce. *The Bolivia-Chile-Peru Dispute in the Atacama Desert.* Durham, NC: International Boundaries Research Unit, Department of Geography, University of Durham, 1994.
Sullivan, John P. "How Illicit Networks Impact Sovereignty." In *Convergence: Illicit Networks and National Security in the Age of Globalization*, Miklaucic, Michael and Brewer, Jacqueline, eds. 171–188. Washington, DC: National Defense University Press, 2013.
Thies, Cameron G. "Territorial Nationalism in Spatial Rivalries: An Institutionalist Account of the Argentine-Chilean Rivalry." *International Interactions* 27:4 (2001): 399–431.
Todorov, Andrey. "Dire Straits of the Russian Arctic: Options and Challenges for a Potential US FONOP in the Northern Sea Route." *Marine Policy* 139 (2022): 105020.
Todorov, Andrey A. "The Russia-USA Legal Dispute over the Straits of the Northern Sea Route and Similar Case of the Northwest Passage." *Arctic and North* 29:1 (2017): 62–75.
Tremolada Alvarez, Eric. "The Recent Land and Maritime Delimitation of the Court of the Hague in the Affairs of Costa Rica v. Nicaragua, in Light of Their Proposals." *Paix et Securite Internationales – Journal of International Law and International Relations* 7 (2019): 47–84.
Vallet, Élisabeth. "State of Border Walls in a Globalized World." In *Borders and Border Walls: In-Security, Symbolism, Vulnerabilities*, Bissonnette, Andréanne and Vallet, Élisabeth, eds. 7–24. Oxford and New York, NY: Routledge, 2021.

Van Cott, Donna Lee. "Broadening Democracy: Latin America's Indigenous Peoples' Movements." *Current History* 103:670 (2004): 80–85.
van der Haar, Gemma. "The Zapatista Uprising and the Struggle for Indigenous Autonomy." *European Review of Latin American and Caribbean Studies* 76 (2004): 98–108.
Van Genugten, Willem and Camillo Perez-Bustillo. "The Emerging International Architecture of Indigenous Rights: The Interaction between Global, Regional, and National Dimensions." *International Journal on Minority and Group Rights* 11:4 (2004): 379–409.
Van Sang, Nguyen, Le Thanh Nam and Luu Trang. "Independent or Annexation: The Texas Issue in the British-American Relations (1836–1846)." *Academic Journal of Interdisciplinary Studies* 10:5 (2021): 201–215.
Vander Linden, H. "Alexander VI and the Demarcation of the Maritime and Colonial Domains of Spain and Portugal, 1493–1494." *The American Historical Review* 22:1 (1916): 1–20.
Villani, Chiara. "Regional Peace in Latin America: A Multifaceted Explanation." *Revista da Escola de Guerra Naval* 23:3 (2017): 721–754.
Villar Gertner, Andrés. "The Beagle Channel Frontier Dispute between Argentina and Chile: Converging Domestic and International Conflicts." *International Relations* 28:2 (2014): 207–227.
Voeten, Erik. *Ideology and International Institutions.* Princeton, NJ: Princeton University Press, 2021.
Wang, Jingyao and Qi Xu. "Reflections on the Nicaragua v. Colombia Case (2022): From the Perspective of Traditional Fishing Rights." *Frontiers in Marine Science* 10 (2023): 255–267.
Wiegand, Krista E. "Peaceful Dispute Resolution by Authoritarian Regimes." *Foreign Policy Analysis* 15:3 (2019): 303–321.
Wilgus, A. Curtis. "The Leticia Incident." *World Affairs* 95:3 (1932): 179–181.
Woolsey, Lester H. "The New Cuban Treaty." *The American Journal of International Law* 28:3 (1934): 530–534.
Zendejas, Juan H. Flores. "The Entanglements of Domestic Polities: Public Debt and European Interventions in Latin America." In *A World of Public Debts*, Barreyre. N. and Delalande, N., eds. 111–133. Cham: Palgrave Macmillan, 2020.
Zendejas, Juan H. Flores and Felipe Ford Cole. "Sovereignty and Debt in Nineteenth-Century Latin America." In *Sovereign Debt Diplomacies: Rethinking Sovereign Debt from Colonial Empires to Hegemony*, Pénet, Pierre and Zendejas, Juan Flores, eds. 49–72. Oxford: Oxford University Press, 2021.
Zou, Fangbin, Miraj Ahmed Bhuiyan, Tiziana Crovella and Annarita Paiano. "Analyzing the Borderlands: A Regional Report on the Colombia–Ecuador Border on Political, Economic, Social, Legal, and Environment Aspects." *International Migration Review* (2023) available at https://doi.org/10.1177/01979183221149019 accessed 27 September 2023.

5 Ongoing European influence in the Americas

Introduction

Despite the fact that the colonial times are long gone, there are still a few remaining cases of direct and indirect European influence in territorial disputes pertaining to America.[1] Arguably, the Falkland/Malvinas Islands dispute[2] between Argentina and the United Kingdom is the most noticeable example of the enduring European colonial legacy in the continent. There are, however, other cases of ongoing European presence in the region such as the Hans Island dispute[3] (Canada and Denmark) and the Marouini (or Maroni)

1 This chapter will only review ongoing territorial disputes in the Americas that include both American and European agents. Therefore, ongoing territorial disputes concerning only American agents will be reviewed in Chapters 6 (Neo-colonialism) and 7 (Americans versus Americans); influence from other non-European agents including Russia, China and India will be reviewed in Chapter 6 (Neo-colonialism). The already settled case of Saint Martin (or Sint Maarten) between France and the Netherlands will not be explored. For further reference to the already settled case of Saint Martin (or Sint Maarten) see the 1648 Treaty of Concordia available at https://www.st-maarten.com/index.php/island/history-overview-st-maarten-st-martin/treaty accessed 10 January 2023. For the 2023 Border Treaty see the Joint Declaration after the Fifth Quadripartite meeting of 15 June 2023 available at https://www.government.nl/documents/diplomatic-statements/2023/06/15/joint-declaration-fifth-quadripartite-meeting-15-june-2023 accessed 10 January 2024.

2 See Jorge E. Núñez, *Territorial Disputes and State Sovereignty: International Law and Politics* (London and New York, NY: Routledge, Taylor & Francis Group, 2020), Chapter 6; Jorge E. Núñez, *Sovereignty Conflicts and International Law and Politics: A Distributive Justice Issue* (London and New York, NY: Routledge, Taylor & Francis Group, 2017), Chapter 7; Alan J. Day, ed., *Border and Territorial Disputes* (Essex: Longman, 1982), 340–345; Peter Beck, *The Falkland Islands as an International Problem* (London and New York, NY: Routledge, 1998); Peter Beck, "The Future of the Falkland Islands: A Solution Made in Hong Kong?" *International Affairs* 61 (1985): 643–660; Peter Beck, "Looking at the Falkland Islands from Antarctica: The Broader Regional Perspective," *Polar Record* 30 (1994): 167–180; Peter Beck, "Britain's Falkland Future—the Need to Look Back," *The Round Table* 73 (1984): 139–152; Peter Beck, "Cooperative Confrontation in the Falkland Island Dispute," *Journal of Inter-American Studies and World Affairs* 24 (1982): 37–57.

3 Christopher Stevenson, "Hans Off!: The Struggle for Hans Island and the Potential Ramifications for International Border Dispute Resolution," *Boston College International and Comparative Law Review* 30:1 (2007): 263–275; A. H. Kessel, "Canadian Arctic Sovereignty: Myths

DOI: 10.4324/9781003350828-7

River tract dispute[4] (Suriname and French Guiana). Furthermore, the settled territorial dispute over the archipelago of San Andrés, Providencia and Santa Catalina provides examples of several issues related to domestic, regional and international contexts, including the tension between a local ethnic and racial minority (Raizal community) and the Colombian state's interests.[5] Similar in that respect to the Falklands/Malvinas case, the San Andrés, Providencia and Santa Catalina situation involves the presence of a population implanted by a former colonial power.[6]

This chapter introduces these cases to demonstrate that, on the surface, the differences seem to center on very clearly defined current claims and issues at stake between specific claiming agents. However, these territorial disputes include a myriad of actual and potential elements such as the historical and legal claims, the "right-peopling"[7] of the territory with settlers, the principle of territorial integrity, the economic value of natural resources and their exploration and exploitation, the geostrategic location and, in some cases, their importance as a link to claims in Antarctica. It is in the intricate combination of these and other elements where the stalemate finds its bases.

More precisely, these disputes include a combination of domestic, regional and international agents and contexts fostering the stalemate. For instance, domestically, although a stalemate may seem negative and governments are assumed to seek peaceful and permanent dispute settlements, the *status quo* serves other purposes for local politics because it guarantees an endless legal and political limbo that benefits a leader's position.[8] Moreover, Núñez (2020) included some partial conclusions that indicated that any population in a disputed territory, whether implanted for "right-peopling" reasons or indigenous, may present a different interest to the ones represented by the claimant sovereign states.[9] Regionally, the competing interests of neighbor

---

and Realities," in D. A. Berry, N. Bowles and H. Jones, eds., *Governing the North American Arctic* (London: Palgrave Macmillan, 2016), 242–246.

4 Thomas W. Donovan, "The Marouini River Tract and Its Colonial Legacy in South America," *Chicago-Kent Journal of International and Comparative Law* 4 (2004): 1–28.

5 Pablo Alonso González, Wilhelm Londoño and Eva Parga-Dans, "Equality and Hierarchy, Sovereignty and Multiculturalism: The Heritagisation of Raizals in Santa Catalina (Colombia)," *Journal of Ethnic and Migration Studies* 46:19 (2018): 4066–4085; James Ross, "Routes for Roots: Entering the 21st Century in San Andrés Island, Colombia," *Caribbean Studies* 35:1 (2007): 3–36.

6 The case of implanted populations will be addressed extensively in Chapter 8.

7 Brendan O'Leary, "The Elements of Right-Sizing and Right-Peopling the State," in Brendan O'Leary, Ian S. Lustick and Thomas Callaghy, eds., *Right-Sizing the State: The Politics of Moving Borders* (Oxford: Oxford University Press, 2001), 15–73. This notion of "right-peopling" will be addressed extensively in Chapter 8.

8 Huth explains how an ongoing dispute can benefit leaders. Paul K. Huth, *Standing Your Ground: Territorial Disputes and International Conflict* (Ann Arbor, MI: University of Michigan Press, 2001), 171–172 and 178–179.

9 Jorge E. Núñez, *Territorial Disputes and State Sovereignty: International Law and Politics* (London and New York, NY: Routledge, Taylor & Francis Group, 2020), Chapter 9.

states and communities encompass several elements and features such as natural resources, borders, bordering minorities, migration, defense and security. Finally, the international context plays a role in terms of prestige because great powers would opt to go to war to preserve their status, even if the practical results seemed trivial,[10] and also because of the geostrategic location of the disputed territories.

As stated in Núñez (2020),[11] any territorial dispute is a combination of several issues at stake—i.e. in terms of territory, population, government and law. More precisely, these issues at stake are related to the several pluralisms that characterize territorial disputes. Therein, issues at stake can be assessed in terms of their individuality or together, with reference to a particular or several pluralisms. With this frame in mind, the following sections will introduce four cases: the Falkland/Malvinas Islands (Argentina and the United Kingdom); San Andrés, Providencia and Santa Catalina (Colombia and Nicaragua); the Hans Island dispute (Canada and Denmark); and the Marouini (or Maroni) River tract dispute (Suriname and French Guiana). All these differences present various issues at stake including ongoing European influence in the Americas, colonial roots, bordering minorities, leader's prestige, natural resources and geostrategic location, to name a few, and these can appear in a combination of pluralisms. Each of these issues at stake and any pluralisms may be assessed individually. Alternatively, each of them may be assessed using a broader approach as one of several components in a given territorial dispute. The latter is the aim of the final section: to incorporate a multidimensional view of these disputes by showcasing the different issues at stake and their pluralisms. Understandably, these sections will give the reader only a glimpse of such a multi-layered approach. For a thorough and more meaningful analysis, each individual territorial dispute deserves a dedicated multidimensional study that embraces all the issues and pluralisms.

Falkland/Malvinas Islands (Argentina and the United Kingdom)

This current dispute between Argentina and the United Kingdom started as early as 1833, when the British expelled Argentina's residents from the Falkland/Malvinas Islands and settled their people.[12] However, there are views

10 Matthieu Grandpierron, "Preserving 'Great Power Status': The Complex Case of the British Intervention in the Falklands (1982)," *Croatian International Relations Review* 23:79 (2017): 127–156.

11 See Jorge E. Núñez, *Territorial Disputes and State Sovereignty: International Law and Politics* (London and New York, NY: Routledge, Taylor & Francis Group, 2020).

12 For official historical accounts see https://www.falklands.gov.fk/our-history (UK) and https://www.cancilleria.gob.ar/es/politica-exterior/cuestion-malvinas/antecedentes/antecedentes-historicos (Argentina), both accessed 12 January 2024. The list of books and academic journal articles on the Falklands/Malvinas issue and, in particular, the 1982 war between Argentina and the United Kingdom is vast. For several examples, including the

that maintain the islands were first discovered by the English navigator John Davis in 1592.[13] Arguably, the first British claim dates back to 1690, just after the first recorded landing in the Falklands/Malvinas by Captain John Strong. Controversially, the first permanent settlement might have been in 1764 by France, followed later by a British settlement. Therefore, even if the British discovered the islands as early as the alleged first event, they were occupied only by the French in 1764—i.e. 172 years after the alleged British discovery.[14] Until the 1810s, there were British, French and Spanish settlements and claims.[15] In 1816, Argentina became independent and claimed the former Spanish territories, including the Falklands/Malvinas, taking actual possession of the islands in 1820.[16] The British then expelled Argentine settlers in 1833.[17] Since then, Argentina and the United Kingdom have claimed exclusive sovereign rights over the islands, both bilaterally and internationally, with the dispute reaching a climax in 1982 when a war broke out between the two countries.[18]

The Falkland/Malvinas Islands territorial dispute has been in a deadlock since its origin. Technically, the territory at issue between Argentina and the United Kingdom includes the islands and their dependencies, the South Georgia and South Sandwich Islands. Regardless of whether Argentina and/or the United Kingdom have grounds for their claims or not, their arguments and counterarguments guarantee a stalemate because they are based on unidimensional approaches that fail to consider the issue in all its intricacy. Therein, while Argentina bases its position on international law and their historical right to the islands, Britain focuses on their *de facto* control of the islands, the length of their occupation and the principle of self-determination. More precisely, Argentina's official position is that it has sovereignty over the islands

---

author's work, see fn 2. For some of the latest publications see, for example, Louise A. Clare, *Politics, Propaganda and the Press: International Reactions to the Falklands/Malvinas Conflict* (London and New York, NY: Routledge, 2023); Graham Pascoe and Peter Pepper, *Falklands Facts and Fallacies: The Falkland Islands in History and International Law* (Surrey: Grosvenor House Publishing, 2022); Fernando Pedrosa and Guillermo C. Mira Delli-Zotti, *Revisiting the Falklands-Malvinas Question: Transnational and Interdisciplinary Perspectives* (London: University of London Press, 2021); and many more.

13 For an account of the history behind the dispute see Julius Goebel, *The Struggle for the Falklands: A Study in Legal and Diplomatic History* (New Haven, CT: Yale University Press, 1982); Ian Strange, *The Falkland Islands* (Devon: David and Charles, 1972).

14 Lowell Steven Gustafson, *The Sovereignty Dispute over the Falkland (Malvinas) Islands* (Oxford: Oxford University Press, 1988).

15 Farooq Hassan, "The Sovereignty Dispute over the Falkland Islands," *Virginia Journal of International Law* 23:1 (1982): 53–74.

16 Ricardo Caillet-Bois, *Una Tierra Argentina: Las Islas Malvinas* (Buenos Aires: Peuser, 1948).

17 Christopher C. Joyner, "Anglo-Argentine Rivalry After the Falklands/Malvinas War: Laws, Geopolitics, and the Antarctic Connection," *Lawyer of the Americas* 15:3 (1984): 467–502.

18 For a multi-faceted and multidisciplinary vision of the Malvinas war including historical, sociological, international relations and political science see Érico Esteves Duarte, ed., *The Falklands/Malvinas War in the South Atlantic* (Cham: Palgrave Macmillan, 2021).

based on historical entitlement and on the fact the United Kingdom is in direct violation of the principle of territorial integrity.[19] In turn, the United Kingdom maintains that the Falkland/Malvinas Islands are a British Overseas Territory.[20] Finally, sovereignty for the islanders, therefore, is not up for discussion.[21] The Falkland/Malvinas Islands' official position is to acknowledge the right to self-determination and the aim to retain its links with the United Kingdom as a British Overseas Territory, with self-governance except for defense and foreign affairs.

Internationally, according to the United Nations (UN), the Falklands/Malvinas have been a non-self-governing territory since 1946.[22] Moreover, the UN acknowledges that a "dispute exists between the Governments of Argentina and the United Kingdom of Great Britain and Northern Ireland concerning sovereignty over the Falkland Islands (Malvinas)."[23] There have been several United Nations General Assembly (UNGA) Resolutions directly and indirectly related to this issue such as UNGA Resolution 1514 (XV) "Declaration on the Granting of Independence to Colonial Countries and Peoples,"[24] UNGA Resolution 2065 (XX) "Question of the Falkland Islands (Malvinas),"[25] UNGA Resolution 3160 (XXVIII) "Question of the Falkland Islands (Malvinas)"[26] and several others.[27] Regionally,[28] the Organization of

19 Argentina's official position at the United Nations available at https://www.cancilleria.gob.ar/es/politica-exterior/cuestion-malvinas/malvinas-en-naciones-unidas accessed 12 January 2024.

20 Official United Kingdom government website available at https://www.gov.uk/foreign-travel-advice/falkland-islands accessed 15 January 2024.

21 Official Falkland/Malvinas Islands position available at https://www.falklands.gov.fk/our-home accessed 12 January 2024.

22 See the United Nations official website at https://www.un.org/dppa/decolonization/en/content/falkland-islands-malvinas accessed 15 January 2024.

23 See the United Nations official website at https://www.un.org/dppa/decolonization/en/content/falkland-islands-malvinas accessed 15 January 2024.

24 UNGA Resolution 1514 (XV) complete text available at https://www.ohchr.org/en/instruments-mechanisms/instruments/declaration-granting-independence-colonial-countries-and-peoples accessed 15 January 2024.

25 UNGA Resolution 2065 (XX) complete text available at https://treaties.un.org/doc/source/docs/A_RES_2065-Eng.pdf accessed 15 January 2024.

26 UNGA Resolution 3160 (XXVIII) complete text available at https://www.staff.city.ac.uk/p.willetts/SAC/UN/RES3160.PDF https://treaties.un.org/doc/source/docs/A_RES_3160-Eng.pdf accessed 15 January 2024.

27 For a complete list see the South Atlantic Council available at https://www.staff.city.ac.uk/p.willetts/SAC/UN/UN-LIST.HTM#:~:text=Resolution%202065%20(XX)%2C%2016,of%20the%20drive%20for%20decolonisation accessed 15 January 2024 and the United Nations and Decolonization webpage available at https://www.un.org/dppa/decolonization/en/content/falkland-islands-malvinas accessed 15 January 2024.

28 For a complete list of regional organizations see Chapter 2.

American States (OAS),[29] the Southern Common Market (MERCOSUR)[30] and several others have recommended the peaceful and definitive settlement of the difference. According to Argentina's National Constitution, the Falkland/Malvinas Islands, and the South Georgia and South Sandwich Islands, including maritime and insular spaces, are an integral part of the national territory and, therefore, under their exclusive sovereignty.[31] Pre-Brexit, as an Overseas Territory of the United Kingdom, the Falklands/Malvinas were considered an Associated Territory of the European Union (EU).[32] This situation, however, was left in a legal and political limbo after Brexit with the EU not setting a clear position about the sovereignty dispute.[33] Finally, for the Falkland/Malvinas Islanders, there is no question about sovereignty that needs to be answered. According to the 2021 census the islands had a resident population of 3,662, with 60% of them being Falkland/Malvinas Islanders, 10% permanent residents and 28% work permit holders and their dependents.[34] Most of them (almost 70%) considered themselves "Falkland Islanders, British or a combination of both."[35] Over a decade ago, in March 2013, there was a

29 OAS official website available at https://www.oas.org/en/ accessed 15 January 2024.
30 MERCOSUR official website available at https://www.mercosur.int/en/ accessed 15 January 2024.
31 Argentina's National Constitution (in Spanish) complete text available at https://www.argentina.gob.ar/normativa/nacional/ley-24430-804/texto accessed 15 January 2024.
32 See, relating to before Brexit, the United Kingdom Parliament files, The House of Lords (27 March 2017) available at https://researchbriefings.files.parliament.uk/documents/LIF-2017-0028/LIF-2017-0028.pdf accessed 15 January 2024.
33 See the House of Commons Research Briefing Paper (dated 1 August 2022) on "Brexit and the UK's Overseas Territories" available at https://researchbriefings.files.parliament.uk/documents/CBP-9592/CBP-9592.pdf accessed 15 January 2024; and the European Union Parliamentary Question (dated 21 March 2023) concerning "Trade Relations between the EU and the Falkland Islands (Malvinas)" available at https://www.europarl.europa.eu/doceo/document/E-9-2022-001140_EN.html accessed 15 January 2024. Controversially, since Brexit, the European Union has used interchangeably the names "Falklands" and "Malvinas." See "Rishi Sunak hits out at EU calling Falklands Islands 'Islas Malvinas'" available at https://www.bbc.co.uk/news/uk-politics-66258669 accessed 23 January 2025; "Islas Malvinas: EU Signs Deal Using Falklands' Argentine Name" available at https://www.theguardian.com/uk-news/2023/jul/20/islas-malvinas-brexit-cited-as-eu-endorses-falklands-argentine-name accessed 23 January 2025; European Commission, ***European Union, Trade in Goods with Falkland Islands*** available at https://webgate.ec.europa.eu/isdb_results/factsheets/country/details_falkland-islands_en.pdf accessed 23 January 2025.
34 Falkland/Malvinas Islands Census Statistics (2021) available at https://www.falklands.gov.fk/policy/2021-census/census accessed 15 January 2024. For information about the 2016 and 2012 censuses see the Falklands/Malvinas official webpage including "Census and Statistical Reports" available at https://www.falklands.gov.fk/policy/downloads/category/13-falkland-islands-census-reports accessed 15 January 2024.
35 Falkland/Malvinas Islands Census Statistics (2021) available at https://www.falklands.gov.fk/policy/2021-census/census accessed 15 January 2024. For information about the 2016 and 2012 censuses see the Falklands/Malvinas official webpage including "Census and Statistical Reports" available at https://www.falklands.gov.fk/policy/downloads/category/13-falkland-islands-census-reports accessed 15 January 2024.

referendum asking the Falkland/Malvinas Islanders whether they wanted to remain as a British Overseas Territory. The number of ballot papers issued was 1,522 while the votes cast at the referendum were 1,518. With a 92% turnout, there were 1,513 (99.8%) "Yes" votes and three (0.2%) "No" votes.[36]

Pertaining to issues of geographical location and the wider implications that are intertwined with domestic, regional and international law and politics, it is important to note the area's actual and potential relevance in terms of the exploration and exploitation of natural resources, geopolitics and the connection with Antarctica.[37] Arguably aware of the possible natural wealth in the area, prior to the 1982 war, the United Kingdom had commissioned what was then known as the Shackleton report[38] in order to assess the islands' economic importance. Natural resources include hydrocarbons on the islands and offshore, fisheries and mineral deposits.[39] Unilateral acts pertaining to the exploration and exploitation of these resources in the disputed area are controversial.[40] Because of their geographical location, the islands are important geopolitically[41] and in connection to claims over Antarctica.[42] With regard to the

36 Official results of the referendum on the Political Status of the Falkland/Malvinas Islands available at https://www.fiassociation.com/news/press-release-result-of-referendum-remains-clear-10-years-on/ accessed 23 January 2025.

37 Territorial claims over Antarctica will be reviewed extensively in Chapter 9. Christopher C. Joyner, "Anglo-Argentine Rivalry After the Falklands/Malvinas War: Laws, Geopolitics, and the Antarctic Connection," *Lawyer of the Americas* 15:3 (1984): 467–502.

38 1976 Shackleton (volume 1 of 2) report available at https://www.nationalarchives.gov.fk/jdownloads/Trade%20and%20Industry/R-TRA-ECO-1-7.%20Economic%20Survey%20of%20the%20Falkland%20Islands%20Volume%201%20of%202%20Resources%20and%20Development%20Potential%20July%201976%20-%20The%20Rt%20Hon%20Lord%20Shackleton.pdf accessed 16 January 2024. Lord Shackleton's subsequent 1982 Falkland Islands Economic Study is available at https://www.nationalarchives.gov.fk/jdownloads/Trade%20and%20Industry/R-TRA-ECO-1-10.%20Falkland%20Islands%20economic%20survey%201982.pdf accessed 16 January 2024.

39 Jorge Gabriel Perez, "El Conflicto de las Malvinas a través del Prisma de la Geopolítica de Recursos Naturales," *Coleção Meira Mattos: Revista das Ciências Militares* 14:51 (2020): 331–356; Grace Livingstone, "Oil and the Falklands/Malvinas: Oil Companies, Governments and Islanders," *The Round Table* 111:1 (2022): 91–103; Rogério Do Nascimento Carvalho, "New Alliances for Argentina with the Discovery of Mineral Reserves in the Falkland Islands," *The Round Table* 111:1 (2022): 141–142; and many more.

40 Youri van Logchem, "Exploration and Exploitation of Oil and Gas Resources in Maritime Areas of Overlap under International Law: The Falklands (Malvinas)," in Ruth A. Kok and Jure Vidmar, eds., *Hague Yearbook of International Law/Annuaire de La Haye de Droit International* (Leiden: Brill, Nijhoff, 2015), 29–64.

41 D. J. Keeling, "A Geopolitical Perspective on Argentina's Malvinas/Falkland Claims," *Global Discourse* 3:1 (2013): 158–165. This is a very brief article. However, it includes several references to texts in Spanish originally published in Argentina.

42 Adrian Howkins, "Latin America and Antarctica," in *Oxford Research Encyclopedia of Latin American History* (2017) available at https://oxfordre.com/latinamericanhistory/display/10.1093/acrefore/9780199366439.001.0001/acrefore-9780199366439-e-434 accessed 9 May 2024; Robert Keith Headland, "Territory and Claims in the Antarctic Treaty Region:

latter, according to the British Letters Patent of 1908 and 1917[43] the Antarctic territories had long been British possessions and had been utilized and administered by the Falkland/Malvinas Islands Government. Interestingly, the United Kingdom later distinguished between the titles to the territories concerning the Falkland/Malvinas Islands and Antarctica.[44]

A further layer worth mentioning relates to non-rational elements and features pertaining to this difference; it includes national culture, nationalism, patriotism and emotion on both sides and even involves language and place names.[45] Indeed, the Falklands/Malvinas territorial dispute encompasses an identity dispute.[46] Therein, it has been part of the political agenda in Argentina and the United Kingdom for decades and has served different governments and leaders.[47] Even after the 1982 war, issues such as galvanized interpretations of the conflict and a "patriotic cult" persist to the present day.[48] In terms of polemics, as in other territorial disputes, governments and leaders on both sides use views that are extremely biased and polarized with "positive self-presentation and negative other-presentation"[49] to divert from internal

A Disquisition on Historical and Recent Developments," *The Cartographic Journal* 57:2 (2020): 160–174.

43 "British Letters Patent of 1908 and 1917 constituting the Falkland Islands Dependencies," *Polar Record* 5:35–36 (1948): 241–243. Complete texts of the British Letters Patent of 1908 and 1917 available at https://www.cambridge.org/core/journals/polar-record/all-issues accessed 19 February 2025.

44 See paragraph 2 and its note 2 in ICJ Pleadings, Oral Arguments, Documents Antarctica Cases (United Kingdom v. Argentina; United Kingdom v. Chile) [1956] where it says "It will be understood that although, for reasons of convenience, the territories to which the present Application relates were constituted part of the Falkland Islands Dependencies for administrative purposes, the British *title* to these territories is a separate and independent one which in no way derives from or depends on the title to the Falkland Islands themselves." Complete text available at https://www.icj-cij.org/sites/default/files/case-related/27/027-19550504-APP-1-00-EN.pdf accessed 16 January 2024.

45 Yliana V. Rodríguez and Adolfo Elizaincín, "Competing Place Names: Malvinas vs. Falklands: When a Sovereignty Conflict Becomes a Name Conflict," *Journal of Language Aggression and Conflict* 11:2 (2023): 226–255.

46 Magdalena Lisińska, "The Falklands/Malvinas as an Identity Dispute: A Constructivist Analysis of the British and Argentinian Positions," *The International Spectator* 59:2 (2023): 95–111.

47 Louise A. Clare, *Politics, Propaganda and the Press: International Reactions to the Falklands/Malvinas Conflict* (New York, NY and London: Routledge, 2023); Matthieu Grandpierron, "The British Use of Domestic Political Situations during the Falklands War," *The Round Table* 111:1 (2022): 56–68.

48 Federico Lorenz, "Malvinas/Falklands War: Changes in the Idea of Nationhood, the Local and National, in a Post-Dictatorship Context—Argentina, 1982–2007," in J. Grigera and L. Zorzoli, eds., *The Argentinian Dictatorship and Its Legacy. Studies of the Americas* (Cham: Palgrave Macmillan, 2020), 197–209.

49 Ray Chung Hang Leung, "The Discursive Positioning of the Falkland Islands (Las Islas Malvinas): A Corpus-Based Collocational Analysis of British and Argentinian Websites," *Global: A Journal of Language, Culture and Communication* 5 (2017): 1–31.

problematic situations.[50] Unsurprisingly, Argentine and British governments and leaders have not reached a settlement to the dispute since the internal, regional and international payoffs are higher if they simply maintain the *status quo*. The direct influence over the domestic political status of the ruling power at the time of the Falkland/Malvinas 1982 war and during the ongoing territorial dispute over the islands today is unquestionable.[51] Furthermore, the international context plays a role in terms of prestige because great powers would elect to go to war as a means to preserve their status even if the practical results seem trivial.[52]

San Andrés, Providencia and Santa Catalina (Colombia and Nicaragua)

Similar to other cases in the Americas, the territorial dispute over the archipelago of San Andrés, Providencia and Santa Catalina is rooted in colonialism.[53] The archipelago was discovered by Europeans in the sixteenth century,[54] colonized by Spain, and later occupied by English Puritans from Bermuda. Slaves arrived in 1633 from other Caribbean islands. Breaking up with Spain, Colombia and Nicaragua became independent states. At that time the

50 Krista E. Wiegand, "Territorial Dispute Strategies as Diversionary Behavior," *Journal of Territorial and Maritime Studies* 5:1 (2018): 42–63.

51 David Sanders, Hugh Ward, David Marsh and Tony Fletcher, "Government Popularity and the Falklands War: A Reassessment," *British Journal of Political Science* 17:3 (1987): 281–313; Helmut Norpoth, "The Falklands War and Government Popularity in Britain: Rally without Consequence or Surge without Decline?" *Electoral Studies* 6:1 (1987): 3–16; David Monoghan, *The Falklands War* (London: Palgrave Macmillan, 1998), 1–38; James Aulich, *Framing the Falklands War: Nationhood, Culture, and Identity* (Milton Keynes: Open University Press, 1992), 133; Jack S. Levy and Lily I. Vakili, "Diversion Action by Authoritarian Regimes: Argentina and the Falklands/Malvinas Case," in Manus I. Midlarsky, ed., *The Internationalization of Communal Strife* (London: Routledge, 1992), 118–146; Helardo Muñoz, "Efectos y Lecciones del Conflicto de las Malvinas," *Estudios Internacionales* 15:60 (1982): 499–512; Sabrina Morán, "The Malvinas War in the Democratic Transition in Argentina. Conflicts and Tension within A Demalvinized Political Agenda," *Cuadernos de Marte* 9:15 (2018): 173–207; Vaughne Miller, "Argentina and the Falkland Islands," *House of Commons Library* (2012) available at https://researchbriefings.parliament.uk/ResearchBriefing/Summary/SN05602 accessed 25 January 2024; and many others. For a very detailed and current study of the Falklands/Malvinas case, see Norberto Consani, Federico Martín Gomez and Leandro Enrique Sánchez, *Malvinas y la Construcción de un Reclamo Soberano: Pasado, Presente y Futuro* (La Plata: Universidad Nacional de La Plata, 2017) available at http://www.iri.edu.ar/wp-content/uploads/2017/03/libro_refem_malvinas_construccion.pdf accessed 25 January 2024.

52 Matthieu Grandpierron, "Preserving 'Great Power Status': The Complex Case of the British Intervention in the Falklands (1982)," *Croatian International Relations Review* 23:79 (2017): 127–156.

53 See Chapter 4.

54 Arthur P. Newton, *The Colonising Activities of the English Puritans* (New York, NY: Kennikat Press, 1966).

archipelago—which then included the Islas Mangles (Cum Islands)—and the Mosquito Coast were part of the Spanish Virreinato de Santa Fe or Virreinato de Nueva Granada (Viceroyalty of New Granada). According to Colombia, the archipelago has since then been fully and exclusively under their sovereignty and administration. Indeed, according to this account the islands joined the then independent Gran Colombia in 1822.[55] However, according to Nicaragua, these islands have always been under their jurisdiction, first as part of the Spanish colony and later as part of the Captaincy-General of Guatemala, of which Nicaragua was a province, and the United Provinces of Central America, of which Nicaragua was a part. By application of the principle of *uti possidetis juris* since the colonial period and as an independent state, Nicaragua claims exclusive sovereignty.[56]

In 1923, the Colombian government started the "Colombianization" of the islands by supporting Catholics, removing the Baptist Church and prohibiting the use of English in schools.[57] In 1928, Colombia and Nicaragua signed the Esguerra-Bárcenas Treaty by which the former recognized Nicaragua's sovereignty over the Mosquito Coast between Cape Gracias a Dios and the San Juan River, and over Mangle Grande and Mangle Chico Islands in the Atlantic Ocean (Great Corn Island and Little Corn Island); and the latter recognized Colombia's sovereignty over the islands of San Andrés, Providencia and Santa Catalina.[58]

In February 1980, the Esguerra-Bárcenas Treaty was declared void by the new Sandinista government in Nicaragua.[59] In 2001, Nicaragua presented its sovereignty claims at the International Court of Justice (ICJ).[60] In 2007, the ICJ recognized Colombian sovereignty. In 2012, the ICJ ruled that the Esguerra-Bárcenas Treaty did not include a maritime delimitation—i.e.

55 Donald Rowland, "Spanish Occupation of the Island of Old Providence, or Santa Catalina, 1641–1670," *The Hispanic American Historical Review* 15:3 (1935): 298–312; Peter J. Wilson, *Crab Antics: The Social Anthropology of English-Speaking Negro Societies of the Caribbean* (New Haven, CT: Yale University Press, 1973).

56 For a detailed account of the history behind the dispute according to both Colombia and Nicaragua see the International Court of Justice (ICJ) Territorial and Maritime Dispute (Nicaragua v. Colombia) available at https://www.icj-cij.org/case/124 in particular, the preliminary objections of Colombia and the memorial of Nicaragua, both available at https://www.icj-cij.org/case/124/preliminary-objections. All documents accessed on 12 January 2024.

57 Klaus de Albuquerque and William F. Stinner, "The Colombianization of Black San Andreans," *Caribbean Studies* 17:3/4 (1977–1978): 171–181.

58 Rafael Nieto-Navia, "Some Remarks on the Territorial and Maritime Dispute (Nicaragua v. Colombia) Case," in Lilian del Castillo, ed., *Law of the Sea, From Grotius to the International Tribunal for the Law of the Sea* (Leiden: Brill, Nijhoff, 2015), 545–562.

59 J. G. Tokatlian, "Colombia at War: The Search for a Peace Diplomacy," *International Journal of Politics, Culture, and Society* 14 (2000): 333–362.

60 Christian Diemer and Amalija Šeparović, "Territorial Questions and Maritime Delimitation with Regard to Nicaragua's Claims to the San Andrés Archipelago," *Heidelberg Journal of International Law* 66 (2006): 167–185.

there was no agreed maritime boundary between Colombia and Nicaragua.[61] Moreover, because Colombia is not a party to the United Nations Convention on the Law of the Sea (UNCLOS), by application of customary international law,[62] the ICJ used a novel and controversial interpretation—i.e. a mixture of weighted base points, geodetic lines, parallels of latitude and enclaving—and confirmed Colombian sovereignty and granted Nicaragua control over part of the western coastline of the archipelago.[63]

In the bilateral and regional dimensions,[64] the archipelago presents a tension stemming from European past activities between a local ethnic and racial minority and the Colombian state's interests.[65] As a result of migration, slavery and the different cultural influences at play, the Raizal community has struggled as they are caught between Anglophone/Protestant and Hispanic/Catholic views.[66] Islanders are sociologically linked with the English and Creole-speaking community on the Nicaraguan coast.[67] Controversially, there seems to still be a dominant national vision overriding the local Raizal community involving imposition by the Colombian state coupled with private sector interests.[68]

61 Walter Arévalo Ramírez, "Resistance to Territorial and Maritime Delimitation Judgments of the International Court of Justice and Clashes with 'Territory Clauses' in the Constitutions of Latin American States," *Leiden Journal of International Law* 35:1 (2022): 185–208.
62 Jingyao Wang and Qi Xu, "Reflections on the Nicaragua v. Colombia Case (2022): From the Perspective of Traditional Fishing Rights," *Frontiers in Marine Science* 10 (2023): 1–13.
63 Lorenzo Palestini, "The Territorial and Maritime Dispute (Nicaragua v. Colombia): On Territorial Sovereignty and the International Court of Justice's Failure to Rule on the Geographical Scope of the Archipelago of San Andrés," *The Law and Practice of International Courts and Tribunals Journal* 15:1 (2016): 56–80; Nienke Grossman, "Territorial and Maritime Dispute," *American Journal of International Law* 107:2 (2013): 396–403. For an overview of the case and relevant judgments see *Territorial and Maritime Dispute (Nicaragua v. Colombia)*, International Court of Justice available at https://www.icj-cij.org/en/case/124 accessed 20 June 2019.
64 See Chapter 7.
65 Pablo Alonso González, Wilhelm Londoño and Eva Parga-Dans, "Equality and Hierarchy, Sovereignty and Multiculturalism: The Heritagisation of Raizals in Santa Catalina (Colombia)," *Journal of Ethnic and Migration Studies* 46:19 (2018): 4066–4085.
66 James Ross, "Routes for Roots: Entering the 21st Century in San Andrés Island, Colombia," *Caribbean Studies* 35:1 (2007): 3–36.
67 James Ross, "Routes for Roots: Entering the 21st Century in San Andrés Island, Colombia," *Caribbean Studies* 35:1 (2007): 3–36.
68 Pablo Alonso González, Wilhelm Londoño and Eva Parga-Dans, "Equality and Hierarchy, Sovereignty and Multiculturalism: The Heritagisation of Raizals in Santa Catalina (Colombia)," *Journal of Ethnic and Migration Studies* 46:19 (2020): 4066–4085.

The Hans Island dispute (Canada and Denmark)

In the last few years, islands have gained a more central role in territorial disputes.[69] The Arctic Ocean area is not an exception. Legally, the area is under customary international law and the law of the sea, including the 1982 UNCLOS and the 1958 Geneva Conventions on the Law of the Sea.[70] Similar to other areas of territorial dispute in the world pertaining to islands, including the Falkland/Malvinas Islands and the San Andrés, Providencia and Santa Catalina archipelago, the usual reasons for controversy among the Arctic states have to do with maritime boundaries, and rights for exploration and exploitation of the seabed and natural resources including the actual and potential existence of oil, natural gas and mineral deposits. Moreover, global warming and the consequent heating of the Arctic seas have resulted in navigable waters between Canada and Greenland throughout most of the year.[71]

The sovereignty over Hans Island, a 1.3 square kilometer uninhabited rock formation, had been claimed since the 1970s by Canada and Denmark. More precisely, both Canada and Denmark agreed on the Arctic border demarcation.[72] However, named after the Inuit guide from Greenland, Hans Hendrik, the Hans Island became more relevant in 1971 when Canada and Greenland (an autonomous territory of the Kingdom of Denmark) discussed their boundary. Since then, Denmark had argued for the exclusive sovereignty of the island citing several reasons that include a territorial claim[73] based on geological

69 Robert W. Smith and L. Thomas Bradford, "Island Disputes and the Law of the Sea: An Examination of Sovereignty and Delimitation Disputes," *Maritime Briefing, International Boundary Research Unit* 2:4 (1998): 1–26.

70 Eight states possess territories extending beyond the 66th Parallel and are known as Arctic states: Norway, Sweden, Finland, Russia, the United States (Alaska), Denmark (Greenland), Iceland and Canada. Four Arctic coastal states, Canada, Norway, Denmark and Russia, have ratified these international conventions, while the US accepts its main provisions as norms of customary international law, but is also in the process of ratifying UNCLOS. See Ermal Xhelilaj and Kristofor Lapa, "Territorial Claims in North Polar Maritime Zone in View of International Security," *Transactions on Maritime Science* 11:01 (2022): 278–285; Clive Schofield and Andreas Østhagen, "A Divided Arctic: Maritime Boundary Agreements and Disputes in the Arctic Ocean," in Joachim Weber, ed., *Handbook on Geopolitics and Security in the Arctic: The High North Between Cooperation and Confrontation* (Cham: Springer, 2020), 171–191.

71 For a brief yet informative account see Christopher Stevenson, "Hans Off!: The Struggle for Hans Island and the Potential Ramifications for International Border Dispute Resolution," *Boston College International and Comparative Law Review* 30:1 (2007): 263–275.

72 Agreement between the Government of Canada and the Government of the Kingdom of Denmark, relating to the delimitation of the continental shelf between Greenland and Canada, entered in force on 13 March, 1974. Full text of the treaty is available at https://treaties.un.org/doc/Publication/UNTS/Volume%20950/volume-950-I-13550-English.pdf accessed 23 January 2025.

73 For different kinds of claims pertaining to territorial disputes and sovereignty conflicts see Jorge E. Núñez, *Cosmopolitanism, State Sovereignty, International Law and Politics: A Theory* (London and New York, NY: Routledge, Taylor & Francis Group, 2023), Chapter 7; Jorge E. Núñez, *Territorial Disputes and State Sovereignty: International Law and Politics* (London

similarities with Greenland and a historical claim based on the arguable fact that it was discovered by Hendrik himself. Different from the Falkland/Malvinas Islands and the San Andrés, Providencia and Santa Catalina archipelago cases, the Hans Island is uninhabited. Interestingly, although there is no permanent population, Denmark included among the arguments the historical and sociological claim that the Greenlandic Inuit (but not Canadian Inuit) had used the rock for surveying ice and hunting.[74] In turn, Canada's claim was based on the control transfer by the 1880 British order in council and the island's location.[75]

The dispute was finally settled in 2022 when Canada and Denmark signed an agreement. The border resulted in an allocation of 40% of the island to Canada and 60% to Denmark.[76] In addition to the inclusion of issues pertaining to cooperation in ocean matters, the agreement considers the access of indigenous Inuit people to Hans Island[77] and other provisions concerning limits of the continental shelf between southern Greenland and Canada (near Newfoundland and Labrador).[78]

---

and New York, NY: Routledge, Taylor & Francis Group, 2020), Chapter 4; Jorge E. Núñez, *Sovereignty Conflicts and International Law and Politics: A Distributive Justice Issue* (London and New York, NY: Routledge, Taylor & Francis Group, 2017), Chapter 6.

74 Dwayne Ryan Menezes, "Canada, Indigenous Peoples and Northern Borders," *The Round Table* 106:5 (2017): 579–581.

75 P. Whitney Lackenbauer and Rasmus Leander Nielsen, "Close, Like-Minded Partners Committed to Democratic Principles: Settling the Hans Island/Tartupaluk Territorial Dispute," *Briefing Notes, Arctic Yearbook* (2022) available at https://arcticyearbook.com/images/yearbook/2022/Briefing-Notes/3BN_-_AY2022_Lackenbauer_Nielsen.pdf accessed 12 January 2024.

76 Mathieu Landriault, Pauline Pic and Frédéric Lasserre, "Beyond Hans Island: The Canada-Denmark Agreement's Possible Impact on Mobility and Continental Shelves," *International Journal* 78:1–2 (2023): 243–253. Complete agreement between Canada and Denmark available at https://www.ft.dk/ripdf/samling/20231/beslutningsforslag/b14/20231_b14_som_fremsat.pdf accessed 12 January 2024.

77 J. J. P. Smith, "Canada: The Arctic's Final Frontier: Canada and Denmark Settle the Territorial Question of Hans Island," *Asia-Pacific Journal of Ocean Law and Policy* 8:1 (2023): 156–164; Apostolos Tsiouvalas and Endalew Lijalem Enyew, "The Legal Implications of the 2022 Canada-Denmark/Greenland Agreement on Hans Island (Tartupaluk) for the Inuit Peoples of Greenland and Nunavut," *The Arctic Institute: Center for Circumpolar Security Studies*, 24 January 2023 available at https://www.thearcticinstitute.org/legal-implications-2022-canada-denmark-greenland-agreement-hans-island-tartupaluk-inuit-peoples-greenland-nunavut/ accessed 12 January 2024.

78 Mathieu Landriault, Pauline Pic and Frédéric Lasserre, "Beyond Hans Island: The Canada-Denmark Agreement's Possible Impact on Mobility and Continental Shelves," *International Journal* 78:1–2 (2023): 243–253.

The Marouini (or Maroni) River tract dispute (Suriname and French Guiana)

The Marouini (or Maroni) River was intended to act as an extension of the border between Suriname and French Guiana and to the Brazilian border.[79] The disputed area between the first two states covers approximately 5,000 square miles of the Amazon forest and may be rich in natural resources such as precious metals, minerals and hydroelectric potential.[80] Similar to other territorial differences in the Americas, the Marouini River tract dispute stems from a common colonial past in which European empires had little or no regard for the exact demarcation of boundaries.[81]

What is nowadays French Guiana was discovered in 1496 by Spain. Thereafter, the Dutch established settlements. Under the 1667 Treaty of Breda, the Dutch left the area. French settlements began in the late 1700s. The French government's intent at the time was to claim the area for France, and, in order to do so, they began to occupy the region with French colonialists. This was an attempt by means of "right-peopling"[82] the territory with French settlers to have grounds to claim sovereignty. However, the settlers moved on to larger cities.[83]

Legally and politically, the dispute seems to have been settled. With the 2021 protocol,[84] between the French and Surinamese authorities, the parties reached an agreement.[85] Technically, there is still a dispute over the area further south between the Litani and Marouini Rivers—i.e. Suriname claims the

79 Thomas W. Donovan, "The Marouini River Tract and Its Colonial Legacy in South America," *Chicago-Kent Journal of International and Comparative Law* 4 (2004): 1–28.

80 Ivan Sanderson, "A Journey in Dutch Guiana," *The Geographical Journal* 93:6 (1939): 468–489.

81 See Chapter 4.

82 Brendan O'Leary, "The Elements of Right-Sizing and Right-Peopling the State," in Brendan O'Leary, Ian S. Lustick and Thomas Callaghy, eds., *Right-Sizing the State: The Politics of Moving Borders* (Oxford: Oxford University Press, 2001), 15–73. This notion of "right-peopling" will be addressed extensively in Chapter 8.

83 Thomas W. Donovan, "The Marouini River Tract and Its Colonial Legacy in South America," *Chicago-Kent Journal of International and Comparative Law* 4 (2004): 1–28.

84 For an accessible yet thorough account of the preceding events see Patrick Blancodini, "The Suriname – French Guiana Border: Geopolitics of a Route that Remains to be Fixed," *Géoconfluences* (October 2019) available at https://geoconfluences.ens-lyon.fr/informations-scientifiques/dossiers-thematiques/la-frontiere-discontinuites-et-dynamiques/articles-scientifiques/maroni-frontiere-guyane-suriname/@@download_pdf?id=maroni-frontiere-guyane-suriname&uid=da98cb905dfa4bc2940331ebb2c26884 accessed 12 January 2024. Complete 2021 Protocol available at https://www.dna.sr/media/330804/21_1437__Pres._Ch._Santokhi__aanb._overeenkomst_protocol_tussen_Rep._Suriname_en_Franse_Rep._op_de_regeling_van_de_Grens_tussen_Suriname_en_Frans_Guyana_verdrag_parijs_30sept.1915_tot_vaststellen_van_de_Grens.pdf accessed 12 January 2024.

85 "A New Border on the River Maroni," *Initiatives for the Future of Great Rivers* available at https://www.initiativesrivers.org/actualites/a-border-on-the-river-maroni/ accessed 12 January 2024.

border is along the Marouini River to the east while France argues it is along the Litani River to the west.[86]

Regardless of the issues pertaining to law and politics, in terms of population, the area is characteristically multi-ethnic and includes among others the earliest inhabitants called Carib Indians, other Amerindian groups such as the Arawak Indians and the Maroons—in French Guiana referred to as Bushinenge—who are former African slaves that were brought to the region by Europeans and escaped captivity.[87] In fact, it has acted as a "refuge zone" as well for Amerindians fleeing European colonization.[88]

Maroons are present in both French Guiana—as an estimated 22 percent of the French Guiana population[89]—and in Suriname. As a result of the failed state situation during Suriname's civil war (1986–1992), Suriname's Maroon population moved to the Marouini River basin.[90] This is because, in contrast to the political turmoil in Suriname and the socioeconomic situation in neighbor states—e.g. Brazilian gold diggers—the multi-ethnic area is fairly peaceful because of the alliances and treaties between the various Maroon groups and regional indigenous peoples.[91] Finally, because of the informally established gold economy in the area,[92] there is an influx of Brazilian *garimpeiros*. This has led Brazilian migrants to accept transport protection by local Maroons, agree payment of informal taxes and respect customary laws.[93]

86 "Suriname," *CIA's The World Factbook (2022 Archive)* available at https://www.cia.gov/the-world-factbook/about/archives/2022/countries/suriname/#transnational-issues accessed 12 January 2024.

87 Thomas W. Donovan, "The Marouini River Tract and Its Colonial Legacy in South America," *Chicago-Kent Journal of International and Comparative Law* 4 (2004): 1–28.

88 Silvia Espelt-Bombin, "Makers and Keepers of Networks: Amerindian Spaces, Migrations, and Exchanges in the Brazilian Amazon and French Guiana, 1600–1730," *Ethnohistory* 65:4 (2018): 597–620.

89 T. Bellardie and M. Heemskerk, "Maroons in French Guiana: History, Culture, Demographics, and Socioeconomic Development along the Maroni and Lawa Rivers" available at https://social-solutions.net/data/images/reports/french-guiana-maroons.pdf accessed 12 January 2024.

90 Dirk Kruijt and Wim Hoogbergen, "Peaceful Relations in a Stateless Region: The Post-War Maroni River Borders in the Guianas," *Tijdschrift voor Economische en Sociale Geografie* 96:2 (2005): 199–208.

91 Shelby Matthew Givens, *An Ethnographic Study of Social Control and Dispute Settlement among the Aluku Maroons of French Guiana and Surinam South America* (Berkeley, CA: University of California, 1984).

92 Marjo de Theije, "Small-Scale Gold Mining in the Guianas: Mobility and Policy across National Borders," in Rosemarijn Hoefte, Matthew L. Bishop and Peter Clegg, eds., *Post-Colonial Trajectories in the Caribbean: The Three Guianas* (London and New York, NY: Routledge, 2016), 112–126.

93 Michel Jébrak, Arnauld Heuret and Pierre Rostan, "The Gold, Peoples and Multiple Frontiers of French Guiana," *The Extractive Industries and Society* 8:1 (2021): 8–22.

A multidimensional approach

While all the territorial disputes in the Americas have common roots, and these roots include a historical component stemming from a common colonial past, there are in all cases several pluralisms at play in which different agents interrelate in the domestic, regional and international contexts. These interrelations fuel intra-society differences resulting in ongoing differences and, at times, escalation into conflict.

A traditional scholarly approach in disciplines like law, political science and international relations would appeal to unidimensional views[94] and understand, for example, that a dispute, normatively, is between sovereign states only, i.e. for a linear vertical understanding, the only agents that can have legal and political sovereignty are states and, therefore, individuals and communities would not count. Another interpretation might be that a claiming party in a territorial dispute may perceive another agent as a mere attendee or viewer while another claiming party may recognize them as participants—i.e. a linear horizontal understanding. In turn, a nonlinear regressive view may help understand some disputes in the Americas. Although European colonialism is now non-existent, there are still some territorial disputes in the Americas, as this chapter has shown, that directly or indirectly involve European states. One consequence of this, for example, is that although American states are recognized in law as sovereign states, their European counterparts—and scholars—continue to justify their interference.

Territorial disputes encompass different issues at stake.[95] Obviously, depending on the dispute under study, these issues may be more tightly related to a particular pluralism. In that vein, agents such as individuals, communities and states may take a more visible role as a host of or a mere participant in the dispute while in some other cases it may be the local, regional and/or international contexts that take the center stage. Similarly, any of the realms—i.e. factual, normative and/or axiological—might help explain how and why a particular object—i.e. ideal, natural, cultural or metaphysical—could have triggered the escalation into conflict or could enable a peaceful settlement.

Scientific disciplines such as the legal and political sciences and international relations characterize these issues at stake by reference to the elements that make a political community or state—i.e. territory, population, government and law. For example, issues at stake pertaining to "territory" include strategic

94 For an understanding of dimensional approaches, including unidimensionality and multidimensionality, see Jorge E. Núñez, *Cosmopolitanism, State Sovereignty, International Law and Politics: A Theory* (London and New York, NY: Routledge, Taylor & Francis Group, 2023), Chapter 6.

95 See Jorge E. Núñez, *Territorial Disputes and State Sovereignty: International Law and Politics* (London and New York, NY: Routledge, Taylor & Francis Group, 2020), Chapter 4. See also Paul K. Huth, *Standing Your Ground. Territorial Disputes and International Conflict* (Ann Arbor, MI: University of Michigan Press, 2001), 72–85.

location, territorial integrity and natural resources; issues at stake pertaining to "population" may be related to bordering minorities, a refugee crisis, common ethnicity, etc. Finally, issues at stake pertaining to "government and law" could mean political unification, a leader's prestige, legal entitlement, etc.

The aforementioned issues at stake may be defined and characterized individually by different scientific disciplines. Unsurprisingly, real case territorial disputes involve a combination of these and other issues at stake. Similarly, legal and political sciences and international relations explore territorial disputes by reference to a particular pluralism, either incorporating a particular agent—e.g. individuals, communities or states; a particular role any of these agents may play—i.e. either hosts, participants, attendees or viewers; a particular context where their interrelations develop—i.e. domestic, regional or international; a particular realm of reference taken to understand, explain and assess these interrelations—i.e. factual, normative or axiological; or a particular object or subject of study—i.e. ideal, factual, natural or metaphysical. However, a more robust understanding of territorial disputes and their intricacy requires the study of all the different pluralisms at play and, consequently, should embrace all the issues at stake. The assessment and explanation of territorial disputes in the Americas are not an exception. Consequently, it is important to acknowledge that territorial disputes are multi-layered phenomena with different reasons behind them that have to do with cultural, legal, historical, sociological, geographical, financial and many other elements and features. The subsections below incorporate a multidimensional view of the four previously presented disputes by showcasing their different issues at stake and pluralisms.

Agents and players

The territorial disputes in the Americas that include European influence contain a permanent sociological feature that is present in other territorial disputes: pluralism in terms of agents and the roles they play. Whether acknowledged or not in law and politics, in all the cases referred to in this chapter, there are individuals, communities and states with common and conflicting interests.

In terms of individuals, it is important to discern between representatives and those being represented and their different interests. For instance, to assume that all governments, leaders and political parties aim to resolve the aforementioned territorial disputes permanently and peacefully is a simplistic idea. Domestic political prestige is an important motivator to start and maintain territorial disputes.[96] Cases such as the Falkland/Malvinas Islands dispute

96 See Chapter 4. See also Paul K. Huth, *Standing Your Ground. Territorial Disputes and International Conflict* (Ann Arbor, MI: University of Michigan Press, 2001); Youngho Kim, "Does Prestige Matter in International Politics?" *Journal of International and Area Studies* 11:1 (2004): 39–55; Brandon J. Kinne, "Dependent Diplomacy: Signalling, Strategy, and Prestige in the Diplomatic Network," *International Studies Quarterly* 58:2 (2014): 247–259; Daniel Markey, "Prestige and the Origins of War: Returning to Realism," *Security Studies* 8:4 (1999):

clearly show that emotive and symbolic elements and factors can be manipulated. As stated in Núñez (2020),[97] the use of territorial disputes in this way is twofold. Firstly, a linear vertical dimensional view acknowledges that the leader's prestige directly feeds their personal and political internal influence. Secondly, a nonlinear dimensional self-referred approach helps explain how and why governments and leaders use territorial disputes to divert internal attention away from problems such as inflation, corruption, lack of security and unemployment, while they legitimize ordinary and extraordinary measures such as financial endowment, political intervention and censorship.[98]

With reference to communities, the Falklands/Malvinas case and examples like the San Andrés, Providencia and Santa Catalina archipelago and the Marouini (or Maroni) River tract demonstrate that there are other agents to be considered in addition to sovereign states—i.e. indigenous peoples and/or implanted populations. Therefore, a multidimensional understanding of these differences enables the acknowledgment that any agreement between states involved in these differences should foster the inclusion of those inhabiting and/or historically making use of the territory and somehow accommodate their communities' interests—as Canada and Denmark are doing with the Inuit people in the Hans Island case.[99] A point worth noting, and dissimilar to the Hans Island case in which both Canada and Denmark perceive indigenous peoples in the same manner, is that in the Falkland/Malvinas Islands case the islanders are mere attendees for Argentina because the Argentine government has systematically neglected their right to participate in any negotiation about sovereignty over the territory in question, whereas the United Kingdom accepts them as participants.[100]

Finally, it is puzzling that—in a time in which decolonial positions are gaining momentum[101]—central states that are alien to the region, such as the

---

126–172; Barry O'Neill, *Honor, Symbols and War* (Ann Arbor, MI: University of Michigan Press, 1999).

97 Jorge E. Núñez, *Territorial Disputes and State Sovereignty: International Law and Politics* (London and New York, NY: Routledge, Taylor & Francis Group, 2020), Chapter 6.

98 Paul K. Huth, *Standing Your Ground: Territorial Disputes and International Conflict* (Ann Arbor, MI: University of Michigan Press, 2001), 171–172 and 178–179.

99 The cases of indigenous rights and implanted populations will be addressed extensively in Chapter 8.

100 For the notion and characterization of agents such as hosts, participants, attendees and viewers see Jorge E. Núñez, *Cosmopolitanism, State Sovereignty, International Law and Politics: A Theory* (London and New York, NY: Routledge, Taylor & Francis Group, 2023), Chapter 4.

101 The amount written on decolonial positions is vast. See, for example, Gustavo Quintero, "Transnational Legacies of Revolt: Approaching Decolonial Struggles in the Americas," *Journal of Latin American Cultural Studies* 29:3 (2020): 469–478; Sergio Wanderley and Amon Barros, "Decoloniality, Geopolitics of Knowledge and Historic Turn: Towards a Latin American Agenda," *Management & Organizational History* 14:1 (2019): 79–97; Kiran Asher, "Latin American Decolonial Thought, or Making the Subaltern Speak," *Geography Compass* 7:12 (2013): 832–842.

United Kingdom and France, still have a direct and indirect presence in the Americas through their involvement in these territorial disputes and, consequently, in domestic and regional law and politics. Therein, a dimensional nonlinear regressive approach applied to these situations raises questions about the viability of international law principles like the non-intervention of European states in the affairs of America based on the Monroe, Calvo and Drago doctrines.[102]

Contexts

The domestic context seems to influence territorial disputes and whether they result in peaceful and permanent settlements or unstable situations, even in cases in which the disputes have been resolved. For instance, the agreement over Hans Island between Canada and Denmark suggests the likelihood for a peaceful understanding between challenger and challenged agents if they both have stable legal and political internal situations. Conversely, when internal situations encompass issues such as financial, legal and political instability including inflation, hyperinflation, unemployment and corruption, there seems to be a tendency to maintain these disputes as partly or completely unresolved—as in the Marouini (or Maroni) River tract and Falklands/Malvinas cases. Internal issues can also result in an opt out from fully enforcing international decisions and agreements—as in the case of the archipelago of San Andrés, Providencia and Santa Catalina.

The regional context adds several facets. Firstly, neighbor states and their populations may have competing interests with those of the challenger and challenged agents. These interests may refer, for example, to issues related to the territory itself—e.g. natural resources, borders, defense; population—e.g. minorities' rights, migration, asylum seekers, nationalism; and government—e.g. leader's internal prestige directly linked to the state's regional relevance in terms of, for example, security. Secondly, another aspect is the existence of regional organizations such as the OAS and, because of the direct and indirect presence of European states in the cases referred to in this chapter, supranational and intergovernmental organizations such as the EU. Interestingly, American states tend to deal with their European counterparts in territorial disputes as solo players. In the Falklands/Malvinas and the Marouini (or Maroni) River tract cases, Argentina and Suriname seem to leave the regional context outside of the dispute, unless it can help garner support from other continental actors. Arguably, Argentina's and Suriname's bargaining positions could be strengthened by shifting the national-cause stance toward a more regional approach. For example, instead of stating "the Malvinas/Falklands

102 See Chapter 4.

are Argentine,"[103] they could claim "the Malvinas/Falklands are American (or Latin American)."[104]

The influence of the international context in the territorial disputes described in this chapter is evident. Central states like France and the United Kingdom have a constant presence—i.e. financially, militarily, politically, etc.—in disputes that have little to do with their own legally defined domestic jurisdiction. These direct and indirect influences by European states that are alien to the region suggest they still follow a unidimensional linear vertical approach when dealing with their American, and arguably weaker, counterparts. Controversially, these central states are meant to have horizontal respect for their peers in law and politics under the principle of equality of the states-e.g. art. 2, paragraph 1 of the United Nations Charter. Furthermore, in addition to the influence of European states, there are several other central states, such as the United States, the Russian Federation, India and China, with direct and indirect influence in the Americas.[105] Therefore, excluding the international context in the study of territorial disputes will result in a narrow and, arguably, incomplete view.

Realms

Like other territorial disputes in the Americas, the cases explored in this chapter raise issues pertaining to the factual, normative and axiological realms. Depending on the realm of reference, different scholarly disciplines such as legal and political sciences and international relations take different unidimensional approaches. For instance, all theories applied in the legal and political sciences that refer to the state have to do with the same necessary elements: population, territory and government. Depending on which element the theory focuses on, either population, territory or government, the factual, normative or axiological realm may seem to take center stage. For example, in law, sovereignty is currently characterized by reference to territorial sovereignty. In turn, political science, when considering the state, looks mainly at the relationship

103 Magdalena Lisińka, "Is the Archipelago a Political Tool? The Role of the Falkland Islands Sovereignty Dispute in Argentina Policy During the Kirchner Era," *Ad Americam. Journal of American Studies* 17 (2016): 119–134; Silvia R. Tandeciarz, *Citizens of Memory: Affect, Representation, and Human Rights in Postdictatorship Argentina* (Lewisburg, WV: Bucknell University Press, 2017), xvii.

104 Ignacio Gutierrez Bróndolo, "Malvinas en la Nueva Perspectiva Latinoamericana," *Universidad Nacional de Rosario* (2017) available at https://rephip.unr.edu.ar/items/8d2f1624-2706-4254-ad1b-7ff25898a774 accessed 26 January 2024; Alberto Monzón and Claudio Briceño, "Las Islas del Atlántico Sur y la Integración Latinoamericana," *Humania del Sur* 7:12 (2012): 51–72; Stella Krepp, "A View from the South: the Falklands/Malvinas and Latin America," *Journal of Transatlantic Studies* 15:4 (2017): 348–265; and many others.

105 The influence of these states in territorial disputes in the Americas will be reviewed in Chapter 6.

between two necessary conditions: population and government.[106] This is neither an epistemological and methodological difference nor is it minor. The different stands on realms are the roots behind scholarly understandings of concepts such as self-determination. More precisely, because state sovereignty is normatively understood as territorial sovereignty, self-determination might challenge one of the elements that integrates a sovereign state, such as territory—by giving preeminence to another element such as population.

On the surface, the Falklands/Malvinas, the San Andrés, Providencia and Santa Catalina archipelago, the Marouini (or Maroni) River tract and the Hans Island cases appear to have different factual elements and features. In terms of space, according to its scope in a narrow sense, i.e. territory, or space according to the way it is perceived as physical space,[107] there are obvious differences between disputes that include islands and disputes that are within mainland states. Normatively, these factual differences may bring about different consequences in, for example, the applicable law—e.g. whether the Law of the Sea is applicable or not. Moreover, the different terrain or actual and potential changes over time—e.g. the change of a river course or overlapping areas when two or more states are bordering neighbors—may present challenges in terms of the enforcement of a legal norm or agreement.

Taking into account the three realms, a more complex point, controversially, seems to be about the different ways in which the peoples concerned with the disputed territories are acknowledged. In fact, these peoples might have been somehow connected to the land for generations—e.g. indigenous populations; they might have been brought by former colonial empires to justify a claim to sovereignty—i.e. by means of "right-peopling" the territory; or they might have settled a long time ago because of any other reason but colonial intent—i.e. settlers, as broadly understood. Therefore, it is relatively simple to understand factually how and why these peoples are related to the territory in question. However simple in fact, axiologically, these peoples have been consistently treated differently by sovereign states involved in territorial disputes. These different axiological choices concerning these peoples have resulted in different ways to deal with them normatively. Clearly, the Falklands/Malvinas and the San Andrés, Providencia and Santa Catalina archipelago cases show implanted populations—by means of "right-peopling," brought to the land originally as slaves, or settlers arriving for any other reason—and these populations, axiologically, are perceived differently by the challenger and challenging sovereign states. As a result, normatively, the Falkland/Malvinas Islanders

106 For more detail about the state, including a conceptual view and different theories, see Jorge E. Núñez, *Territorial Disputes and State Sovereignty: International Law and Politics* (London and New York, NY: Routledge, Taylor & Francis Group, 2020), Chapter 2.

107 For different notions of space see Jorge E. Núñez, *Cosmopolitanism, State Sovereignty, International Law and Politics: A Theory* (London and New York, NY: Routledge, Taylor & Francis Group, 2023), Chapter 6.

and the Raizals are either acknowledged as having legal and political standing to decide their legal or political status as communities or as not having this standing—i.e. it is acknowledged if they have or do not have the right to self-determination. Conversely, the Hans Island case demonstrates that sovereign states might take a different approach and agree on the kind of standing peoples concerned in the territorial dispute could have. Despite the fact the latter case refers to an indigenous population, i.e. the Inuit people, and the former two cases have to do with implanted populations, i.e. the Falkland/Malvinas Islanders and the Raizals, it is interesting to observe that sovereign states make these different axiological choices that result in, normatively, different consequences.[108]

Modes of existence

The ideal object called "justice" is an abstract notion that can imply myriad things.[109] Addressing this feature at the individual level, Rawls explains that questions of distributive justice arise only under certain circumstances of justice, that is to say in cases of limited resources and limited altruism.[110] In territorial disputes, what Rawls labels at the individual level in ideal terms as moderate scarcity or limited resources finds its parallel in the non-sovereign third territory under dispute—i.e. the only "thing" all the agents are claiming exclusive sovereignty over.[111] In all the cases included in this chapter, the non-sovereign third territories under dispute stem from colonialism and are still influenced by former colonial powers. Therein, the question about historical entitlement to these territories is tightly linked to the question about the justice behind their acquisition. Faced with the idea of applying any kind of principle based on a historical entitlement, there are two main problems. First, based on natural and cultural objects, it is of utmost importance to demonstrate the historical account—i.e. what actually happened, who was the first one to discover the territory, or to have a population there, etc. Second, the challenger and challenged agents would need to decide what type of act makes their claimed rights just—i.e. the first one setting foot on the territory, the first one to have a permanent settlement, etc.[112]

108 The cases of indigenous rights and implanted populations will be addressed extensively in Chapter 8.

109 For a sample of notions regarding justice see Hans Kelsen, "What is Justice?," in Hans Kelsen, ed., *Essays in Legal and Moral Philosophy* (Dordrecht: D. Reidel Publishing Company, 1973), 1–26.

110 John Rawls, *Justice as Fairness* (Cambridge, MA: Harvard University Press, 2003), 109.

111 Jorge E. Núñez, *Sovereignty Conflicts and International Law and Politics: A Distributive Justice Issue* (London and New York, NY: Routledge, Taylor & Francis Group, 2017), Chapter 6.

112 For a detailed discussion about the just acquisition principle applied to territorial disputes and sovereignty conflicts see Jorge E. Núñez, *Sovereignty Conflicts and International Law*

In addition to the discussion about ideal objects and notions such as justice and, for example, whether it is just or not to still count on the European presence in territorial disputes in the Americas, the cases explored in this chapter encompass several natural and cultural elements that go beyond any discussion about historical entitlement. The previous sections have included brief accounts in each case about these natural and cultural objects. For instance, there were references to natural objects that may include rivers, forests, the seabed, fauna and flora; and cultural objects that may involve agreed boundaries, the means for the exploration and exploitation of natural resources, and the norms of international law. These and other objects may influence territorial disputes in different ways. First, the objects themselves may change over time—e.g. characteristics of the terrain can fluctuate and may make it easier or more difficult to enforce the agreed border; they may currently present problematic circumstances—e.g. access to the exploration and exploitation of natural resources in the seabed may be impossible or onerous. Second, there is the perception of these objects according to different agents—e.g. new technologies may bring about new ways to maximize the use of the territory under dispute and their existing natural resources. Tightly linked to perceptions, some of these disputes clearly show that they are often highly emotional, with the participants taking the view that "victory for us is to see you suffer."[113] Interestingly, existing scholarship tends to carefully neglect non-rational cultural elements and features such as national culture, nationalism, patriotism and emotion. Cases like the Falkland/Malvinas Islands and the San Andrés, Providencia and Santa Catalina archipelago suggest that there is a pressing need for a multidimensional approach that moves away from disciplinary unidimensionality and embraces rationality, emotion, nationalism, prejudice and different perspectives. Ergo, a multidimensional approach that includes interdisciplinary as well as non-disciplinary understandings is needed because of the multi-faceted and multi-layered nature of territorial disputes.

Conclusion

This chapter presented current territorial disputes in the Americas in which there is direct and/or indirect European influence. First, it was shown that there are common roots in all cases concerning the historical component based on colonial times and the lack of clear border demarcation at the time the territory was established or, in the cases in which the demarcation had taken place in law, the difficulty in applying a decision to the areas in question.

and Politics: A Distributive Justice Issue (London and New York, NY: Routledge, Taylor & Francis Group, 2017), Chapter 6.

113 Philip C. Winslow, *Victory for Us Is to See You Suffer: In the West Bank with the Palestinians and the Israelis* (Boston, MA: Beacon Press, 2007).

The brief account provided in each case demonstrated that multi-faceted and multi-layered territorial disputes are the result not only of the historical background and the lack of clearly defined boundaries in colonial times but also a number of contemporary factors, including current international law such as the Law of the Sea; new technologies for exploration and exploitation of natural resources; the existence or absence of indigenous or implanted populations in the territories under question; and non-rational elements and factors such as nationalism.

Some partial conclusions indicate that any population in a disputed territory, whether implanted for "right-peopling" reasons or indigenous, may present a different interest to the ones represented by the claimant sovereign states. Regardless of these reasons, it is clear these peoples should be somehow included in any study and, arguably, any negotiation concerning the sovereignty in question, if the aim is to understand the dispute's intricate nature and find a peaceful and permanent settlement between the claimant agents.

Furthermore, all the cases explored in this chapter provided evidence that these differences are influenced by the domestic, regional and international contexts. Therefore, to leave any of these contexts aside when explaining and assessing these differences is to have a partial and, arguably, a biased view about them. A controversial issue that appears in all cases was the dichotomy between current international law and political culture supporting the notion of sovereign equality of states and realpolitik clearly demonstrating there is still interference in the Americas by former colonial powers.

Finally, the aforementioned dichotomy in the territorial disputes explored in this chapter, and in particular in cases such as the Falkland/Malvinas Islands and the Marouini (or Maroni) River tract, opens up the question of whether a regional approach in the form of a bloc, sub-continental or continental alliance could strengthen the position of continental actors against external interests in the region by bettering the bargaining power of what could otherwise be individually weak international actors.

The following chapters will explore other existing territorial disputes that encompass central and non-central states. In contrast to this chapter, the focus will be on disputes pertaining to regional agents only and, using cases of the interference of agents alien to the region, the study will include non-European states such as Russia, China and India. Despite the circumstantial differences between the cases reviewed in this chapter and those that will be reviewed in subsequent ones, common threads will be evident, including their common historical roots, the several agents at play, the way the different contexts influence each other and the tension between international law and politics and realpolitik.

Bibliography

Asher, Kiran. "Latin American Decolonial Thought, or Making the Subaltern Speak." *Geography Compass* 7:12 (2013): 832–842.

Aulich, James. *Framing the Falklands War: Nationhood, Culture, and Identity.* Milton Keynes: Open University Press, 1992.
Beck, Peter. "Britain's Falkland Future—the Need to Look Back." *The Round Table* 73 (1984): 139–152.
Beck, Peter. "Cooperative Confrontation in the Falkland Island Dispute." *Journal of Interamerican Studies and World Affairs* 24 (1982): 37–57.
Beck, Peter. "Looking at the Falkland Islands from Antarctica: The Broader Regional Perspective." *Polar Record* 30 (1994): 167–180.
Beck, Peter. *The Falkland Islands as an International Problem.* London and New York, NY: Routledge, 1998.
Beck, Peter. "The Future of the Falkland Islands: A Solution Made in Hong Kong?" *International Affairs, Royal Institute of International Affairs* 61 (1985): 643–660.
Bellardie, T. and M. Heemskerk. "Maroons in French Guiana: History, Culture, Demographics, and Socioeconomic Development along the Maroni and Lawa Rivers" available at https://social-solutions.net/data/images/reports/french-guiana-maroons.pdf accessed 12 January 2024.
Blancodini, Patrick. "The Suriname—French Guiana Border: Geopolitics of a Route that Remains to Be Fixed." *Géoconfluences*, October 2019 available at https://geoconfluences.ens-lyon.fr/informations-scientifiques/dossiers-thematiques/la-frontiere-discontinuites-et-dynamiques/articles-scientifiques/maroni-frontiere-guyane-suriname/@@download_pdf?id=maroni-frontiere-guyane-suriname&uid=da98cb905dfa4bc2940331ebb2c26884 accessed 12 January 2024.
Caillet-Bois, Ricardo. *Una Tierra Argentina: Las Islas Malvinas.* Buenos Aires: Peuser, 1948.
Carvalho, Rogério Do Nascimento. "New Alliances for Argentina with the Discovery of Mineral Reserves in the Falkland Islands." *The Round Table* 111:1 (2022): 141–142.
Clare, Louise A. *Politics, Propaganda and the Press: International Reactions to the Falklands/Malvinas Conflict.* London and New York, NY: Routledge, 2023.
Consani, Norberto, Federico Martín Gomez and Leandro Enrique Sánchez. *Malvinas y la Construcción de un Reclamo Soberano: Pasado, Presente y Futuro.* La Plata: Universidad Nacional de La Plata, 2017.
Day, Alan J., ed. *Border and Territorial Disputes.* Essex: Longman, 1982.
de Albuquerque, Klaus and William F Stinner. "The Colombianization of Black San Andreans." *Caribbean Studies* 17:3/4 (1977–1978): 171–181.
de Theije, Marjo. "Small-Scale Gold Mining in the Guianas: Mobility and Policy across National Borders." In *Post-Colonial Trajectories in the Caribbean: The Three Guianas*, Hoefte, Rosemarijn, Bishop, Matthew L. and Clegg, Peter, eds. 112–126. London and New York, NY: Routledge, 2016.
Diemer, Christian and Amalija Šeparović. "Territorial Questions and Maritime Delimitation with Regard to Nicaragua's Claims to the San Andrés Archipelago." *Heidelberg Journal of International Law* 66 (2006): 167–185.
Donovan, Thomas W. "The Marouini River Tract and Its Colonial Legacy in South America." *Chicago-Kent Journal of International and Comparative Law* 4 (2004): 1–28.
Espelt-Bombin, Silvia. "Makers and Keepers of Networks: Amerindian Spaces, Migrations, and Exchanges in the Brazilian Amazon and French Guiana, 1600–1730." *Ethnohistory* 65:4 (2018): 597–620.
Esteves Duarte, Érico, ed. *The Falklands/Malvinas War in the South Atlantic.* Cham: Palgrave Macmillan, 2021.

Givens, Shelby Matthew. *An Ethnographic Study of Social Control and Dispute Settlement among the Aluku Maroons of French Guiana and Surinam South America.* Berkeley, CA: University of California, 1984.

Goebel, Julius. *The Struggle for the Falklands: A Study in Legal and Diplomatic History.* New Haven, CT: Yale University Press, 1982.

González, Pablo Alonso, Wilhelm Londoño, and Eva Parga-Dans. "Equality and Hierarchy, Sovereignty and Multiculturalism: The Heritagisation of Raizals in Santa Catalina (Colombia)." *Journal of Ethnic and Migration Studies* 46:19 (2018): 4066–4085.

Grandpierron, Matthieu. "Preserving 'Great Power Status': The Complex Case of the British Intervention in the Falklands (1982)." *Croatian International Relations Review* 23:79 (2017): 127–156.

Grandpierron, Matthieu. "The British Use of Domestic Political Situations during the Falklands War." *The Round Table* 111:1 (2022): 56–68.

Grossman, Nienke. "Territorial and Maritime Dispute." *American Journal of International Law* 107:2 (2013): 396–403.

Gustafson, Lowell Steven. *The Sovereignty Dispute over the Falkland (Malvinas) Islands.* Oxford: Oxford University Press, 1988.

Gutierrez Bróndolo, Ignacio. "Malvinas en la Nueva Perspectiva Latinoamericana." *Universidad Nacional de Rosario,* 2017 available at https://rephip.unr.edu.ar/bitstream/handle/2133/9011/MALVINAS%20EN%20LA%20NUEVA%20PERSPECTIVA%20%20LATINOAMERICANA.pdf accessed 26 January 2024.

Hassan, Farooq. "The Sovereignty Dispute over the Falkland Islands." *Virginia Journal of International Law* 23:1 (1982): 53–74.

Headland, Robert Keith. "Territory and Claims in the Antarctic Treaty Region: A Disquisition on Historical and Recent Developments." *The Cartographic Journal* 57:2 (2020): 160–174.

Howkins, Adrian. "Latin America and Antarctica." In *Oxford Research Encyclopedia of Latin American History,* 2017 available at https://oxfordre.com/latinamericanhistory/display/10.1093/acrefore/9780199366439.001.0001/acrefore-9780199366439-e-434 accessed 9 May 2024.

Huth, Paul K. *Standing Your Ground: Territorial Disputes and International Conflict.* Ann Arbor, MI: University of Michigan Press, 2001.

Jébrak, Michel, Arnauld Heuret and Pierre Rostan. "The Gold, Peoples and Multiple Frontiers of French Guiana." *The Extractive Industries and Society* 8:1 (2021): 8–22.

Joyner, Christopher C. "Anglo-Argentine Rivalry After the Falklands/Malvinas War: Laws, Geopolitics, and the Antarctic Connection." *Lawyer of the Americas* 15:3 (1984): 467–502.

Keeling, D. J. "A Geopolitical Perspective on Argentina's Malvinas/Falkland Claims." *Global Discourse* 3:1 (2013): 158–165.

Kelsen, Hans. "What is Justice?" In *Essays in Legal and Moral Philosophy,* Kelsen, Hans, ed. 1–26. Dordrecht: D. Reidel Publishing Company, 1973.

Kessel, A. H. "Canadian Arctic Sovereignty: Myths and Realities." In *Governing the North American Arctic,* Berry, D. A., Bowles, N. and Jones, H., eds. 242–246. London: Palgrave Macmillan, 2016.

Kim, Youngho. "Does Prestige Matter in International Politics?" *Journal of International and Area Studies* 11:1 (2004): 39–55.

Kinne, Brandon J. "Dependent Diplomacy: Signalling, Strategy, and Prestige in the Diplomatic Network." *International Studies Quarterly* 58:2 (2014): 247–259.
Krepp, Stella. "A View from the South: the Falklands/Malvinas and Latin America." *Journal of Transatlantic Studies* 15:4 (2017): 348–265.
Kruijt, Dirk and Wim Hoogbergen. "Peaceful Relations in a Stateless Region: The Post-War Maroni River Borders in the Guianas." *Tijdschrift voor Economische en Sociale Geografie* 96:2 (2005): 199–208.
Lackenbauer, P. Whitney and Rasmus Leander Nielsen. "Close, Like-Minded Partners Committed to Democratic Principles: Settling the Hans Island/Tartupaluk Territorial Dispute." *Briefing Notes, Arctic Yearbook*, 2022 available at https://arcticyearbook.com/images/yearbook/2022/Briefing-Notes/3BN_-_AY2022_Lackenbauer_Nielsen.pdf accessed 12 January 2024.
Landriault, Mathieu, Pauline Pic and Frédéric Lasserre. "Beyond Hans Island: The Canada-Denmark Agreement's Possible Impact on Mobility and Continental Shelves." *International Journal* 78:1–2 (2023): 243–253.
Leung, Ray Chung Hang. "The Discursive Positioning of the Falkland Islands (Las Islas Malvinas): A Corpus-Based Collocational Analysis of British and Argentinian Websites." *Global: A Journal of Language, Culture and Communication* 5 (2017): 1–31.
Levy, Jack S. and Lily I. Vakili. "Diversion Action by Authoritarian Regimes: Argentina and the Falklands/Malvinas Case." In *The Internationalization of Communal Strife*, Midlarsky, Manus I., ed. 118–146. London: Routledge, 1992.
Lisińka, Magdalena. "Is the Archipelago a Political Tool? The Role of the Falkland Islands Sovereignty Dispute in Argentina Policy During the Kirchner Era." *Ad American. Journal of American Studies* 17 (2016): 119–134.
Lisińska, Magdalena. "The Falklands/Malvinas as an Identity Dispute: A Constructivist Analysis of the British and Argentinian Positions." *The International Spectator* 59:2 (2023): 95–111.
Livingstone, Grace. "Oil and the Falklands/Malvinas: Oil Companies, Governments and Islanders." *The Round Table* 111:1 (2022): 91–103.
Lorenz, Federico. "Malvinas/Falklands War: Changes in the Idea of Nationhood, the Local and National, in a Post-Dictatorship Context—Argentina, 1982–2007." In *The Argentinian Dictatorship and its Legacy. Studies of the Americas*, Grigera, J. and Zorzoli, L., eds. 197–209. Cham: Palgrave Macmillan, 2020.
Markey, Daniel. "Prestige and the Origins of War: Returning to Realism." *Security Studies* 8:4 (1999): 126–172.
Menezes, Dwayne Ryan. "Canada, Indigenous Peoples and Northern Borders." *The Round Table* 106:5 (2017): 579–581.
Miller, Vaughne. "Argentina and the Falkland Islands," *House of Commons Library*, 2012 available at https://researchbriefings.parliament.uk/ResearchBriefing/Summary/SN05602 accessed 17 May 2025.
Monoghan, David. *The Falklands War*. London: Palgrave Macmillan, 1998.
Monzón, Alberto and Claudio Briceño. "Las Islas del Atlántico Sur y la Integración Latinoamericana." *Humania del Sur* 7:12 (2012): 51–72.
Morán, Sabrina. "The Malvinas War in the Democratic Transition in Argentina. Conflicts and Tension within a Demalvinized Political Agenda." *Cuadernos de Marte* 9:15 (2018): 173–207.
Muñoz, Helardo. "Efectos y Lecciones del Conflicto de las Malvinas." *Estudios Internacionales* 15:60 (1982): 499–512.

Newton, Arthur P. *The Colonising Activities of the English Puritans.* New York, NY: Kennikat Press, 1966.

Nieto-Navia, Rafael. "Some Remarks on the Territorial and Maritime Dispute (Nicaragua v. Colombia) Case." In *Law of the Sea, From Grotius to the International Tribunal for the Law of the Sea*, del Castillo, Lilian, ed. 545–562. Leiden: Brill, Nijhoff, 2015.

Norpoth, Helmut. "The Falklands War and Government Popularity in Britain: Rally without Consequence or Surge without Decline?" *Electoral Studies* 6:1 (1987): 3–16.

Núñez, Jorge E. *Cosmopolitanism, State Sovereignty, International Law and Politics: A Theory.* London and New York, NY: Routledge, Taylor & Francis Group, 2023.

Núñez, Jorge E. *Sovereignty Conflicts and International Law and Politics: A Distributive Justice Issue.* London and New York, NY: Routledge, Taylor & Francis Group, 2017.

Núñez, Jorge E. *Territorial Disputes and State Sovereignty: International Law and Politics.* London and New York, NY: Routledge, Taylor & Francis Group, 2020.

O'Leary, Brendan. "The Elements of Right-Sizing and Right-Peopling the State." In *Right-Sizing the State: The Politics of Moving Borders*, O'Leary, Brendan, Lustick, Ian S. and Callaghy, Thomas, eds. 15–73. Oxford: Oxford University Press, 2001.

O'Neill, Barry. *Honor, Symbols and War.* Ann Arbor, MI: The University of Michigan Press, 1999.

Palestini, Lorenzo. "The Territorial and Maritime Dispute (Nicaragua v. Colombia): On Territorial Sovereignty and the International Court of Justice's Failure to Rule on the Geographical Scope of the Archipelago of San Andrés." *The Law and Practice of International Courts and Tribunals Journal* 15:1 (2016): 56–80.

Pascoe, Graham and Peter Pepper. *Falklands Facts and Fallacies: The Falkland Islands in History and International Law.* Surrey: Grosvenor House Publishing, 2022.

Pedrosa, Fernando and Guillermo C. Mira Delli-Zotti. *Revisiting the Falklands-Malvinas Question: Transnational and Interdisciplinary Perspectives.* London: University of London Press, 2021.

Perez, Jorge Gabriel. "El Conflicto de las Malvinas a través del Prisma de la Geopolítica de Recursos Naturales." *Coleção Meira Mattos: Revista das Ciências Militares* 14:51 (2020): 331–356.

Quintero, Gustavo. "Transnational Legacies of Revolt: Approaching Decolonial Struggles in the Americas." *Journal of Latin American Cultural Studies* 29:3 (2020): 469–478.

Ramírez, Walter Arévalo. "Resistance to Territorial and Maritime Delimitation Judgments of the International Court of Justice and Clashes with 'Territory Clauses' in the Constitutions of Latin American States." *Leiden Journal of International Law* 35:1 (2022):185–208.

Rawls, John. *Justice as Fairness.* Cambridge, MA: Harvard University Press, 2003.

Rodríguez, Yliana V. and Adolfo Elizaincín. "Competing Place Names: Malvinas vs. Falklands: When a Sovereignty Conflict Becomes a Name Conflict." *Journal of Language Aggression and Conflict* 11:2 (2023): 226–255.

Ross, James. "Routes for Roots: Entering the 21st Century in San Andrés Island, Colombia." *Caribbean Studies* 35:1 (2007): 3–36.

Rowland, Donald. "Spanish Occupation of the Island of Old Providence, or Santa Catalina, 1641–1670." *The Hispanic American Historical Review* 15:3 (1935): 298–312.

Sanders, David, Hugh Ward, David Marsh and Tony Fletcher. "Government Popularity and the Falklands War: A Reassessment." *British Journal of Political Science* 17:3 (1987): 281–313.

Sanderson, Ivan. "A Journey in Dutch Guiana." *The Geographical Journal* 93:6 (1939): 468–489.

Schofield, Clive and Andreas Østhagen. "A Divided Arctic: Maritime Boundary Agreements and Disputes in the Arctic Ocean." In *Handbook on Geopolitics and Security in the Arctic: The High North Between Cooperation and Confrontation*, Weber, Joachim, ed. 171–191. Cham: Springer: 2020.

Smith, J. J. P. "Canada: The Arctic's Final Frontier: Canada and Denmark Settle the Territorial Question of Hans Island." *Asia-Pacific Journal of Ocean Law and Policy* 8:1 (2023): 156–164.

Smith, Robert W. and L. Thomas Bradford. "Island Disputes and the Law of the Sea: An Examination of Sovereignty and Delimitation Disputes." *Maritime Briefing, International Boundary Research Unit* 2:4 (1998): 1–26.

Stevenson, Christopher. "Hans Off!: The Struggle for Hans Island and the Potential Ramifications for International Border Dispute Resolution." *Boston College International and Comparative Law Review* 30:1 (2007): 263–275.

Strange, Ian. *The Falkland Islands.* Devon: David and Charles, 1972.

Tandeciarz, Silvia R. *Citizens of Memory: Affect, Representation, and Human Rights in Postdictatorship Argentina.* Lewisburg, WV: Bucknell University Press, 2017.

Tokatlian, J. G. "Colombia at War: The Search for a Peace Diplomacy." *International Journal of Politics, Culture, and Society* 14 (2000): 333–362.

Tsiouvalas, Apostolos and Endalew Lijalem Enyew. "The Legal Implications of the 2022 Canada-Denmark/Greenland Agreement on Hans Island (Tartupaluk) for the Inuit Peoples of Greenland and Nunavut." *The Arctic Institute: Center for Circumpolar Security Studies,* 24 January 2023 available at https://www.thearcticinstitute.org/legal-implications-2022-canada-denmark-greenland-agreement-hans-island-tartupaluk-inuit-peoples-greenland-nunavut/ accessed 12 January 2024.

van Logchem, Youri. "Exploration and Exploitation of Oil and Gas Resources in Maritime Areas of Overlap under International Law: The Falklands (Malvinas)." In *Hague Yearbook of International Law/Annuaire de La Haye de Droit International*, Kok, Ruth A. and Vidmar, Jure, eds. 29–64. Leiden: Brill, Nijhoff, 2015.

Wanderley, Sergio and Amon Barros. "Decoloniality, Geopolitics of Knowledge and Historic Turn: Towards a Latin American Agenda." *Management & Organizational History* 14:1 (2019): 79–97.

Wang, Jingyao and Qi Xu. "Reflections on the Nicaragua v. Colombia Case (2022): From the Perspective of Traditional Fishing Rights." *Frontiers in Marine Science* 10 (2023): 1–13.

Wiegand, Krista E. "Territorial Dispute Strategies as Diversionary Behavior." *Journal of Territorial and Maritime Studies* 5:1 (2018): 42–63.

Wilson, Peter J. *Crab Antics: The Social Anthropology of English-Speaking Negro Societies of the Caribbean.* New Haven, CT: Yale University Press, 1973.

Winslow, Philip C. *Victory for Us Is To See You Suffer: In the West Bank with the Palestinians and the Israelis.* Boston, MA: Beacon Press, 2007.

Xhelilaj, Ermal and Kristofor Lapa. "Territorial Claims in North Polar Maritime Zone in View of International Security." *Transactions on Maritime Science* 11:01 (2022): 278–285.

6 Neo-colonialism and colonial mindset

Introduction

The previous chapters showed that several territorial disputes in the Americas are rooted in a similar colonial past. Chapter 4 provided a broad introduction to three different historical stages in the Americas: pre-Columbian, post-Columbian but pre-independence and post-independence. Chapter 5 referred to the ongoing direct and indirect influence of some European states on the continent. In turn, this chapter will continue the exploration of the past and ongoing influences pertaining to the origin, continuation and potential escalation into conflict of territorial disputes in the region, but with a focus on the interference by other central sovereign states. For instance, in modern times, Latin America has been under the influence of either the United States or Russia. More currently, while the United States and Russia have had (and still do have) different degrees of interference in domestic and regional legal and political agendas of other states on the continent, there are other sovereign states such as China and India that have a strong direct and indirect presence and are in the ascendancy.[1] That is because, after the end of the Soviet Union era and the emergence of new central agents such as China and India, there is an evident shift to a multipolar world. Therein, it is not surprising that these states have a direct and indirect involvement in territorial disputes on the continent.

A multidimensional understanding of these interferences helps to discern, for example, linear vertical and horizontal dimensional differences in the interrelation of American states and those other central, strong or advantaged agents like the United States, Russia, China and India. Explored by means of a multidimensional understanding, these interferences regarding territorial disputes clearly show the tension between law and politics. In brief, although public international law acknowledges sovereign equality, i.e. the linear horizontal dimension, realpolitik suggests the bargaining power of the most advantaged party in the bilateral relationship in a territorial dispute between

1 The ongoing European influence in the Americas is addressed in Chapter 5.

DOI: 10.4324/9781003350828-8

challenger and challenged agents jeopardizes the legally and politically presupposed equilibrium, i.e. the linear vertical dimension. In other words, when a regional state counts on the support of a strong peer alien to the region and forms, for example, a bloc or alliance, arguably, the dynamics of the relationships with neighbor states will shift. Moreover, when the colonial past or neocolonial practices are still present in the way in which agents such as individuals and communities perceive central states—i.e. there is a colonial mindset—the influence of this mindset is still prevalent on the continent.

The first part of the chapter will refer to the overarching notion of domination applied to the interrelation between agents such as individuals, communities and sovereign states. Some territorial disputes in the Americas can be characterized as being intertwined with different forms of domination, namely colonialism, neo-colonialism and colonial mindset. By presenting several examples, the rest of the chapter discusses these different forms of domination that have resulted in territorial disputes. Broadly, domination implies the ability agents may have to pursue their own interests at the expense of others in an unrestrained and systematic way.[2] The cases explored in the chapter are brought to show that central states like the United States, Russia, China and India use different means to involve themselves in the region, either directly through the roles they play in territorial disputes, i.e. from a neo-colonial perspective, or indirectly, by manipulating the way in which they are perceived by regional agents in order to secure them regional standing, i.e. with a colonial mindset. Furthermore, these interferences may be government-led, but there is also evidence clearly indicating privately-led influence in domestic and regional law and politics by multinational corporations.

Although traditional scholarly literature in legal and political sciences and international relations may offer a unidimensional understanding about these different kinds of domination in the form of a variety of direct and indirect interferences, the chapter's final section applies the multidimensional approach to show how the many pluralisms at play interrelate. Therefore, a comprehensive understanding of these interferences and their impact on territorial disputes, arguably, requires a view beyond traditionally applied scholarly methods.

2 Cecile Laborde, "Republicanism and Global Justice: A Sketch," *European Journal of Political Theory* 9 (2010): 48–69. For a more detailed account about republican freedom and non-domination see Lena Halldenius, "Building Blocks of Cosmopolitanism: The Modality of Being Free," *European Journal of Political Theory* 9 (2010): 12–30; and Philip Pettit, "A Republican Law of Peoples," *European Journal of Political Theory* 9 (2010): 70–94. For the author's views on domination and non-domination see Jorge E. Núñez, *Sovereignty Conflicts and International Law and Politics: A Distributive Justice Issue* (London and New York, NY: Routledge, Taylor & Francis Group, 2017), Chapter 4.

Different forms of domination: colonialism, neo-colonialism and colonial mindset

The author has explained elsewhere that, in principle, domination means the ability or capacity somebody has to exercise power arbitrarily for their own benefit over others, regardless of the consequences for others. Conversely, non-domination implies the ability or capacity for someone's affairs not to be arbitrarily interfered with by someone else.[3] Applied to territorial disputes, when an agent such as a sovereign state dominates another agent, there is arbitrary power. On the contrary, when an agent willingly accepts the limitations another agent imposes, there is non-domination.

Obviously, in the specific case of sovereign states, they may enter into commitments and limit their own sovereignty factually and normatively. Domination, however, implies a particular kind of limitation (an axiological choice) that results in arbitrary power over someone else—e.g. another state, pseudo-states, failed states and communities. The distinction between domination and non-domination, arbitrary and non-arbitrary is more clearly understood when the multidimensional analysis is applied.[4] For instance, a linear horizontal dimensional view encompasses the understandings in public international law of sovereign equality of the states. For example, according to art. 2.1 of the United Nations (UN) Charter, sovereign equality is a core principle. This indicates that sovereign states ought to treat each other on an equal standing or equal footing basis. However, a linear vertical dimensional view acknowledges in fact that central, strong or advantaged states may do as they wish with their weaker or least advantaged peers—e.g. the realpolitik view. Indeed, a multidimensional approach helps in understanding that although law may recognize sovereign equality, that recognition may not translate into empirical equality. To reiterate, it is a fact that some states are more equal than others in realpolitik despite public international law granting legal sovereign equality.[5]

Colonialism as a form of domination implies the control by agents such as states, communities and individuals over other states, communities and individuals, and over their territories and behaviors.[6] Colonialism so characterized

3 Jorge E. Núñez, *Territorial Disputes and State Sovereignty: International Law and Politics* (London and New York, NY: Routledge, Taylor & Francis Group, 2020), Chapter 3.

4 For unidimensional and multidimensional approaches see Jorge E. Núñez, *Cosmopolitanism, State Sovereignty, International Law and Politics: A Theory*, Chapter 6.

5 R. P. Anand, "Sovereign Equality of States in International Law," *International Studies* 8:3 (1966): 213–224; Hans Kelsen, "The Principle of Sovereign Equality of States as a Basis for International Organization," *Yale Law Journal* 53:2 (1944): 207–220; R. Hjorth, "Equality in the Theory of International Society: Kelsen, Rawls and the English School," *Review of International Studies* 37:5 (2011): 2585–2602.

6 Notion adapted from Ronald J. Horvath, "A Definition of Colonialism," *Current Anthropology* 13:1 (1972): 45–57. The author does not distinguish here between colonialism and imperialism. For this distinction see Krishan Kumar, "Colony and Empire, Colonialism and Imperi-

may be subdivided into intergroup and intragroup domination. While the former refers to the domination process in culturally heterogeneous agents, the latter involves homogeneous ones.[7] State sovereignty, both in fact and in law, is limited, but the axiological choice made by the agent in question determines its final absoluteness or limitedness.[8] Historically, in the time of colonial empires, several cases in the Americas showed that states such as France, Portugal, Spain and Great Britain claimed to have absolute sovereignty, yet only recognized the sovereignty of selected peers; at the same time, they considered other entities as non-sovereigns, and therefore, did as they wished with their territories and populations.[9]

More currently, states like the United States, Russia, China and India have direct and indirect involvement in legal and political issues pertaining to other American peers, including territorial disputes. Whether these practices involve neo-colonialism or a colonial mindset, in all cases, they have to do with a form of domination. Neo-colonialism, a kind of adapted colonialism, includes different means of domination such as political, financial, military and technical control.[10] The neo-colonial form of domination implies that an agent such as a sovereign state is directly and/or indirectly controlled and/or influenced from outside.[11] In turn, a more subtle and often ignored form of domination, described as colonial mindset or colonial syndrome, refers to the psychologically embedded preconceptions of agents, such as individuals and communities, that are conditioned by colonial and/or neo-colonial norms and/or facts as well as the actual and/or potential exertion of psychological oppression upon formerly colonial agents like individuals and/or communities. This subtle form of domination, colonial mindset, can be better comprehended when explored by means of nonlinear dimensional understandings, such as the self-referred or regressive approach.[12] For instance, a dimensional nonlinear

alism: A Meaningful Distinction?" *Comparative Studies in Society and History* 63:2 (2021): 280–309; James Thuo Gathii, "Imperialism, Colonialism, and International Law," *Buffalo Law Review* 54:4 (2006): 1013–1066; Michael Adas, "Imperialism and Colonialism in Comparative Perspective," *The International History Review* 20:2 (1998): 371–388; and many others.

7 Ronald J. Horvath, "A Definition of Colonialism," *Current Anthropology* 13:1 (1972): 45–57.

8 Jorge E. Núñez, *Cosmopolitanism, State Sovereignty, International Law and Politics: A Theory* (London and New York, NY: Routledge, Taylor & Francis Group, 2023), Chapter 2.

9 For more details about colonial times in the Americas see Chapter 4.

10 G. Martin, "The Historical, Economic, and Political Bases of France's African Policy," *The Journal of Modern African Studies* 23:2 (1985): 189–208.

11 Notion based on Kwame Nkrumah, *Neo-colonialism: The Last Stage of Imperialism* (London: Panaf Ltd., 1974).

12 For linear and nonlinear dimensional approaches see Jorge E. Núñez, *Territorial Disputes and State Sovereignty: International Law and Politics* (London and New York, NY: Routledge, Taylor & Francis Group, 2020), Chapter 6. For an application of nonlinear approaches to better understand colonial mindset see Rafael V. Capó García, "(De)colonizing Critiques: Critical Pedagogy, Currere, and the Limits of the Colonial Mentality," *Journal of Curriculum Theorizing* 36:2 (2021): 43–55.

self-referred view on agents would accept, for example, that some individuals and communities in the Americas may be the sole cause to originate or to maintain a territorial dispute because of the way they perceive themselves—i.e. although they may be part of an already sovereign state and, hence, possess a defined nationality with relevant rights and obligations, they still consider themselves as non-nationals or second-class citizens. In turn, a nonlinear regressive view may help to understand why some states in the Americas are considered, politically, pseudo, failed or quasi states by their peers. Therein, central, strong or advantaged states are able to justify their interference under the involvement of institutions, for example, in the cases of humanitarian intervention and humanitarian aid.

United States

The United States' influence on the continent is self-evident. This influence, both direct and indirect, comprises several issues including law and politics and has to do with different kinds of agents—e.g. individuals, communities and states—in bilateral and multilateral interrelations. Furthermore, the influence has been historically stemming from different fronts: government and privately-led. More accurately, the United States' government-led direct and indirect influence on the rest of the continent has been present since the early days of independence.[13] More recent examples, such as the Mexico–United States border, intervention in Central America, Guantanamo Bay and Operation Condor, are introduced below to demonstrate that the United States has had (and still has), for different reasons, direct and indirect government-led involvement in territorial disputes on the continent. In addition to the government-led interference, from the early days of the post-independence period with the United Fruit Company to the more current situation with Amazon, Tesla and others, privately-led interference by multinational corporations has been a constant issue.[14] Intertwining geopolitics and business, arguably, these corporations encompass elements and features that characterize a sovereign state including the use of coercive power to the extent that some of them are more powerful than states themselves.[15]

13 Joseph Smith, *The United States and Latin America: A History of American Diplomacy, 1776–2000* (London and New York, NY: Routledge, 2005).

14 See the case of the United Fruit Company and their influence in Central and South America. For an account refer to Marcelo Bucheli, "Multinational Corporations, Totalitarian Regimes and Economic Nationalism: United Fruit Company in Central America, 1899–1975," *Business History* 50:4 (2008): 433–454. See also Kema Irogbe, "Global Political Economy and the Power of Multinational Corporations," *Journal of Third World Studies* 30:2 (2013): 223–247; Patrick J. W. Egan, "Hard Bargains: The Impact of Multinational Corporations on Economic Reform in Latin America," *Latin American Politics and Society* 52:1 (2010): 1–32.

15 Čedomir Nestorović, "Business Geopolitics," in Čedomir Nestorović, ed., *Geopolitics and Business: Relevance and Resonance* (Cham: Springer Nature, 2023), 219–303.

Disputes that directly involve the United States in the Americas[16] include those concerning the Bajo Nuevo and Serranilla Banks (Colombia, Honduras and the United States) and Navassa Island (Haiti and the United States).[17] Furthermore, with the longest international border between them, the United States and Canada have several territorial disputes including those over the Machias Seal Island[18] and the North Rock.[19] However, the United States' recent involvement in territorial disputes pertaining to other areas in the continent, like the Guyana–Venezuela[20] difference over the Essequibo region, simply shows a sustained practice the northern state has had over the years in other disputes.

The long-settled border between Mexico and the United States is an ongoing center of controversy that includes the estimated transit[21] of one million people and US$1.5 billion worth of goods as well as a potential humanitarian crisis.[22] Migration issues, nationalism and actions intended to enhance political prestige that include militarization are arguably turning Mexico into a great south border.[23] Although there is not a territorial dispute *per se*, the hallmarks of this kind of difference are present.

16 The disputes that involve the United States directly will be reviewed in more detail in Chapter 7.

17 For a more comprehensive and up-to-date understanding of the United States' rationale behind these claims see the US Department of the Interior, Acquisition Process of Insular Areas available at https://www.doi.gov/oia/islands/acquisitionprocess accessed 27 March 2024. For an account see Kacper Grass, "Geopolitics in the Western Hemisphere after Trump: Has the United States Abandoned Hegemony in Latin America?" *Revista Internacional de Pensamiento Politico* 16 (2021): 473–492.

18 Sara McLaughlin Mitchell, "Clashes at Sea: Explaining the Onset, Militarization, and Resolution of Diplomatic Maritime Claims," *Security Studies* 29:4 (2020): 637–670.

19 Ted L. McDorman, *Salt Water Neighbors: International Ocean Law Relations between the United States and Canada* (Oxford: Oxford University Press, 2009).

20 For a recent media article on this particular issue and the United States involvement see *US Throws Weight behind Guyana in Territorial Dispute with Venezuela*, AlJazeera, published on 07 December 2023 available at https://www.aljazeera.com/news/2023/12/7/us-throws-weight-behind-guyana-in-territorial-dispute accessed 1 February 2024.

21 Jacqueline Mazza, "The US-Mexico Border and Mexican Migration to the United States: A 21st Century Review," *SAIS Review of International Affairs* 37:2 (2017): 33–47.

22 Austin Kocher, "Migrant Protection Protocols and the Death of Asylum," *Journal of Latin American Geography* 20:1 (2021): 249–258; William C. Gruben and Tony Payan, "Illegal Immigration on the U.S.-Mexico Border: Is It Really a Crisis?" The James A. Baker III Institute for Public Policy, Rice University, 2014 available at https://www.bakerinstitute.org/sites/default/files/2014-10/import/MC-Immig-Gruben_Payan-101714.pdf accessed 24 January 2025; Maureen Meyer, Adam Isacson and Carolyn Scorpio, "Not a National Security Crisis: The U.S.-Mexico Border and Humanitarian Concerns, Seen from El Paso," *Advocacy for Human Rights in the Americas*, 2016 available at https://www.wola.org/wp-content/uploads/2016/10/WOLA_NoNationalSecurityCrisis_October2016.pdf accessed 23 June 2023.

23 Ewa Antoszek, "Immigration and the Expanding U.S. Southern Border: Casa en Tierra Ajena (2016)," *European Journal of American Studies* 16:1 (2021) available at https://journals.openedition.org/ejas/16822 accessed 23 June 2023.

Former disputes related to the United States' presence in the Central America and Caribbean regions include those concerning Panama, Honduras-El Salvador, Guatemala-Belize and Cuba. These disputes combined several elements such as financial and social crises, guerrilla warfare, ideological views and geopolitical location.[24] In the Caribbean, the ongoing situation of Guantanamo Bay finds its roots in colonial times like other territorial disputes in the area.[25] Bilaterally, there have been rhetorical announcements but no sign of changing the current arrangements.[26] Regionally, Latin America is assertively articulating its position as a bloc through different means such as the Organization of American States (OAS),[27] the Community of Latin American and Caribbean States (CELAC),[28] and the Latin American Parliament (Parlatino).[29] In the case of Central America,[30] the United States has had clear interference in conflicts like the Nicaraguan case[31] that have gained international attention.[32] In fact, despite the intervention of the International Court of Justice (ICJ), the United States did not accept the ruling and continued to support those who were operating against the Nicaraguan government.[33]

24 J. Child, "Interstate Relations in Latin America: Peaceful or Conflictual?" *International Journal* 43:3 (1988): 378–403.

25 Lynn Bender, *Cuba vs. United States* (San Juan: Inter American University Press, 1981).

26 "Cuba: U.S. Policy in the 115th Congress," *Congressional Research Service*, 2018, available at https://www.hsdl.org/?view&did=818557 accessed 23 June 2023; "Obama Administration Efforts to Close the Guantanamo Bay Detention Facility," *White House Archives* available at https://obamawhitehouse.archives.gov/sites/whitehouse.gov/files/images/Obama_Administration_Efforts_to_Close_Guantanamo.pdf accessed 23 June 2023.

27 "Towards the Closure of Guantanamo," *Inter-American Commission on Human Rights, Organization of American States*, 2015, available at http://www.oas.org/en/iachr/reports/pdfs/Towards-Closure-Guantanamo.pdf accessed 23 June 2023.

28 Nicolás Boeglin, "La Devolución de la Base de Guantánamo: Primeras Consideraciones de la CELAC," *SciencePo*, available at https://www.sciencespo.fr/opalc/content/la-devolucion-de-la-base-de-guantanamo-primeras-consideraciones-de-la-celac accessed 24 January 2025.

29 "Declaración Guantánamo," Parlatino, 2009, available at http://parlatino.org/pdf/organos-principales/otras-instancias/mesa-directiva/declaraciones/declaracion-guantanamo.pdf accessed 23 June 2023.

30 For a historical account of the United States presence in Central America see Thomas M. Leonard, *Central America and the United States: The Search for Stability* (Athens, GA: University of Georgia Press, 1991). See also Thomas David Schoonover, *The United States in Central America, 1860–1911: Episodes of Social Imperialism and Imperial Rivalry in the World System* (Durham, NC and London: Duke University Press, 1991).

31 Kenneth Roberts, "Bullying and Bargaining: The United States, Nicaragua, and Conflict Resolution in Central America," *International Security* 15:2 (1990): 67–102.

32 See the ICJ Judgment Military and Paramilitary Activities in and against Nicaragua (Nicaragua v. United States of America) 26 November 1984 available at https://www.icj-cij.org/case/70/judgments accessed 1 February 2024.

33 Richard J. Kilroy, "Maritime and Territorial Boundary Disputes in Latin America," *The Journal of Territorial and Maritime Studies* 1:1 (2014): 91–111.

Operation Condor[34] was a system designed by the United States to support military regimes in South America and included states like Argentina, Bolivia, Brazil, Chile, Ecuador, Paraguay and Peru.[35] The Condor system had a strong influence in the region and this influence included how territorial disputes developed. Arguably, the role military governments played in the Condor agenda can explain the long-standing territorial dispute concerning Argentina and Chile related to the Beagle Channel border that almost resulted in war.[36]

Historically, the United States has had different approaches toward regional organizations.[37] Depending on the interests at the time, since World War II, the United States' positioning in relation to these organizations can be distinguished into four different clusters: (1) hemispheric influence; (2) containment; (3) economic development; and (4) conflict prevention and management.[38] The fourth cluster—i.e. conflict prevention and management—includes territorial disputes. The United States' rationale toward their presence in regional organizations for resolution of this kind of differences, arguably, can be understood as both an interest in peacebuilding in the region and the blocking of other central, strong or advantaged states being involved.[39]

Traditionally, the United States' relationship with the OAS[40] has had two main aims in terms of territorial disputes: to prevent the influence of other central, strong or advantaged states such as Russia and China—i.e. a defensive aim; and to support progress in the region—i.e. a constructive aim.[41] Importantly, the OAS has not been a substitute for the United States' own

34 Note the expression "Operation Condor" does not refer in this monograph to the 1960s events concerning the Falkland/Malvinas Islands between Argentina and the United Kingdom. For this "Operation Condor" see Steven G. Stransky, "Re-Examining the Falkland Islands War: The Necessity for Multi-Level Deterrence in Preventing Wars of Aggression," *Georgia Journal of International and Comparative Law* 40:2 (2011): 473–526; Michael P. Socarras, "The Argentine Invasion of the Falklands and International Norms of Signalling," *Yale Journal of International Law* 10:2 (1985): 356–383.

35 Barbara Zanchetta, "Between Cold War Imperatives and State-Sponsored Terrorism: The United States and 'Operation Condor,'" *Studies in Conflict & Terrorism* 39:12 (2016): 1084–1102; Patrice McSherry, "Tracking the Origins of a State Terror Network: Operation Condor," *Latin American Perspectives* 29:1 (2002): 38–60; and many more.

36 Francesca Lessa, *The Condor Trials: Transnational Repression and Human Rights in South America* (New Haven, CT: Yale University Press, 2022), 110–135.

37 Carlos Gustavo Poggio Teixeira, *Brazil, the United States, and the South American Subsystem: Regional Politics and the Absent Empire* (Plymouth: Lexington Books, 2012); Carolyn M. Shaw, *Cooperation, Conflict, and Consensus in the Organization of American States* (New York, NY: Palgrave Macmillan, 2004).

38 Joseph S. Nye, "United States Policy toward Regional Organization," *International Organization* 23:3 (1969): 719–740.

39 Brooke N. Coe, *Sovereignty in the South: Intrusive Regionalism in Africa, Latin America, and Southeast Asia* (Cambridge: Cambridge University Press, 2019).

40 For regional organizations in the Americas see Chapter 2.

41 John C. Dreier, "The Organization of American States and United States Policy," *International Organization* 17:1 (1963): 36–53.

foreign policy. Arguably, the OAS has enabled the legitimization of unilateral actions by the northern state. In fact, realpolitik shows that the United States has taken unilateral actions to manage conflict in cases of a lack of support within the OAS.[42]

Russia

The interference of the United States over the years in issues pertaining to other states on the continent helped to create fractures in the Monroe Doctrine.[43] Whether heightened because of these fractures or rising during the Soviet era, Russia's interest and interference in the continent started long ago. Indeed, Russia's direct and indirect influence in the Americas can be traced back to the pre-independence period.[44] Thereafter, the Soviet legacy in the region and the strategic bilateral relations with states like Mexico, Colombia, Venezuela, Cuba, Brazil and Argentina are undeniable.[45] The changes over time in the relationship between the United States and Latin America have been seen by Russia as an opportunity to influence the area.[46] For instance, during the Cold War period, a clear example is the Soviet Union's involvement with armed revolutions in Cuba and Nicaragua against regimes supported by the United States.

Disputes that directly involve Russia in the Americas are the cases of the Canada Basin/Alpha Rise (Canada–Russia) and the Northern Sea Route, also known as the Northeast Passage (United States–Russia).[47] The Canada Basin/Alpha Rise issue concerns overlapping ocean jurisdictional claims made by Canada and Russia.[48] In that respect, the Arctic Ocean is subject to the United Nations Convention on the Law of the Sea (UNCLOS) except for

42 Muthiah Alagappa, "Regionalism and Conflict Management: A Framework for Analysis," *Review of International Studies* 21:4 (1995): 359–387.

43 Originally conceived to prevent European interference in the Americas, the Monroe Doctrine seems to have enabled the United States' practices toward Latin America. See Chapter 4 for more details about the Calvo, Drago and Monroe doctrines.

44 Russell H. Bartley, *Imperial Russia and the Struggle for Latin American Independence, 1808–1828* (Austin, TX: University of Texas Press, 1978).

45 Vladimir Rouvinski and Victor Jeifets, eds., *Rethinking Post-Cold War Russian–Latin American Relations* (London and New York, NY: Routledge, 2022); Elena Pavlova, "A Russian Challenge to Multipolarity? The Prospects for Political Cooperation between Russia and Latin America," *Problems of Post-Communism* 65:6 (2018): 394–408; and many others.

46 Douglas Farah and Román D. Ortiz, "Russian Influence Campaigns in Latin America," Special Report Number 525, *United States Institute of Peace* (2023) available at https://www.usip.org/sites/default/files/2023-10/sr_525-russian_influence_campaigns_latin_america.pdf accessed 9 February 2024.

47 Adnan Dal, "Introducing Territorial Disputes in the Arctic," in Kamrul Hossain and J. Miguel Roncero, eds., *Arctic Law in 1000 Words* (Rovaniemi: Northern Institute for Environmental and Minority Law, Arctic Centre, University of Lapland, 2023), 87–90.

48 Viatcheslav Gavrilov, Ted L. McDorman and Clive Schofield, "Canada and the Russian Federation," *Arctic Review on Law and Politics* 13 (2022): 219–231.

art. 234, negotiated by Canada, the United States and the former Union of Soviet Socialist Republics (USSR).[49] Geopolitically important,[50] the Northern Sea Route dispute involves the shipping route between Europe and Asia and comprises the questions regarding if and to what extent there is freedom of navigation in these waters or whether they are sovereign waters of the coastal states and are subject to domestic law.[51]

Russia's influence in the area, which includes territorial disputes, is evident in states like Venezuela and Bolivia.[52] The Essequibo dispute, a difference between Guyana and Venezuela, offers a clear example of the Russian interest in the region that includes Sino-American presences.[53] The difference between Bolivia and Chile over the Pacific coast access offers another example. In partnership with Bolivia, Russia is involved in transcontinental gas pipeline systems, encompassing Argentina, Brazil, Paraguay and Uruguay.[54] Concerning Argentina, Russia's support for the country on the Falklands/Malvinas sovereignty question has to do with their common past as great nations. For instance, the British demands against Russia relating to the situation in Crimea and Ukraine face Russia's counterargument asking the United Kingdom to accept Argentina's sovereignty over the Falkland/Malvinas Islands.[55] Interestingly, Argentina did not accept the 2014 referendum in Crimea and condemned the violation of Ukraine's territorial integrity.[56]

49 Viatcheslav Gavrilov, Roman Dremliuga and Rustambek Nurimbetov, "Article 234 of the 1982 United Nations Convention on the Law of the Sea and Reduction of Ice Cover in the Arctic Ocean," *Marine Policy* 106 (2019): 103518.

50 Ján Koper, Branislav Kováčik and Rudolf Kučharčík, "Northern Sea Route: Geopolitical Importance," in Egor V. Pak, Artem I. Krivtsov and Natalia S. Zagrebelnaya, eds., *The Handbook of the Arctic: A Broad and Comprehensive Overview* (Singapore: Springer Nature, 2022), 561–574.

51 Andrey Todorov, "Dire Straits of the Russian Arctic: Options and Challenges for a Potential US FONOP in the Northern Sea Route," *Marine Policy* 139 (2022): 105020; Andrey A. Todorov, "The Russia-USA Legal Dispute over the Straits of the Northern Sea Route and Similar Case of the Northwest Passage," *Arctic and North* 29:1 (2017): 62–75.

52 Ekaterina Kosevich, "Russia's Relations with the Countries of Latin America at the Beginning of the 21st Century: Four Levels of Interstate Interaction," *Russian Politics* 7:3 (2022): 450–484.

53 Raphael Padula, Matheus de Freitas Cecílio, Igor Candido de Oliveira and Caio Jorge Prado, "Guyana: Oil, Internal Disputes, the USA and Venezuela," *Contexto Internacional* 45:1 (2023): 1–25.

54 Ekaterina Kosevich, "Russia's Relations with the Countries of Latin America at the Beginning of the 21st Century: Four Levels of Interstate Interaction," *Russian Politics* 7:3 (2022): 450–484.

55 Douglas Farah and Román D. Ortiz, "Russian Influence Campaigns in Latin America," Special Report Number 525, *United States Institute of Peace* (2023) available at https://www.usip.org/sites/default/files/2023-10/sr_525-russian_influence_campaigns_latin_america.pdf accessed 9 February 2024.

56 Elena Pavlova, "A Russian Challenge to Multipolarity? The Prospects for Political Cooperation between Russia and Latin America," *Problems of Post-Communism* 65:6 (2018): 394–408.

In terms of regional organizations, the Bolivarian Alliance for the Peoples of Our America (ALBA), a bloc of ten full member states—i.e. Antigua and Barbuda, Bolivia, Cuba, Dominica, the Federation of Saint Kitts and Nevis, Grenada, Nicaragua, Saint Lucia, Saint Vincent and the Grenadines, and Venezuela—has clear links with Russia[57] and, arguably, allows these states to have an ally on the United Nations Security Council (UNSC) when there are issues concerning human rights violations.[58]

Originally conceived as a grouping of emerging economies, BRICS (Brazil, Russia, India, China and South Africa) enables states like Russia to have legal and political influence over, arguably, a new global order.[59] For instance, regardless of their differences, BRICS members followed the same approach when voting on the Crimea issue at the UN General Assembly 2014.[60] The reinvigorated interest in the Americas, both to keep Russia's influence in the domestic and regional agendas and to keep the support of historical allies ideologically aligned could be part of the current multipolar world because, arguably, Latin America might play a key part in Russia's political, economic and foreign policy.[61]

China

An increasingly globalized world results in influences emerging beyond those rooted in the colonial past or from the traditional superpowers like the United States and Russia. China's interest in the Americas, and in particular Latin America and the Caribbean, has grown over the past few decades.[62] This has even led to competition with other central peers like the United States and,

57 Bruce M. Bagley and Magdalena Defort, eds. *Decline of the US Hegemony?: A Challenge of ALBA and a New Latin American Integration of the Twenty-First Century* (London: Lexington Books, 2015).

58 Douglas Farah and Liana Eustacia Reyes, "Russia in Latin America," *Prism* 5:4 (2016): 100–117.

59 Cedric de Coning, Thomas Mandrup and Liselotte Odgaard, eds., *The BRICS and Coexistence: An Alternative Vision of World Order* (London and New York, NY: Routledge, Taylor & Francis, 2014).

60 Boris Martynov, "BRICS' Perspectives on International Law," *International Trends* 2:2 (2016): 25–34.

61 Victor Jeifets, "The Place of Latin America in a Multipolar World: Views and Approaches of Russian Researchers," *Latin America* 5 (2021): 50–68.

62 Rhys Jenkins, "China and Latin America," in Rhys Jenkins, *American Hegemony and the Rise of Emerging Powers* (London and New York, NY: Routledge, Taylor & Francis, 2017), 182–197; Carol Wise and Victoria Chonn Ching, "Conceptualizing China–Latin America Relations in the Twenty-First Century: The Boom, the Bust, and the Aftermath," *The Pacific Review* 31:5 (2018): 553–572; Haibin Niu, "A New Era of China-Latin America Relations," *Anuario de la Integración Regional de América Latina y el Gran Caribe* 11 (2015): 39–51; and many others.

arguably, a new dependency of a center-periphery form.[63] Moreover, these relatively new relationships pose a question in terms of public international law and relevant tenets like the Monroe Doctrine.[64]

China's interference in the continent has different forms and includes economic engagement, technology sharing, military collaboration, party-to-party training, united front work, people-to-people exchanges, ideology and soft power influence.[65] For instance, BRICS offers a clear example of a multilateral relationship between China, Latin America and the Caribbean that goes beyond economic ties.[66] Moreover, regional organizations such as the CELAC are influenced both by China's soft and hard power.[67]

China's interests in Latin America and the Caribbean can also be explained by following a dimensional nonlinear self-referred view.[68] More precisely, China's interference in the Americas is in part a response to its own geopolitical situation. Indeed, China's place in Latin America and the Caribbean faces the Taiwanese agenda.[69] States such as El Salvador, Panama, the Dominican Republic, Honduras, Nicaragua and Paraguay find themselves caught between the influences of Beijing and/or Taipei. In addition to diplomatic exchanges, technical and medical aid, both China and Taiwan use military training and military and financial assistance to gather support in the region.[70]

63 Barbara Stallings, *Dependency in the Twenty-First Century?: The Political Economy of China-Latin America Relations* (Cambridge: Cambridge University Press, 2020); Rhys Jenkins, "Latin America and China—A New Dependency?" Third World Quarterly 33:7 (2012): 1337–1358.

64 Marcos Cordeiro Pires and Lucas Gualberto do Nascimento, "The Monroe Doctrine 2.0 and US-China-Latin America Trilateral Relations," *International Organisations Research Journal* 15:3 (2020): 202–222.

65 For an insight see Ryan C. Berg, "China in Latin America and the Caribbean," *Center for Strategic and International Studies* (2021) available at https://www.jstor.org/stable/pdf/resrep37529.pdf accessed 16 February 2024.

66 Ana Saggioro Garcia and Rodrigo Curty Pereira, "Political Economy of South–South Relations: An Analysis of BRICS' Investment Protection Agreements in Latin America and the Caribbean," *Third World Quarterly* 44:1 (2023): 57–75; Bas Hooijmaaijers, "China, the BRICS, and the Limitations of Reshaping Global Economic Governance," *The Pacific Review* 34:1 (2021): 29–55; Hee-Yong Yang and Seungho Lee, "China's Engagement with Latin America and Its Implications for Soft Balancing against the United States," *Asian Perspective* 44:4 (2020): 587–615; and many others.

67 Javier Vadell, "China's Bilateral and Minilateral Relationship with Latin America and the Caribbean: the Case of China–CELAC Forum," *Area Development and Policy* 7:2 (2022): 187–203.

68 For linear and nonlinear dimensional approaches see Jorge E. Núñez, *Territorial Disputes and State Sovereignty: International Law and Politics* (London and New York, NY: Routledge, Taylor & Francis Group, 2020), Chapter 6.

69 Elisa Hsiu-chi Wang, "Challenges for the Republic of China: Diplomatic Relations within Latin America after the Regime Rotation in 2016," *Revista UNISCI (Unidad de Investigación sobre Seguridad y Cooperación Internacional)* 46 (2018): 69–86.

70 Lorenzo Maggiorelli, "Taiwan's Development Aid to Latin America and the Caribbean and the One China Policy," *Razón Crítica* 7 (2019): 177–208; Daniel P. Erikson and Janice

Brevitatis causa, both directly and indirectly relevant to territorial disputes, the Chinese military influence in Latin America and the Caribbean can be classified by regime as follows:[71] (1) anti-United States communist and populist regimes like the cases in Venezuela, Cuba, Ecuador, Argentina and Bolivia, depending on the ruling power at the time; (2) diversity-of-partner and in-transition regimes that include states that may not share the ideological component and have relationships with China as well as the United States and others (e.g. Peru, Barbados, Guyana); (3) diplomatically "off-the-table" regimes that do not diplomatically recognize China (e.g. Paraguay, Nicaragua, Guatemala, Honduras, Belize) but may still have some bilateral dealings with them, for example, buying military equipment or institutional exchanges (e.g. Chile); and (4) strongly United States allied regimes (e.g. Chile, Colombia and Argentina, depending on the ruling power at the time) that limit their bilateral relationships to purchases of military equipment, technological and infrastructure exchanges.

India

For different reasons that include historical and geographical elements, there seems to be a scholarly understanding that India's influence in the Americas, in particular Latin America and the Caribbean, is more recent in comparison to that of the United States, Russia and China.[72] Traditionally, it appeared that India had tenuous (if any) relations with the American continent.[73] More currently, scholarly literature suggests that India's interest in the Americas is increasing.[74] However, a closer look reveals that India's interest in the region has been ongoing for decades. For instance, India's policy relating to Latin America and the Caribbean can be characterized, at least during the Cold War period, as the support of the former against the interferences of the United States. There are several examples in which India's position is evident: (1) US intervention in Guatemala in 1954; (2) the Cuban Crisis; (3) the case of

---

Chen, "China, Taiwan, and the Battle for Latin America," *The Fletcher Forum of World Affairs* 31:2 (2007): 69–89; He Li, "Rivalry between Taiwan and the PRC in Latin America," *Journal of Chinese Political Science* 10:2 (2005): 77–102.

71 Taxonomy by R. Evan Ellis, "Chinese Security Engagement in Latin America," *Center for Strategic and International Studies* (2020): 1–11 available at https://www.jstor.org/stable/pdf/resrep27000.pdf accessed 18 July 2024.

72 See, for example, Deepak Bhojwani, "India and Latin America: Looking Ahead," *India Quarterly* 70:1 (2014): 33–46; Vivek Katju, R. Viswanathan and Jorge Heine, "Latin America and the Caribbean: Next Step for India," *Indian Foreign Affairs Journal* 6:1 (2011): 1–27.

73 R. Narayanan, "India and Latin America," *International Studies* 17:3–4 (1978): 655–675.

74 Mauricio Mesquita Moreira, *India: Latin America's Next Big Thing?* (Washington, DC: Inter-American Development Bank, 2018).

the Panama Canal; (4) the Chilean Crisis of 1973; (5) the 1982 Falkland/ Malvinas Islands war; and (6) US intervention in Nicaragua.[75]

As in China's case, India's interest in Latin America and the Caribbean seems to be multi-layered. India's interference has many forms and includes natural resources, technology exchange and entrepreneurial initiatives.[76] India–Latin America relations have increased substantially, and in part this may be due to deliberate governmental actions.[77] However, unlike China's government-led interference, India's influence is mainly led by the private sector and appears to have different drivers.[78] India's main economic partner in the region is the Common Market of the South (MERCOSUR).[79] Additionally, together with Russia, China and other states, India is a member of BRICS. BRICS has enabled India to have direct and indirect influence in the region.[80] Although there may be similarities in the way these central, strong or advantaged states engage via BRICS with Latin America and the Caribbean, for example, in terms of self-identity and their status as rising powers, research suggests that India's foreign policy drivers may include solidarity.[81]

Concerning territorial disputes, conflict resolution and India's positioning as a world peacebuilding leader, there are several issues worth noting in respect to the Americas. First, India accepts the need to resolve the Falklands/ Malvinas dispute. Secondly, it is aligned with Brazil in arguing for a reform of the UNSC.[82]

75 Cesar Ross, "India, Latin America, and the Caribbean during the Cold War," *Revista Brasileira de Política Internacional* 56 (2013): 23–44.

76 Deepak Bhojwani, "India and Latin America: Looking Ahead," *India Quarterly* 70:1 (2014): 33–46.

77 Jorge I. Domínguez, "India-Latin America Relations, 2000–22: Their Encounter and Shared Gains," *Diplomacy & Statecraft* 34:4 (2023): 777–799.

78 Jorge Heine and Hari Seshasayee, "From Tagore to IT: India's Changing Presence in Latin America," in Gian Luca Gardini, ed., *External Powers in Latin America: Geopolitics between Neo-Extractivism and South-South Cooperation* (London and New York, NY: Routledge, Taylor & Francis, 2021), 106–122.

79 Georgina M. Pagola Rodríguez, Rajiv Ranjan and Liber S. Di Paulo Torterolo, "India's G20 Presidency: Implications for the Latin American Region in the Framework of the Global South," *India Quarterly* 79:4 (2023): 514–524; Ignacio Bartesaghi, "Relations between Latin America and India in the BRICS Context: The Role of Brazil," *Relaciones Internacionales* 24:49 (2015): 127–148.

80 Mikio Kuwayama, *Brazil and India: Two BRICs as a "Building Bloc" for South-South Cooperation* (Santiago: Economic Commission for Latin America and the Caribbean, ECLAC, 2010) available at https://repositorio.cepal.org/items/aa97f32c-e80c-46ef-a88f-3e4c0a054cd2 accessed 16 February 2024.

81 Andrew F. Cooper, "China, India and the Pattern of G20/BRICS Engagement: Differentiated Ambivalence between 'Rising' Power Status and Solidarity with the Global South," *Third World Quarterly* 42:9 (2021): 1945–1962.

82 Ariel González Levaggi, "The South Atlantic and the Global Strategic Competition," in Ariel González Levaggi, ed., *Great Power Competition in the Southern Oceans: From the Indo-Pacific to the South Atlantic* (Cham: Springer Nature, 2023), 185–226.

A multidimensional approach

While the previous chapters showed that several territorial disputes in the Americas are rooted in a similar colonial past, this chapter reveals that there are central, strong or advantaged agents like the United States, Russia, China and India with direct and indirect interference in the continent. These interferences incorporate hard and soft approaches that include political, financial, military and technical elements and features. Whether these influences are a form of domination that may be characterized as neo-colonialism or whether they may be based on a colonial mindset or motivated by goodwill, cooperation and solidarity, they deserve more comprehensive analyses.

Traditionally, by the application of unidimensional approaches,[83] legal and political sciences and international relations would focus the attention on a particular agent and issue. For example, a study might explore the legal title the United States had over Texas or Alaska in relation to Mexico and Russia, respectively. Yet, another study could assess whether Antarctica,[84] Amazonia or the Amazon rainforest[85] should be internationalized. But all these studies would fail to acknowledge that any changes pertaining to Antarctica or Amazonia could result in outcomes beyond those expected in law and politics by the involved agents. More precisely, seemingly proposed for the common good of humanity by central, strong or advantaged agents like the United States, Russia, China and India, these kinds of legal and political changes, as has been shown in the cases of Texas and Alaska, would bring consequences not just to the directly involved states at the time of signing the relevant agreement. For instance, those individuals and communities in the territory and their lives—and that of their future generations—would be affected more than any others by any arrangements.

By moving toward a multidimensional view of these interferences, it is possible to know, understand and assess law and realpolitik simultaneously. For instance, by application of a nonlinear chaotic approach it is possible to question why and how agents such as communities and states may be characterized as having different interrelations within and without their spheres of influence. This could help explain why, for example, although some Latin American and Caribbean states and their governments may seem to follow the United States' foreign policy, their communities may be more aligned toward Russian, Chinese or Indian world visions and ideologies. Moreover, the scholar could apply nonlinear random views and include non-rational elements and

83 For an understanding of dimensional approaches, including unidimensionality and multidimensionality, see Jorge E. Núñez, *Cosmopolitanism, State Sovereignty, International Law and Politics: A Theory* (London and New York, NY: Routledge, Taylor & Francis Group, 2023), in particular Chapter 6.

84 Territorial claims over Antarctica will be addressed extensively in Chapter 9.

85 Note the author uses the terms Amazonia or Amazon rainforest to refer to the geographical area in which many sovereign states in South America make sovereignty claims.

features—e.g. emotion, nationalism—in order to speculate about the reasons behind the apparent commonalities between otherwise different individuals and communities.

Domestic and regional cultural, legal, historical, sociological, geographical, financial and many other elements and features could be intertwined with the direct and indirect influence of these central, strong or advantaged agents. Therefore, comprehensive explanations and analyses of territorial disputes in the Americas require the incorporation of these elements. The subsections below apply multidimensional approaches to discern whether the United States, Russia, China and India could influence territorial disputes in the Americas and, if they did, to what extent.

Agents and players

A multidimensional perspective does not only consider the evident agents—i.e. sovereign states—but also those who might have involvement and/or be somehow affected by these interferences such as communities and individuals. Moreover, this methodology helps to discern the different roles that might be played by the government-led influence of central, strong or advantaged agents like the United States, Russia, China and India and the privately-led ascendancy of multinational corporations.

The actual and potential presence of natural resources seems to suggest a higher likelihood of a variety of non-traditional agents playing different roles. For instance, although most of the territorial disputes in the area are now resolved, the Amazon rainforest presents different agents such as sovereign states, indigenous peoples, non-governmental organizations, multinational private companies and scientists.[86] In fact, cutting across territorially defined boundaries, multinational corporations have extended their influence and there is clear evidence of mutual bargaining between them and Latin American and Caribbean host states.[87]

Regardless of territorially defined boundaries and the influence of multinational corporations, there appears to be a move in the Americas toward the recognition of indigenous peoples as not simply attendees or viewers but participants or stakeholders.[88] Interestingly, a multidimensional approach shows

86 Paul E. Little, *Amazonia: Territorial Struggles on Perennial Frontiers* (Baltimore, MD: Johns Hopkins University Press, 2001).

87 Caner Bakir and Judith Woods, "Host State Bargaining with Multinationals," in Andreas Nölke and Christian May, eds., *Handbook of the International Political Economy of the Corporation* (Cheltenham and Northampton, MA: Edward Elgar Publishing, 2018), 279–294; Robert Grosse, *Multinationals in Latin America* (London and New York, NY: Routledge, Taylor & Francis, 2013).

88 For a notion and characterization of agents such as hosts, participants, attendees and viewers, see Jorge E. Núñez, *Cosmopolitanism, State Sovereignty, International Law and Politics: A Theory* (London and New York, NY: Routledge, Taylor & Francis Group, 2023), Chap-

that communities such as indigenous populations may be opposed to local government's intentions for different reasons. Not only do these reasons include their fight against neo-colonial practices, but they might also be motivated by external support to their cause against local governments—support that is designed only to fulfill the agendas of central, strong or advantaged agents. Linear diagonal or curved dimensional views help demonstrate that neo-colonial practices encompass legal, political, economic, security and cultural ties. For example, China's growing influence in Latin America is unquestionable.[89] However, Chinese efforts to influence Latin American governments in terms of exploration and exploitation of natural resources have found indigenous resistance.[90] Controversially, nonlinear self-referred and chaotic dimensional views could explain how neo-colonial practices might take the form of terrorism against local governments by means of alien interference in the region supporting indigenous peoples' claims to territory.[91]

Contexts

The shift to a multipolar world in which not only the United States and Russia but also states such as China and India are exercising their influence toward other agents in several areas, including law, politics, financial markets, health and security, indicates a growing entanglement of domestic, regional and international affairs.

Domestically, it is important to acknowledge that in addition to the government there are private agents such as local companies. These local agents are subject to domestic and regional realities such as inflation, unemployment, natural resources wealth and scarcity and support (or lack of support) from individuals. Moreover, they are subject to external factors such as oil and gas prices. Intertwined with these internal and external factors, including nationalism and actions intended to bolster political prestige, the domestic realities

ter 4. See also Gerald P. Neugebauer III, "Indigenous Peoples as Stakeholders: Influencing Resource-Management Decisions Affecting Indigenous Community Interests in Latin America," *New York University Law Review* 78:3 (2003): 1227–1261.

89 For an up-to-date report see Diana Roy, "China's Growing Influence in Latin America," *Council on Foreign Relations* last updated 15 June 2023 available at https://www.cfr.org/backgrounder/china-influence-latin-america-argentina-brazil-venezuela-security-energy-bri accessed 14 March 2024.

90 Wenyuan Wu, *Chinese Oil Enterprises in Latin America: Corporate Social Responsibility* (Cham: Palgrave Macmillan, 2019); Cintia Quiliconi and Pablo Rodríguez Vasco, "Chinese Mining and Indigenous Resistance in Ecuador," *Carnegie Endowment for International Peace* (2021) available at https://carnegieendowment.org/2021/09/20/chinese-mining-and-indigenous-resistance-in-ecuador-pub-85382 accessed 7 March 2024.

91 See, for example, a United Kingdom–based organization allegedly accused by the Argentine government of supporting the Mapuche community. Press release by the Mapuche International Link, United Kingdom published on 1 September 2017 available at https://www.mapuche-nation.org/english/html/news/pr-119.html accessed 14 March 2024.

in Latin America and the Caribbean seem to favor a welcoming attitude in relation to interferences from central, strong or advantaged agents like the United States, Russia, China and India that can translate, arguably, into both mutual benefits and dependency.[92] Assuming the latter, a nonlinear chaotic dimensional approach could help explain how: (1) these interferences might constitute a variable that increases the likelihood of escalation into conflict; and (2) they might be directly linked to the domestic and international political agenda of the government in power.[93]

Regionally, there are several elements and features that may work in synergy both positively and negatively. Neighbor states, overlapping areas concerning natural resources both in land and water, migrants, guerrilla warfare that does not recognize legally established borders and regional organizations are but a few of these elements and features.

The international context is characterized by central, strong or advantaged agents like the United States, Russia, China and India that have a constant direct and indirect financial, military, political, etc. influence in differences that have little to do with their own jurisdictions.[94] Indeed, great power competition in Latin America and the Caribbean is a reality and affects local and regional situations including territorial disputes. For example, Russia has supported regimes in states like Venezuela and Nicaragua and their respective territorial and maritime claims against Colombia while the United States has aided the latter.[95]

Realms

The previous paragraphs have shown that whether an agent can influence others or be influenced by others is a matter that encompasses factual, normative and axiological issues. Factually, an agent may be more central, stronger

92 Stuti Banerjee, "India and Latin America: Partners in Development," in N. K. Mahawar and D. Battachargee, eds., *India's Development Partnership: Expanding Vision* (London and New York, NY: Routledge, Taylor & Francis, 2024), 235–248; Barbara Stallings, *Dependency in the Twenty-First Century?: The Political Economy of China-Latin America Relations* (Cambridge: Cambridge University Press, 2020); Damares Lopes Afonso, Suzana Quinet de Andrade Bastos and Fernando Salgueiro Perobelli, "Latin America and China: Mutual Benefit or Dependency?" *CEPAL Review* 135 (2021) available at https://repositorio.cepal.org/server/api/core/bitstreams/f57b749c-78d5-4e7f-ab05-859fd20db144/content accessed 29 March 2024; and many others.

93 Paul K. Huth, *Standing Your Ground: Territorial Disputes and International Conflict* (Ann Arbor, MI: University of Michigan Press, 2001).

94 Douglas Farah and Kathryn Babineau, "Extra-Regional Actors in Latin America," *Prism* 8:1 (2019): 96–113.

95 Irina A. Chindea, Elina Treyger, Raphael S. Cohen, Christian Curriden, Kurt Klein, Carlos Sanchez, Holly Gramkow and Khrystyna Holynska, "Great-Power Competition and Conflict in Latin America" (Santa Monica, CA: RAND, 2023) available at https://apps.dtic.mil/sti/trecms/pdf/AD1203939.pdf accessed 21 March 2024.

or advantaged than others depending on a multiplicity of elements and features, such as geographical location, level of development, financial stability, economic and technological development and the presence of greater natural resources and the ability to exploit them. For example, cases like the United States and China can be considered where natural resources are present and they have the means to explore and exploit them. Conversely, other states in the Americas, more precisely Latin America and the Caribbean, might be as rich in natural resources as the United States and China but might have to depend on external aid for their exploration and exploitation due to lack of financial means or technological development. Normatively, an agent may be more central, stronger or advantaged than others depending on elements and features pertaining to systems such as law, morality and religion. Consider, for example, cases in which certain belief systems characterize a particular group of people as the "chosen" ones and the UN Charter that clearly guarantees a different treatment for some states at UNSC level. To choose which element or feature defines the "most advantaged" or "least advantaged" agent is an axiological matter. Indeed, as explained elsewhere,[96] there are two intertwined considerations here: (a) which feature or element will be considered to determine the most or least advantaged; and (b) variability.

Brevitatis causa, several cases in Latin America and the Caribbean can be considered where states might be rich in natural resources, but they might have small populations and might not have means for defense. Clearly, the most advantaged in terms of ownership and/or possession of natural resources seem to be the states in Latin America and the Caribbean area in this broad example. However, in many cases, they might not be able to explore or exploit their resources or they might have to rely on external aid to do so. Therein, the most advantaged in terms of exploration and exploitation of natural resources might be other agents such as the United States, Russia, China and India. The same could be said about defense. Indeed, to define the "most advantaged" or "least advantaged" agent depends on an axiological choice, that is, deciding which element or feature would be counted as relevant. Moreover, even if there were an agreement on the element or feature to be considered, this element or feature and/or the perception about their value might change and, consequently, being defined as the least and the most advantaged agent might vary in time. For example, natural resources might be depleted; natural boundaries might move or cease to exist; domestic, regional and global power dynamics might shift; and bilateral or multilateral agreements might be amended. These factual, normative and axiological changes have resulted in a multipolar world where the United States and Russia still directly and indirectly influence the Americas while states like China and India have a growing involvement in the affairs of the continent.

96 Jorge E. Núñez, *Sovereignty Conflicts and International Law and Politics: A Distributive Justice Issue* (London and New York, NY: Routledge, Taylor & Francis Group, 2017), Chapter 6.

Modes of existence

The influence of central, strong or advantaged agents in the Americas involves myriad ideal, natural, cultural and metaphysical elements. Clearly, ideology has helped develop the roots behind both the United States and Russia's influences in Latin America and the Caribbean.[97] The presence of natural resources on the continent has been one of the driving forces that helps in understanding why these central states prioritize the region in their regional (United States) and international agendas (Russia, China and India).[98] In terms of cultural objects, while the United States has been able to maintain an almost monopoly in terms of foreign aid, military and policy training and development assistance in Latin America and the Caribbean, it is clear that Russia and more recently China are either strengthening or expanding, respectively, their influence in states like Cuba, Nicaragua and Venezuela by means of, for example, technology sharing and soft power influence.[99] Finally, the soft power influence of these central states encompasses metaphysical elements as well. Consider, for instance, Latin American and Caribbean's permeability toward China and India's views on theology heightened by decolonial trends.[100]

Conclusion

This chapter explored the past and ongoing influence pertaining to the origin, continuation and potential escalation into conflict of territorial disputes in the Americas with focus on the interference by central sovereign states, namely the United States, Russia, China and India. Regardless of their peculiarities and whether there were historical roots in each case, the selected examples highlighted the interconnections these different agents might have; the domestic, regional and international contexts in which their interrelations might happen; some factual, normative and axiological issues related to these influences; and some of the several elements at play.

97 José de Arimatéia da Cruz, "Strategic Insights: From Ideology to Geopolitics: Russian Interests in Latin America," *Current Politics and Economics of Russia, Eastern and Central Europe* 30:1/2 (2015): 175; Stephen J. Randall, "Ideology, National Security, and the Corporate State: The Historiography of US-Latin American Relations," *Latin American Research Review* 27:1 (1992): 205–217; and many others.

98 Riordan Roett and Guadalupe Paz, eds., *Latin America and the Asian Giants: Evolving Ties with China and India* (Washington, DC: Brookings Institution Press, 2016); Stephen Blank and Younkyoo Kim, "Russia and Latin America: The New Frontier for Geopolitics, Arms Sales and Energy," *Problems of Post-Communism* 62:3 (2015): 159–173; and many others.

99 Douglas Farah and Caitlyn Yates, "Great Power Competition in Latin America: A New Normal," *The Fletcher Forum of World Affairs* 44:2 (2020): 45–64.

100 Nelson Maldonado-Torres, "Epistemology, Ethics, and the Time/Space of Decolonization: Perspectives from the Caribbean and the Latina/o Americas," in Ada María Isasi-Díaz and Eduardo Mendieta, eds., *Decolonizing Epistemologies: Latina/o Theology and Philosophy: Latina/o Theology and Philosophy* (New York, NY: Fordham University Press, 2012), 193–206.

Whether these more central, stronger or advantaged states use hard or soft power to influence individuals, communities and states in Latin America and the Caribbean, and regardless of whether these influences are government-led or privately-led, it is unquestionable that they do interfere with issues pertaining to law and politics, including territorial disputes. The nature of these interferences and the degree of influence in particular territorial disputes deserve further, more comprehensive and multidimensional exploration. This chapter has painted a first outline of some of these interferences. The question remains as to whether these interferences could constitute a form of domination, that is arbitrary power, or if the individuals, communities and states affected by these interferences might willingly accept them. Moreover, in the case of the former, the chapter has highlighted that although the distinction may be subtle, it is important to discern what type of domination might take place, that is whether it is a form of colonialism, neo-colonialism or a colonial mindset. Therefore, any future study concerning the influence that central, strong or advantaged agents might have regarding the origin, continuation and potential escalation into conflict of territorial disputes should take into account the intrinsic intricate nature of these interferences. Because these interferences comprise several pluralisms that include agents, contexts, realms and modes of existence, these studies should incorporate both linear and nonlinear dimensional approaches.

While this chapter explored the influence of central, strong or advantaged agents such as the United States, Russia, China and India in the region, the next chapter will focus on cases in which the involved agents have a similar legal understanding and factual bargaining power when considering territorial disputes. In other words, the next chapter will focus on territorial disputes involving agents only located in the Americas and cases in which the claiming and claimant agents acknowledge reciprocally in law and in fact the principle of sovereign equality.

Bibliography

Adas, Michael. "Imperialism and Colonialism in Comparative Perspective." *The International History Review* 20:2 (1998): 371–388.

Afonso, Damares Lopes, Suzana Quinet de Andrade Bastos and Fernando Salgueiro Perobelli. "Latin America and China: Mutual Benefit or Dependency?" *CEPAL Review* 135 (2021) available at https://repositorio.cepal.org/server/api/core/bitstreams/f57b749c-78d5-4e7f-ab05-859fd20db144/content accessed 29 March 2024.

Alagappa, Muthiah. "Regionalism and Conflict Management: A Framework for Analysis." *Review of International Studies* 21:4 (1995): 359–387.

Anand, R. P. "Sovereign Equality of States in International Law." *International Studies* 8:3 (1966): 213–224.

Antoszek, Ewa. "Immigration and the Expanding U.S. Southern Border: Casa en Tierra Ajena (2016)." *European Journal of American Studies* 16:1 (2021) available at https://journals.openedition.org/ejas/16822 accessed 23 June 2023.

Bagley, Bruce M. and Magdalena Defort, eds. *Decline of the US Hegemony?: A Challenge of ALBA and a New Latin American Integration of the Twenty-First Century*. London: Lexington Books, 2015.

Bakir, Caner and Judith Woods. "Host State Bargaining with Multinationals." In *Handbook of the International Political Economy of the Corporation*, Nölke, Andreas and May, Christian, eds. 279–294. Cheltenham and Northampton, MA: Edward Elgar Publishing, 2018.

Banerjee, Stuti. "India and Latin America: Partners in Development." In *India's Development Partnership: Expanding Vistas*, Mahawar, N. K. and Battacharjee, D., eds. 235–248. London and New York, NY: Routledge, Taylor & Francis, 2024.

Bartesaghi, Ignacio. "Relations between Latin America and India in the BRICS Context: The Role of Brazil." *Relaciones Internacionales* 24:49 (2015): 127–148.

Bartley, Russell H. *Imperial Russia and the Struggle for Latin American Independence, 1808–1828*. Austin, TX: University of Texas Press, 1978.

Bender, Lynn. *Cuba vs. United States*. San Juan: Inter American University Press, 1981.

Berg, Ryan C. "China in Latin America and the Caribbean." *Center for Strategic and International Studies* (2021) available at https://www.jstor.org/stable/pdf/resrep37529.pdf accessed 16 February 2024.

Bhojwani, Deepak. "India and Latin America: Looking Ahead." *India Quarterly* 70:1 (2014): 33–46.

Blank, Stephen and Younkyoo Kim. "Russia and Latin America: The New Frontier for Geopolitics, Arms Sales and Energy." *Problems of Post-Communism* 62:3 (2015): 159–173.

Bucheli, Marcelo. "Multinational Corporations, Totalitarian Regimes and Economic Nationalism: United Fruit Company in Central America, 1899–1975." *Business History* 50:4 (2008): 433–454.

Capó García, Rafael V. "(De)colonizing Critiques: Critical Pedagogy, Currere, and the Limits of the Colonial Mentality." *Journal of Curriculum Theorizing* 36:2 (2021): 43–55.

Child, J. "Interstate Relations in Latin America: Peaceful or Conflictual?" *International Journal* 43:3 (1988): 378–403.

Chindea, Irina A., Elina Treyger, Raphael S. Cohen, Christian Curriden, Kurt, Klein, Carlos Sanchez, Holly Gramkow and Khrystyna Holynska. "Great-Power Competition and Conflict in Latin America." Santa Monica, CA: RAND, 2023 available at https://apps.dtic.mil/sti/trecms/pdf/AD1203939.pdf accessed 21 March 2024.

Coe, Brooke N. *Sovereignty in the South: Intrusive Regionalism in Africa, Latin America, and Southeast Asia*. Cambridge: Cambridge University Press, 2019.

Cooper, Andrew F. "China, India and the Pattern of G20/BRICS Engagement: Differentiated Ambivalence between 'Rising' Power Status and Solidarity with the Global South." *Third World Quarterly* 42:9 (2021): 1945–1962.

da Cruz, José de Arimatéia. "Strategic Insights: From Ideology to Geopolitics: Russian Interests in Latin America." *Current Politics and Economics of Russia, Eastern and Central Europe* 30:1/2 (2015): 175–185.

Dal, Adnan. "Introducing Territorial Disputes in the Arctic." In *Arctic Law in 1000 Words*, Hossain, Kamrul and Roncero, J. Miguel, eds. 87–90. Rovaniemi: Northern Institute for Environmental and Minority Law, Arctic Centre, University of Lapland, 2023.

de Coning, Cedric, Thomas Mandrup and Liselotte Odgaard, eds. *The BRICS and Coexistence: An Alternative Vision of World Order*. London and New York, NY: Routledge, Taylor & Francis, 2014.

Domínguez, Jorge I. "India-Latin America Relations, 2000–22: Their Encounter and Shared Gains." *Diplomacy & Statecraft* 34:4 (2023): 777–799.

Dreier, John C. "The Organization of American States and United States Policy." *International Organization* 17:1 (1963): 36–53.

Egan, Patrick J. W. "Hard Bargains: The Impact of Multinational Corporations on Economic Reform in Latin America." *Latin American Politics and Society* 52:1 (2010): 1–32.

Ellis, R. Evan. "Chinese Security Engagement in Latin America," *Center for Strategic and International Studies* (2020): 1–11 available at https://www.jstor.org/stable/pdf/resrep27000.pdf accessed 18 July 2024.

Erikson, Daniel P. and Janice Chen. "China, Taiwan, and the Battle for Latin America." *The Fletcher Forum of World Affairs* 31:2 (2007): 69–89.

Farah, Douglas and Kathryn Babineau. "Extra-Regional Actors in Latin America." *Prism* 8:1 (2019): 96–113.

Farah, Douglas and Román D. Ortiz. "Russian Influence Campaigns in Latin America." Special Report Number 525, *United States Institute of Peace,* 2023 available at https://www.usip.org/sites/default/files/2023-10/sr_525-russian_influence_campaigns_latin_america.pdf accessed 9 February 2024.

Farah, Douglas and Liana Eustacia Reyes. "Russia in Latin America." *Prism* 5:4 (2016): 100–117.

Farah, Douglas and Caitlyn Yates. "Great Power Competition in Latin America: A New Normal." *The Fletcher Forum of World Affairs* 44:2 (2020): 45–64.

Gathii, James Thuo. "Imperialism, Colonialism, and International Law." *Buffalo Law Review* 54:4 (2006): 1013–1066.

Gavrilov, Viatcheslav, Roman Dremliuga and Rustambek Nurimbetov. "Article 234 of the 1982 United Nations Convention on the Law of the Sea and Reduction of Ice Cover in the Arctic Ocean." *Marine Policy* 106 (2019): 103518.

Gavrilov, Viatcheslav, Ted L. McDorman and Clive Schofield. "Canada and the Russian Federation." *Arctic Review on Law and Politics* 13 (2022): 219–231.

Grass, Kacper. "Geopolitics in the Western Hemisphere after Trump: Has the United States Abandoned Hegemony in Latin America?" *Revista Internacional de Pensamiento Politico* 16 (2021): 473–492.

Grosse, Robert. *Multinationals in Latin America*. London and New York, NY: Routledge, Taylor & Francis, 2013.

Gruben, William C. and Tony Payan. "Illegal Immigration on the U.S.-Mexico Border: Is It Really a Crisis?" *The James A. Baker III Institute for Public Policy,* Rice University, 2014 available at https://www.bakerinstitute.org/sites/default/files/2014-10/import/MC-Immig-Gruben_Payan-101714.pdf accessed 24 January 2025.

Halldenius, Lena. "Building Blocks of Cosmopolitanism: The Modality of Being Free." *European Journal of Political Theory* 9:1 (2010): 12–30.

Heine, Jorge and Hari Seshasayee. "From Tagore to IT: India's Changing Presence in Latin America." In *External Powers in Latin America: Geopolitics between Neo-Extractivism and South-South Cooperation*, Gardini, Gian Luca, ed. 106–122. London and New York, NY: Routledge, Taylor & Francis, 2021.

Hjorth, R. "Equality in the Theory of International Society: Kelsen, Rawls and the English School." *Review of International Studies* 37:5 (2011): 2585–2602.

Hooijmaaijers, Bas. "China, the BRICS, and the Limitations of Reshaping Global Economic Governance." *The Pacific Review* 34:1 (2021): 29–55.

Horvath, Ronald J. "A Definition of Colonialism." *Current Anthropology* 13:1 (1972): 45–57.

Huth, Paul K. *Standing Your Ground: Territorial Disputes and International Conflict.* Ann Arbor, MI: University of Michigan Press, 2001.

Irogbe, Kema. "Global Political Economy and the Power of Multinational Corporations." *Journal of Third World Studies* 30:2 (2013): 223–247.

Jeifets, Victor. "The Place of Latin America in a Multipolar World: Views and Approaches of Russian Researchers." *Latin America* 5 (2021): 50–68.

Jenkins, Rhys. "China and Latin America." In *American Hegemony and the Rise of Emerging Powers*, Jenkins, Rhys, ed. 182–197. London and New York, NY: Routledge, Taylor & Francis, 2017.

Jenkins, Rhys. "Latin America and China—A New Dependency?" *Third World Quarterly* 33:7 (2012): 1337–1358.

Katju, Vivek, R. Viswanathan, and Jorge Heine. "Latin America and the Caribbean: Next Step for India." *Indian Foreign Affairs Journal* 6:1 (2011): 1–27.

Kelsen, Hans. "The Principle of Sovereign Equality of States as a Basis for International Organization." *Yale Law Journal* 53:2 (1944): 207–220.

Kilroy, Richard J. "Maritime and Territorial Boundary Disputes in Latin America." *The Journal of Territorial and Maritime Studies* 1:1 (2014): 91–111.

Kocher, Austin. "Migrant Protection Protocols and the Death of Asylum." *Journal of Latin American Geography* 20:1 (2021): 249–258.

Koper, Ján, Branislav Kováčik and Rudolf Kucharčík. "Northern Sea Route: Geopolitical Importance." In *The Handbook of the Arctic: A Broad and Comprehensive Overview*, Pak, Egor V., Krivtsov, Artem I. and Zagrebelnaya, Natalia S., eds. 561–574. Singapore: Springer Nature, 2022.

Kosevich, Ekaterina. "Russia's Relations with the Countries of Latin America at the Beginning of the 21st Century: Four Levels of Interstate Interaction." *Russian Politics* 7:3 (2022): 450–484.

Kumar, Krishan. "Colony and Empire, Colonialism and Imperialism: A Meaningful Distinction?" *Comparative Studies in Society and History* 63:2 (2021): 280–309.

Kuwayama, Mikio. *Brazil and India: Two BRICs as a "Building Bloc" for South-South Cooperation.* Santiago: Economic Commission for Latin America and the Caribbean, ECLAC, 2010.

Laborde, Cecile. "Republicanism and Global Justice: A Sketch." *European Journal of Political Theory* 9 (2010): 48–69.

Leonard, Thomas M. *Central America and the United States: The Search for Stability.* Athens, GA: University of Georgia Press, 1991.

Lessa, Francesca. *The Condor Trials: Transnational Repression and Human Rights in South America.* New Haven, CT: Yale University Press, 2022).

Levaggi, Ariel González. "The South Atlantic and the Global Strategic Competition." In *Great Power Competition in the Southern Oceans: From the Indo-Pacific to the South Atlantic*, Levaggi, Ariel González, 185–226. Cham: Springer Nature, 2023.

Li, He. "Rivalry between Taiwan and the PRC in Latin America." *Journal of Chinese Political Science* 10:2 (2005): 77–102.

Little, Paul E. *Amazonia: Territorial Struggles on Perennial Frontiers.* Baltimore, MD: Johns Hopkins University Press, 2001.

Maggiorelli, Lorenzo. "Taiwan's Development Aid to Latin America and the Caribbean and the One China Policy." *Razón Crítica* 7 (2019): 177–208.

Maldonado-Torres, Nelson. "Epistemology, Ethics, and the Time/Space of Decolonization: Perspectives from the Caribbean and the Latina/o Americas." In *Decolonizing Epistemologies: Latina/o Theology and Philosophy: Latina/o Theology and Philosophy*, Isasi-Díaz, Ada María and Mendieta, Eduardo, eds. 193–206. New York, NY: Fordham University Press, 2012.

Martin, G. "The Historical, Economic, and Political Bases of France's African Policy." *The Journal of Modern African Studies* 23:2 (1985): 189–208.

Martynov, Boris. "BRICS' Perspectives on International Law." *International Trends* 2:2 (2016): 25–34.

Mazza, Jacqueline. "The US-Mexico Border and Mexican Migration to the United States: A 21st Century Review." *SAIS Review of International Affairs* 37:2 (2017): 33–47.

McDorman, Ted L. *Salt Water Neighbors: International Ocean Law Relations between the United States and Canada.* Oxford: Oxford University Press, 2009.

McSherry, Patrice. "Tracking the Origins of a State Terror Network: Operation Condor." *Latin American Perspectives* 29:1 (2002): 38–60.

Meyer, Maureen, Adam Isacson and Carolyn Scorpio. "Not a National Security Crisis: The U.S.-Mexico Border and Humanitarian Concerns, Seen from El Paso." *Advocacy for Human Rights in the Americas*, 2016 available at https://www.wola.org/wp-content/uploads/2016/10/WOLA_NoNationalSecurityCrisis_October2016.pdf accessed 23 June 2023.

Mitchell, Sara McLaughlin. "Clashes at Sea: Explaining the Onset, Militarization, and Resolution of Diplomatic Maritime Claims." *Security Studies* 29:4 (2020): 637–670.

Moreira, Mauricio Mesquita. *India: Latin America's Next Big Thing?* Washington, DC: Inter-American Development Bank, 2018.

Narayanan, R. "India and Latin America." *International Studies* 17:3–4 (1978): 655–675.

Nestorović, Čedomir. "Business Geopolitics." In *Geopolitics and Business: Relevance and Resonance*, Nestorović, Čedomir, ed. 219–303. Cham: Springer Nature, 2023.

Neugebauer III, Gerald P. "Indigenous Peoples as Stakeholders: Influencing Resource-Management Decisions Affecting Indigenous Community Interests in Latin America." *New York University Law Review* 78:3 (2003): 1227–1261.

Niu, Haibin. "A New Era of China-Latin America Relations." *Anuario de la Integración Regional de América Latina y el Gran Caribe* 11 (2015): 39–51.

Nkrumah, Kwame. *Neo-colonialism: The Last Stage of Imperialism.* London: Panaf Ltd., 1974.

Núñez, Jorge E. *Cosmopolitanism, State Sovereignty, International Law and Politics: A Theory.* London and New York, NY: Routledge, Taylor & Francis Group, 2023.

Núñez, Jorge E. *Sovereignty Conflicts and International Law and Politics: A Distributive Justice Issue.* London and New York, NY: Routledge, Taylor & Francis Group, 2017.

Núñez, Jorge E. *Territorial Disputes and State Sovereignty: International Law and Politics.* London and New York, NY: Routledge, Taylor & Francis Group, 2020.

Nye, Joseph S. "United States Policy toward Regional Organization." *International Organization* 23:3 (1969): 719–740.

Padula, Raphael, Matheus de Freitas Cecílio, Igor Candido de Oliveira and Caio Jorge Prado. "Guyana: Oil, Internal Disputes, the USA and Venezuela." *Contexto Internacional* 45:1 (2023): 1–25.

Pavlova, Elena. "A Russian Challenge to Multipolarity? The Prospects for Political Cooperation between Russia and Latin America." *Problems of Post-Communism* 65:6 (2018): 394–408.

Pettit, Philip. "A Republican Law of Peoples." *European Journal of Political Theory* 9:1 (2010): 70–94.

Pires, Marcos Cordeiro and Lucas Gualberto do Nascimento. "The Monroe Doctrine 2.0 and US-China-Latin America Trilateral Relations." *International Organisations Research Journal* 15:3 (2020): 202–222.

Quiliconi, Cintia and Pablo Rodríguez Vasco. "Chinese Mining and Indigenous Resistance in Ecuador." *Carnegie Endowment for International Peace* (2021) available at https://carnegieendowment.org/2021/09/20/chinese-mining-and-indigenous-resistance-in-ecuador-pub-85382 accessed 7 March 2024.

Randall, Stephen J. "Ideology, National Security, and the Corporate State: The Historiography of US-Latin American Relations." *Latin American Research Review* 27:1 (1992): 205–217.

Roberts, Kenneth. "Bullying and Bargaining: The United States, Nicaragua, and Conflict Resolution in Central America." *International Security* 15:2 (1990): 67–102.

Rodríguez, Georgina M. Pagola, Rajiv Ranjan and Liber S. Di Paulo Torterolo. "India's G20 Presidency: Implications for the Latin American Region in the Framework of the Global South." *India Quarterly* 79:4 (2023): 514–524.

Roett, Riordan and Guadalupe Paz, eds. *Latin America and the Asian Giants: Evolving Ties with China and India*. Washington, DC: Brookings Institution Press, 2016.

Ross, Cesar. "India, Latin America, and the Caribbean during the Cold War." *Revista Brasileira de Política Internacional* 56 (2013): 23–44.

Rouvinski, Vladimir and Victor Jeifets, eds. *Rethinking Post-Cold War Russian–Latin American Relations*. London and New York, NY: Routledge, 2022.

Roy, Diana. "China's Growing Influence in Latin America." *Council on Foreign Relations*, 15 June 2023 available at https://www.cfr.org/backgrounder/china-influence-latin-america-argentina-brazil-venezuela-security-energy-bri accessed 14 March 2024.

Saggioro Garcia, Ana and Rodrigo Curty Pereira. "Political Economy of South–South Relations: An Analysis of BRICS' Investment Protection Agreements in Latin America and the Caribbean." *Third World Quarterly* 44:1 (2023): 57–75.

Schoonover, Thomas David. *The United States in Central America, 1860–1911: Episodes of Social Imperialism and Imperial Rivalry in the World System*. Durham, NC; London: Duke University Press, 1991.

Shaw, Carolyn M. *Cooperation, Conflict, and Consensus in the Organization of American States*. New York, NY: Palgrave Macmillan, 2004.

Smith, Joseph. *The United States and Latin America: A History of American Diplomacy, 1776–2000*. London and New York, NY: Routledge, 2005.

Socarras, Michael P. "The Argentine Invasion of the Falklands and International Norms of Signalling." *Yale Journal of International Law* 10:2 (1985): 356–383.

Stallings, Barbara. *Dependency in the Twenty-First Century?: The Political Economy of China-Latin America Relations*. Cambridge: Cambridge University Press, 2020.

Stransky, Steven G. "Re-Examining the Falkland Islands War: The Necessity for Multi-Level Deterrence in Preventing Wars of Aggression." *Georgia Journal of International and Comparative Law* 40:2 (2011): 473–526.

Teixeira, Carlos Gustavo Poggio. *Brazil, the United States, and the South American Subsystem: Regional Politics and the Absent Empire.* Lanham, MD: Lexington Books, 2012.

Todorov, Andrey. "Dire Straits of the Russian Arctic: Options and Challenges for a Potential US FONOP in the Northern Sea Route." *Marine Policy* 139 (2022): 105020.

Todorov, Andrey A. "The Russia-USA Legal Dispute over the Straits of the Northern Sea Route and Similar Case of the Northwest Passage." *Arctic and North* 29:1 (2017): 62–75.

Vadell, Javier. "China's Bilateral and Minilateral Relationship with Latin America and the Caribbean: the Case of China–CELAC Forum." *Area Development and Policy* 7:2 (2022): 187–203.

Wang, Elisa Hsiu-chi. "Challenges for the Republic of China: Diplomatic Relations within Latin America after the Regime Rotation in 2016." *Revista UNISCI (Unidad de Investigación sobre Seguridad y Cooperación Internacional)* 46 (2018): 69–86.

Wise, Carol and Victoria Chonn Ching. "Conceptualizing China–Latin America Relations in the Twenty-first Century: The Boom, the Bust, and the Aftermath." *The Pacific Review* 31:5 (2018): 553–572.

Wu, Wenyuan. *Chinese Oil Enterprises in Latin America: Corporate Social Responsibility.* Cham: Palgrave Macmillan, 2019.

Yang, Hee-Yong and Seungho Lee. "China's Engagement with Latin America and its Implications for Soft Balancing against the United States." *Asian Perspective* 44:4 (2020): 587–615.

Zanchetta, Barbara. "Between Cold War Imperatives and State-Sponsored Terrorism: The United States and 'Operation Condor.'" *Studies in Conflict & Terrorism* 39:12 (2016): 1084–1102.

7 Americans versus Americans

Introduction

In contrast to the cases reviewed in Chapters 5 and 6, such as those concerning the Mexico–United States border, the Falkland/Malvinas Islands and Guantanamo Bay, other territorial disputes on the continent present agents with similar bargaining power.[1] More precisely, cases explored in previous chapters that included central, strong or advantaged agents such as the United Kingdom, the United States, Russia, China and India characterize themselves by their different realpolitik influences in comparison to other agents involved in the relevant territorial dispute despite, for example, public international law granting legal sovereign equality to states.[2] Conversely, while legal sovereign equality is still present, this chapter focuses on cases in which the involved agents have similar situations with regard to their bargaining power in the territorial dispute at hand, whether they are the challenger or the challenged agent.

Broadly, the territorial disputes between American states reviewed in this chapter originated and are fueled by several elements and features, such as historical roots, the exploration and exploitation of natural resources and the sociological, ethnic and cultural components. Therein, the first part of the chapter will introduce a basic typology of these differences to distinguish between border disputes, resource disputes, ideological disputes, influence disputes, migratory disputes and leaders' prestige disputes.[3]

To more comprehensively present and assess these cases, the territorial disputes are divided into three clusters that correspond to three different geopolitical regions: North America, Central America and the Caribbean Basin and South America. Thus, the second part of the chapter will focus on North America and the disputes between the United States and Canada centered

1 The author is indebted to Fabio Fernández for his research assistance on this chapter.

2 For factual sovereignty, normative sovereignty, axiological sovereignty and the difference between sovereignty in law and sovereignty in realpolitik see Chapter 2.

3 Typology based on J. Child, "Interstate Relations in Latin America: Peaceful or Conflictual?" *International Journal* 43:3 (1988): 378–403.

DOI: 10.4324/9781003350828-9

on maritime claims.[4] The third part will show how different elements and features have worked together in negative synergy to foster differences in Central America and the Caribbean Basin. Colonial seeds, the 1982 United Nations Convention on the Law of the Sea (UNCLOS) and the redefinition of areas such as the exclusive economic zone (EEZ), new technologies and the presence of natural resources have resulted in several differences, such as in the cases of Guatemala and Belize,[5] Guyana and Suriname,[6] Venezuela and Guyana,[7] Nicaragua and Costa Rica and El Salvador and Honduras.[8]

Most of the territorial disputes in South America are now resolved. They all had roots in colonial times. There are, however, several hallmarks of territorial disputes that are present in areas like the Amazon[9] and the Southern Cone that will be explored in the fourth part of the chapter: it is a territory rich in natural resources that attracts domestic, regional and international agents[10] such as sovereign states, indigenous peoples, non-governmental organizations, multinational private companies and scientists; politicians and academics seem to agree that the internationalization[11] of the Amazon is not advisable; current

4 Note the Mexico–United States border is settled and, therefore, not included here. For a view on this border and ongoing controversies see Chapter 6.

5 Alma H. Young and Dennis H. Young, "The Impact of the Anglo-Guatemalan Dispute on the Internal Politics of Belize," *Latin American Perspectives* 15:2 (1988): 6–30; William Bianchi, *Belize: The Controversy between Guatemala and Great Britain over the Territory of British Honduras in Central America* (New York, NY: Las Americas, 1959).

6 Thomas W. Donovan, "Suriname-Guyana Maritime and Territorial Disputes: A Legal and Historical Analysis," *Journal of Transnational Law and Policy* 13:1 (2003): 41–98.

7 Thomas W. Donovan, "Challenges to the Territorial Integrity of Guyana: A Legal Analysis," *Georgia Journal of International and Comparative Law* 32 (2004): 661–724; Jacqueline Braveboy-Wagner, *The Venezuela-Guyana Border Dispute* (Boulder, CO: Westview Press, 1984).

8 L. H. Martin and Y. B. Parkhomenko, "The Territorial and Maritime Dispute (Nicaragua v. Colombia) and Its Implications for Future Maritime Delimitations in the Caribbean Sea and Elsewhere," in E. Sobenes Obregon and B. Samson, eds., *Nicaragua Before the International Court of Justice* (Cham: Springer, 2018), 113–141; Martin Pratt, "The Maritime Boundary Dispute between Honduras and Nicaragua in the Caribbean Sea," *Boundary and Security Bulletin* 9:2 (2001): 106–116.

9 Note the author uses the terms Amazonia or Amazon rainforest to refer to the geographical area in which many sovereign states in South America may have sovereignty claims.

10 Paul E. Little, *Amazonia: Territorial Struggles on Perennial Frontiers* (Baltimore, MD: Johns Hopkins University Press, 2001).

11 See the speech by Cristovam Buarque, Professor at the University of Brasilia, former candidate for the Presidency of Brazil (2006), former District Governor and Senator, in *Revista Diálogo Educacional* 3:5 (2002): 107–108 available (in Portuguese) at https://periodicos.pucpr.br/index.php/dialogoeducacional/article/download/4753/4705 accessed 23 June 2023. There are many resources in Portuguese opposed to the internationalization of Amazonia that are not translated into English. See, for example, Pio Penna Filho, "Interações Regionais e Pressões Internacionais sobre a Pan-Amazônia: Perspectivas Brasileiras," in Gilberto F. Gheller, Selma L. M. Gonzales and Laerte P. Mello, eds., *Amazônia e Atlântico Sul: Desafios e Perspectivas para a Defesa no Brasil* (Brasilia: IPEA, 2015), 17–38; Arthur C. F. Reis, "A Amazônia e a Integridade do Brasil," in *Brasília: Senado Federal* (Brasilia: Conselho Editorial, 2001); and many more.

issues[12] include illegal cross-border immigration and differences over resource extraction; border reconfiguration[13] can emerge as a social construction; indigenous communities[14] do not necessarily conform to legally defined borders and their claims to ethno-territorial rights are usually opposed to the interests of sovereign states and private companies; and the presence of external guarantors suggests an arguably more robust peaceful agreement. For example, the guarantors[15] were key in the final dispute resolution between Ecuador and Peru[16] achieved in the 1998 Brasilia Peace Agreement.[17]

As in the previous chapters, the final section will incorporate the multidimensional approach to explain and assess key elements and features pertaining to the cases explored below.

Types of disputes

Evidently, each territorial dispute has its own characteristics. However, all territorial disputes encompass a challenger, a challenged agent, different kinds of claims, issues at stake and contexts.[18] The claims include legal and non-legal reasons, such as effective control, historical accounts, culture, territorial integrity, economic relevance, elitist and/or ideological elements and features. In turn, the issues at stake comprise characteristics including the strategic and economic value of the territory, ties to bordering minorities and political unification. Finally, the domestic, regional and international contexts are intertwined to different degrees. For instance, the prior loss of territory or a prior unresolved dispute in the domestic context may foster regional and interna-

12 Ligia T. L. Simonian and Rubens da Silva Ferreira, "Brazilian Migrant Workers in French Guiana," in Ruben Gowricharn, ed., *Caribbean Transnationalism: Migration, Pluralization, and Social Cohesion* (Lanham, MD: Lexington Books, 2006), 99–116, Chapter 6.

13 Laetitia Perrier Bruslé, "Multi-Scalar Perspectives and Multi-Agent Process in a South American Borderland Region," *Geopolitics* 18: 3 (2013): 584–611.

14 Markus Kröger and Rickard Lalander, "Ethno-Territorial Rights and the Resource Extraction Boom in Latin America: Do Constitutions Matter?" *Third World Quarterly* 37:4 (2016): 682–702.

15 Complete text of the 1942 Rio de Janeiro Protocol available at https://www.cia.gov/library/readingroom/docs/CIA-RDP08C01297R000700110015-9.pdf accessed 23 June 2023.

16 David Scott Palmer, "Peru-Ecuador Border Conflict: Missed Opportunities, Misplaced Nationalism, and Multilateral Peacekeeping," *Journal of Interamerican Studies and World Affairs* 39:3 (1997): 109–148.

17 Complete text of the 1998 Brasilia Peace Agreement (in Spanish) available at https://www.usip.org/sites/default/files/file/resources/collections/peace_agreements/ep_brasilia10261998.pdf accessed 23 June 2023; Monica Herz and João Pontes Nogueira, *Ecuador vs. Peru: Peacemaking Amid Rivalry* (London: Lynne Rienner, 2002), 97–100.

18 For details about categories of claims, issues at stake and contexts relevant to territorial disputes see Jorge E. Núñez, *Territorial Disputes and State Sovereignty: International Law and Politics* (London and New York, NY: Routledge, Taylor & Francis Group, 2020), Chapter 4.

tional alliances. Taking into account the different categories of claims, the different issues at stake and the possible contexts at play, a typology[19] of territorial disputes can be outlined as follows:

Border disputes

These disputes happen when two or more sovereign states share common borders. In the Americas at the time of the colonial empires, it was common for there to be a lack of actual demarcation or a clear principle to stipulate a boundary, arising in differences in the post-independence period between newly formed states.[20] In addition to a normative lacuna or the legal imprecision, factual circumstances related to territory (e.g. high mountains, jungles and swamps) and population (e.g. the presence of former slaves, indigenous populations and drug traffickers) challenged (and in some cases, still do challenge) the effective control of legally established borders.

Resource disputes

Related to territory, of both land and sea, the actual or perceived presence of natural resources contributes to differences. Energy resources in the form of hydrocarbons and hydroelectricity and food and water resources (e.g. fisheries, subterranean water) are examples of elements and features that are linked with the economic and strategic value of the disputed territory. Importantly, resource disputes are related to factual and normative elements and features. Factually, in addition to the location of resources in areas in which borders overlap, technological developments continue to add new and more effective ways to explore and exploit resources that would otherwise be inaccessible or unknown. Normatively, changes in the relevant law, like the UNCLOS, bring about new ways to interpret key concepts relevant to resource ownership and, consequently, their exploration and exploitation.

Ideological disputes

The Americas include disputes that stem from and/or are maintained by arguments based on purely ideological premises. Broadly, and by application of political theory, the continent could be divided into those agents—e.g. individuals, communities and states—that follow liberalism and those that support Marxism (or variants of these two).[21] Most states in the Americas

19 Typology based on J. Child, "Interstate Relations in Latin America: Peaceful or Conflictual?" *International Journal* 43:3 (1988): 378–403.

20 See Chapter 4.

21 For details about liberalism, Marxism and other political theories pertaining to the state see Jorge E. Núñez, *Territorial Disputes and State Sovereignty: International Law and Politics* (London and New York, NY: Routledge, Taylor & Francis Group, 2020), Chapter 2.

have or define themselves as liberal democracies. Liberalism, at least from one point of view, defends values such as toleration and personal liberty that allow pluralism.[22] Conversely, Marxists maintain liberalism is in fact an instrument for class domination. By controlling the state, and therefore the means of production, the dominant class secures its place of privilege in society.[23] Often endorsed by central, strong or advantaged agents like the United States and Russia,[24] this kind of dispute, therefore, flows from agents intending to influence others by means of their dogmatic credos.

Influence disputes

This kind of difference relates to the maintenance and projection of domestic power and prestige at regional and international level. Indeed, as an agent, states have domestic, regional and international agendas. Some states like the United States[25] include in their agendas the extension of their power and prestige beyond their legally defined borders. This influence may be direct and indirect and include the use of hard and soft power. Examples of hard power include economic sanctions, military invasion and military aid. Examples of soft power comprise targeted investments or loans, media and foreign policy that uses institutions—for instance in humanitarian intervention—to fulfill domestic agendas.

Migratory disputes

Due to domestic conflict or financial crisis, refugees and exiles have often been a characteristic of the American landscape. Moreover, cultural, ethnic, religious, sociological or linguistic homogeneity between populations living close by (e.g. natives and former slaves) may contribute to the origin and development of territorial disputes. In addition to individuals and communities willingly migrating, as with the gold diggers or *garimpeiros*,[26] the Americas also experience forced migrations caused by governments, e.g. military coups, and non-governmental groups like *guerrilleros*, e.g. the Sandinista National Liberation Front in Nicaragua (FSLN), the Zapatista Army of National Liberation (EZLN) in Mexico and the Revolutionary Armed Forces of Colombia (FARC).

22 George Crowder, "Two Value-Pluralist Arguments for Liberalism," *Australian Journal of Political Science* 37:3 (2002): 457–473.

23 Olusegun Oladipo, "The Marxist Theory of the State," in F. A. Adeigbo, ed., *Readings in Social and Political Philosophy* (Ibadan: Claverianum Press, 1991), Vol. I.

24 For the ongoing European influence in the Americas see Chapter 5. For the interference of central, strong or advantaged agents like the United States, Russia, China and India see Chapter 6.

25 For further details about the United States and its influence in the Americas see Chapter 6.

26 See Chapter 5.

Leaders' prestige disputes

While influence disputes are those related to the projection of states' domestic power, leaders' prestige disputes are fueled by the interests of other agents such as individuals or groups—e.g. political parties. Internal political prestige can be a strong reason to start a territorial dispute and keep it unresolved.[27] Americas' history shows many cases in which political leaders, *caudillos* and *libertadores* arguably justified territorial disputes based on assumed entitlement, natural resources, actual or perceived economic potential of the territory in question or prior loss of the territory. Indeed, the domestic political needs of state leaders can heavily influence their foreign policy agenda.[28]

Territorial disputes in North America

Historically, the United States and Canada have been able to settle border differences peacefully.[29] However, they still have several territorial disputes centered on maritime claims based on border and resource issues. These differences relate to the Dixon Entrance (Alaska and British Columbia), the Northwest Passage, the Beaufort Sea (Yukon-Alaska), the Strait of Juan de Fuca (Washington state and British Columbia) and the Machias Seal Island and the North Rock.

The Dixon Entrance dispute stems from the establishment in 1903 by the Alaska Boundary Tribunal of the "A-B line" between Alaska and Canada that comprises the land boundary.[30] The maritime boundary, however, is still in question. While Canada argues the A-B line is an international maritime boundary, the United States counterargues with a different interpretation—i.e. claiming that the equidistance principle between the two land masses applies and, therefore, the boundary would be 12 miles south of the A-B line, granting them a larger space.[31] The Dixon Entrance dispute is centered on natural resources—i.e. fish, principally salmon.[32]

27 Paul K. Huth, *Standing Your Ground: Territorial Disputes and International Conflict* (Ann Arbor, MI: University of Michigan Press, 2001), 101.

28 Jorge E. Núñez, *Territorial Disputes and State Sovereignty: International Law and Politics* (London and New York, NY: Routledge, Taylor & Francis Group, 2020), Chapter 4.

29 For a comprehensive list of relevant provisions see Franklin K. Van Zandt, *Boundaries of the United States and the Several States: Geological Survey Bulletin 1212* (Washington, DC: United States Government Printing Office, 1966) available at https://pubs.usgs.gov/bul/1212/report.pdf accessed 2 April 2024.

30 Sara McLaughlin Mitchell and Andrew P. Owsiak, "Judicialization of the Sea: Bargaining in the Shadow of UNCLOS," *American Journal of International Law* 115:4 (2021): 579–621.

31 Sara McLaughlin Mitchell, "Clashes at Sea: Explaining the Onset, Militarization, and Resolution of Diplomatic Maritime Claims," *Security Studies* 29:4 (2020): 637–670.

32 David H. Gray, "Canada's Unresolved Maritime Boundaries," *IBRU Boundary and Security Bulletin* 5:3 (1997): 61–70.

The Northwest Passage can be characterized as a boundary, resources and influence dispute, with Canada claiming these are internal waters and the United States supporting the notion that this is an international strait.[33] On the one hand, the Passage is tightly linked to the Canadian national interest and Canada's Arctic presence. On the other hand, the United States considers the Northwest Passage should be open to international navigation and not under the exclusive sovereignty of any state.[34] The different positions resulted in the 1969 SS *Manhattan* incident and, more recently, issues with commercial agents intending to explore and exploit oil.[35] Moreover, despite the steady increase of vessel traffic and commercial interest, both states are failing to respond with adequate infrastructure in terms of a marine transportation system and search and rescue support.[36]

The Beaufort Sea dispute refers to a maritime area 200 nautical miles north of the border between Yukon and Alaska.[37] Both of the highest courts, that of Canada and that of the United States, have confirmed that the federal governments and not the provinces or states own the area in question.[38] Interestingly, this difference includes other agents in addition to sovereign states, and these are the indigenous populations. More precisely, there is acknowledgment by the Canadian government of the Inuvialuit (or Inuit) rights in the region and their growing influence in the future of the territory.[39] Importantly, because the United States has not ratified the UNCLOS, arguments about the applicable mechanisms to resolve the situation can be expected.[40] Finally, as in

33 Jeremy Seth Geddert, "Right of (Northwest) Passage: Toward a Responsible Canadian Arctic Sovereignty," *Canadian Journal of Political Science/Revue canadienne de science politique* 52:3 (2019): 595–612.

34 Donald R. Rothwell, "The Canadian-US Northwest Passage Dispute: A Reassessment," *Cornell International Law Journal* 26:2 (1993): 331–372.

35 D. C. Burke, "The Northwest Passage Dispute," Oxford Research Group, 2018 available at https://findresearcher.sdu.dk/ws/portalfiles/portal/136624827/The_Northwest_Passage_Dispute.pdf accessed 8 April 2024.

36 Rebecca Sheehan, Dimitrios Dalaklis, Anastasia Christodoulou, Megan Drewniak, Peter Raneri and Angelos Dalaklis, "The Northwest Passage in the Arctic: A Brief Assessment of the Relevant Marine Transportation System and Current Availability of Search and Rescue Services," *Logistics* 5:2 (2021): 23.

37 James S. Baker and Michael Byers, "Crossed Lines: The Curious Case of the Beaufort Sea Maritime Boundary Dispute," *Ocean Development & International Law* 43:1 (2012): 70–95.

38 Nora Refai, "The Beaufort Sea Boundary Dispute: A Consideration of Rights of Inuit in Canada and the United States," *Alberta Law Review* 60:1 (2022): 267–306.

39 Rob Huebert, "Drawing Boundaries in the Beaufort Sea: Different Visions/Different Needs," *Journal of Borderlands Studies* 33:2 (2018): 203–223.

40 Pieter Bekker and Robert van de Poll, "Unlocking the Arctic's Resources Equitably: Using a Law-and-Science Approach to Fix the Beaufort Sea Boundary," *The International Journal of Marine and Coastal Law* 35:2 (2019): 163–200.

the previous cases, the boundary dispute encompasses natural resources—i.e. hydrocarbons.[41]

Settled in 1846, the boundary between Canada and the United States within the Strait of Juan de Fuca is not in question.[42] Development of new technologies and offshore rights, however, led to a dispute between these states concerning the area beyond the strait's entrance and relevant EEZ and continental shelf.[43] Although Canada and the United States apply the principle of equidistance to this difference, they select a different starting point.[44] Particular to this case, the province of British Columbia has a distinctive claim; but, similar to the Dixon Entrance dispute, this difference is centered on natural resources—i.e. fish.[45] There seems to be little concern on both sides to resolve the dispute, arguably because a compromise on a principle applicable to the boundary delimitation could jeopardize their position in relation to other differences.[46]

Finally, the Machias Seal Island[47] and the North Rock,[48] as with the previous cases, are disputes related to location and resource issues based on imprecise agreements and/or contradictory agreements. Located between New Brunswick (Canada) and the state of Maine (United States), the Machias Seal Island was placed, according to the 1783 Treaty of Paris between the United States and Great Britain,[49] under the control of the former. But, according to the 1621 Royal Charter, Nova Scotia (including islands within six leagues) was

41 I. V. Bunik, "US–Canada Beaufort Sea Maritime Boundary Dispute in the Perspective of International Law," *Moscow Journal of International Law* 2 (2018): 126–137.

42 Treaty Establishing the Boundary in the Territory on the Northwest Coast of America Lying Westward of the Rocky Mountains, 15 June 1846 available at https://web.archive.org/web/20091113034143/http://www.lexum.umontreal.ca/ca_us/en/cus.1846.28.en.html accessed 9 April 2024.

43 J. K. Renouf, *Canada's Unresolved Maritime Boundaries* (Fredericton, NB: Canada, 1988), 73–82.

44 David A. Colson and Robert W. Smith, *International Maritime Boundaries (Vol. V)* (Dordrecht and Boston, MA: Martinus Nijhoff, 2005), 3403.

45 Douglas M. Johnston and Mark J. Valencia, *Pacific Ocean Boundary Problems: Status and Solutions* (Dordrecht and Boston, MA: Martinus Nijhoff, 1991), 101–104.

46 M. Byers and A. Østhagen, "Why Does Canada Have So Many Unresolved Maritime Boundary Disputes?" *Canadian Yearbook of International Law* 54 (2017): 1–62.

47 Sara McLaughlin Mitchell, "Clashes at Sea: Explaining the Onset, Militarization, and Resolution of Diplomatic Maritime Claims," *Security Studies* 29:4 (2020): 637–670.

48 Ted L. McDorman, *Salt Water Neighbors: International Ocean Law Relations between the United States and Canada* (Oxford: Oxford University Press, 2009).

49 1783 Treaty of Paris complete text available at https://www.oas.org/sap/peacefund/VirtualLibrary/Inter-StateDisputes/Belize-Guatemala/Treaties/ParisPeaceTreaty1783.pdf accessed 15 April 2024. See in particular art. 2 that referred to Nova Scotia and the islands "within twenty leagues of any of the shores of the United States...excepting the islands as now are or heretofore have been within the limits of the said province of Nova Scotia."

granted to Sir William Alexander.[50] The smaller North Rock lies in the same disputed area where both states argue they have overlapping jurisdictions.[51]

Territorial disputes in Central America and the Caribbean

Geopolitically, this cluster of disputes is in the United States vicinity and some of them are influenced by either direct or indirect interference.[52] For instance, the now resolved situation in Panama involved the *de facto* ruler General Manuel Noriega, ideological differences, drug trafficking, security needs and military installations.[53] Other United States' involvements in the area that can be characterized as ideological disputes between this superpower and, at the time, the Union of Soviet Socialist Republics (USSR) are the cases of Cuba, in particular under Fidel Castro's administration, and Nicaragua under the Sandinista leadership.[54]

Differing from the North American cluster, the Central America and the Caribbean Basin controversies involve continental inland and insular agents, and some of them can be characterized as being ideological, influence and leaders' prestige disputes. Like the disputes in the northern region, the differences in the Central American and the Caribbean Basin cluster encompass issues relating to colonial roots, the UNCLOS, relevant terms such as the continental shelf and EEZ, new technologies and the actual and potential presence of natural resources. Examples are the disputes between Guatemala and Belize,[55] Guyana and Suriname,[56] Venezuela and Guyana,[57] Nicaragua and Costa Rica and El Salvador and Honduras.[58]

50 Alexander Fraser, *Nova Scotia, The Royal Charter of 1621 to Sir William Alexander* (Toronto: University of Toronto Press, 1922), 25–51 available at https://dn790005.ca.archive.org/0/items/novascotiaroyalc00frasuoft/novascotiaroyalc00frasuoft.pdf accessed 15 April 2024.

51 Henry T. King Jr., "Settlement of International Disputes between Canada and the USA," *Canada-United States Law Journal* 35:1–2 (2011): 46–85.

52 See Chapter 6.

53 J. Child, "Interstate Relations in Latin America: Peaceful or Conflictual?" *International Journal* 43:3 (1988): 378–403.

54 For a thorough account of the period see Jennie K. Lincoln and Elizabeth G. Ferris, eds., *The Dynamics of Latin American Foreign Policies: Challenges for the 1980s* (New York, NY and Oxford: Routledge, Taylor & Francis, 1984).

55 Alma H. Young and Dennis H. Young, "The Impact of the Anglo-Guatemalan Dispute on the Internal Politics of Belize," *Latin American Perspectives* 15:2 (1988): 6–30; William Bianchi, *Belize: The Controversy between Guatemala and Great Britain over the Territory of British Honduras in Central America* (New York, NY: Las Americas, 1959).

56 Thomas W. Donovan, "Suriname-Guyana Maritime and Territorial Disputes: A Legal and Historical Analysis," *Journal of Transnational Law and Policy* 13:1 (2003): 41–98.

57 Thomas W. Donovan, "Challenges to the Territorial Integrity of Guyana: A Legal Analysis," *Georgia Journal of International and Comparative Law* 32 (2004): 661–724; Jacqueline Braveboy-Wagner, *The Venezuela-Guyana Border Dispute* (Boulder, CO: Westview Press, 1984).

58 L. H. Martin and Y. B. Parkhomenko, "The Territorial and Maritime Dispute (Nicaragua v. Colombia) and Its Implications for Future Maritime Delimitations in the Caribbean Sea and Elsewhere," in E. Sobenes Obregon and B. Samson, eds., *Nicaragua Before the International*

The dispute between Guatemala and Belize is ongoing. The two countries were once under Spanish and British sovereignty, respectively. After gaining independence from Spain, Guatemala recognized British sovereignty over what is currently Belize (Wyke-Aycinena Treaty, 1859).[59] Following Belize's independence, controversies in respect of Guatemala's claim to Belize's territory have continued until recently.[60] In 2019, both states had referendums concerning the dispute and the case, it was decided, would be submitted to the International Court of Justice (ICJ).[61] The case is still decision pending.[62]

As with the historical background behind the Guatemala-Belize dispute, the difference between Guyana and Suriname stems from an agreement between the former colonial powers of Great Britain and the Netherlands. First, the 1799 agreement between the Dutch colonies of Berbice (part of present-day Guyana) and Suriname set the banks of the Courantyne River as a natural border.[63] After the Napoleonic wars, by the 1814 Treaty of London, territories were ceded to Great Britain and, therefore, the border was between British Guiana (now, Guyana) and Dutch Guiana (now, Suriname).[64] Because the agreements did not consider the source of the Courantyne River, claims appeared over what is known as the "New River Triangle" or "Tigri" area.[65] A region rich in natural resources,[66] the ongoing dispute over the territory includes land and maritime claims.[67]

Court of Justice (Cham: Springer, 2018), 113–141; Martin Pratt, "The Maritime Boundary Dispute between Honduras and Nicaragua in the Caribbean Sea," *Boundary and Security Bulletin* 9:2 (2001): 106–116.

59 Complete text of the 1859 Wyke-Aycinena Treaty available at http://www.belizereferendum.gov.bz/files/Treaty-1859%20-%20Text.pdf accessed 12 April 2024.

60 Maria Zhomartkyzy, "Mediation in Diplomatic Conflicts. Examples from Latin America," *ScienceRise: Juridical Science* 3:25 (2023): 72–84; Arlenie Perez, Chuang Chin-Ta and Farok Afero, "Belize-Guatemala Territorial Dispute and its Implications for Conservation," *Tropical Conservation Science* 2:1 (2009): 11–24; John R. Crook, "The Special Agreement Between Belize and Guatemala to Submit Guatelmala's Territorial, Insular and Maritime Claims to the International Court of Justice," *International Legal Materials* 48:2 (2009): 250–255.

61 Katherine Collin, "Peacemaking Referendums: The Use of Direct Democracy in Peace Processes," *Democratization* 27: 5 (2020): 717–736.

62 For all relevant information concerning the ICJ's involvement in the Guatemala-Belize territorial dispute, including the latest updates, see https://www.icj-cij.org/case/177 accessed 12 April 2024.

63 Thomas W. Donovan, "Challenges to the Territorial Integrity of Guyana: A Legal Analysis," *Georgia Journal of International and Comparative Law* 32 (2004): 661–724.

64 For the complete text of the 1814 Convention between Great Britain and the Netherlands see https://hansard.parliament.uk/Commons/1815-06-09/debates/0e7491ad-421f-4e13-9843-e5a4e4591f6c/ConventionBetweenGreatBritainAndTheNetherlands accessed 12 April 2024.

65 Patricia Marín Luján, "Geopolítica, Conflictos Fronterizos en América Latina," *Revista Geopolítica Transfronteiriça* 1:1 (2017): 1–14.

66 Raphael Padula, Matheus de Freitas Cecílio, Igor Candido de Oliveira and Caio Jorge Prado, "Guyana: Oil, Internal Disputes, the USA and Venezuela," *Contexto Internacional* 45:1 (2023): 1–25.

67 Pascale Ricard and Denys-Sacha Robin, "The Superposition of National Legal Regimes in Maritime Disputed Areas," *Maritime Safety and Security Journal* 10 (2022): 37–58.

Another difference involving an area rich in natural resources is the Venezuela and Guyana territorial dispute over the Essequibo region,[68] an area that encompasses two-thirds of Guyana's land territory. The region was occupied by Great Britain in 1814 after Venezuela's independence; in 1899, the Paris Arbitral Award determined the boundary line between British Guiana (nowadays, Guyana) and Venezuela.[69] Since 1962, Venezuela has officially claimed the territory based on historical entitlement.[70] The 1966 Geneva Agreement, by which Venezuela and the United Kingdom accepted the nullity of the Paris Arbitral Award, was followed by the 1970 Port of Spain Protocol and the involvement of the Organization of American States (OAS) and the United Nations (UN).[71] Recently, there have been developments regarding the difference that have attracted the attention of the UN Security Council.[72]

In the dispute between Nicaragua and Costa Rica, there were many steps to settle the border including the 1858 Cañas-Jerez Treaty,[73] the 1888 Cleveland Award,[74] and the 1897 First and Second Alexander Awards.[75] In short, Nicaragua has sovereignty over Rio San Juan while Costa Rica has navigation rights subject to conditions. Because of different claims concerning the violation of navigation rights by Nicaragua and other issues in the same area,

68 Anthony R. Cummings, "How Guyana's Oil Discovery Rekindled a Border Controversy," *Journal of Latin American Geography* 17:3 (2018): 183–211.

69 The complete 1899 Arbitral Award Regarding the Boundary between the Colony of British Guiana and the United States of Venezuela available at https://legal.un.org/riaa/cases/vol_XXVIII/331-340.pdf accessed 12 April 2024.

70 See the 1962 Venezuelan Official Statement at https://digitallibrary.un.org/record/862319?v=pdf accessed 12 April 2024.

71 For an up-to-date account see Rafael Ramírez, "The Venezuela-Guyana Dispute over the Essequibo," Istituto Affari Internazionali (2024) available at https://www.iai.it/sites/default/files/iaicom2407.pdf accessed 12 April 2024; Raghunath Mahabir and Keron Ganpat, "Border Security and Oil War in the Latin America and Caribbean Region: A Case Study of the Dispute between Guyana and Venezuela," *News. Series: International Relations and Area Studies* 55:1 (2024) available at https://bulletin-irr.ablaikhan.kz/index.php/j1/article/view/384 accessed 12 April 2024.

72 See "Private Meeting on the Territorial Dispute between Guyana and Venezuela," published on 9 April 2024 available at https://www.securitycouncilreport.org/whatsinblue/2024/04/private-meeting-on-the-territorial-dispute-between-guyana-and-venezuela.php accessed 16 April 2024.

73 The 1858 Cañas-Jerez Treaty complete text available at https://jusmundi.com/en/document/treaty/en-treaty-of-limits-between-costa-rica-and-nicaragua-1858-canas-jerez-treaty-1858-thursday-15th-april-1858 accessed 16 April 2024.

74 The 1888 Cleveland Award complete text available at https://legal.un.org/riaa/cases/vol_XXVIII/189-213.pdf accessed 16 April 2024.

75 The 1897 First Alexander Award complete text available at https://legal.un.org/riaa/cases/vol_XXVIII/215-222.pdf; and the 1897 Second Alexander Award complete text available at https://legal.un.org/riaa/cases/vol_XXVIII/223-225.pdf both accessed 16 April 2024.

the ICJ has intervened on several occasions.[76] Notably, in all cases, both parties have resorted to peaceful means to solve their differences.

The difference between El Salvador and Honduras over the Gulf of Fonseca and the maritime spaces within and outside it was settled by the ICJ in 1992.[77] In 2002, El Salvador requested a revision of this judgment based on different and new facts in comparison to the original case which, in turn, the ICJ considered not to be "decisive factors."[78]

At times, regional organizations have played a central role in terms of dispute resolution. For instance, the Central American (CACJ) and the Caribbean Courts of Justice (CCJ) have no jurisdiction, in principle, over territorial disputes.[79] Interestingly, in 2011, the CACJ intervened in the territorial dispute between Costa Rica and Nicaragua.[80] Importantly, the Organization of American States (OAS) Peace Fund has been instrumental in the peaceful resolution of the disputes between Honduras and Nicaragua, El Salvador and Honduras and Belize and Guatemala.[81]

It is important to note that in addition to traditional agents such as sovereign states and regional organizations, there are others involved in territorial disputes in Central America and the Caribbean.[82] Ethnic and cultural diversity characterize the area. For example, in terms of indigenous peoples, the Mesoamerican cultures spread from Mexico (Yucatan and Chiapas) to Costa Rica, Guatemala, Honduras, El Salvador and Nicaragua. These communities tend to reject the "mono-ethnic and homogeneous" sovereign state

76 See, for example, in 2017, ICJ's "Land Boundary in the Northern Part of Isla Portillos (Costa Rica v. Nicaragua)" available at https://www.icj-cij.org/case/165; and in 2005, ICJ's "Dispute regarding Navigational and Related Rights (Costa Rica v. Nicaragua)" available at https://www.icj-cij.org/case/133 both accessed 16 April 2024.

77 See ICJ's "Land, Island and Maritime Frontier Dispute (El Salvador/Honduras: Nicaragua intervening)" available at https://www.icj-cij.org/case/75 accessed 16 April 2024.

78 See ICJ's "Application for Revision of the Judgment of 11 September 1992 in the Case concerning the Land, Island and Maritime Frontier Dispute (El Salvador/Honduras: Nicaragua intervening) (El Salvador v. Honduras)" available at https://www.icj-cij.org/case/127 accessed 16 April 2024.

79 See the Statue of the Central American Court of Justice, Article 22; "The Court's competence includes the following: a) To hear, at the request of any of the Member States, the controversies that arise among them. Excepted are frontier, territorial or maritime controversies, which may not be heard without the consent of all parties concerned." Complete text available at https://treaties.un.org/doc/Publication/UNTS/Volume%201821/volume-1821-I-31191-English.pdf accessed 11 April 2024. See also "Costa Rica, El Salvador, Guatemala, Honduras, Nicaragua, Panama: Statute of the Central American Court of Justice," *International Legal Materials* 34:4 (1995): 921–934, 930.

80 Salvatore Caserta, "Regional International Courts in Search of Relevance: Adjudicating Politically Sensitive Disputes in Central America and the Caribbean," *Duke Journal of Comparative and International Law* 28:1 (2017): 59–97.

81 For detailed information about the OAS Peace Fund and the involvement in dispute resolution see https://www.oas.org/sap/peacefund/peacefund/ accessed 16 April 2024.

82 The cases of indigenous and implanted populations are explored in Chapter 8.

model and, instead, allow for "new multinational or multi-ethnic" informal arrangements.[83] These multi-ethnic and multi-cultural aspects together with individual agents such as *caudillos* have fueled territorial disputes in the past and are still intertwined with ongoing differences. Other non-traditional agents in the region that have had (and still have in some cases) influence in domestic governments and legal and political situations, and therefore, territorial disputes, include drug traffickers and guerrilla forces.[84]

In the intersection between the Central American and Caribbean and the South American clusters, the settled territorial dispute of San Andrés, Providencia and Santa Catalina between Colombia and Nicaragua has several issues relating to the domestic, regional and international contexts.[85] First, although the ICJ determined the sovereign boundaries exclusive to Nicaragua and Colombia, arguments between both states are common.[86] Geographically, the archipelago is situated on the Nicaraguan Rise, approximately 185 kilometers off the Nicaraguan coast. Comprising a total land area of approximately 44 square kilometers and an overall coastline of about 20 kilometers, the archipelago includes three inhabited islands—i.e. San Andrés, Providencia and Santa Catalina; two uninhabited islands, Albuquerque and Bolivar; and uninhabited keys—i.e. Crab Cay, Cotton Cay, Johnny Cay, Haynes Cay, Rose Cay, Three Brothers Cay and Rocky Cay. The inhabitants live mainly from tourism and fishing, but the area may be rich in hydrocarbon deposits and oil fields.[87] Legally, the invocation of the Colombian Constitutional Territory Clause to the interpretation of the ICJ award brings further arguments. Because this kind of clause defines the national territory from a constitutional law point of view, Colombia maintains that only domestic authorities can exercise treaty powers regarding boundary treaties, including specific concepts defined by the international law of the sea.[88] Second, although in principle the dispute is between Nicaragua and Colombia, there are negative impacts on peace, security, natural resources exploration and exploitation at the regional level.

83 Emilio Sánches de Rojas Díaz, "Analysis of the Conflict in the Central American Corridor: Network Geopolitics," Geopolitical Overview of Conflicts 2014 (Madrid: Spanish Institute of Strategic Studies, 2014), 269–306, in particular 274–276.

84 Richard J. Kilroy, "Maritime and Territorial Boundary Disputes in Latin America," *The Journal of Territorial and Maritime Studies* 1:1 (2014): 91–111; Jack Child, "Interstate Relations in Latin America: Peaceful or Conflictual?" *International Journal* 43:3 (1988): 378–403; and many others.

85 See Chapter 5.

86 Mariano V. Ospina, "Nicaragua v. Colombia: A Stalemate in the Caribbean," *Global Security Studies* 4:4 (2013): 31–40.

87 Christian Diemer and Amalija Šeparović, "Territorial Questions and Maritime Delimitation with Regard to Nicaragua's Claims to the San Andrés Archipelago," *Heidelberg Journal of International Law* 66 (2006): 167–185.

88 Walter Arévalo-Ramírez, "Constitutions Challenging the International Court of Justice's Jurisdiction to Adjudicate Territorial Disputes in Latin America," *Heidelberg Journal of International Law* 82:2 (2022): 425–448.

Indeed, the increased value of natural resources found in maritime territory creates a greater incentive for neighbor states to claim jurisdiction over these areas.[89]

Territorial disputes in South America

All the territorial disputes in the South American cluster stem from the colonial past and encompass a variety of types, including border, migratory, natural resources and leaders' prestige disputes. Most of these disputes are now settled.[90]

Brevitatis causa, similar to the rest of the continent, after achieving independence from European empires, the newly formed states in South America found themselves with either unclearly defined or completely undefined borders and the application of the *uti possidetis* principle.[91] Introduced in the Americas with the 1811 Lozano-Cortes Treaty in an attempt to merge the United Provinces of New Granada and Venezuela into a confederation, the *uti possidetis* principle would later be applied to settle the borders between Latin American countries.[92] The principle has two variants: the first is *uti possidetis juris*, the most widely used throughout Hispanic America that gives birth to the doctrine of the same name, which consists of the premise that a newly formed sovereign state inherits its border from the territories it administered as a former colony; and the second is *uti possidetis de facto*, used by Brazil, which is based on the notion that the newly formed sovereign state draws its border from where it had the effective possession of the territory at the time of independence.[93]

The now resolved Peruvian-Ecuadorian difference offers a clear example that brings together the colonial past, the *uti possidetis* principle and leaders' prestige. Finding its roots in the creation of the Viceroys of Peru and New

89 Maria Otero, "Problems in the Caribbean: The Absence of Finality to the Territorial Dispute in Nicaragua v. Colombia Will Have Negative Impacts in the Region," *University of Toledo Law Review* 46:3 (2015): 617–646.

90 Beth A. Simmons, "Territorial Disputes and Their Resolution: The Case of Ecuador and Peru," United States Institute of Peace (USIP) Press, Washington, DC (1999) available at https://www.usip.org/sites/default/files/resources/pwks27.pdf accessed 6 May 2024.

91 See also Chapter 4.

92 Raimundo Rivas, *Historia Diplomática de Colombia (1810–1934)* (Bogotá: Ministerio de Relaciones Exteriores, 1961).

93 For a very detailed historical account of the formation of limits in South America, including applicable legal norms such as international treaties and legal principles, see Fábio Aristimunho Vargas, *Formação das Fronteiras Latino-Americanas* (Brasilia: Fundação Alexandre de Gusmão, 2017) available at https://funag.gov.br/loja/download/FORMACAO-DE-FRONTEIRAS_19_06_v_11.pdf accessed 6 May 2024. See also Jorge Domínguez, *Conflictos Territoriales y Democracia en América Latina* (Buenos Aires: Editorial Siglo XXI, 2003); Percy Cayo, *Perú y Ecuador: Antecedentes de un Largo Conflicto* (Lima: Centro de Investigación de la Universidad del Pacífico, 1995).

Granada (or Santa Fe) and the civil, military and religious administration of the provinces of Tumbes, Jaen, Guayaquil and Maynas,[94] the struggle started with discrepancies over these territories between Bolivar and San Martin, two of the main *libertadores* at the time, and their repartition of the newly formed republics of Peru and Gran Colombia. More precisely, the main controversy revolved around Tumbes and Guayaquil. Based on the *uti possidetis juris* doctrine and the self-determination principle, Tumbes would become part of Peru by pledging allegiance to San Martin.[95] In turn, Guayaquil[96] was claimed by the recently formed congress of Gran Colombia in 1820 alleging the *uti possidetis juris*[97] doctrine, and it was finally annexed in 1822 by Simon Bolivar.[98] Importantly, the presence of external guarantors suggests an arguably more robust peaceful agreement. For example, the guarantors[99] were key in the final dispute resolution between Ecuador and Peru[100] achieved in the 1998 Brasilia Peace Agreement.[101]

Peru, Chile and Bolivia were involved in the war of the Pacific concerning the Atacama Desert. Following their independence from Spain—and arguments about the interpretation of the exact location of former administrative sub-division boundaries, the application of the *uti possidetis* doctrine and the difficulties the terrain presented in conclusively discerning their borders—conflict started.[102] Settlement resulted in a landlocked Bolivia,[103] and Chile

94 William L. Krieg, *Ecuadorean-Peruvian Rivalry in the Upper Amazon* (Washington, DC: United States Department of State, 1978).

95 Germán Leguía y Martínez, *Historia de la Emancipación del Perú: El Protectorado*, 3rd ed. (Lima: Publicaciones de la Comisión Nacional del Sesquicentenario de la Independencia, 1972), 460–490.

96 William L. Krieg, *Ecuadorean-Peruvian Rivalry in the Upper Amazon* (Washington, DC: United States Department of State, 1978), 31.

97 For the difference between *uti possidetis de facto* and *uti possidetis juris* see Chapter 4.

98 Scarlett O'Phelan Godoy, "La Independencia del Perú ntes y después de la Entrevista de Guayaquil entre San Martín y Bolívar en 1822," *Anales del Museo de América* 29 (2021): 141–164; Daniel Gutíerrez Ardila, *El Reconocimiento de Colombia: Diplomacia y Propaganda en la Coyuntura de las Restauraciones (1819–1831)* (Bogotá: Universidad Externado de Colombia, 2012), 171.

99 Complete text of the 1942 Rio de Janeiro Protocol available at https://www.cia.gov/library/readingroom/docs/CIA-RDP08C01297R000700110015-9.pdf accessed 23 June 2023.

100 David Scott Palmer, "Peru-Ecuador Border Conflict: Missed Opportunities, Misplaced Nationalism, and Multilateral Peacekeeping," *Journal of Interamerican Studies and World Affairs* 39:3 (1997): 109–148.

101 Complete text of the 1998 Brasilia Peace Agreement (in Spanish) available at https://www.usip.org/sites/default/files/file/resources/collections/peace_agreements/ep_brasilia10261998.pdf accessed 23 June 2023; Monica Herz and João Pontes Nogueira, *Ecuador vs. Peru: Peacemaking Amid Rivalry* (London: Lynne Rienner, 2002), 97–100.

102 Ronald Bruce St. John, *The Bolivia-Chile-Peru Dispute in the Atacama Desert* (Durham, NC: International Boundaries Research Unit, University of Durham, 1994).

103 Ronald Bruce St. John, *Bolivia: Geopolitics of a Landlocked State* (London: Routledge, 2019).

granted them access to the Chilean port of Arica via road and railway.[104] While Bolivia maintains a pipeline to the sea, it arguably gives Chile a certain degree of control over Bolivian trade and that is a continuous cause of arguments.[105] In turn, Chile and Peru agreed that Chile retained control of Arica and that Tacna was reincorporated by Peru.[106] Regardless of the peaceful resolution between Chile and Peru, and in addition to the importance of geopolitical and natural resources, there are cultural, historical and political ingredients that have influenced their bilateral relationships. For instance, some of the other drivers behind their foreign policies include political figures such as Pinochet in Chile and Fujimori in Peru and their respective domestic, regional and international interests; the 1995 Alto Cenepa conflict between Peru and Ecuador; the maritime boundary;[107] and terrorist groups such as Sendero Luminoso and Movimiento Revolucionario Túpac Amaru.[108]

In the past, the Amazon and Southern Cone regions featured bloody conflicts such as the 1864–1870 Triple Alliance War (Argentina, Brazil, Uruguay and Paraguay)[109] and the 1932–1935 Chaco War (Bolivia and Paraguay).[110] Although these situations belong in the past, these differences encompassed several aspects that are nowadays entangled with more current elements and features. Key traits include the fact that these areas are rich in natural resources and attract domestic, regional and international agents[111] such as sovereign states, indigenous peoples, non-governmental organizations, multinational private companies and scientists. Moreover, politicians and academics seem to

104 Complete text of the Treaty of Peace and Friendship between Chile and Bolivia available at https://upload.wikimedia.org/wikipedia/commons/8/81/Treaty_of_Peace_and_Friedship_between_Chile_and_Bolivia_of_1904.pdf accessed 30 April 2024.

105 See, for example, the 2013–2018 ICJ case Obligation to Negotiate Access to the Pacific Ocean (Bolivia v. Chile) available at https://www.icj-cij.org/case/153 accessed 30 April 2024.

106 Complete text of the 1929 Treaty of Lima between Chile and Peru (in Spanish) available at https://www.memoriachilena.gob.cl/602/w3-article-92277.html accessed 30 April 2024.

107 For the maritime boundary between Chile and Peru see 2008–2014 ICJ Maritime Dispute (Peru v. Chile) available at https://www.icj-cij.org/case/137 accessed 30 April 2024. See also Ana Lucía Gutiérrez González, "Peru vs Chile – The Role of International Communications in a Maritime Dispute," *Journal of Latin American Communication Research* 7:1–2 (2019): 170–191; Julio Faúndez, *The International Court of Justice in Maritime Disputes: The Case of Chile and Peru* (London: Routledge, 2018).

108 Lester Cabrera, "Territorial Discourses Opposed in the 21st Century: The Case of the Chile-Peru Relationship from a Critical Geopolitics Perspective," *Estudios Fronterizos* 19 (2018) available at https://www.scielo.org.mx/scielo.php?pid=S0187-69612018000100121&script=sci_arttext&tlng=en accessed 30 April 2024.

109 Vitor Izecksohn, "State Formation and Identity: Historiographical Trends Concerning South America's War of the Triple Alliance," *History Compass* 17:9 (2019): 1–11.

110 Bridget María Chesterton, ed., *The Chaco War: Environment, Ethnicity, and Nationalism* (London and New York, NY: Bloomsbury Publishing, 2017).

111 Paul E. Little, *Amazonia: Territorial Struggles on Perennial Frontiers* (Baltimore, MD: Johns Hopkins University Press, 2001).

agree that the internationalization of the Amazon is not advisable.[112] Pressing matters[113] encompass illegal cross-border immigration and differences over resource extraction; border reconfiguration[114] can emerge as a social construction; and indigenous communities[115] do not necessarily conform to legally defined borders and their claims to ethno-territorial rights are usually opposed to the interests of sovereign states and private companies.

Currently, these areas are largely free of inter-state disputes and those still ongoing seem not likely to result in conflict. Brazil has two current differences, one with Uruguay over Isla Brasilera, and another one with Bolivia over Isla Suárez.[116] The disputes between Argentina and Chile have involved several factors including territorial expansion, geopolitical strategy, leaders' prestige, natural resources, indigenous communities, the formation of national identities, consolidation, state-building and nationalism.[117] Having solved all their territorial disputes, it is worth mentioning the last two settlements between Argentina and Chile. In the 1970s and 1980s, the dispute over the Beagle Channel encompassed issues pertaining to geopolitical location, natural resources, leaders' prestige and nationalism and, therefore, the domestic, regional and international contexts were converging in negative synergy fostering conflict.[118] Both Argentina and Chile had authoritarian military

112 See the speech by Cristovam Buarque, Professor at the University of Brasilia, former candidate for the Presidency of Brazil (2006), former District Governor and Senator, in *Revista Diálogo Educacional* 3:5 (2002): 107–108 available (in Portuguese) at https://periodicos.pucpr.br/index.php/dialogoeducacional/article/download/4753/4705 accessed 23 June 2023. There are many resources in Portuguese opposed to the internationalization of Amazonia that are not translated into English. See, for example, Pio Penna Filho, "Interações Regionais e Pressões Internacionais sobre a Pan-Amazônia: Perspectivas Brasileiras," in Gilberto F. Gheller, Selma L. M. Gonzales and Laerte P. Mello, eds., *Amazônia e Atlântico Sul: Desafios e Perspectivas para a Defesa no Brasil* (Brasilia: IPEA, 2015): 17–38; Arthur C. F. Reis, "A Amazônia e a Integridade do Brasil" (Brasilia: Senado Federal Conselho Editorial, 2001); and many more.

113 Ligia T. L. Simonian and Rubens da Silva Ferreira, "Brazilian Migrant Workers in French Guiana," in Ruben Gowricharn, ed., *Caribbean Transnationalism: Migration, Pluralization, and Social Cohesion* (Lanham, MD: Lexington Books, 2006), 99–116, Chapter 6.

114 Laetitia Perrier Bruslé, "Multi-Scalar Perspectives and Multi-Agent Process in a South American Borderland Region," *Geopolitics* 18:3 (2013): 584–611.

115 Markus Kröger and Rickard Lalander, "Ethno-Territorial Rights and the Resource Extraction Boom in Latin America: Do Constitutions Matter?" *Third World Quarterly* 37:4 (2016): 682–702.

116 Letícia Núñez Almeida, Agnes Félix, Rafael Masson, Nathan Bueno and Jennifer Silva, "Brazil and Its Borders: History and Limits of a Sovereign State," in Beatriz Zepeda, Fernando Carrión Mena and Francisco Enríquez Bermeon, eds., *Latin America's Global Border System* (New York, NY: Routledge, 2022), 195–220.

117 Cameron G. Thies, "Territorial Nationalism in Spatial Rivalries: An Institutionalist Account of the Argentine-Chilean Rivalry," *International Interactions* 27:4 (2001): 399–431.

118 For positive and negative synergy concerning territorial disputes see Jorge E. Núñez, *Territorial Disputes and State Sovereignty: International Law and Politics* (London and New York, NY: Routledge, Taylor & Francis Group, 2020), Chapter 8. In short, synergy implies a par-

dictatorships at the time that had seized power illegally in 1976 and 1973, respectively.[119] This difference almost ended in war after British involvement but was finally resolved due to the participation of the Vatican.[120] Interestingly, this case shows that religious agents may play an important role in peace-building.[121] In 1994, the Laguna del Desierto dispute was resolved by a Latin American tribunal.[122] Notably, this was the first time in South America that such a decision was made without European or United States involvement.[123]

In terms of maritime claims including the EEZ and continental shelf,[124] Latin America and the Caribbean have had several differences that can be divided into three historical periods relating to pre-codification (1942–1958), the Geneva Conventions (1958–1982) and the UNCLOS (since 1982). In short, although there are still more than 30 maritime boundaries that require

---

ticular relationship among the members, components or objects of the whole given entity. The individual components of the whole can exist on their own, autonomously and independently; however, working together in a synergetic manner may improve their performance in terms of the whole entity (positive synergy) or may work against it (negative synergy).

119 Andrés Villar Gertner, "The Beagle Channel Frontier Dispute between Argentina and Chile: Converging Domestic and International Conflicts," *International Relations* 28:2 (2014): 207–227; Peter Van Aert, "The Beagle Conflict," *Island Studies Journal* 11:1 (2016): 307–314; Cameron G. Thies, "Territorial Nationalism in Spatial Rivalries: An Institutionalist Account of the Argentine-Chilean Rivalry," *International Interactions* 27:4 (2001): 399–431; and many more.

120 Complete text of the 1984 Treaty of Peace and Friendship between Argentina and Chile (in Spanish) available at obtienearchivo.bcn.cl/obtienearchivo?id=recursoslegales/10221.3/35109/1/Tratado_de_Paz_y_Amistad.PDF accessed 30 April 2024. See also Andrés Villar Gertner, "The Beagle Channel Frontier Dispute between Argentina and Chile: Converging Domestic and International Conflicts," *International Relations* 28:2 (2014): 207–227.

121 Alexander Bramble, Ayse S. Kadayifci and Thania Paffenholz, *Religious Actors in Formal Peace Processes* (Washington, DC: United States Institute of Peace, 2023) available at https://www.usip.org/sites/default/files/PW_194_Religious_Actors_in_Formal_Peace_Processes_Bramble.pdf accessed 9 May 2024. For two in-depth studies on the role religion plays in peacebuilding see Tsjeard Bouta, S. Ayse Kadayifci-Orellana and Mohammed Abu-Nimer, *Faith-Based Peace-Building: Mapping and Analysis of Christian, Muslim and Multi-Faith Actors* (The Hague: Netherlands Institute of International Relations Clingendael, 2005); and Kristian Berg Harpviken and Hanne Eggen Røislien, "Mapping the Terrain: The Role of Religion in Peacemaking," International Peace Research Institute, Oslo (PRIO) (2005) available at https://www.files.ethz.ch/isn/38134/2005_07_mapping_the_terrain_stateoftheartpaper__jul05_.pdf accessed 9 May 2024.

122 Complete text of the Award on the Boundary dispute between Argentina and Chile Concerning the Frontier Line Between Boundary Post 62 and Mount Fitzroy available at https://legal.un.org/riaa/cases/vol_XXII/3-149.pdf accessed 30 April 2024.

123 Maria de la Fuente, "Argentina–Chile Laguna del Desierto Arbitration," in K. W. Gray, ed., *Global Encyclopedia of Territorial Rights* (Cham: Springer International Publishing, 2022), 1–6.

124 For a very thorough analysis of relevant law and practice concerning maritime claims in Latin America and the Caribbean see Angel Horna, *Law of the Sea and Maritime Delimitation: State Practice and Case Law in Latin America and the Caribbean* (London and New York, NY: Routledge, Taylor & Francis, 2022).

delimitation in Latin America and the Caribbean, the creation of more than 40 maritime delimitation agreements between 1942 and 2021 suggests that state practice favors peaceful means to resolve these issues.

Neighboring the South American cluster, Antarctica presents several continental agents with claims. These claims can be broadly classified into two groups: (a) those based on connection grounds such as first exploration and discovery (Argentina and Chile), scientific explorations and expeditions, exploitation of natural resources and state activity; and (b) those based on official documents and geographical doctrines like the *uti possidetis juris* principle, transfer of territory, geographic continuity and contiguity and the sector principle.[125] Together with the United Kingdom, Argentina and Chile have claims that overlap. In addition to the legal and political question related to sovereignty, Antarctica is part of Argentina and Chile's national narrative.[126] Other states in South America (Brazil, Peru, Uruguay and Ecuador) have reserved their right to make future claims.[127]

As in the North American, Central American and Caribbean clusters, the territorial disputes in South America include agents other than sovereign states and regional organizations. European practices in colonial times help gain an understanding of current issues.[128] Having conquered part of the territories and settled in the form of haciendas, fincas, etc., Spain and Portugal, the states with the most presence in pre-independence South America, were not able to control all spaces. Therefore, indigenous peoples migrated to places not controlled by the Iberian states. Coupled with slaves who fled from their settlements, *maroons* and *quilombos* were born in Spanish America and Portuguese America, respectively. Decades of land occupation in several states in post-independence South America result nowadays in social movements claiming land redistribution. Furthermore, indigenous peoples challenge the notions of international borders accepted by sovereign states.[129]

125 Classification from Alejandra Mancilla, "The Moral Limits of Territorial Claims in Antarctica," *Ethics & International Affairs* 32:3 (2018): 339–360.

126 Florian Vidal, "The Antarctic Peninsula: Argentina and Chile in the Era of Global Change," *The Polar Journal* 13:1 (2023): 13–30.

127 Adrian Howkins, "Latin America and Antarctica," in *Oxford Research Encyclopedia of Latin American History* (2017) available at https://oxfordre.com/latinamericanhistory/display/10.1093/acrefore/9780199366439.001.0001/acrefore-9780199366439-e-434 accessed 9 May 2024.

128 Bernardo Mançano Fernandes and Cliff Welch, "Movements and Territorial Conflicts in Latin America," in Federico M. Rossi, ed., *The Oxford Handbook of Latin American Social Movements* (New York, NY: Oxford University Press, 2023), 266–282.

129 The cases of indigenous and implanted populations are explored in Chapter 8. See, for example, the Mapuche case in Argentina and Chile in Pablo Arturo Mansilla Quiñones and Miguel Melin Pehuen, "A Struggle for Territory, a Struggle Against Borders: The Mapuche Conflict in Argentina and Chile Contests Notions of Borders Promulgated by the Nation-State," *NACLA Report on the Americas* 51:1 (2019): 41–48.

Regardless of the characteristics of each territorial dispute, it is relevant to consider that, by the end of 1980s, most of the states in the South American cluster had peacefully ended their differences.[130] For example, most South American states face the Atlantic or the Pacific Oceans. Although domestic law may need updating in some cases because of natural resources exploration and exploitation considering their environmental impact, maritime boundaries have mostly been agreed amicably.[131] A combination of several domestic, regional and international factors[132] characterize the region, including identification, cohesiveness, type of regime, motivation, previous and ongoing relationships, distribution of power, regional institutions like the OAS, regional arbitrators and guarantors. Arguably, this suggests that a plurality of institutions, a legal framework that fosters non-interventionism, the distinction between domestic crises and international peacebuilding, the inclusion of other normative systems in addition to law such as a religion interpreted and applied in a way that favors peace, and the involvement of individuals have contributed toward solving territorial disputes amicably.[133]

A multidimensional approach

Although some territorial disputes remain, the Americas are largely free of territorial conflict. For example, in Latin America, most neighboring states (92%) have delimited their borders entirely. About a third of them (29%) partly argue about the legal settlements but without resorting to threat or use of force. Research suggests that there are several necessary and sufficient conditions to settle these territorial disputes amicably. Indeed, the cases in the Americas show that there seems to be a likelihood to peaceful resolution when a multidimensional approach that encompasses several elements and features is applied—e.g. attention should be replaced and reprioritized in

130 See Chapter 4. See also Jorge Mario Battaglino, "The Coexistence of Peace and Conflict in South America: Toward a New Conceptualization of Types of Peace," *Revista Brasileira de Política Internacional* 55:2 (2012): 131–151.

131 Eduardo Jiménez Pineda, "South American Region and Seabed Mining," in Virginie Tassin, ed., *Routledge Handbook of Seabed Mining and the Law of the Sea* (London: Routledge, 2023), 324–332.

132 Marieke Kleiboer, "Understanding Success and Failure of International Mediation," *The Journal of Conflict Resolution* 40:2 (1996): 360–389; J. Bercovitch, "International Mediation and Dispute Settlement: Evaluating the Conditions for Successful Mediation," *Negotiation Journal* 7:1 (1991): 17–30.

133 Monica Herz, Maira Siman and Ana Clara Telles, "Regional Organizations, Conflict Resolution and Mediation in South America," in Marcial A. G. Suarez, Rafael Duarte Villa and Brigitte Weiffen, eds., *Power Dynamics and Regional Security in Latin America* (London: Palgrave Macmillan, 2017), 123–148.

the domestic and, arguably, regional and international agendas; preferences should be altered to move away from deadlock; and there should be third-party assistance.[134]

The cases briefly introduced in this chapter encompass a variety of intertwined hallmarks pertaining to border, resource, ideological, influence, migratory and leaders' prestige disputes. Clearly, these differences are not limited to space in the narrow or physical sense,[135] and, hence, a unidimensional assessment is not enough. Indeed, these disputes require a multidimensional analysis because of the complex socioterritorial relations they present.[136] Consequently, the subsections below apply a brief outline of multidimensional approaches to the aforementioned disputes.

Agents and players

Agents such as individuals, communities and states have played (and still do play) different roles in the origin, continuation and potential escalation into conflict of territorial disputes. The Americas are no exception. Regardless of whether these different agents play a role as the host of the dispute by initiating or keeping the difference in a legal and political limbo, or act in a less central capacity as a participant or an attendee,[137] all clusters in the Americas show a variety of agents that go beyond the traditional two-state or inter-state territorial dispute.

Several cases show that individuals ranging from democratically elected state leaders to *caudillos* may use territorial disputes to generate internal support and, therefore, retain or reinforce their domestic political power and,

134 For figures, different hypotheses, models, research design and other elements see Luis L. Schenoni, Gary Goertz, Andrew P. Owsiak and Paul F. Diehl, "Settling Resistant Territorial Disputes: The Territorial Boundary Peace in Latin America," *International Studies Quarterly* 64:1 (2020): 57–70.

135 "Space" is the actual or virtual area where pluralisms and their interrelations happen such as land, water, outer space and cyberspace. The notion encompasses material (natural) as well as abstract (cultural) elements and features and can be classified: (a) according to its scope; and (b) according to the way it is perceived. In turn, space according to its scope can be subclassified in the narrow, integral and representational sense while space according to the way it is perceived may be sub-divided into physical, social and mental space. For further details see Jorge E. Núñez, *Territorial Disputes and State Sovereignty: International Law and Politics* (London and New York, NY: Routledge, Taylor & Francis Group, 2020), Chapter 6.

136 José Sobreiro Filho, Bernardo M. Fernandes and Tassio B. Cunha, "Water, Land, Socioterritorial Movements, Labour, and Capital: Territorial Disputes and Conflictuality in Brazil," in A. Ioris, ed., *Agriculture, Environment and Development: International Perspectives on Water, Land and Politics* (Cham: Palgrave Macmillan, 2016), 123–148.

137 For a notion and characterization of agents such as hosts, participants, attendees and viewers see Jorge E. Núñez, *Cosmopolitanism, State Sovereignty, International Law and Politics: A Theory* (London and New York, NY: Routledge, Taylor & Francis Group, 2023), Chapter 4.

potentially, regional and international influence.[138] The Americas offer several clear examples from San Martin and Bolivar and the independence movements to the several military governments in the Central American, Caribbean and South American clusters between the 1970s and 1990s. However, individuals may foster peaceful understanding between otherwise competing agents as the Beagle Channel crisis demonstrates with the figure of Pope John Paul II and the Vatican's involvement that resulted in a peaceful settlement between Argentina and Chile, both under authoritarian military dictatorships at the time.

Domestic political groups,[139] communities such as indigenous peoples and multinational corporations directly and indirectly influence (and arguably in some cases, shape) the domestic and foreign policy choices of ruling parties and political leaders to advance their interests. Common ethnic ties between groups that are based on different sides of a border may influence the dynamics in the relationship between bordering sovereign states.[140] In fact, common language and ethnicity may increase the likelihood of a territorial dispute.[141]

Cases in the Americas illustrate several issues at stake that explain the behavior of states. These issues at stake include strategic location of the territory, ties to a bordering minority, political unification and economic value of the territory. For instance, to gain control over a strategically located territory may not be a necessary condition for a territorial dispute to exist, but it is a powerful motivator that helps understand its rationale.[142] There seems to be a correlation between the balance of military forces capabilities between the challenger and the challenged sovereign states.[143] Furthermore, there seems to be a direct relationship between how democratic the states involved are and the probability of a peaceful settlement.[144]

Contexts

Although in some cases one context—either the domestic, the regional or the international—may have more prominent influence, all three are important

138 Paul K. Huth, *Standing Your Ground: Territorial Disputes and International Conflict* (Ann Arbor, MI: University of Michigan Press, 2001), 41.
139 Paul K. Huth, *Standing Your Ground: Territorial Disputes and International Conflict* (Ann Arbor, MI: University of Michigan Press, 2001), 43.
140 Paul K. Huth, *Standing Your Ground: Territorial Disputes and International Conflict* (Ann Arbor, MI: University of Michigan Press, 2001), 50–52.
141 Paul K. Huth, *Standing Your Ground: Territorial Disputes and International Conflict* (Ann Arbor, MI: University of Michigan Press, 2001), 78.
142 Paul K. Huth, *Standing Your Ground: Territorial Disputes and International Conflict* (Ann Arbor, MI: University of Michigan Press, 2001), 73–75.
143 Paul K. Huth, *Standing Your Ground: Territorial Disputes and International Conflict* (Ann Arbor, MI: University of Michigan Press, 2001), 53–54.
144 Paul K. Huth, *Standing Your Ground: Territorial Disputes and International Conflict* (Ann Arbor, MI: University of Michigan Press, 2001), 62–62.

in understanding territorial disputes. In terms of the international context, despite a few cases that still show the presence of non-regional agents—e.g. the Falkland/Malvinas Islands—it seems that common alliances and relevant public international law doctrines—i.e. Calvo, Drago, Monroe—have acted as a deterrent and impeded hostile interventions from more central, stronger or advantaged powers outside the region.[145]

All three clusters in the Americas show that most of the security threats, disputes and conflicts came from within the region.[146] In the same vein, several peaceful settlements that followed these disputes and conflicts were attained regionally and counted with regional guarantors. Whether the success in the peaceful resolution of conflict and peacebuilding in the region is because of this approach that incorporates regional institutions and regional guarantors or because a dominant power like the United States has offered security assistance[147] is a matter for further research.

Evidently, the domestic context has been influential in the origin, continuation and potential escalation into conflict over territorial disputes, their peaceful settlement and, in some cases, their revival. For instance, a domestic change in regime and leaders, the discovery of natural resources and internal socio-political turmoil have been some of the reasons that help explain why states did (and do) not comply with past agreements. For example, cases like Nicaragua vs. Colombia, Ecuador vs. Peru and Venezuela vs. Guyana clearly show that those deciding not to comply with previously agreed settlements to disputes did so by arguing that these earlier arrangements were accepted under coercive circumstances.[148] Furthermore, the historical roots of the disputes in the area have influenced (and to some extent, continue to influence) the decision-making of political leaders. Many disputes in Latin America and the Caribbean stem from the colonial past, numerous confrontations and wars. Ruling powers balance out a peaceful settlement and respective conditions against their own agendas, national interests and perceptions because any decision in that regard could be perceived as a political setback.[149] Indeed, in these cases, leaders' prestige is at stake and political leaders might risk having to face

145 See Chapter 6 for further details about the direct and indirect influence of the United States, Russia, China and India.

146 Paul K. Huth, *Standing Your Ground: Territorial Disputes and International Conflict* (Ann Arbor, MI: University of Michigan Press, 2001), 89.

147 Paul K. Huth, *Standing Your Ground: Territorial Disputes and International Conflict* (Ann Arbor, MI: University of Michigan Press, 2001), 89.

148 Paul K. Huth, *Standing Your Ground: Territorial Disputes and International Conflict* (Ann Arbor, MI: University of Michigan Press, 2001), 91.

149 Paul K. Huth, *Standing Your Ground: Territorial Disputes and International Conflict* (Ann Arbor, MI: University of Michigan Press, 2001), 95.

the opposition of the military[150] and the electorate if they do not maintain the dispute.

Realms

The factual, the normative and the axiological realms are entangled in territorial disputes in the Americas. Issues at stake pertaining to the factual realm include the strategic location of the disputed territories, minority groups such as the indigenous peoples, the economic importance of the territory (e.g. the actual or potential presence of natural resources), the balance of military capabilities and the historical roots of the differences.[151] Furthermore, each of these issues at stake encompasses myriad elements and features of their own. For example, the historical roots that are common to most territorial disputes in the Americas range from the lack of border demarcation in colonial times to unsettled prior territorial disputes and difficulty in effectively demarcating a settled border because of the terrain—e.g. high mountains, swamps and impenetrable jungles.[152]

Normatively, issues that influence territorial disputes comprise defense alliances, regional organizations, prior settlements by means of international agreements and awards, decolonization norms and the presence (or not) of democratic legal systems. Like the issues related to the factual realm, each of those that are normative in nature presents a complexity of their own that deserves further exploration. For example, the presence (or not) of a democratic legal system in the challenger agent and how long democratic institutions and practices have been part of that system might help explain how the domestic sphere influences the origin, continuation and potential escalation of territorial disputes into conflict as well as their potential peaceful resolution. A point worth highlighting that seems to be a constant feature in territorial disputes in the Americas and their peaceful settlements has to do with a normative system other than law, that is religion. All states in the Americas in some way follow and/or officially support the Judeo-Christian tradition. Research shows that the Judeo-Christian tradition, in comparison to others, fosters peacebuilding by additional means than holy scriptures and individual figures such as institutions and practices dedicated to that effect.[153]

150 Paul K. Huth, *Standing Your Ground: Territorial Disputes and International Conflict* (Ann Arbor, MI: University of Michigan Press, 2001), 97.

151 For details about each issue at stake relevant to territorial disputes see Jorge E. Núñez, *Territorial Disputes and State Sovereignty: International Law and Politics* (London and New York, NY: Routledge, Taylor & Francis Group, 2020), Chapter 4.

152 Paul K. Huth, *Standing Your Ground: Territorial Disputes and International Conflict* (Ann Arbor, MI: University of Michigan Press, 2001), 256–263.

153 Alexander Bramble, Ayse S. Kadayifci and Thania Paffenholz, *Religious Actors in Formal Peace Processes* (Washington, DC: United States Institute of Peace, 2023) available at https://www.usip.org/sites/default/files/PW_194_Religious_Actors_in_Formal_Peace

In contrast to colonial and early post-independence times when strong states intervened as they wished in the internal and external affairs of their weaker peers (axiological realm),[154] nowadays most states in the Americas, regardless of their empirical differences (factual realm), seem to respect the international legal principle of sovereign equality (normative realm). This equal footing may help explain the preference for peacebuilding on the continent. However, it is important to note that although public international law acknowledges sovereign equality, i.e. the linear horizontal dimension, realpolitik suggests that the bargaining power of the most advantaged party in the bilateral relationship in a territorial dispute between the challenger and the challenged agents jeopardizes the legally and politically presupposed equilibrium, i.e. the linear vertical dimension. Although to define the "most advantaged" or "least advantaged" agent in any situation depends on an axiological choice, that is, to choose which element or feature would be counted as relevant, arguably, the United States is the most central, strongest or advantaged agent in the region when considering elements and features like financial development, defense capabilities and democratic history. Therefore, the influence of the United States in territorial disputes in the region and their development deserves further study.[155]

Modes of existence

The cases presented in this chapter share a multiplicity of elements and features that characterize them and deserve detailed analyses. *Brevitatis causa*, to different degrees, they all encompass ideal, natural, cultural and metaphysical objects. For instance, several examples in the Americas can be characterized as ideological, influence and/or leaders' prestige disputes because they are based on ideal objects in the form of ideologies—i.e. the main reason behind the difference has to do with the propagation or annihilation of certain beliefs. Natural objects such as rivers, high mountains, swamps and impenetrable jungles that are distinctive in the Americas add to the intricacy of these disputes. The challenges they present are numerous and comprise the difficulties the terrain may present in effectively demarcating a border, and the fact that the

_Processes_Bramble.pdf accessed 9 May 2024. For two in-depth studies on the role religion plays in peacebuilding see Tsjeard Bouta, S. Ayse Kadayifci-Orellana and Mohammed Abu-Nimer, *Faith-Based Peace-Building: Mapping and Analysis of Christian, Muslim and Multi-Faith Actors* (The Hague: Netherlands Institute of International Relations Clingendael, 2005); and Kristian Berg Harpviken and Hanne Eggen Røislien, "Mapping the Terrain: The Role of Religion in Peacemaking," International Peace Research Institute, Oslo (PRIO) (2005) available at https://www.files.ethz.ch/isn/38134/2005_07_mapping_the_terrain_stateoftheartpaper__jul05_.pdf accessed 9 May 2024.

154 Examples in the previous chapters show how former colonial powers treated themselves reciprocally as equals in law and politics while they discarded native populations.

155 For the influence of the United States in territorial disputes in the Americas see Chapter 6.

technologies to do it are non-existent. Furthermore, new technologies continue to be developed and, therefore, enable the making of new discoveries, such as the existence of previously unknown natural resources. There are also issues with the changes any territory may have over time—e.g. a river changing its course, a flood, newly formed barren areas. Similarly, cultural objects such as man-made structures and the ongoing development of technology, the way in which each sovereign state defines in domestic law the term "territory" and notions like nationalism, national identity, culture and identification present another pluralism of elements and features that should be carefully considered in order to more comprehensively understand these debates. Finally, metaphysical objects can be defining issues in some cases. For example, while it was both possible and achievable that Argentina and Chile accepted similar legal concepts and implications relevant to terms like "sovereignty" and "territory," the native Mapuches, located between these two states, might have different understandings based on their own belief system.[156]

Conclusion

This chapter presented a sample of the territorial disputes in the Americas with a focus on those in which the challenger and the challenged agents had similar situations concerning their bargaining power in the dispute. First, it introduced a typology that encompassed border, resource, ideological, influence, migratory and leaders' prestige disputes. Thereafter, three clusters were presented and reviewed separately: North America, Central America and the Caribbean and South America. These accounts included relevant legal and factual elements and features and provided some indications of the origin of these disputes, why some of them are still ongoing and how some were amicably solved. Therein, regardless of their particularities, it was possible to identify some commonalities in these cases, such as the historical background, the lack of clearly defined boundaries in colonial times, current international law such as the Law of the Sea, new technologies for exploration and exploitation of natural resources, and the existence or absence of indigenous or implanted populations in the territories under question.

The chapter brought evidence of the multi-faceted and multi-layered nature of these territorial disputes. Some partial conclusions suggest that to more robustly comprehend and, arguably, address their complexity, there are several points that should be carefully considered. These points include the fact that population and government may but not necessarily have the same interest in relation to a dispute; how the domestic, regional and international contexts influence each other; questions of identification; the type of regime; leaders' prestige; regional involvement in the form of institutions, arbitrators

156 See Chapters 4 and 8 for further details about the Mapuche case between Argentina and Chile.

and guarantors and non-interventionism; the distinction between domestic crises and international peacebuilding; and the inclusion of other normative systems in addition to law such as a religion.

Among the commonalities in different cases in the Americas, there is a constant characteristic: the presence of indigenous and implanted populations. Therefore, the next chapter will focus on the role they play in territorial disputes. More precisely, the attention will be on indigenous peoples, the historical reasons that explain current practices in law and politics concerning their rights to territory and how the domestic, regional and international contexts are dealing with their situation. There will also be a focus on implanted populations that settled in the Americas either willingly or forcibly.

Bibliography

Almeida, Letícia Núñez, Agnes Félix, Rafael Masson, Nathan Bueno and Jennifer Silva. "Brazil and Its Borders: History and Limits of a Sovereign State." In *Latin America's Global Border System*, Zepeda, Beatriz, Carrión Mena, Fernando and Enríquez Bermeon, Francisco, eds. 195–220. New York, NY: Routledge, 2022.

Arévalo-Ramírez, Walter. "Constitutions Challenging the International Court of Justice's Jurisdiction to Adjudicate Territorial Disputes in Latin America." *Heidelberg Journal of International Law* 82:2 (2022): 425–448.

Baker, James S. and Michael Byers. "Crossed Lines: The Curious Case of the Beaufort Sea Maritime Boundary Dispute." *Ocean Development & International Law* 43:1 (2012): 70–95.

Battaglino, Jorge Mario. "The Coexistence of Peace and Conflict in South America: Toward a New Conceptualization of Types of Peace." *Revista Brasileira de Política Internacional* 55:2 (2012): 131–151.

Bekker, Pieter and Robert van de Poll. "Unlocking the Arctic's Resources Equitably: Using a Law-and-Science Approach to Fix the Beaufort Sea Boundary." *The International Journal of Marine and Coastal Law* 35:2 (2019): 163–200.

Bercovitch, J. "International Mediation and Dispute Settlement: Evaluating the Conditions for Successful Mediation." *Negotiation Journal* 7:1 (1991): 17–30.

Bianchi, William. *Belize: The Controversy between Guatemala and Great Britain over the Territory of British Honduras in Central America.* New York, NY: Las Americas, 1959.

Bouta, Tsjeard, S. Ayse Kadayifci-Orellana and Mohammed Abu-Nimer. *Faith-Based Peace-Building: Mapping and Analysis of Christian, Muslim and Multi-Faith Actors.* The Hague: Clingendael—Netherlands Institute of International Relations, 2005.

Bramble, Alexander, Ayse S. Kadayifci and Thania Paffenholz. *Religious Actors in Formal Peace Processes* (Washington, DC: United States Institute of Peace, 2023) available at https://www.usip.org/sites/default/files/PW_194_Religious_Actors_in_Formal_Peace_Processes_Bramble.pdf accessed 9 May 2024.

Braveboy-Wagner, Jacqueline. *The Venezuela-Guyana Border Dispute.* Boulder, CO: Westview Press, 1984.

Buarque, Cristovam. "A internacionalização do mundo." *Revista Diálogo Educacional* 3:5 (2002): 107–108.

Bunik, I. V. "US–Canada Beaufort Sea Maritime Boundary Dispute in the Perspective of International Law." *Moscow Journal of International Law* 2 (2018): 126–137.

Burke, D. C. "The Northwest Passage Dispute." Oxford Research Group, 2018 available at https://findresearcher.sdu.dk/ws/portalfiles/portal/136624827/The_Northwest_Passage_Dispute.pdf accessed 8 April 2024.

Byers, M. and A. Østhagen. "Why Does Canada Have So Many Unresolved Maritime Boundary Disputes?" *Canadian Yearbook of International Law* 54 (2017): 1–62.

Cabrera, Lester. "Territorial Discourses Opposed in the 21st Century: The Case of the Chile-Peru Relationship from a Critical Geopolitics Perspective." *Estudios Fronterizos* 19 (2018) available at https://www.scielo.org.mx/scielo.php?pid=S0187-69612018000100121&script=sci_arttext&tlng=en accessed 30 April 2024.

Caserta, Salvatore. "Regional International Courts in Search of Relevance: Adjudicating Politically Sensitive Disputes in Central America and the Caribbean." *Duke Journal of Comparative and International Law* 28:1 (2017): 59–97.

Cayo, Percy. *Perú y Ecuador: Antecedentes de un Largo Conflicto.* Lima: Centro de Investigación de la Universidad del Pacífico, 1995.

Chesterton, Bridget María, ed. *The Chaco War: Environment, Ethnicity, and Nationalism.* London and New York, NY: Bloomsbury Publishing, 2017.

Child, Jack. "Interstate Relations in Latin America: Peaceful or Conflictual?" *International Journal* 43:3 (1988): 378–403.

Collin, Katherine. "Peacemaking Referendums: The Use of Direct Democracy in Peace Processes." *Democratization* 27:5 (2020): 717–736.

Colson, David A. and Robert W. Smith. *International Maritime Boundaries (Vol. V).* Dordrecht and Boston, MA: Martinus Nijhoff, 2005.

Crook, John R. "The Special Agreement Between Belize and Guatemala to Submit Guatelmala's Territorial, Insular and Maritime Claims to the International Court of Justice." *International Legal Materials* 48:2 (2009): 250–255.

Crowder, George. "Two Value-Pluralist Arguments for Liberalism." *Australian Journal of Political Science* 37:3 (2002): 457–473.

Cummings, Anthony R. "How Guyana's Oil Discovery Rekindled a Border Controversy." *Journal of Latin American Geography* 17:3 (2018): 183–211.

de la Fuente, Maria. "Argentina–Chile Laguna del Desierto Arbitration." In *Global Encyclopedia of Territorial Rights*, Gray, K. W., ed. 1–6. Cham: Springer International Publishing, 2022.

Diemer, Christian and Amalija Šeparović. "Territorial Questions and Maritime Delimitation with Regard to Nicaragua's Claims to the San Andrés Archipelago." *Heidelberg Journal of International Law* 66 (2006): 167–185.

Domínguez, Jorge. *Conflictos Territoriales y Democracia en América Latina.* Buenos Aires: Editorial Siglo XXI, 2003.

Donovan, Thomas W. "Challenges to the Territorial Integrity of Guyana: A Legal Analysis." *Georgia Journal of International and Comparative Law* 32 (2004): 661–724.

Donovan, Thomas W. "Suriname-Guyana Maritime and Territorial Disputes: A Legal and Historical Analysis." *Journal of Transnational Law and Policy* 13:1 (2003): 41–98.

Faúndez, Julio. *The International Court of Justice in Maritime Disputes: The Case of Chile and Peru.* London: Routledge, 2018.

Fernandes, Bernardo Mançano and Cliff Welch. "Movements and Territorial Conflicts in Latin America." In *The Oxford Handbook of Latin American Social Movements*, Rossi, Federico M., ed. 266–282. New York, NY: Oxford University Press, 2023.

Fraser, Alexander. *Nova Scotia, The Royal Charter of 1621 to Sir William Alexander*. Toronto: University of Toronto Press, 1922.

Geddert, Jeremy Seth. "Right of (Northwest) Passage: Toward a Responsible Canadian Arctic Sovereignty." *Canadian Journal of Political Science/Revue canadienne de science politique* 52:3 (2019): 595–612.

Gray, David H. "Canada's Unresolved Maritime Boundaries." *IBRU Boundary and Security Bulletin* 5:3 (1997): 61–70.

Gutíerrez Ardila, Daniel. *El Reconocimiento de Colombia: Diplomacia y Propaganda en la Coyuntura de las Restauraciones (1819–1831)*. Bogotá: Universidad Externado de Colombia, 2012.

Gutiérrez González, Ana Lucía. "Peru vs Chile—The Role of International Communications in a Maritime Dispute." *Journal of Latin American Communication Research* 7:1–2 (2019): 170–191.

Harpviken, Kristian Berg and Hanne Eggen Røislien. "Mapping the Terrain: The Role of Religion in Peacemaking." International Peace Research Institute, Oslo (PRIO), 2005 available at https://www.files.ethz.ch/isn/38134/2005_07_mapping_the_terrain_stateoftheartpaper__jul05_.pdf accessed 9 May 2024.

Herz, Monica and João Pontes Nogueira. *Ecuador vs. Peru: Peacemaking Amid Rivalry*. London: Lynne Rienner, 2002.

Herz, Monica, Maira Siman and Ana Clara Telles. "Regional Organizations, Conflict Resolution and Mediation in South America." In *Power Dynamics and Regional Security in Latin America*, Suarez, Marcial A. G., Villa, Rafael Duarte and Weiffen, Brigitte, eds. 123–148. London: Palgrave Macmillan, 2017.

Horna, Angel. *Law of the Sea and Maritime Delimitation: State Practice and Case Law in Latin America and the Caribbean*. London and New York, NY: Routledge, Taylor & Francis, 2022.

Howkins, Adrian. "Latin America and Antarctica." In *Oxford Research Encyclopedia of Latin American History* (2017) available at https://oxfordre.com/latinamericanhistory/display/10.1093/acrefore/9780199366439.001.0001/acrefore-9780199366439-e-434 accessed 9 May 2024.

Huebert, Rob. "Drawing Boundaries in the Beaufort Sea: Different Visions/Different Needs." *Journal of Borderlands Studies* 33:2 (2018): 203–223.

Huth, Paul K. *Standing Your Ground: Territorial Disputes and International Conflict*. Ann Arbor, MI: University of Michigan Press, 2001.

Izecksohn, Vitor. "State Formation and Identity: Historiographical Trends Concerning South America's War of the Triple Alliance." *History Compass* 17:9 (2019): 1–11.

Jiménez Pineda, Eduardo. "South American Region and Seabed Mining." In *Routledge Handbook of Seabed Mining and the Law of the Sea*, Tassin, Virginie, ed. 324–332. London: Routledge, 2023.

Johnston, Douglas M. and Mark J. Valencia. *Pacific Ocean Boundary Problems: Status and Solutions*. Dordrecht and Boston, MA: Martinus Nijhoff, 1991.

Kilroy, Richard J. "Maritime and Territorial Boundary Disputes in Latin America." *The Journal of Territorial and Maritime Studies* 1:1 (2014): 91–111.

King Jr., Henry T. "Settlement of International Disputes between Canada and the USA." *Canada-United States Law Journal* 35:1–2 (2011): 46–85.

Kleiboer, Marieke. "Understanding Success and Failure of International Mediation." *The Journal of Conflict Resolution* 40:2 (1996): 360–389.

Krieg, William L. *Ecuadorean-Peruvian Rivalry in the Upper Amazon.* Washington, DC: United States Department of State, 1978.

Kröger, Markus and Rickard Lalander. "Ethno-Territorial Rights and the Resource Extraction Boom in Latin America: Do Constitutions Matter?" *Third World Quarterly* 37:4 (2016): 682–702.

Leguía y Martínez, Germán. *Historia de la Emancipación del Perú: El Protectorado.* 3rd ed. Lima: Publicaciones de la Comisión Nacional del Sesquicentenario de la Independencia, 1972.

Lincoln, Jennie K. and Elizabeth G. Ferris, eds., *The Dynamics of Latin American Foreign Policies: Challenges for the 1980s.* New York, NY and Oxford: Routledge, Taylor & Francis, 1984.

Little, Paul E. *Amazonia: Territorial Struggles on Perennial Frontiers.* Baltimore, MD: Johns Hopkins University Press, 2001.

Luján, Patricia Marín. "Geopolítica, Conflictos Fronterizos en América Latina." *Revista Geopolítica Transfronteiriça* 1:1 (2017): 1–14.

Mahabir, Raghunath and Keron Ganpat. "Border Security and Oil War in the Latin America and Caribbean Region: A Case Study of the Dispute between Guyana and Venezuela." *News. Series: International Relations and Area Studies* 55:1 (2024) available at https://bulletin-irr.ablaikhan.kz/index.php/j1/article/view/384 accessed 12 April 2024.

Mancilla, Alejandra. "The Moral Limits of Territorial Claims in Antarctica." *Ethics & International Affairs* 32:3 (2018): 339–360.

Mansilla Quiñones, Pablo Arturo and Miguel Melin Pehuen. "A Struggle for Territory, a Struggle Against Borders: The Mapuche Conflict in Argentina and Chile Contests Notions of Borders Promulgated by the Nation-State." *NACLA Report on the Americas* 51:1 (2019): 41–48.

Martin, L. H. and Y. B. Parkhomenko. "The Territorial and Maritime Dispute (Nicaragua v. Colombia) and Its Implications for Future Maritime Delimitations in the Caribbean Sea and Elsewhere." In *Nicaragua Before the International Court of Justice*, Sobenes Obregon, E. and Samson, B., eds. 113–141. Cham: Springer, 2018.

McDorman, Ted L. *Salt Water Neighbors: International Ocean Law Relations between the United States and Canada.* Oxford: Oxford University Press, 2009.

Mitchell, Sara McLaughlin. "Clashes at Sea: Explaining the Onset, Militarization, and Resolution of Diplomatic Maritime Claims." *Security Studies* 29:4 (2020): 637–670.

Mitchell, Sara McLaughlin and Andrew P. Owsiak. "Judicialization of the Sea: Bargaining in the Shadow of UNCLOS." *American Journal of International Law* 115:4 (2021): 579–621.

Núñez, Jorge E. *Cosmopolitanism, State Sovereignty, International Law and Politics: A Theory.* London and New York, NY: Routledge, Taylor & Francis Group, 2023.

Núñez, Jorge E. *Territorial Disputes and State Sovereignty: International Law and Politics.* London and New York, NY: Routledge, Taylor & Francis Group, 2020.

O'Phelan Godoy, Scarlett. "La Independencia del Perú ntes y después de la Entrevista de Guayaquil entre San Martín y Bolívar en 1822." *Anales del Museo de América* 29 (2021): 141–164.

Oladipo, Olusegun. "The Marxist Theory of the State." In *Readings in Social and Political Philosophy*, Vol. I., Adeigbo, F. A., ed. Ibadan: Claverianum Press, 1991.

Ospina, Mariano V. "Nicaragua v. Colombia: A Stalemate in the Caribbean." *Global Security Studies* 4:4 (2013): 31–40.

Otero, Maria. "Problems in the Caribbean: The Absence of Finality to the Territorial Dispute in Nicaragua v. Colombia Will Have Negative Impacts in the Region." *University of Toledo Law Review* 46:3 (2015): 617–646.

Padula, Raphael, Matheus de Freitas Cecílio, Igor Candido de Oliveira and Caio Jorge Prado. "Guyana: Oil, Internal Disputes, the USA and Venezuela." *Contexto Internacional* 45:1 (2023): 1–25.

Palmer, David Scott. "Peru-Ecuador Border Conflict: Missed Opportunities, Misplaced Nationalism, and Multilateral Peacekeeping." *Journal of Interamerican Studies and World Affairs* 39:3 (1997): 109–148.

Penna Filho, Pio. "Interações Regionais e Pressões Internacionais sobre a Pan-Amazônia: Perspectivas Brasileiras." In *Amazônia e Atlântico Sul: Desafios e Perspectivas para a Defesa no Brasil*, Gheller, Gilberto F., Gonzales, Selma L. M., Mello, Laerte P., eds., 17-38, Brasilia: IPEA, 2015.

Perez, Arlenie, Chuang Chin-Ta and Farok Afero. "Belize-Guatemala Territorial Dispute and Its Implications for Conservation." *Tropical Conservation Science* 2:1 (2009): 11–24.

Perrier Buslé, Laetitia. "Multi-Scalar Perspectives and Multi-Agent Process in a South American Borderland Region." *Geopolitics* 18:3 (2013): 584–611.

Pratt, Martin. "The Maritime Boundary Dispute between Honduras and Nicaragua in the Caribbean Sea." *Boundary and Security Bulletin* 9:2 (2001): 106–116.

Ramírez, Rafael. "The Venezuela-Guyana Dispute over the Essequibo." *Istituto Affari Internazionali* (2024) available at https://www.iai.it/sites/default/files/iaicom2407.pdf accessed 12 April 2024.

Refai, Nora. "The Beaufort Sea Boundary Dispute: A Consideration of Rights of Inuit in Canada and the United States." *Alberta Law Review* 60:1 (2022): 267–306.

Reis, Arthur C. F. "A Amazônia e a Integridade do Brasil." Brasilia: Senado Federal Conselho Editorial, 2001.

Renouf, J. K. *Canada's Unresolved Maritime Boundaries.* (Fredericton, NB: Canada, 1988).

Ricard, Pascale and Denys-Sacha Robin. "The Superposition of National Legal Regimes in Maritime Disputed Areas." *Maritime Safety and Security Journal* 10 (2022): 37–58.

Rivas, Raimundo. *Historia Diplomática de Colombia (1810–1934)*. Bogotá: Ministerio de Relaciones Exteriores, 1961.

Rothwell, Donald R. "The Canadian-US Northwest Passage Dispute: A Reassessment." *Cornell International Law Journal* 26:2 (1993): 331–372.

Sánches de Rojas Díaz, Emilio. "Analysis of the Conflict in the Central American Corridor: Network Geopolitics." Geopolitical Overview of Conflicts 2014, 269–306. Madrid: Spanish Institute of Strategic Studies, 2014.

Schenoni, Luis L., Gary Goertz, Andrew P. Owsiak and Paul F. Diehl. "Settling Resistant Territorial Disputes: The Territorial Boundary Peace in Latin America." *International Studies Quarterly* 64:1 (2020): 57–70.

Sheehan, Rebecca, Dimitrios Dalaklis, Anastasia Christodoulou, Megan Drewniak, Peter Raneri and Angelos Dalaklis. "The Northwest Passage in the Arctic: A Brief Assessment of the Relevant Marine Transportation System and Current Availability of Search and Rescue Services." *Logistics* 5:2 (2021): 23.

Simmons, Beth A. "Territorial Disputes and Their Resolution: The Case of Ecuador and Peru." United States Institute of Peace (USIP) Press, Washington, DC, 1999 available at https://www.usip.org/sites/default/files/resources/pwks27.pdf accessed 6 May 2024.

Simonian, Ligia T. L. and Rubens da Silva Ferreira. "Brazilian Migrant Workers in French Guiana." In *Caribbean Transnationalism: Migration, Pluralization, and Social Cohesion*, Gowricharn, Ruben, ed., 99–116. Lanham, MD: Lexington Books, 2006.

Sobreiro Filho, José, Bernardo M. Fernandes and Tassio B. Cunha. "Water, Land, Socioterritorial Movements, Labour, and Capital: Territorial Disputes and Conflictuality in Brazil." In *Agriculture, Environment and Development: International Perspectives on Water, Land and Politics*, Ioris, A., ed. 123–148. Cham: Palgrave Macmillan, 2016.

St. John, Ronald Bruce. *Bolivia: Geopolitics of a Landlocked State.* London: Routledge, 2019.

St. John, Ronald Bruce. *The Bolivia-Chile-Peru Dispute in the Atacama Desert.* Durham, NC: International Boundaries Research Unit, University of Durham, 1994.

Thies, Cameron G. "Territorial Nationalism in Spatial Rivalries: An Institutionalist Account of the Argentine-Chilean Rivalry." *International Interactions* 27:4 (2001): 399–431.

van Aert, Peter. "The Beagle Conflict." *Island Studies Journal* 11:1 (2016): 307–314.

Van Zandt, Franklin K. *Boundaries of the United States and the Several States: Geological Survey Bulletin 1212.* Washington, DC: United States Government Printing Office, 1966, available at https://pubs.usgs.gov/bul/1212/report.pdf accessed 2 April 2024.

Vargas, Fábio Aristimunho. *Formação das Fronteiras Latino-Americanas.* Brasilia: Fundação Alexandre de Gusmão, 2017 available at https://funag.gov.br/loja/download/FORMACAO-DE-FRONTEIRAS_19_06_v_11.pdf accessed 6 May 2024.

Vidal, Florian. "The Antarctic Peninsula: Argentina and Chile in the Era of Global Change." *The Polar Journal* 13:1 (2023): 13–30.

Villar Gertner, Andrés. "The Beagle Channel Frontier Dispute between Argentina and Chile: Converging Domestic and International Conflicts." *International Relations* 28:2 (2014): 207–227.

Young, Alma H. and Dennis H. Young. "The Impact of the Anglo-Guatemalan Dispute on the Internal Politics of Belize." *Latin American Perspectives* 15:2 (1988): 6–30.

Zhomartkyzy, Maria. "Mediation in Diplomatic Conflicts. Examples from Latin America." *ScienceRise: Juridical Science* 3:25 (2023): 72–84.

8 Indigenous rights and implanted populations

Introduction

While the legal and political status of indigenous peoples is often contested in territorial disputes,[1] the Americas also include populations that were at one time settlers. The latter encompasses those who relocated willingly such as the Falkland/Malvinas Islanders, and those who were forced as in the case of former African slaves in the archipelago of San Andrés, Providencia and Santa Catalina, i.e. the Raizal community. Regardless of their different circumstances, several of these groups nowadays claim self-determination.[2] By considering a variety of cases, this chapter exposes a puzzling issue in law and politics: in the context of international law and politics, settlers or implanted populations are considered "persons" and may be able to claim the territory they inhabit, whereas the legal and political status of indigenous populations is still only vaguely acknowledged.

The chapter is divided into three main sections. The first part will briefly explain the relevance in law and politics of the notion of self-determination and the role it may play in territorial disputes, in particular those including indigenous peoples and/or implanted populations. The second part will focus on indigenous populations,[3] the historical reasons that explain current practices in law and politics concerning their rights to territory and how the domestic, regional and international contexts are dealing with their situation. In turn,

1 Rachel Sieder, "Indigenous People's Rights and the Law in Latin America," in Corinne Lennox and Damien Short, eds., *Handbook of Indigenous Peoples' Rights* (London and New York, NY: Routledge, 2016), 414–423.

2 For the author's previous work on self-determination in the context of territorial disputes see Jorge E. Núñez, *Territorial Disputes and State Sovereignty: International Law and Politics* (London and New York, NY: Routledge, Taylor & Francis Group, 2020), Chapter 3.

3 For the notion of indigenous peoples see the Indigenous and Tribal Peoples Convention (Convention 169, *International Labour Organization*, 1989) available at https://normlex.ilo.org/dyn/normlex/en/f?p=NORMLEXPUB:12100:0::NO::P12100_ILO_CODE:C169 accessed 12 November 2024. For other relevant international and regional law see the specific subsection below.

DOI: 10.4324/9781003350828-10

the third part will shift the attention toward implanted populations that settled in the Americas either willingly or forcibly.

In certain situations, self-determination may challenge the public international law principle of territorial integrity. To bring more precision, the chapter will make clear that self-determination centers on people, implies different degrees of autonomy and does not necessarily mean secession. Indeed, public international law empowers populations to freely decide what is best for them even in cases of territorial disputes. However, sovereignty and self-determination may also draw together agents with opposing claims over territorial disputes, and there may be room for territorial disputes to be resolved by cooperative approaches.

The way in which indigenous peoples are currently considered in law and politics in the Americas, unsurprisingly, can be traced back to colonial times. Both legally and politically, indigenous peoples were not legally "persons" or they were considered inferior.[4] Therefore, colonial empires discarded territorial claims made by these native populations.[5] Internationally, there seems to be a move toward supporting indigenous rights but in relation to issues other than territorial claims.[6] In the same manner, regional states are reviewing[7] the way they interact with these populations.[8] Arguably, self-determination and consequent self-government could be the next steps in this legal evolution toward the recognition of indigenous rights in relation to territorial disputes.[9]

4 Jérémie Gilbert, *Indigenous Peoples' Land Rights under International Law: From Victors to Actors* (Ardsley, NY: Transnational, 2006), 1–2.

5 M. F. Lindley, *The Acquisition and Government of Backward Territory in International Law: Being a Treatise on the Law and Practice Relating to Colonial Expansion* (New York, NY: Negro University Press, 1969), 11–12.

6 Jérémie Gilbert, "Indigenous Rights in the Making: The United Nations Declaration on the Rights of Indigenous Peoples," *International Journal on Minority and Group Rights* 14 (2007): 207–230.

7 Allen Gerlach, *Indians, Oil, and Politics: A Recent History of Ecuador* (Wilmington, NC: Scholarly Resources, 2003).

8 Austen L. Parrish, "Changing Territoriality, Fading Sovereignty, and the Development of Indigenous Rights," *American Indian Law Review* 31:2 (2006/2007): 291–314; Willem van Genugten and Camillo Perez-Bustillo, "The Emerging International Architecture of Indigenous Rights: The Interaction Between Global, Regional, and National Dimensions," *International Journal on Minority and Group Rights* 11:4 (2004): 379–409; Gemma van der Haar, "The Zapatista Uprising and the Struggle for Indigenous Autonomy," *European Review of Latin American and Caribbean Studies* 76 (2004): 98–108; Donna Lee Van Cott, "Broadening Democracy: Latin America's Indigenous People's Movements," *Current History* 103:670 (2004): 80–85; Shane Greene, "Getting Over the Andes: The Geo-Eco-Politics of Indigenous Movements in Peru's Twenty-First Century Inca Empire," *Journal of Latin American Studies* 38:2 (2006): 327–354.

9 See, for example, the United States and the case of Hawaii in Keri E. Iyall Smith, *The State and Indigenous Movements* (New York, NY: Routledge, 2006).

In contrast, "right-peopling"[10] the territory with settlers willing to relocate from their native land was a way in which some former colonial powers (and, arguably, some modern states like Israel) secured their claim to sovereignty over new territories by means of self-determination. Moreover, whether or not the intention was to use the same means to achieve the same goal, a similar situation has stemmed from those who were originally brought to the Americas by former colonial empires as slaves.

As the chapter will show, several ongoing territorial disputes in the Americas that include indigenous populations and settlers are examples of the tension between self-determination and territorial integrity. Unsurprisingly, in the scholarly literature there is support for both the preeminence of self-determination over territorial integrity and vice versa.[11] In relation to territorial disputes the choice between self-determination and territorial integrity shows a similar experience, with some cases suggesting preeminence to the former and some to the latter.[12] Consequently, self-determination does not necessarily override territorial integrity.[13] The decision on whether to apply self-determination or territorial integrity to a territorial dispute depends on interpreting, weighing and balancing different elements particular to that dispute.[14] Scholarly literature and public international law seem to suggest that self-determination may take priority over territorial integrity unless, for example, an administering authority attempts to use it as a means to an end—e.g. in the case of "plantations."[15] It is clear that the choice between self-determination and territorial integrity is as complex as it is controversial. Therein,

10 Brendan O'Leary, "The Elements of Right-Sizing and Right-Peopling the State," in Brendan O'Leary, Ian S. Lustick and Thomas Callaghy, eds., *Right-Sizing the State: The Politics of Moving Borders* (Oxford: Oxford University Press, 2001), 15–73.

11 For an analysis of the relationship between self-determination and territorial integrity see Miguel Antonio Sánchez, "Self-Determination and the Falkland Islands Dispute," *Columbia Journal of Transnational Law* 21 (1983): 557–584. For self-determination overriding territorial integrity see Thomas M. Franck and Paul Hoffman, "The Right to Self-Determination in Very Small Places," *New York University Journal of International Law and Politics* 8 (1975): 331–386; Rupert Emerson, "Self-Determination," *American Journal of International Law* 65 (1971): 459–475; Advisory Opinion by Judge Dillard on Western Sahara, International Court of Justice, 12, 120 n.1 (Advisory Opinion of 16 October 1975). For territorial integrity overriding self-determination see Roger S. Clark, "The Decolonization of East Timor and the United Nations Norms on Self-Determination and Aggression," *Yale Journal of World Public Order* 7:2 (1980): 30.

12 For details about different cases, including factual and legal analysis, see S. K. N. Blay, "Self-Determination Versus Territorial Integrity in Decolonization," *NYU Journal of International Law and Politics* 18 (1986): 441–472.

13 J. Robert Maguire, "The Decolonization of Belize. Self-Determination v. Territorial Integrity," *Virginia Journal of International Law* 22:4 (1982): 849–881, 871.

14 Hurst Hannum, *Autonomy, Sovereignty, and Self-determination: The Accommodation of Conflicting Rights* (Philadelphia, PA: University of Pennsylvania Press, 1996).

15 S. K. N. Blay, "Self-Determination Versus Territorial Integrity in Decolonization," *NYU Journal of International Law and Politics* 18 (1986): 441–472.

in order to better comprehend the role they play in territorial disputes in the Americas, the following sections will review different situations that include indigenous peoples and implanted populations, "plantations" or those who settled in previously inhabited or uninhabited territories.[16]

Sovereignty and self-determination

While current understandings of sovereignty center on the state and, more precisely, one of its elements, that is its territory, self-determination focuses on people.[17] Therefore, in certain situations, self-determination appears to challenge the principle of territorial integrity as defined in public international law. Consequently, territorial disputes often include situations in which at least part of the population of a sovereign state may wish to have a different government and, therefore, divide the territory as in the case of some indigenous peoples. In other cases, like the Falkland/Malvinas Islands and San Andrés, Providencia and Santa Catalina, populations are in a legal and political limbo because they wish to exercise self-determination while a sovereign state denies them that right. It is important to note, however, that self-determination may lead to solutions other than secession.

The concept of self-determination is not stipulated in public international law and, therefore, has several hermeneutical problems including how to understand the following notions: dismemberment of territory, the right to determine political status and the concept of "people."

Dismemberment of territory

Self-determination enables people to decide their political status, and this may result in the physical dismemberment of the state. In that sense, self-determination challenges the public international law principle of territorial integrity.[18]

16 The author refers to "previously inhabited or uninhabited territories" intentionally because it may be epistemologically impossible to demonstrate whether there was habitation or not in a territory. For an extensive analysis on this point see Jorge E. Núñez, *Sovereignty Conflicts and International Law and Politics: A Distributive Justice Issue* (London and New York, NY: Routledge, Taylor & Francis Group, 2017), Chapter 6; in particular "Why 'Just Acquisition' Cannot Work," 117–120.

17 For the author's previous work on self-determination in the context of territorial disputes see Jorge E. Núñez, *Territorial Disputes and State Sovereignty: International Law and Politics* (London and New York, NY: Routledge, Taylor & Francis Group, 2020), Chapter 3. See also P. H. Kooijmans, "Tolerance, sovereignty and self-determination," *Netherlands International Law Review* 43:2 (1996): 211–217.

18 For a detailed analysis of the concept of territorial integrity see Christian Marxsen, "Territorial Integrity in International Law—Its Concept and Implications for Crimea," *Heidelberg Journal of International Law* 75:1 (2015): 7–26. See also S. Lalonde, *Determining Boundaries in a Conflicted World: The Role of Uti Possidetis* (Montreal: McGill-Queen's University Press, 2002), 158–164.

As mentioned above, there is scholarly literature supporting both the preeminence of self-determination over territorial integrity and vice versa.[19]

The right to determine the political status

Self-determination may result in secession,[20] but it does not need to. Secession is an *ultimum remedium*[21] in situations in which the sovereign state and the population that wishes to secede are in conflict. Public international law enables people to choose their political status by means of self-determination. The political status in any community may imply independence and the formation of a new sovereign state as well as other outcomes such as administration, integration, free association or shared sovereignty.[22]

People

The term "people" in self-determination, as a legal concept, is hermeneutically challenging. Public international law does not include any legal norm, either legislation or case law, with a clear, unequivocal and prescriptive definition. This circumstance results in arguments in many ongoing territorial disputes. The International Court of Justice (ICJ) provides some clarification in the Western Sahara Advisory Opinion that the right of that population to self-determination is assumed; in the East Timor case (Portugal v. Australia), that both parties recognize that the people of East Timor have the right to

19 For an analysis of the relationship between self-determination and territorial integrity see Miguel Antonio Sánchez, "Self-Determination and the Falkland Islands Dispute," *Columbia Journal of Transnational Law* 21 (1983): 557–584. For self-determination overriding territorial integrity see Thomas M. Franck and Paul Hoffman, "The Right to Self-Determination in Very Small Places," *New York University Journal of International Law and Politics* 8 (1975): 331–386; Rupert Emerson, "Self-Determination," *American Journal of International Law* 65 (1971): 459–475, 464; Advisory Opinion by Judge Dillard on Western Sahara, International Court of Justice, 12, 120 n.1 (Advisory Opinion of 16 October 1975). For territorial integrity overriding self-determination see Roger S. Clark, "The Decolonization of East Timor and the United Nations Norms on Self-Determination and Aggression," *Yale Journal of World Public Order* 7:2 (1980): 30.

20 For a comprehensive list of scholarly legal literature on secession see Mary D. Hood, "Bibliography on Secession and International Law," *Santa Clara University School of Law* (2001) available at https://digitalcommons.law.scu.edu/cgi/viewcontent.cgi?referer=https://www.google.com/&httpsredir=1&article=1042&context=facpubs accessed 6 June 2024.

21 P. H. Kooijmans, "Tolerance, sovereignty and self-determination," *Netherlands International Law Review* 43:2 (1996): 211–217.

22 For details about these and other remedies to sovereignty conflicts see Jorge E. Núñez, *Sovereignty Conflicts and International Law and Politics: A Distributive Justice Issue* (London and New York, NY: Routledge, Taylor & Francis Group, 2017), Chapter 5.

self-determination; and the Israeli Wall Advisory Opinion explains that the rights of the Palestinian people include self-determination.[23]

Despite these preliminary setbacks, Núñez (2020) drew some conclusions:[24]

- Self-determination enables people to choose their political status.
- Self-determination is an *erga omnes* right.
- Self-determination does not necessarily result in secession.
- Secession is an extreme, ultimate means to resolve a dispute that includes a party claiming self-determination.
- Self-determination can be external or internal.
- External self-determination implies secession in cases in which people are being oppressed by their government and/or their interests are continuously overridden or ignored.
- Internal self-determination implies any other instance in which people are not being oppressed but they wish a degree of autonomy in relation to their state's government.
- Internal self-determination includes any degree of autonomy such as free association, integration or shared sovereignty.
- "People" as a concept of the right to self-determination is defined by internal and external elements.
- "People," internally defined, has to do with characteristics that make the individuals in the group somehow homogeneous—e.g. a common wish to decide their political status, national legal order, common social, cultural, historical, ethnic and linguistic background.
- "People," externally defined, has to do with the way the group is oppressed (or not) by the state's government and/or how their wishes are continuously ignored.
- "Plantations" or populations that were settled by formerly colonial powers in previously inhabited or uninhabited territories[25] are an exceptional case that should be explored in detail, in law and in fact, taking all the claiming agents and the above considerations into account.

23 For more details see Daniel Thürer and Thomas Burri, "Self-Determination," in *Max Planck Encyclopedia of Public International Law* (2008) available at https://opil.ouplaw.com/view/10.1093/law:epil/9780199231690/law-9780199231690-e873 accessed 6 June 2024.

24 Jorge E. Núñez, *Territorial Disputes and State Sovereignty: International Law and Politics* (London and New York, NY: Routledge, Taylor & Francis Group, 2020), Chapter 3.

25 The author refers to "previously inhabited or uninhabited territories" intentionally because it may be epistemologically impossible to demonstrate whether there was habitation or not in a territory. For an extensive analysis on this point see Jorge E. Núñez, *Sovereignty Conflicts and International Law and Politics: A Distributive Justice Issue* (London and New York, NY: Routledge, Taylor & Francis Group, 2017), Chapter 6; in particular "Why 'Just Acquisition' Cannot Work," 117–120.

Indigenous peoples

The end of colonial times left an ongoing dilemma in the Americas, with many indigenous groups in territorial disputes with "civilized" states over what had been classed as "non-civilized" territories.[26] *Brevitatis causa*, the population in the New World was between 54 and 112 million in pre-Columbian times.[27] However, as a result of colonization, fewer than 10 million indigenous peoples survived.[28] European rulers created borders using a European understanding of concepts such as sovereignty and state: see, for example, the Papal bulls of Alexander VI. Unsurprisingly, none of these documents mention the indigenous population.[29]

From Canada to Argentina, there are still several indigenous peoples intertwined with territorial disputes. For instance, the Beaufort Sea dispute between Yukon and Alaska includes the acknowledgment by the Canadian government of the Inuvialuit (or Inuit) rights in the region and their growing influence in the future of the territory.[30] The Mexico–United States border has been continuously occupied by natives for millennia. Either inhabited by tribes or integrated into the Aztec Empire in pre-Columbian times, the international border was agreed by the Treaty of Guadalupe Hidalgo in 1848.[31] Similarly, Central America and the Caribbean are characterized by ethnic and cultural diversity. For example, the Mesoamerican cultures spread from Mexico (Yucatan and Chiapas) to Costa Rica, Guatemala, Honduras, El Salvador and Nicaragua. These communities tend to reject the "mono-ethnic and homogeneous" sovereign state model and, instead, allow for "new multinational or multi-ethnic" informal arrangements.[32] Unsurprisingly, as with the rest of the continent, in South America indigenous communities do not necessarily conform to legally defined borders and their claim to ethno-territorial rights is usually opposed to the interests of sovereign states and private companies.[33]

This section is divided into two subsections. The first subsection will refer to the relevant regional and international reception in law in terms of territorial rights pertaining to indigenous peoples. The second subsection will bring evidence of different domestic case studies in North America, Central America and the Caribbean and South America in which natives are intertwined with territorial disputes.

26 M. F. Lindley, *The Acquisition and Government of Backward Territory in International Law: Being a Treatise on the Law and Practice Relating to Colonial Expansion* (New York, NY: Negro University Press, 1969), 11–12.

27 William M. Denevan, *The Native Population of the Americas in 1492* (Madison, WI: University of Wisconsin Press, 1992); Henry F. Dobyns, "An Appraisal of Techniques with a New Hemispheric Estimate," *Current Anthropology* 7:4 (1966): 395–416.

28 Noble David Cook, *Born to Die: Disease and the New World Conquest, 1492–1650* (Cambridge: Cambridge University Press, 1998).

29 See Chapter 4.

30 See Chapter 7.

31 See Chapters 4 and 6.

32 See Chapter 7.

33 See Chapter 7.

International and regional law, indigenous peoples, territorial rights and native self-determination

Public international law includes some rules regarding indigenous peoples such as, indirectly, the 1948 Universal Declaration of Human Rights;[34] globally, the 2007 United Nations (UN) Declaration on the Rights of Indigenous Peoples;[35] and, regionally, directly referred to the Americas, the 2016 American Declaration on the Rights of Indigenous Peoples.[36]

Internationally, there seems to be a move toward supporting indigenous rights that include human rights, health and education. In what is relevant to indigenous peoples and territory, the 2007 United Nations (UN) Declaration on the Rights of Indigenous Peoples states:[37]

> Article 8:
>
> 2. States shall provide effective mechanisms for prevention of, and redress for: (b) Any action which has the aim or effect of dispossessing them of their lands, territories or resources;
>
> Article 10: Indigenous peoples shall not be forcibly removed from their lands or territories. No relocation shall take place without the free, prior and informed consent of the indigenous peoples concerned and after agreement on just and fair compensation and, where possible, with the option of return.
>
> Article 25: Indigenous peoples have the right to maintain and strengthen their distinctive spiritual relationship with their traditionally owned or otherwise occupied and used lands, territories, waters and coastal seas and other resources and to uphold their responsibilities to future generations in this regard.
>
> Article 26:
>
> 1. Indigenous peoples have the right to the lands, territories and resources which they have traditionally owned, occupied or otherwise used or acquired.
> 2. Indigenous peoples have the right to own, use, develop and control the lands, territories and resources that they possess by reason of

34 Complete text available at https://www.un.org/en/about-us/universal-declaration-of-human-rights accessed 29 May 2024.

35 Overview and complete text available at https://www.un.org/development/desa/indigenouspeoples/declaration-on-the-rights-of-indigenous-peoples.html accessed 29 May 2024.

36 Complete text available at https://www.oas.org/en/sare/documents/DecAmIND.pdf accessed 29 May 2024.

37 Only relevant articles and paragraphs are included here. The complete text is available at https://www.un.org/development/desa/indigenouspeoples/wp-content/uploads/sites/19/2018/11/UNDRIP_E_web.pdf accessed 29 May 2024.

> traditional ownership or other traditional occupation or use, as well as those which they have otherwise acquired.
>
> 3. States shall give legal recognition and protection to these lands, territories and resources. Such recognition shall be conducted with due respect to the customs, traditions and land tenure systems of the indigenous peoples concerned.
>
> Article 27: States shall establish and implement, in conjunction with indigenous peoples concerned, a fair, independent, impartial, open and transparent process, giving due recognition to indigenous peoples' laws, traditions, customs and land tenure systems, to recognize and adjudicate the rights of indigenous peoples pertaining to their lands, territories and resources, including those which were traditionally owned or otherwise occupied or used. Indigenous peoples shall have the right to participate in this process.
>
> Article 28:
>
> 1. Indigenous peoples have the right to redress, by means that can include restitution or, when this is not possible, just, fair and equitable compensation, for the lands, territories and resources which they have traditionally owned or otherwise occupied or used, and which have been confiscated, taken, occupied, used or damaged without their free, prior and informed consent.
>
> 2. Unless otherwise freely agreed upon by the peoples concerned, compensation shall take the form of lands, territories and resources equal in quality, size and legal status or of monetary compensation or other appropriate redress.
>
> Article 32:
>
> 2. States shall consult and cooperate in good faith with the indigenous peoples concerned through their own representative institutions in order to obtain their free and informed consent prior to the approval of any project affecting their lands or territories and other resources, particularly in connection with the development, utilization or exploitation of mineral, water or other resources.

Importantly, despite these rules, the UN Declaration is not legally binding.[38] Consequently, although the human rights of indigenous peoples are acknowledged by global international law,[39] their territorial claims remain unanswered. In turn, the ICJ still ignores the territorial occupation of indigenous popula-

38 Jérémie Gilbert, "Indigenous Rights in the Making: The United Nations Declaration on the Rights of Indigenous Peoples," *International Journal on Minority and Group Rights* 14 (2007): 207–230.

39 S. James Anaya, *Indigenous Peoples in International Law* (Oxford: Oxford University Press, 2004).

tions as "effective" occupation in cases of territorial disputes. Arguably, the current interpretation of notions such as effective occupation in cases encompassing natives is an embryo of assumptions and beliefs that stem from the colonial past.[40] In that vein, any current legal and political justification to claim a territory through *terra nullius*, the rule of effective occupation or the principle of *uti possidetis* opens the question of whether indigenous populations legally "exist" and, consequently, rejects their connection with the territory and any actual or potential claim.[41]

Regionally, the Americas are recognizing in law some legal rights to indigenous peoples and their moral and historical entitlement to the territory is being reviewed.[42] The Organization of American States (OAS) has been instrumental in the recognition of their collective rights.[43] Furthermore, the development in the legal regime of restitution—the right of indigenous peoples to participate in the decision-making process related to the lands they inhabit and their rights to natural resources in these territories[44]—suggests a move toward acknowledgment of their legal status. In what is relevant to indigenous peoples and territory, the 2016 American Declaration on the Rights of Indigenous Peoples, Section Five (Social, economic and property rights), Article XXV (Traditional forms of property and cultural survival. Right to land, territory and resources) states:[45]

1. Indigenous peoples have the right to maintain and strengthen their distinctive spiritual, cultural, and material relationship with their lands, territories, and resources and to uphold their responsibilities to preserve them for themselves and for future generations.
2. Indigenous peoples have the right to the lands, territories and resources which they have traditionally owned, occupied or otherwise used or acquired.
3. Indigenous peoples have the right to own, use, develop and control the lands, territories and resources that they possess by reason of traditional

40 Jérémie Gilbert, *Indigenous Peoples' Land Rights under International Law: From Victors to Actors* (Ardsley, NY: Transnational, 2006), 35.

41 Jérémie Gilbert, *Indigenous Peoples' Land Rights under International Law: From Victors to Actors* (Ardsley, NY: Transnational, 2006), 40.

42 Allen Gerlach, *Indians, Oil, and Politics: A Recent History of Ecuador* (Wilmington, NC: Scholarly Resources, 2003).

43 Megan Mooney, "How the Organization of American States Took the Lead: The Development of Indigenous Peoples' Rights in the Americas," *American Indian Law Review* 31:2 (2006): 553–572.

44 For the legal regime on restitution see Chapter 4. For indigenous peoples' rights to participate in the decision-making process in relation to the land they inhabit and their rights over natural resources see Jérémie Gilbert, *Indigenous Peoples' Land Rights under International Law: From Victors to Actors* (Ardsley, NY: Transnational, 2006), Chapter 5.

45 Complete text available at https://www.oas.org/en/sare/documents/DecAmIND.pdf accessed 29 May 2024.

ownership or other traditional occupation or use, as well as those which they have otherwise acquired.

4. States shall give legal recognition and protection to these lands, territories and resources. Such recognition shall be conducted with due respect to the customs, traditions and land tenure systems of the indigenous peoples concerned.
5. Indigenous peoples have the right to legal recognition of the various and particular modalities and forms of property, possession and ownership of their lands, territories, and resources, in accordance with the legal system of each State and the relevant international instruments. States shall establish special regimes appropriate for such recognition and for their effective demarcation or titling.

On the surface, the international and regional legal regimes pertaining to indigenous peoples in what concerns territory are very similar.[46] Their rights are limited to possession and ownership and the applicable domestic, regional and international law. Therefore, currently, there is no recognition of native self-determination. However, there is a clear indication of the right to self-determination, and consequent self-government could be the next steps in this legal evolution toward the recognition of indigenous rights in relation to territorial disputes.[47]

Domestic case studies, law and politics: indigenous peoples and territorial rights

Most of the territorial disputes in the Americas that include natives are confined to a single sovereign state. Therefore, according to the methodological choices set out in this monograph,[48] only cases in which indigenous peoples are involved in a territorial dispute pertaining to more than one sovereign state will be explored more extensively. Broadly, in terms of the domestic legal and political orders throughout the Americas, there seems to be a bottom-up advancement in terms of indigenous peoples and legal and political recognition of their rights, including territorial claims. More specifically, the legal and

46 For a detailed comparison between the 2007 UN Declaration on the Rights of Indigenous Peoples and the 2016 American Declaration on the Rights of Indigenous Peoples see "The American Declaration on the Rights of Indigenous Peoples: Background Materials and Strategies for Implementation," Indiana Law Resource Center available at https://indianlaw.org/sites/default/files/ADRIP%20Booklet%20(web%20version).pdf accessed 30 May 2024.

47 See, for example, the United States and the case of Hawaii in Keri E. Iyall Smith, *The State and Indigenous Movements* (New York, NY: Routledge, 2006).

48 See Chapter 1. In terms of what is relevant here, as with its predecessors, Núñez (2017), Núñez (2020) and Núñez (2023), this monograph is concerned with territorial disputes pertaining to two or more fully sovereign states (both *de jure* and *de facto*).

political developments seem to start at the domestic level and then expand regionally and internationally.

Section 35 of Canada's 1982 Constitution Act recognizes and affirms Aboriginal rights.[49] Furthermore, the Indian Act in Canada provides a body of law pertaining to Indian life.[50] Regardless of these norms and attempts to reconcile Canada's and indigenous peoples' claims to land, self-determination applies narrowly.[51] Most of Canada's territorial disputes with indigenous peoples are intra-state. More precisely, Canada is acknowledging territorial claims made by indigenous peoples while keeping these communities within the state. Broadly, these claims can be divided into comprehensive claims or modern treaties and specific claims.[52] In short, comprehensive claims or modern treaties have to do with First Nations, Métis and Inuit who had no treaties with non-indigenous settlements and, therefore, their Aboriginal titles to land had been overridden or ignored.[53] In turn, specific claims encompass those that are already based on agreed obligations between natives and the Government of Canada—e.g. historic treaties or the Indian Act—but are not fulfilled.[54]

Like Canada, most of the territorial disputes with indigenous peoples in the United States are intra-state. However, differing from the Canadian model, after 1871, these issues are conducted through legislation.[55] In 1934, the United States formally began to recognize the Indian nations or tribes by means of the Indian Reorganization Act.[56] Currently, there are 574 federally

49 For further details about Canada's 1982 Constitution Act, Section 35 and Aboriginal rights refer to the Indigenous Foundations website available at https://indigenousfoundations.arts.ubc.ca/constitution_act_1982_section_35/ accessed 4 June 2024.

50 Complete text of Canada's Indian Act available at https://laws-lois.justice.gc.ca/eng/acts/i-5/ accessed 4 June 2024.

51 Hayden King and Shiri Pasternak, *Canada's Emerging Indigenous Rights Framework: A Critical Analysis* (Toronto: Yellowhead Institute, 2018).

52 Gretchen Albers, "Indigenous Land Claims in Canada," in *The Canadian Encyclopedia* (2020) available at https://www.thecanadianencyclopedia.ca/en/article/land-claims accessed 10 June 2024.

53 For detailed information about modern treaties see the Government of Canada official website available at https://www.rcaanc-cirnac.gc.ca/eng/1677073191939/1677073214344 accessed 10 June 2024.

54 For detailed information about specific claims see the Government of Canada official website available at https://www.rcaanc-cirnac.gc.ca/eng/1100100030291/1539617582343 accessed 10 June 2024.

55 For a detailed account of relevant history, legislation and case law pertaining to the United States, indigenous populations and intra-state territorial disputes refer to the Indian Land Tenure Foundation website available at https://iltf.org/land-issues/history/ accessed 11 June 2024.

56 1934 Indian Reorganization Act complete text available at https://www.govinfo.gov/content/pkg/COMPS-5299/pdf/COMPS-5299.pdf accessed 3 June 2024.

recognized sovereign Indian nations and tribes with their own constitutions and charters. All of them are included in the federal and state structure.[57]

Regardless of their similarities and differences in terms of territorial disputes within their borders that include natives,[58] Canada and the United States share cases in which First Nations and Native Americans challenge both sovereign states.[59] For example, transboundary waters bring about discussions over the environment, decolonization norms, self-determination and self-government.[60] Several other border issues include mobility rights, the Jay Treaty,[61] identity documents and immigration laws.[62]

In terms of intra-state territorial disputes, Mexico seems to be evolving toward the recognition of full citizenship and indigenous autonomy.[63] However, the situation is different in cases in which natives find themselves on the border between the United States and Mexico. Several tribes including the Apache, O'odham and Kumeyaay have members on both sides of the southern border.[64] Clearly, indigenous peoples on the northern and southern borders (Canada–United States and United States–Mexico, respectively) face challenges stemming from international borders agreed by former colonial empires and/or sovereign states with little regard to their presence and interests.[65] In recent years, indigenous leaders from Canada, the United States and

57 For up-to-date information including Indian constitutions and charters see the Library of Congress Collection on Native American Constitutions and Legal Materials available at https://www.loc.gov/collections/native-american-constitutions-and-legal-materials/about-this-collection/ accessed 3 June 2024.

58 James S. Frideres, "Indigenous Peoples of Canada and the United States of America: Entering the 21st Century," in Leen d'Haenens, ed., *Images of Canadianness: Visions on Canada's Politics, Culture, and Economics* (Ottawa: University of Ottawa Press, 1998): 167–196.

59 For a comprehensive analysis of legal and political issues see Patrick Macklem, "Distributing Sovereignty: Indian Nations and Equality of Peoples," in Anthony J. Connolly, ed., *Indigenous Rights* (London and New York, NY: Routledge, 2017), 303–359.

60 Emma S. Norman, *Governing Transboundary Waters: Canada, the United States, and Indigenous Communities* (London and New York, NY: Routledge, 2014).

61 Bryan Nickels, "Native American Free Passage Rights under the 1794 Jay Treaty: Survival under United States Statutory Law and Canadian Common Law," *Boston College International and Comparative Law Review* 24:2 (2001): 313–340. For details about the 1794 Jay Treaty and its complete text refer to the United States Library of Congress official website available at https://guides.loc.gov/jays-treaty accessed 11 June 2024.

62 For First Nations and Native Americans crossing the Canada–US border see Canada's official website available at https://www.sac-isc.gc.ca/eng/1100100032399/1572459562067; and the United States official website available at https://ca.usembassy.gov/first-nations-and-native-americans/ both accessed 11 June 2024.

63 Gemma van der Haar, "The Zapatista Uprising and the Struggle for Indigenous Autonomy," *European Review of Latin American and Caribbean Studies* 76 (2004): 98–108.

64 Eileen M. Luna-Firebaugh, "The Border Crossed Us: Border Crossing Issues of the Indigenous Peoples of the Americas," *Wicazo Sa Review* 17:1 (2002): 159–181.

65 Jacob Moeller, "A Tribe Divided: The Threat of the Loss of Tribal Autonomy and Culture Facing Transnational Tribes on the Northern and Southern Borders of the United States," *Vanderbilt Journal of Transnational Law* 54:5 (2021): 1257–1292.

Mexico formed the Tribal Border Alliance to deal with issues including border crossing and tribal-driven solutions related to border policies, access to tribal land and culture.[66]

States in Central America, the Caribbean and South America, originally opposed to recognition of indigenous rights at the time of the colony and early independence, are leaving behind the European understanding and changing the way they interact with these populations.[67] For instance, most of the Latin American states include norms in their national constitutions recognizing the rights of indigenous peoples to land ownership.[68] However, whether there are new normative grounds for territorial claims based on indigenous rights is still debatable.[69] For example, Nicaragua's infringement of indigenous rights in favor of development and promotion of new regional standards suggest new practices are being explored.[70] Territorial disputes in these states that include indigenous peoples are mainly intra-state and have a tendency to remain peaceful. There are some exceptions that include armed groups—e.g. Colombia, Guatemala and Peru.[71]

Arguably, the two countries at the forefront of recognizing the presence of natives and their claims, in law and politics, are Ecuador and Bolivia. The growing influence of indigenous parties and indigenous individuals in positions of power,[72] and the Peruvian President Alejandro Toledo's self-identification as indigenous,[73] demonstrate the tendency to acknowledge indigenous populations as "persons" in law with legal rights and obligations at the local

66 Brenden W. Rensink, "Indigenous Peoples and Euro-American Frontiers, Borderlands, and Borders in North America," in Jane Dailey, ed., *Oxford Research Encyclopedia of American History* available at https://oxfordre.com/americanhistory/display/10.1093/acrefore/9780199329175.001.0001/acrefore-9780199329175-e-772. For the official Tribal Border Alliance website see https://www.tribalborderalliance.org/about/ both accessed 12 June 2024.

67 Austen L. Parrish, "Changing Territoriality, Fading Sovereignty, and the Development of Indigenous Rights," *American Indian Law Review* 31:2 (2006/2007): 291–314.

68 Jérémie Gilbert, *Indigenous Peoples' Land Rights under International Law: From Victors to Actors* (Ardsley, NY: Transnational, 2006), 299.

69 See, for example, Avery Kolers, *Law, Conflict and Justice: Theory of Territory* (New York, NY: Cambridge University Press, 2009). Kolers introduces a way to assess indigenous peoples' territorial claims that allows the coexistence of different claims in the same state.

70 Willem Van Genugten and Camillo Perez-Bustillo, "The Emerging International Architecture of Indigenous Rights: The Interaction Between Global, Regional, and National Dimensions," *International Journal on Minority and Group Rights* 11 (2004): 379–409.

71 Victoria Tauli-Corpuz, "Conflict, Peace and the Human Rights of Indigenous Peoples," in Elsa Stamatopoulou, ed., *Indigenous Peoples' Rights and Unreported Struggles: Conflict and Peace* (New York, NY: Columbia University Press, 2017), 1–24 available at https://academiccommons.columbia.edu/doi/10.7916/D8PK1PRM accessed 20 June 2024.

72 Donna Lee Van Cott, "Broadening Democracy: Latin America's Indigenous People's Movements," *Current History* 103:670 (2004): 80–85.

73 Shane Greene, "Getting Over the Andes: The Geo-Eco-Politics of Indigenous Movements in Peru's Twenty-First Century Inca Empire," *Journal of Latin American Studies* 38:2 (2006): 327–354.

level first, and from there, regionally. New legal concepts and categories such as "good living" or "mother earth" ("buen vivir" and "Pachamama," respectively, in Spanish and Aymara/Quechua) that are rooted in natives' traditions and understandings were incorporated in Ecuador's national constitution in 2008; and indigenous rights to the environment were included in Bolivia's 2009 reform to their national constitution.[74]

An intricate case in which indigenous people are involved in a territorial dispute pertaining to more than one sovereign state is the Mapuche conflict in Argentina and Chile.[75] Sociologically, like other indigenous populations involved in territorial disputes in the Americas, the Mapuche constitute a nation that is located within nation-states borders and, controversially, across them.[76] The Mapuche are the largest indigenous population in South America with most of them living in Chile; in fact, they constitute about 84% of Chile's indigenous population and about 9% of Chile's total population.[77] Like many cases previously reviewed in this monograph, the current territorial dispute can be traced back to colonial times.[78] Unsurprisingly, like other differences in the Americas, this territorial dispute includes the environment and natural resources and, therefore, practices clashing with decolonial political ecology.[79] Indeed, alongside the Mapuche, Argentina and Chile, this case features private sector agents' extractivism[80] and other practices that encompass appropriation of nature and the dividing of communities.[81] While Chile seems to be

74 Silvina Ramírez, "Pueblos Indígenas, Identidad y Territorio—Sin Territorio no hay Identidad como Pueblo," *Revista Jurídica de la Universidad de Palermo* 15:1 (2017): 11–32.

75 Pablo Arturo Mansilla Quiñones and Miguel Melin Pehuen, "A Struggle for Territory, a Struggle Against Borders: The Mapuche Conflict in Argentina and Chile Contests Notions of Borders Promulgated by the Nation-State," *NACLA Report on the Americas* 51:1 (2019): 41–48. For further details and the most up-to-date information about the Mapuche in Argentina and Chile refer to the Minority Rights Group webpage available at https://minorityrights.org/communities/mapuche/ accessed 20 June 2024.

76 Sarah Warren, "A Nation Divided: Building the Cross-Border Mapuche Nation in Chile and Argentina," *Journal of Latin American Studies* 45:2 (2013): 235–264.

77 Cecilia Brey, "Land Rights and Regime Change: Trends in Mapuche Territorial Conflict from 1970 to Present in South-Central Chile," *Proceedings of GREAT Day* 2019:7 (2020): 49–68; Jack Herscowitz, "The Mapuche-Chilean Land Conflict and Justice: Re-Contextualizing 21st Century Violence," *Towson University Journal of International Affairs* 52:2 (2019): 14–33.

78 Carla Alberti, Juan Pablo Luna, Sergio Toro-Maureira and Eugenia Gayo, "The Long Memory of the Land: Pre-Colonial Origins of Mapuche Mobilization in Chile," *Political Geography* 103 (2023): 1–11.

79 Robinson Torres, Gerardo Azócar, Roberto Gallardo and Julio Mendoza, "Water Extractivism and Decolonial Struggles in Mapuche Territory, Chile," *Water Alternatives* 15:1 (2022): 150–174.

80 Hugo Romero-Toledo and Katy Jenkins, "Contested Waters, Extractivisms, and Territories: Indigenous People in Chile and the Neoliberal Crisis," *Current Directions in Water Scarcity Research* 4 (2022): 189–208.

81 Sarah H. Kelly, "Mapping Hydropower Conflicts: A Legal Geography of Dispossession in Mapuche-Williche Territory, Chile," *Geoforum* 127 (2021): 269–282.

moving back and forth between cooperation and conflict,[82] Argentina is moving toward cooperation with the Mapuche—e.g. in the co-management of the Nahuel Huapi National Park.[83] In addition to the domestic and regional contexts, the case encompasses international components. Indeed, the Mapuche case includes an alien interference in the region supporting the indigenous people's claims to territory.[84] Launched in 1996 to replace the Comité Exterior Mapuche (1978–1996), the Mapuche International Link, a support group based in the United Kingdom, aims to contribute toward the indigenous peoples' development, autonomy and self-determination.[85] An Argentine minister accused the group of supporting terrorism against local governments; whether this is the case or not, or whether it is a means used by the United Kingdom to interfere with the Falklands/Malvinas case, is a matter of further research.[86]

Implanted populations

Alongside the legal and political issues involving indigenous peoples,[87] there are also territorial disputes in the Americas relating to populations that were at one time settlers and nowadays claim self-determination. Such populations include the Falkland/Malvinas Islanders and the Raizal community in San Andrés, Providencia and Santa Catalina. The continent features communities shaped by different immigration processes, involving willing or forced relocation in the Americas: settler colonialism, colonies with settlers and slavery. Moreover, some of these processes were intended to secure claims to

82 Germán Bidegain, "From Cooperation to Confrontation: The Mapuche Movement and its Political Impact, 1990–2014," in Sofia Donoso and Marisa von Bülow, eds., *Social Movements in Chile: Organization, Trajectories, and Political Consequences* (New York, NY: Palgrave Macmillan, 2017): 99–129.

83 Renaud Miniconi and Sylvain Guyot, "Conflicts and Cooperation in the Mountainous Mapuche Territory (Argentina). The Case of the Nahuel Huapi National Park," *Journal of Alpine Research* 98:1 (2010): 138–153.

84 See, for example, a United Kingdom–based organization allegedly accused by the Argentine government of supporting the Mapuche community. Press release by the Mapuche International Link, United Kingdom published on 1 September 2017 available at https://www.mapuche-nation.org/english/html/news/pr-119.html accessed 14 March 2024.

85 Official Mapuche International Link website available at https://www.mapuche-nation.org/about-us/ accessed 13 June 2024. See also Leslie Ray, *Language of the Land: The Mapuche in Argentina and Chile* (Skive: International Work Group for Indigenous Affairs, 2007).

86 See in 2017 Argentina's Minister of Security, Patricia Bullrich, making an accusation regarding the Mapuche Ancestral Resistance (RAM) available at https://www.mapuche-nation.org/blog/false-allegations-against-mapuche-international-link-by-argentinian-government/ and https://www.bristolpost.co.uk/news/bristol-news/bristol-based-organisation-allegedly-accused-426938 both accessed 20 June 2024.

87 Rachel Sieder, "Indigenous People's Rights and the Law in Latin America," in Corinne Lennox and Damien Short, eds., *Handbook of Indigenous Peoples' Rights* (London and New York, NY: Routledge, 2016), 414–423.

sovereignty. For instance, "right-peopling"[88] the territory with settlers was a means employed by some former colonial powers (and, arguably, some modern states such as Israel) to secure their claim to sovereignty over new territories. Indeed, the "right-peopling" strategy consists of relocating people in a territory to shape later claims to sovereignty. By relocating people identified with the same race, ethnicity or national identity from the motherland into newly discovered territories, former colonial powers secured their claim to sovereignty over these territories by means of self-determination.[89] In turn, whether or not the method was intended to achieve the same goal, a similar situation has arisen from those who were originally brought to the Americas as slaves by former colonial powers. The question remains whether these populations have the right to self-determination and, if so, to what extent.

Settler colonialism and colonies with settlers

In short, settlers characterize America's population, whether they arrived willingly, by force, by chance or by design.[90] Whether people moved willingly from their motherland to the new territories, or they were forced to do so (without being slaves), this section focuses on those populations who were not originally from the Americas, moved to the content as free persons and are still intertwined with territorial disputes.

People who moved to the Americas can be subdivided into those who settled on the continent following their own wishes—e.g. largely, immigrants—and those who were sent to the new territories for right-peopling and right-sizing reasons by European empires.[91] Right-peopling and right-sizing are intertwined with colonialism and settler colonialism.[92] More precisely, colonialism was previously characterized in this monograph as a form of domination that implies the control by agents such as states, communities and individuals

88 Brendan O'Leary, "The Elements of Right-Sizing and Right-Peopling the State," in Brendan O'Leary, Ian S. Lustick and Thomas Callaghy, eds., *Right-Sizing the State: The Politics of Moving Borders* (Oxford: Oxford University Press, 2001), 15–73.

89 Oded Haklai and Nephytos Loizides, "Settlers and Conflict Over Contested Territories," in Oded Haklai and Neophytos Loizides, eds., *Settlers in Contested Lands. Territorial Disputes and Ethnic Conflicts* (Stanford, CA: Stanford University Press, 2015), 1–16.

90 For detailed accounts of different cases pertaining to settlers in the Americas see Jayme A. Sokolow, *The Great Encounter: Native Peoples and European Settlers in the Americas, 1492–1800* (New York, NY and London: Routledge, Taylor & Francis, 2016); Henry Schwarz and Sangeeta Ray, eds., *A Companion to Postcolonial Studies* (Oxford: Blackwell Publishing Ltd, 2005).

91 Brendan O'Leary, "The Elements of Right-Sizing and Right-Peopling the State," in Brendan O'Leary, Ian S. Lustick and Thomas Callaghy, eds., *Right-Sizing the State: The Politics of Moving Borders* (Oxford: Oxford University Press, 2001), 15–73.

92 For the difference between settler colonies and colonies with settlers see Chris Youé, "Settler Colonialism or Colonies with Settlers?" *Canadian Journal of African Studies* 52:1 (2018): 69–85.

over other states, communities and individuals, their territories and behaviors.[93] Colonialism so characterized may be subdivided into intergroup and intragroup domination. While intergroup colonialism refers to the domination process in culturally heterogeneous agents, the intragroup colonialism has to do with homogeneous ones. In any case, colonialism is characterized by the permanent subordination of those who are colonized, regardless of whether the relationship between colonizer and colonized stems from colonialism, neo-colonialism or colonial mindset or syndrome.[94] In turn, settler colonialism is characterized by repressing, co-opting and ultimately, extinguishing indigenous agents. As a result, having superseded any other agent and claim, settler colonials later claim to be "settled."[95]

A situation that illustrates European settlement in the Americas and that is still an ongoing territorial dispute is the Falkland/Malvinas Islands case. Depending on the agent at play—that is Argentina, the United Kingdom or the islanders—there might be a case of settlement of originally uninhabited land, colonialism or settler colonialism. Arguably, Argentina, the United Kingdom and the Falkland/Malvinas Islanders would agree on the following account: the islands were originally uninhabited; until the 1810s, there were British, French and Spanish settlements; and since then there have been claims over the Falkland/Malvinas Islands.[96] More specifically, in 1816, Argentina became independent and claimed the former Spanish territories, including the Falklands/Malvinas, taking actual possession of the islands in 1820.[97] The British expelled Argentine settlers in 1833.[98] Since then, Argentina and the United Kingdom have claimed exclusive sovereign rights over the islands, both bilaterally and internationally, with the dispute reaching a climax in 1982 in the outbreak of a war between the two countries. The territory at issue includes the islands and their dependencies, the South Georgia and South Sandwich Islands. Importantly, the Falkland/Malvinas Islanders maintain there is no question about sovereignty that needs to be answered.[99] The Falkland/Malvinas Islands are located between Latin America and Africa and, therefore, it might be possible to control maritime transport and sea lanes in the South Atlantic from them.[100] In addition to their geographical location

93 See Chapter 6.

94 See Chapter 6.

95 For a notion of settler colonial studies see Lorenzo Veracini, "Introducing: Settler Colonial Studies," *Settler Colonial Studies* 1:1 (2011): 1–12.

96 See Chapter 5.

97 Ricardo Caillet-Bois, *Una Tierra Argentina: Las Islas Malvinas* (Buenos Aires: Peuser, 1948).

98 Christopher C. Joyner, "Anglo-Argentine Rivalry after the Falklands/Malvinas War: Laws, Geopolitics, and the Antarctic Connection," *Lawyer of the Americas* 15:3 (1984): 467–450.

99 Official results of the referendum on the Political Status of the Falkland/Malvinas Islands available at https://www.fiassociation.com/news/press-release-result-of-referendum-remains-clear-10-years-on/ accessed 23 January 2025.

100 Detlef Nolte and Leslie E. Wehner, "Geopolitics in Latin America, Old and New," in David R. Mares and Arie M. Kacowicz, eds., *Routledge Handbook of Latin American Security* (Abingdon: Routledge, 2015), 33–43.

and natural resources, it is important to note the area's actual and potential relevance in terms of Antarctica.[101]

Argentina, the United Kingdom and the Falkland/Malvinas Islanders have presented arguments and counterarguments that have only resulted in a stalemate because they are based on unidimensional approaches that fail to consider the issue in its intricacy. The self-determination of the Falkland/Malvinas Islanders is legally and politically controversial.[102] For instance, the islanders maintain the islands "have never had any native inhabitants and no indigenous people have ever been displaced."[103] If that were the case, there could not be colonialism or settler colonialism on the islands because there has never been permanent subordination of colonized peoples or repression of indigenous agents. Conversely, Argentina maintains that in "1833, the Malvinas Islands were illegally occupied by British forces who expelled the Argentine population and authorities established there legitimately, to replace them with British subjects."[104] This account suggests that (a) there were no natives displaced—i.e. Argentines were not natives of the land—hence, there could not be settler colonialism; and (b) the displacement of Argentines was illegal and illegitimate and, therefore, there would be a case of colonialism—i.e. depending on the validity of the title Argentines had at the time, they could be considered, for example, first settlers. If the latter situation were true, it would follow that (a) the Falkland/Malvinas Islanders occupied the islands illegally and illegitimately; (b) the United Kingdom right-peopled the territory to right-size it later. Clearly, the case encompasses different categories of claims including

101 Territorial claims over Antarctica will be reviewed extensively in Chapter 9. Christopher C. Joyner, "Anglo-Argentine Rivalry After the Falklands/Malvinas War: Laws, Geopolitics, and the Antarctic Connection," *Lawyer of the Americas* 15:3 (1984): 467–502.

102 There are several academic publications, both in English and Spanish, in legal and political sciences and international relations pertaining to the self-determination question regarding the Falkland/Malvinas islanders. For examples immediately after the 1982 Falklands/Malvinas war see Houchang E. Chehabi, "Self-Determination, Territorial Integrity, and the Falkland Islands," *Political Science Quarterly* 100:2 (1985): 215–225; Denzil Dunnett, "Self-Determination and the Falklands," *International Affairs (Royal Institute of International Affairs 1944–)* 59:3 (1983): 415–428; W. Michael Reisman, "The Struggle for the Falklands," *The Yale Law Journal* 93:2 (1983): 287–317. For more recent academic research on this point see Peter Clegg, "Political and Constitutional Issues for the Contemporary Falkland Islands," *The Round Table* 111:1 (2022): 69–78; Augusto Javier López, "Ni Autodeterminación, Ni Pueblo. Improcedencia de la Argumentación Inglesa por la Soberanía de Malvinas," *Raigal* 9 (2022): 66–70; Jaime Trinidad, *Self-determination in Disputed Colonial Territories* (Cambridge: Cambridge University Press, 2018); and many more.

103 Official Falkland Islands Government website available at https://falklands.gov.fk/our-history accessed 28 June 2024.

104 Official Ministry of Foreign Affairs, International Trade and Worship, Argentine Republic website available at https://cancilleria.gob.ar/en/188-years-after-illegal-occupation-malvinas-argentina-reaffirms-its-sovereignty-rights-over-islands accessed 25 June 2024.

effective control, historical, territorial and cultural.[105] Furthermore, while it may be evident that the Falkland/Malvinas Islands controversy has to do with legal, political, historical and sociological features, it is also advisable to acknowledge that geopolitics and economics, in the form of exploration and exploitation of natural resources, have a role to play.

Colonialism, slavery and black self-determination

The Americas include some territorial disputes that encompass former slave communities. These cases have some of the hallmarks pertaining to native populations and some of those who settled in the Americas; these qualities make them have a nature of their own. Like settlers, descendants of former slaves find their roots in regions other than the Americas. Like some native populations, some of the descendant communities of former slaves are claiming self-determination.[106] Therefore, the following paragraphs refer to some cases in which there is a territorial dispute that includes people whose origin relates to prior slavery.

The San Andrés, Providencia and Santa Catalina territorial dispute between Colombia and Nicaragua includes the Raizal people. They are a local ethnic and racial minority.[107] With origins in the European colonial past that encompassed slavery, migration and different cultures, the Raizal people have their own culture, including their own language, i.e. Creole, and an overall identity that makes them define themselves as different from the people living on Colombia's mainland.[108] Differences between the islanders and Colombia's mainland population comprise religious discrepancies arising from their respective Anglophone/Protestant and Hispanic/Catholic views.[109] In fact, the Raizal people are sociologically linked with the English and Creole-speaking community on the Nicaraguan coast.[110] Controversially, there seems to be a

105 For different categories of claims in the context of territorial disputes see Jorge E. Núñez, *Territorial Disputes and State Sovereignty: International Law and Politics* (London and New York, NY: Routledge, Taylor & Francis Group, 2020), Chapter 4.

106 The academic literature seems to be acknowledging this issue more recently with labels such as "Black self-determination." See, for example, Manu Karuka, "Black and Native Visions of Self-Determination," *Critical Ethnic Studies* 3:2 (2017): 77–98.

107 See Chapter 5.

108 Dilia Robinson Saavedra, "Pueblo Raiza en Colombia," in Carlos Parra Dussán and Gloria Amparo Rodríguez, eds., *Comunidades Étnicas en Colombia: Cultura y Jurisprudencia* (Bogotá: Centro Editorial Universidad del Rosario, 2013), 1–25.

109 Pablo Alonso González, Wilhelm Londoño and Eva Parga-Dans, "Equality and Hierarchy, Sovereignty and Multiculturalism: The Heritagisation of Raizals in Santa Catalina (Colombia)," *Journal of Ethnic and Migration Studies* 46:19 (2018): 4066–4085; James Ross, "Routes for Roots: Entering the 21st Century in San Andrés Island, Colombia," *Caribbean Studies* 35:1 (2007): 3–36.

110 James Ross, "Routes for Roots: Entering the 21st Century in San Andrés Island, Colombia," *Caribbean Studies* 35:1 (2007): 3–36.

dominant national vision overriding the local Raizal community by means of imposition by the Colombian state coupled with private sector interests.[111] More recently, with the Black Lives Matter movement, the Raizal's claims for self-determination seem to be gaining more visibility domestically, regionally and internationally.[112] Therein, national level organizations such as Proceso de Comunidades Negras (Black Communities' Process, PCN) defend the right to the political–organizational autonomy of the Raizal people.[113]

Like other cases in the Americas, the Marouini (or Maroni) River tract territorial dispute is not limited to sovereign states, that is Suriname and French Guiana, but includes other agents.[114] French settlers, who had originally moved to the area in the 1700s for "right-peopling" reasons, moved on to larger cities.[115] Despite these movements, the multi-ethnic area comprises Carib Indians and other Amerindian groups, such as the Arawak Indians and the Maroons. The Maroons—known in French Guiana as Bushinenge—are former African slaves who were brought to the area by Europeans and escaped captivity.[116] French Guiana is a region of France located in South America.[117] In 2017, France created the Grand Customary Council, a consultative body aimed to strengthen the capacities of self-representation of the Amerindian and Bushinenge peoples.[118] This institution replaced the former Consultative Council of Amerindian and Bushinenge Populations (CCPAB).[119] Regardless of the apparent answer by the French government to the self-representation

111 Pablo Alonso Gonzalez, Wilhelm Londoño and Eva Parga-Dans, "Equality and Hierarchy, Sovereignty and Multiculturalism: The Heritagisation of Raizals in Santa Catalina (Colombia)," *Journal of Ethnic and Migration Studies* 46:19 (2020): 4066–4085.

112 Cassiani Hernàndez and Rubén Darío, "Afro-Colombian, Black, Raizal and Palenquero Participation in Electoral Politics: The Construction of a Distinctive Political Culture in Colombia," in Cloves Luiz Pereira Oliveira, Gladys Lanier Mitchell-Walthour and Minion K. C. Morrison, eds., *Black Lives Matter in Latin America: Continuities in Racism, Cross-National Resistance and Mobilization in the Americas* (Cham: Springer Nature, 2024), 205–227.

113 Viviane Weitzner, "'¡Guardia, Guardia!': Autonomies and Territorial Defense in the Context of Colombia's Post Peace-Accord," in Miguel González, Ritsuko Funaki, Araceli Burguete Cal y Mayor, José Marimán and Pablo Ortiz-T, eds., *Indigenous Territorial Autonomy and Self-Government in the Diverse Americas* (Calgary: University of Calgary Press, 2023), 603–640.

114 See Chapter 5.

115 Thomas W. Donovan, "The Marouini River Tract and Its Colonial Legacy in South America," *Chicago-Kent Journal of International and Comparative Law* 4 (2004): 1–28.

116 Thomas W. Donovan, "The Marouini River Tract and Its Colonial Legacy in South America," *Chicago-Kent Journal of International and Comparative Law* 4 (2004): 1–28.

117 For details about French Guiana's governmental organization see their official website available at https://www.guyane.gouv.fr/Services-de-l-Etat/Organisation-des-services-de-l-Etat accessed 2 July 2024.

118 David Nathaniel Berger, ed., *The Indigenous World 2019* (Copenhagen: International Work Group for Indigenous Affairs, 2019). Complete text available at https://www.iwgia.org/en/resources/publications/305-books/3333-the-indigenous-world-2019.html accessed 2 July 2024.

119 The CCPAB was created by Law No. 2007-24 of 21 February 2007.

claims of these local agents, it is important to highlight that the native people and the Bushinenge have different traditions and customary norms. Indeed, this is a clear case of the dichotomy between universalism and particularism where, on the one hand, France intends to provide a one-size-fits-all solution and, on the other hand, there is evident self-identification of different groups and interests.[120] Moreover, as a consultative body, the Council's decisions are not binding. These elements and features suggest that attempts for self-determination may struggle.[121]

Conclusion

This chapter has exposed a puzzling subject in the context of international law and politics, in which settlers or implanted populations are considered "persons" and may be able to claim the territory they inhabit, whereas by contrast the legal and political status of indigenous populations remains only vaguely recognized. Further research shows that, domestically and regionally, the Americas are moving toward recognizing the legal personhood of native populations and relevant rights and obligations such as the capacity for self-governing. In a similar way, some implanted populations—in particular, those with their origins in former enslaved communities—are gaining a similar recognition. Whether as a cause of this acknowledgment in law or as a consequence, native populations and some implanted people are uniting in domestic, regional and international organizations to both gather support for their claims and to support legal and political changes concerning their status in terms of territorial use and ownership.

The chapter explained why sovereign states may face a problem with claims to territories of this type—i.e. involving internal groups such as indigenous peoples and implanted populations arguing for their right to self-determination. Indeed, self-determination may result in secession of part of the territory of the sovereign state in question. However, the chapter brought precision by clarifying that although self-determination may imply secession, this does not need to be the outcome. Secession is an *ultimum remedium* in situations in which the sovereign state and the population that wishes to secede are in conflict. In fact, self-determination may lead to several other results.

The ways in which self-determination and secession are characterized and applied are fundamental in the resolution of territorial disputes. As explained

120 Fred Réno and Bernard Phipps, "The Dichotomy of Universalism and Particularism in French Guiana," in Rosemarijn Hoefte, Matthew L. Bishop and Peter Clegg, eds., *Postcolonial Trajectories in the Caribbean: The Three Guianas* (London and New York, NY: Routledge, 2016), 66–78.

121 Christopher Mark Macneill, "Europe's Last Continental America Colony: French Guiana's Subjugation Struggles," *International Journal of Law Management & Humanities* 4:6 (2021): 1–24.

in detail in Núñez (2020),[122] when there is a territorial dispute and the claiming parties only disagree about their rights over a territory, self-determination in the form of secession is not an advisable solution. It goes against the principle of territorial integrity. Second, it guarantees the disagreement of the agent left outside the arrangement. Third, and most importantly, as long as there is no oppression, there are other remedies that can secure a permanent and peaceful understanding among all the involved agents.

Arrangements such as the co-management of the Nahuel Huapi National Park between Argentina and the Mapuche and the proposal by the PCN to grant the Raizal people the right to political-organizational autonomy show that it is possible to accommodate both self-determination and territorial integrity. Therefore, in situations where there is a peaceful understanding between the state and internal communities that fulfill certain legal criteria, but there may be disagreements about territorial claims, solutions may be found by means of cooperation rather than conflict. Importantly, since there is no unequivocal and binding legal definition of self-determination, the concept of "who counts?"[123] should be clearly articulated. Once the "who counts" is determined, further questions such as "on what grounds" or according to what category of claim can be explored.[124] Finally, these different agents—i.e. sovereign states and communities that fulfill the self-determination criteria—can move toward finding mutually beneficial solutions.

Since self-determination centers on people, implies different degrees of autonomy and does not necessarily mean secession (which requires oppression by the government, an internal way of domination), public international law empowers populations to freely decide what is best for them even in cases of territorial disputes. However, sovereignty and self-determination may also draw together agents with opposing claims over territorial disputes. If territorial disputes can be centered on elements other than territory, and if sovereignty can be shared in a way that is beneficial to all the claiming agents, then self-determination may lead to solutions other than secession, and there is room for territorial disputes to be resolved by cooperative approaches.

122 For the author's previous work on self-determination in the context of territorial disputes see Jorge E. Núñez, *Territorial Disputes and State Sovereignty: International Law and Politics* (London and New York, NY: Routledge, Taylor & Francis Group, 2020), Chapter 3.

123 For the author's view on "who counts" in negotiations about territorial disputes and sovereignty conflicts see Jorge E. Núñez, *Sovereignty Conflicts and International Law and Politics: A Distributive Justice Issue* (London and New York, NY: Routledge, Taylor & Francis Group, 2017), Chapter 6; and Jorge E. Núñez, *Territorial Disputes and State Sovereignty: International Law and Politics* (London and New York, NY: Routledge, Taylor & Francis Group, 2020), Chapter 4.

124 For details about different categories of claims relevant to territorial disputes see Jorge E. Núñez, *Territorial Disputes and State Sovereignty: International Law and Politics* (London and New York, NY: Routledge, Taylor & Francis Group, 2020), Chapter 4.

Bibliography

Albers, Gretchen. "Indigenous Land Claims in Canada." In *The Canadian Encyclopedia* (2020) available at https://www.thecanadianencyclopedia.ca/en/article/land-claims accessed 10 June 2024.

Alberti, Carla, Juan Pablo Luna, Sergio Toro-Maureira and Eugenia Gayo. "The Long Memory of the Land: Pre-Colonial Origins of Mapuche Mobilization in Chile." *Political Geography* 103 (2023): 1–11.

Alonso González, Wilhelm Pablo Londoño and Eva Parga-Dans. "Equality and Hierarchy, Sovereignty and Multiculturalism: The Heritagisation of Raizals in Santa Catalina (Colombia)." *Journal of Ethnic and Migration Studies* 46:19 (2018): 4066–4085.

Anaya, S. James. *Indigenous Peoples in International Law*. Oxford: Oxford University Press, 2004.

Berger, David Nathaniel, ed. *The Indigenous World 2019*. Copenhagen: International Work Group for Indigenous Affairs, 2019, available at https://www.iwgia.org/en/resources/publications/305-books/3333-the-indigenous-world-2019.html accessed 2 July 2024.

Bidegain, Germán. "From Cooperation to Confrontation: The Mapuche Movement and its Political Impact, 1990–2014." In *Social Movements in Chile: Organization, Trajectories, and Political Consequences*, Donoso, Sofia and von Bülow, Marisa, eds. 99–129. New York, NY: Palgrave Macmillan, 2017.

Blay, S. K. N. "Self-Determination Versus Territorial Integrity in Decolonization." *NYU Journal of International Law and Politics* 18 (1986): 441–472.

Brey, Cecilia. "Land Rights and Regime Change: Trends in Mapuche Territorial Conflict from 1970 to Present in South-Central Chile." *Proceedings of GREAT Day* 2019:7 (2020): 49–68.

Caillet-Bois, Ricardo. *Una Tierra Argentina: Las Islas Malvinas*. Buenos Aires: Peuser, 1948.

Chehabi, Houchang E. "Self-Determination, Territorial Integrity, and the Falkland Islands." *Political Science Quarterly* 100:2 (1985): 215–225.

Clark, Roger S. "The Decolonization of East Timor and the United Nations Norms on Self-Determination and Aggression." *Yale Journal of World Public Order* 7:2 (1980): 30.

Clegg, Peter. "Political and Constitutional Issues for the Contemporary Falkland Islands." *The Round Table* 111:1 (2022): 69–78.

Cook, Noble David. *Born to Die: Disease and the New World Conquest, 1492–1650*. Cambridge: Cambridge University Press, 1998.

Denevan, William M. *The Native Population of the Americas in 1492*. Madison, WI: University of Wisconsin Press, 1992.

Dobyns, Henry F. "An Appraisal of Techniques with a New Hemispheric Estimate." *Current Anthropology* 7:4 (1966): 395–416.

Donovan, Thomas W. "The Marouini River Tract and Its Colonial Legacy in South America." *Chicago-Kent Journal of International and Comparative Law* 4 (2004): 1–28.

Dunnett, Denzil. "Self-Determination and the Falklands." *International Affairs (Royal Institute of International Affairs 1944–)* 59:3 (1983): 415–428.

Emerson, Rupert. "Self-Determination." *American Journal of International Law* 65: 3 (1971): 459–475.

Franck, Thomas M. and Paul Hoffman. "The Right to Self-Determination in Very Small Places." *New York University Journal of International Law and Politics* 8 (1975): 331–386.

Frideres, James S. "Indigenous Peoples of Canada and the United States of America: Entering the 21st Century." In *Images of Canadianness: Visions on Canada's Politics, Culture, and Economics*, d'Haenens, Leen, ed. 167–196. Ottawa: University of Ottawa Press, 1998.

Gerlach, Allen. *Indians, Oil, and Politics: A Recent History of Ecuador*. Wilmington, NC: Scholarly Resources, 2003.

Gilbert, Jérémie. "Indigenous Rights in the Making: The United Nations Declaration on the Rights of Indigenous Peoples." *International Journal on Minority and Group Rights* 14 (2007): 207–230.

Gilbert, Jérémie. *Indigenous Peoples' Land Rights under International Law: From Victors to Actors*. Ardsley, NY: Transnational, 2006.

Greene, Shane. "Getting Over the Andes: The Geo-Eco-Politics of Indigenous Movements in Peru's Twenty-First Century Inca Empire." *Journal of Latin American Studies* 38:2 (2006): 327–354.

Haklai, Oded and Nephytos Loizides. "Settlers and Conflict Over Contested Territories." In *Settlers in Contested Lands. Territorial Disputes and Ethnic Conflicts*, Haklai, Oded and Loizides, Neophytos, eds. 1–16. Stanford, CA: Stanford University Press, 2015.

Hannum, Hurst. *Autonomy, Sovereignty, and Self-determination: The Accommodation of Conflicting Rights*. Philadelphia, PA: University of Pennsylvania Press, 1996.

Hernàndez, Cassiani and Rubén Darío. "Afro-Colombian, Black, Raizal and Palenquero Participation in Electoral Politics: The Construction of a Distinctive Political Culture in Colombia." In *Black Lives Matter in Latin America: Continuities in Racism, Cross-National Resistance and Mobilization in the Americas*, Oliveira, Cloves Luiz Pereira, Mitchell-Walthour, Gladys Lanier and Morrison, Minion K. C., eds. 205–227. Cham: Springer Nature, 2024.

Herscowitz, Jack. "The Mapuche-Chilean Land Conflict and Justice: Re-Contextualizing 21st Century Violence." *Towson University Journal of International Affairs* 52:2 (2019): 14–33.

Hood, Mary D. "Bibliography on Secession and International Law." *Santa Clara University School of Law* (2001) available at https://digitalcommons.law.scu.edu/cgi/viewcontent.cgi?referer=https://www.google.com/&httpsredir=1&article=1042&context=facpubs accessed 6 June 2024.

Iyall Smith, Keri E. *The State and Indigenous Movements*. New York, NY: Routledge, 2006.

Joyner, Christopher C. "Anglo-Argentine Rivalry After the Falklands/Malvinas War: Laws, Geopolitics, and the Antarctic Connection." *Lawyer of the Americas* 15:3 (1984): 467–502.

Karuka, Manu. "Black and Native Visions of Self-Determination." *Critical Ethnic Studies* 3:2 (2017): 77–98.

Kelly, Sarah H. "Mapping Hydropower Conflicts: A Legal Geography of Dispossession in Mapuche-Williche Territory, Chile." *Geoforum* 127 (2021): 269–282.

King, Hayden and Shiri Pasternak. *Canada's Emerging Indigenous Rights Framework: A Critical Analysis*. Toronto: Yellowhead Institute, 2018.

Kolers, Avery. *Law, Conflict and Justice: Theory of Territory*. New York, NY: Cambridge University Press, 2009.

Kooijmans, P. H. "Tolerance, Sovereignty and Self-Determination." *Netherlands International Law Review* 43:2 (1996): 211–217.

Lalonde, S. *Determining Boundaries in a Conflicted World: The Role of Uti Possidetis.* Montreal: McGill-Queen's University Press, 2002.

Lindley, M. F. *The Acquisition and Government of Backward Territory in International Law: Being a Treatise on the Law and Practice Relating to Colonial Expansion.* New York, NY: Negro University Press, 1969.

López, Augusto Javier. "Ni Autodeterminación, Ni Pueblo. Improcedencia de la Argumentación Inglesa por la Soberanía de Malvinas." *Raigal* 9 (2022): 66–70.

Luna-Firebaugh, Eileen M. "The Border Crossed Us: Border Crossing Issues of the Indigenous Peoples of the Americas." *Wicazo Sa Review* 17:1 (2002): 159–181.

Macklem, Patrick. "Distributing Sovereignty: Indian Nations and Equality of Peoples." In *Indigenous Rights*, Connolly, Anthony J., ed. 303–359. London and New York, NY: Routledge, 2017.

Macneill, Christopher Mark. "Europe's Last Continental America Colony: French Guiana's Subjugation Struggles." *International Journal of Law Management & Humanities* 4:6 (2021): 1–24.

Maguire, J. Robert. "The Decolonization of Belize. Self-Determination v. Territorial Integrity." *Virginia Journal of International Law* 22:4 (1982): 849–881.

Mansilla Quiñones, Pablo Arturo and Miguel Melin Pehuen. "A Struggle for Territory, a Struggle Against Borders: The Mapuche Conflict in Argentina and Chile Contests Notions of Borders Promulgated by the Nation-State." *NACLA Report on the Americas* 51:1 (2019): 41–48.

Marxsen, Christian. "Territorial Integrity in International Law—Its Concept and Implications for Crimea." *Heidelberg Journal of International Law* 75:1 (2015): 7–26.

Miniconi, Renaud and Sylvain Guyot. "Conflicts and Cooperation in the Mountainous Mapuche Territory (Argentina). The Case of the Nahuel Huapi National Park." *Journal of Alpine Research* 98:1 (2010): 138–153.

Moeller, Jacob. "A Tribe Divided: The Threat of the Loss of Tribal Autonomy and Culture Facing Transnational Tribes on the Northern and Southern Borders of the United States." *Vanderbilt Journal of Transnational Law* 54:5 (2021): 1257–1292.

Mooney, Megan. "How the Organization of American States Took the Lead: The Development of Indigenous Peoples' Rights in the Americas." *American Indian Law Review* 31:2 (2006): 553–572.

Nickels, Bryan. "Native American Free Passage Rights under the 1794 Jay Treaty: Survival under United States Statutory Law and Canadian Common Law." *Boston College International and Comparative Law Review* 24:2 (2001): 313–340.

Nolte, Detlef and Leslie E. Wehner. "Geopolitics in Latin America, Old and New." In *Routledge Handbook of Latin American Security*, Mares, David R. and Kacowicz, Arie M. eds. 33–43. Abingdon: Routledge, 2015.

Norman, Emma S. *Governing Transboundary Waters: Canada, the United States, and Indigenous Communities.* London and New York, NY: Routledge, 2014.

Núñez, Jorge E. *Cosmopolitanism, State Sovereignty, International Law and Politics: A Theory.* London and New York, NY: Routledge, Taylor & Francis Group, 2023.

Núñez, Jorge E. *Sovereignty Conflicts and International Law and Politics: A Distributive Justice Issue.* London and New York, NY: Routledge, Taylor & Francis Group, 2017.

Núñez, Jorge E. *Territorial Disputes and State Sovereignty: International Law and Politics.* London and New York, NY: Routledge, Taylor & Francis Group, 2020.
O'Leary, Brendan. "The Elements of Right-Sizing and Right-Peopling the State." In *Right-Sizing the State: The Politics of Moving Borders*, O'Leary, Brendan, Lustick, Ian S. and Callaghy, Thomas, eds. 15–73. Oxford: Oxford University Press, 2001.
Parrish, Austen L. "Changing Territoriality, Fading Sovereignty, and the Development of Indigenous Rights." *American Indian Law Review* 31:2 (2006/2007): 291–313.
Ramírez, Silvina. "Pueblos Indígenas, Identidad y Territorio—Sin Territorio no hay Identidad como Pueblo." *Revista Jurídica de la Universidad de Palermo* 15:1 (2017): 11–32.
Ray, Leslie. *Language of the Land: The Mapuche in Argentina and Chile.* Skive: International Work Group for Indigenous Affairs, 2007.
Reisman, W. Michael. "The Struggle for the Falklands." *The Yale Law Journal* 93:2 (1983): 287–317.
Réno, Fred and Bernard Phipps. "The Dichotomy of Universalism and Particularism in French Guiana." In *Post-Colonial Trajectories in the Caribbean: The Three Guianas*, Hoefte, Rosemarijn, Bishop, Matthew L. and Clegg, Peter, eds. 66–78. London and New York, NY: Routledge, 2016.
Rensink, Brenden W. "Indigenous Peoples and Euro-American Frontiers, Borderlands, and Borders in North America." In *Oxford Research Encyclopedia of American History*, Dailey, Jane, ed. (2021) available at https://oxfordre.com/americanhistory/display/10.1093/acrefore/9780199329175.001.0001/acrefore-9780199329175-e-772 accessed 12 June 2024.
Robinson Saavedra, Dilia. "Pueblo Raiza en Colombia." In *Comunidades Étnicas en Colombia: Cultura y Jurisprudencia*, Parra Dussán, Carlos and Rodríguez, Gloria Amparo, eds. 1–25. Colombia: Centro Editorial Universidad del Rosario, 2013.
Romero-Toledo, Hugo and Katy Jenkins. "Contested Waters, Extractivisms, and Territories: Indigenous People in Chile and the Neoliberal Crisis." *Current Directions in Water Scarcity Research* 4 (2022): 189–208.
Ross, James. "Routes for Roots: Entering the 21st Century in San Andrés Island, Colombia." *Caribbean Studies* 35:1 (2007): 3–36.
Sánchez, Miguel Antonio. "Self-Determination and the Falkland Islands Dispute." *Columbia Journal of Transnational Law* 21 (1983): 557–584.
Schwarz, Henry and Sangeeta Ray, eds. *A Companion to Postcolonial Studies.* Oxford: Blackwell Publishing, 2005.
Sieder, Rachel. "Indigenous People's Rights and the Law in Latin America." In *Handbook of Indigenous Peoples' Rights*, Lennox, Corinne and Short, Damien, eds. 414–423. New York, NY: Routledge, 2016.
Sokolow, Jayme A. *The Great Encounter: Native Peoples and European Settlers in the Americas, 1492–1800.* New York, NY and London: Routledge, Taylor & Francis, 2016.
Tauli-Corpuz, Victoria. "Conflict, Peace and the Human Rights of Indigenous Peoples." In *Indigenous Peoples' Rights and Unreported Struggles: Conflict and Peace*, Stamatopoulou, Elsa, ed., 1–24. New York, NY: Columbia University Press, 2017 available at https://academiccommons.columbia.edu/doi/10.7916/D8PK1PRM accessed 20 June 2024.
Thürer, Daniel and Thomas Burri. "Self-Determination." In *Max Planck Encyclopedia of Public International Law* (2008) available at https://opil.ouplaw.com/view

/10.1093/law:epil/9780199231690/law-9780199231690-e873 accessed 6 June 2024.

Torres, Robinson, Gerardo Azócar, Roberto Gallardo and Julio Mendoza. "Water Extractivism and Decolonial Struggles in Mapuche Territory, Chile." *Water Alternatives* 15:1 (2022): 150–174.

Trinidad, Jaime. *Self-Determination in Disputed Colonial Territories.* Cambridge: Cambridge University Press, 2018.

Van Cott, Donna Lee. "Broadening Democracy: Latin America's Indigenous People's Movements." *Current History* 103:670 (2004): 80–85.

van der Haar, Gemma. "The Zapatista Uprising and the Struggle for Indigenous Autonomy." *European Review of Latin American and Caribbean Studies* 76 (2004): 98–108.

van Genugten, Willem and Camillo Perez-Bustillo. "The Emerging International Architecture of Indigenous Rights: The Interaction Between Global, Regional, and National Dimensions." *International Journal on Minority and Group Rights* 11:4 (2004): 379–409.

Veracini, Lorenzo. "Introducing: Settler Colonial Studies." *Settler Colonial Studies* 1:1 (2011): 1–12.

Warren, Sarah. "A Nation Divided: Building the Cross-Border Mapuche Nation in Chile and Argentina." *Journal of Latin American Studies* 45:2 (2013): 235–264.

Weitzner, Viviane. "'¡Guardia, Guardia!': Autonomies and Territorial Defense in the Context of Colombia's Post Peace-Accord." In *Indigenous Territorial Autonomy and Self-Government in the Diverse Americas*, González, Miguel, Funaki, Ritsuko, Burguete Cal y Mayor, Araceli, Marimán, José and Ortiz-T, Pablo, eds. 603–640. Calgary: University of Calgary Press, 2023,

Youé, Chris. "Settler Colonialism or Colonies with Settlers?" *Canadian Journal of African Studies* 52: 1 (2018): 69–85.

Part Three

9 Territorial claims over Antarctica

Introduction

Unquestionably, Antarctica is important for many reasons to many different agents, with interested parties including but not limited to sovereign states.[1] For instance, scientific researchers highlight its role as part of the Earth's climate system, as an open laboratory with actual and potential benefits to humanity and as an environment for wildlife.[2] There are several central, strong or advantaged as well as non-central, weak or disadvantaged states that consider Antarctica as part of their geopolitical strategies.[3] Clearly, law and politics are intertwined.[4]

The Antarctic Treaty[5] mostly refers to scientific exploration of Antarctica and, therefore, in terms of sovereignty the legal situation is a *status quo ante*.[6] Whether it is futile or not to refer to the question about sovereign rights in Antarctica in light of the Antarctic Treaty,[7] it is still a fact there are several

1 This chapter will refer only to one kind of agent, that is, sovereign states. For the author's understanding of agents refer to Chapter 3. For further details see Jorge E. Núñez, *Cosmopolitanism, State Sovereignty, International Law and Politics: A Theory* (London and New York, NY: Routledge, Taylor & Francis Group, 2023), Chapter 4.

2 Lydia McLean and Jenny Rock, "The Importance of Antarctica: Assessing the Values Ascribed to Antarctica by Its Researchers to Aid Effective Climate Change Communication," *The Polar Journal* 6:2 (2016): 291–306.

3 Klaus Dodds, "Antarctic Geopolitics," in Klaus Dodds, Alan D. Hemmings and Peder Roberts, eds., *Handbook on the Politics of Antarctica* (Cheltenham: Edward Elgar Publishing, 2017), 199–214; Alan D. Hemmings, "Antarctic Politics in a Transforming Global Geopolitics," in Klaus Dodds, Alan D. Hemmings and Peder Roberts, eds., *Handbook on the Politics of Antarctica* (Cheltenham: Edward Elgar Publishing, 2017), 507–522.

4 Christopher C. Joyner, "Nonmilitarization of the Antarctic: The Interplay of Law and Geopolitics," *Naval War College Review* 42:4 (1989): 83–104.

5 For a complete version of the Antarctic Treaty see http://www.ats.aq/documents/ats/treaty_original.pdf accessed 26 August 2024. For the official Secretariat of the Antarctic Treaty website see https://www.ats.aq/e/antarctictreaty.html accessed 27 August 2024.

6 J. Peter A. Bernhardt, "Sovereignty in Antarctica," *California Western International Journal* 5 (1975): 297–349.

7 Benedetto Conforti, "Territorial Claims in Antarctica: A Modern Way to Deal with an Old Problem," *Cornell International Law Journal* 19:2 (1986): 249–258.

DOI: 10.4324/9781003350828-12

agents involved directly and indirectly in the area with different interests including: seven states with territorial claims, i.e. Argentina, Australia, Chile, France, New Zealand, Norway and the United Kingdom; central, strong or advantaged agents such as the Russian Federation and the United States with research facilities in the area; and many more agents like Brazil, China, India and other Indian Ocean states.[8]

As stated in Núñez (2020),[9] the case of Antarctica, as a territorial dispute, encompasses several unique issues: legally, sovereignty is frozen; there is no indigenous or permanent population living in the area; it is a demilitarized zone; there are several original claimants and even more post-Treaty interested parties; the territory includes land, water and the exclusive economic zone;[10] there are natural resources; and many other matters. Such a complex situation in law and fact requires a multidisciplinary vision[11] to enable the different governments representing each claiming and interested agent to actually give priority to the common global interest of humanity as a whole.

The chapter has three main sections. The first section will outline the historical and current claims over the area while the second one will convey information about Antarctica and the Antarctic Treaty System (ATS). The rationale behind the first two sections is to explain what the situation is in fact and in law. Thereafter, the final section will present and explore guidelines to offer a permanent and peaceful solution.

Núñez (2020)[12] suggested some basic guidelines for a permanent and peaceful understanding in Antarctica. These guidelines outlined the need to share sovereignty; to avoid domination; to guarantee equal footing in the decision-making process; and to be independent from the United Nations (UN) system legally and politically. In that vein, this chapter explores these

8 For a very comprehensive study see Anne-Marie Brady, ed., *The Emerging Politics of Antarctica* (Oxford and New York, NY: Routledge, 2013). See also Klaus Dodds, Alan D. Hemmings and Peder Roberts, eds., *Handbook on the Politics of Antarctica* (Cheltenham: Edward Elgar Publishing, 2017); Wei-chin Lee, "China and Antarctica: So Far and Yet So Near," *Asian Survey* 30:6 (1990): 576–586; Anne-Marie Brady, "China's Rise in Antarctica?" *Asian Survey* 50:4 (2010): 759–785; Jonathan Harrington, "China in Antarctica: A History," *Southeast Review of Asian Studies* 37 (2015): 1–19; Anne-Marie Brady, *China as a Polar Great Power* (Cambridge: Cambridge University Press, 2017); Christopher C. Joyner, "Antarctica and the Indian Ocean States: The Interplay of Law, Interests, and Geopolitics," *Ocean Development and International Law* 21:1 (1990): 41–70; and many others.

9 Jorge E. Núñez, *Territorial Disputes and State Sovereignty: International Law and Politics* (London and New York, NY: Routledge, Taylor & Francis Group, 2020), Chapter 6.

10 Christopher C. Joyner, "The Exclusive Economic Zone and Antarctica: The Dilemmas of Non-Sovereign Jurisdiction," *Ocean Development and International Law* 19:6 (1988): 469–491.

11 Luis Valentín Ferrada, "Five Factors that Will Decide the Future of Antarctica," *The Polar Journal* 8:1 (2018): 84–109.

12 Jorge E. Núñez, *Territorial Disputes and State Sovereignty: International Law and Politics* (London and New York, NY: Routledge, Taylor & Francis Group, 2020), Chapter 6.

guidelines in light of the multidimensional approach introduced in Núñez (2023),[13] briefly sketched in Part One and the partial conclusions from the chapters in Part Two. The exploration will follow ideal circumstances designed in Núñez (2017).[14] *Brevitatis causa*, it is assumed all agents involved are part of a hypothetical situation. In consequence, the only thing needed is that all parties are motivated to obtain a reasonable solution. Therefore, it is assumed that they have appointed free and equal negotiators to achieve this aim. Within this environment, the negotiators will examine the aforementioned guidelines and decide an agreement that free and rational beings could not reasonably reject.

Territorial claims over Antarctica

There are seven states claiming territorial sovereignty over Antarctica. Whether linked to colonial, imperialistic practices or not,[15] these claims precede the ATS and have been made by the United Kingdom (1908), New Zealand (1923), France (1924), Argentina (1890s), Australia (1933), Norway (1939) and Chile (1890s). The bases for these claims include discovery, effective occupation and geographical proximity.[16] Arguably, when considering realpolitik, there seems to be a different standing between central and non-central states on the issue pertaining to the mutual recognition of territorial claims over Antarctica—i.e. only Australia, France, New Zealand, Norway and the United Kingdom mutually recognize the claims of the others.[17]

Considering the monograph's theme and content, the subsections below will refer to agents pertaining to Latin America and those characterized as central, strong or advantaged states that are in one way or another influencing the origin, continuation and potential escalation into conflict of territorial disputes in the region.[18]

13 Jorge E. Núñez, *Cosmopolitanism, State Sovereignty, International Law and Politics: A Theory* (London and New York, NY: Routledge, Taylor & Francis Group, 2023).

14 Jorge E. Núñez, *Sovereignty Conflicts and International Law and Politics: A Distributive Justice Issue* (London and New York, NY: Routledge, Taylor & Francis Group, 2017), Chapter 7.

15 Peder Robertsan and Alejandra Mancilla, eds., *Colonialism and Antarctica: Attitudes, Logics, and Practices* (Manchester: Manchester University Press, 2024).

16 For details about different categories of claims relevant to territorial disputes see Jorge E. Núñez, *Territorial Disputes and State Sovereignty: International Law and Politics* (London and New York, NY: Routledge, Taylor & Francis Group, 2020), Chapter 4.

17 Gillian Triggs, "The Antarctic Treaty System: A Model of Legal Creativity and Cooperation," in Paul Arthur Berkman, Michael A. Lang, David W. H. Walton and Oran R. Young, eds., *Science Diplomacy: Antarctica, Science, and the Governance of International Spaces* (Washington, DC: Smithsonian Institution Scholarly Press, 2011), 39–50. For a detailed examination of the records pertaining to the first Antarctic Treaty Consultative Meetings, including the Special Consultative Meetings on Antarctic Mineral Resources, see Jeffrey D. Myhre, *The Antarctic Treaty System: Politics, Law, and Diplomacy* (London and New York, NY: Routledge, 2019).

18 See Chapter 6.

Latin America and Antarctica

11 of the 20 Latin American states are part of at least one of the ATS legal instruments.[19] Neighboring the South American cluster, Antarctica presents several continental agents with claims. These claims can be broadly classified into two groups: (a) those based on connection grounds such as first exploration and discovery (Argentina and Chile), scientific explorations and expeditions, exploitation of natural resources and state activity; and (b) those based on official documents and geographical doctrines like the *uti possidetis juris* principle, transfer of territory, geographic continuity and contiguity and the sector principle.[20]

Together with the United Kingdom, the Argentine and Chilean claims overlap. Concessions given to third parties by Argentina to exploit natural resources in Antarctica and arguments from Chile regarding these concessions started as early as the 1890s.[21] Discussions between Argentina and Chile to determine their sovereignty by delimiting their respective territories over Antarctica started in 1906.[22] In 1908, Britain claimed Antarctica as part of the "Falklands sector" or the "Falkland Islands Dependencies sector."[23] In 1925, Argentina counterclaimed British sovereignty over Antarctica when the South American state placed a wireless station at the Laurie Island weather observatory. While Britain argued that Argentina should have complied with the International Telegraph Convention and applied for a permission to erect the station, Argentina maintained the territory was under their sovereignty.[24] The bases of the Argentine and British discussion at the time, and after signing the Antarctic Treaty, included effective occupation, *terra nullius*, *animus occupandi*, contiguity, discovery, annexation and peaceful and continuous

19 Luis Valentín Ferranda, "Latin America and the Antarctic Treaty System," *The Polar Journal* 9:2 (2019): 286–299.

20 Classification from Alejandra Mancilla, "The Moral Limits of Territorial Claims in Antarctica," *Ethics & International Affairs* 32:3 (2018): 339–360.

21 Karen Manzano Iturra, "La Competencia por los Derechos Antárticos: Chile y Argentina en la Zona Austral (1890–1910)," *Revista Política y Estrategia* 131 (2018): 41–55, available at https://www.politicayestrategia.cl/index.php/rpye/article/view/205 accessed 29 August 2024.

22 Pablo Mancilla González, "Chile, Argentina y Gran Bretaña en el Continente Antártico, 1906–1961. Una Aproximación a las Controversias Diplomáticas," *Revista de Estudios Históricos* 3:1 (2006): 1–20.

23 For an account that predates the Antarctic Treaty see David Winston Heron, "Antarctic Claims," *Foreign Affairs* 32:4 (1954): 661–667. For historical examples of the diplomatic exchanges between Great Britain, Argentina and Chile predating the Antarctic Treaty see "Antarctic Claims-Diplomatic Exchanges between Great Britain, Argentina and Chile in 1951," *Polar Record* 6:43 (1952): 413–418. For the same period see Walter Sullivan, "Antarctica in a Two-Power World," *Foreign Affairs* 36:1 (1957): 154–166; D. A. Graber, "Struggle for a Continent: Who Will Rule Antarctica?" *World Affairs* 113:1 (1950): 12–16; and many others.

24 Robert E. Wilson, "National Interests and Claims in the Antarctic," *Arctic* 17:1 (1964): 15–31.

display of authority.[25] It is in the 1940s and 1950s, with the first two presidential mandates of General Juan Domingo Perón, that Argentina positions the issue, together with the Falklands/Malvinas question, as being of national interest.[26] Currently, the Antarctic section in which Argentine, British and Chilean claims overlap is considered in Argentina as part of the southernmost "Provincia de Tierra del Fuego, Antártida e Islas del Atlántico Sur" (Province of Tierra del Fuego, Antarctica and South Atlantic Islands) which nominally includes the Falkland/Malvinas Islands. Therein, arguably, any decision over the territorial dispute concerning the Falkland/Malvinas Islands will affect directly Argentina's standing in relation to Antarctica.[27]

Chile's pre-Antarctic Treaty position concerning Antarctica can be divided into two periods: the early 1900s and the 1940s. The early 1900s are characterized by Chilean interest to determine extension and limits of the area, failed negotiations with Argentina to agree on a border between the two in Antarctica to divide the area and, like Argentina, a rejection of the 1908 British patent. It is in 1940 that Chile determines the Chilean Antarctic sector by Decreto N° 1747, that is, 53° to 90° west of Greenwich longitude.[28]

Having signed the Antarctic Treaty, Argentina and Chile still had some disagreements concerning other territorial disputes.[29] Despite their peaceful understandings concerning past differences, Argentina and Chile maintain a separate stand over Antarctica.[30] This is largely because, in addition to the legal and political questions related to sovereignty and issues pertaining to actual

25 Russell W. MacKechnie Jr., "Sovereignty in Antarctica: The Anglo-Argentine Dispute," *Syracuse Journal of International Law and Commerce* 5:1 (1977): 119–148. For a thorough explanation see, in Spanish, Ricardo R. Caillet-Bois, "Las Malvinas y la Antártida Argentina" (1956) available at https://cefadigital.edu.ar/bitstream/1847939/798/1/Revista%20ESG%20no.%20322-1956_Caillet-Bois_84.pdf accessed 28 August 2024.

26 Martín Bertone, Pablo Melara and Tamara Culleton, "Territorio, Conciencia Nacional y Educación. Las Islas Malvinas y la Antártida Argentina en las Políticas de Estado Peronistas (1946–1955)," *Centro Educativo de las Fuerzas Armadas Argentinas* (2023) available at https://cefadigital.edu.ar/handle/1847939/2403 accessed 28 August 2024.

27 Sergio G. Caplan and Sergio Eissa, "Análisis Estratégico del Sistema Malvinas, Antártida y Atlántico Sur," *Centro Educativo de las Fuerzas Armadas Argentinas* (2015) available at https://cefadigital.edu.ar/handle/1847939/1588 accessed 28 August 2024.

28 Mauricio Jara, "Una Disputa Doblemente Pospuesta: Chile y el Territorio Antártico: 1906–1948," *Revista Notas Históricas y Geográficas* (2021): 131–138, available at https://revistanotashistoricasygeograficas.cl/carga/wp-content/uploads/2021/01/n9-10-10.pdf accessed 29 August 2024; Carolina Bugueño and Pablo Mancilla. "Una Aproximación a las Controversias Diplomáticas entre Chile, Argentina y Gran Bretaña en el Continente Antártico, 1906–1961," *Revista de Historia de América* 136 (2005): 9–20; and several others.

29 See Chapter 4.

30 Karen Manazno Iturra and Diego Jiménez Cabrera, "Antártica Chilena. Discusiones en torno a la Plataforma Continental y la Geopolítica Austral," *Revista Política y Estrategia* 139 (2022): 21–37, available at https://www.politicayestrategia.cl/index.php/rpye/article/view/992 accessed 29 August 2024.

and potential natural resources, Antarctica is part of the national narratives of Argentina and Chile.[31]

Other states in South America (Brazil, Peru, Uruguay and Ecuador) have reserved their right to make future claims.[32] For instance, Brazil has developed the dedicated Brazilian Antarctic Program (PROANTAR, in Portuguese).[33] With more than 40 years of research in Antarctica,[34] Brazil's interests include regional and global factors such as foreign policy, defense strategy and scientific and technological goals.[35] In turn, despite Peru's interactions with the area dating back to the 1970s, there seems to be a more limited presence and, therefore, influence, mostly due to the lack of investment.[36] With almost 30 scientific expeditions to date, Peru's agenda has two main fronts, which are strategic-political and scientific-environmental. The former is centered on Peru's interest to maintain Antarctica as a place in which peace and science may blossom; the latter is focused on the regional and global importance of keeping such an ecosystem in equilibrium.[37] The combination of these factors explains the rationale behind Peru's geopolitical interest in keeping a consultative status in the ATS.[38]

The domestic, regional and international situation in the 1950s, including the control of the South Atlantic Ocean and the interest of states like the United States and the former Union of Soviet Socialist Republics (USSR), moved Argentina to invite Uruguay to participate in the Argentine Antarctic campaigns.[39] Thereafter, on 9 October 1956, Uruguay created their First

31 Florian Vidal, "The Antarctic Peninsula: Argentina and Chile in the Era of Global Change," *The Polar Journal* 13:1 (2023): 13–30.

32 Adrian Howkins, "Latin America and Antarctica," in *Oxford Research Encyclopedia of Latin American History* (2017) available at https://oxfordre.com/latinamericanhistory/display/10.1093/acrefore/9780199366439.001.0001/acrefore-9780199366439-e-434 accessed 9 May 2024.

33 Israel de Oliveira Andrade, Leonardo Faria de Mattos, Andrea Cancela da Cruz-Kaled and Giovanni Roriz Lyra Hillebrand, *Brazil in Antarctica: The Scientific and Geopolitical Importance of PROANTAR in the Brazilian Strategic Surrounding Area* (Brasilia: IPEA, Institute for Applied Economic Research, 2020). For a detailed account of the history of Brazil's engagement with Antarctica see Javier Ignacio Cardone, *Antarctic Politics of Brazil: Where the Tropic meets the Pole* (Cham: Palgrave Macmillan, 2022).

34 Paulo E. A. S. Câmara, Ana F. Barros-Platiau, Israel De Oliveira Andrade and Giovanni R. L. Hillebrand, "Brazil in Antarctica: 40 Years of Science," *Antarctic Science* 33:1 (2021): 30–38.

35 Adriana Erthal Abdenur and Danilo Marcondes Neto, "Rising Powers and Antarctica: Brazil's Changing Interests," *The Polar Journal* 4:1 (2014): 12–27.

36 Wilder Alejandro Sánchez and Otto Raul Tielemans Jr., "Reinvigorating Peru's Role in Antarctic Geopolitics," *The Polar Journal* 5:1 (2015): 101–112.

37 Manuel Ruidías Villalaz, "La Antártida y la Importancia de las Actividades Científicas Desarrolladas por el Perú," *Revista de la Escuela Superior de Guerra Naval* 18:1 (2021): 65–78.

38 Wolker Helmer Lozada Maldonado, "Implicancias Geopolíticas de la Presencia del Perú en la Antártida," *Fuerza Aérea del Perú* (2021) available at http://209.45.53.131/handle/fap/381 accessed 2 September 2024.

39 Waldemar Fontes, "Uruguayan Antarctic links during the 1950s Decade," in Consuelo León, Mauricio Jara and Nelson Llanos, eds., *Antarctica in the 1950s: Perspectives from the*

Technical Commission concerning Antarctica. However, at the time, discussions about a potential "Uruguayan Antarctica" remained either stagnant or as press speculation.[40] It is in the 1980s that Uruguay joined the ATS and achieved its consultative status, with one station and three vessels regularly operational in the region.[41] Like other agents, the Antarctic question has become part of Uruguay's strategic vision.[42]

Ecuador is the latest of the Latin American states to join the ATS (1987), creating a dedicated Antarctic Institute.[43] Since then, the creation of the National Commission of Antarctic Issues (CONANT, in Spanish) and the Ecuadorian Antarctic Program (PROANTEC, in Spanish) suggest Ecuador is giving Antarctica a more central place in their national and regional agendas.[44] Like their other South American peers, Ecuador has consultative status in the ATS, has a base and conducts scientific research.[45]

As suggested in Núñez (2020),[46] in terms of the Americas and Antarctica, with Argentina and Chile as original claiming parties and Brazil, Uruguay, Peru and Ecuador as full members of the Antarctic Treaty,[47] Latin America as a region has the opportunity to leave behind the individual and self-centered agendas of states, generate consensus and act as a bloc internationally against the classical colonial powers, such as the United Kingdom and France, and the neo-imperialist ambitions from states like the United States and China. The facts they have in common normatively and factually, such as a shared colonial past, sociological composition, language, culture, geographical proximity in

---

Southern Cone (Chile: LW Editorial, 2021), 141–156, available at https://www.lweditorial.cl/ANTARTIC-book-PDF.pdf#page=141 accessed 4 September 2024.

40 Waldemar Fontes, "Uruguayan Antarctic links during the 1950s Decade," in Consuelo León, Mauricio Jara and Nelson Llanos, eds., *Antarctica in the 1950s: Perspectives from the Southern Cone* (Chile: LW Editorial, 2021), 141–156, 149, available at https://www.lweditorial.cl/ANTARTIC-book-PDF.pdf#page=141 accessed 4 September 2024.

41 Luis Valentín Ferrada, "Latin America and the Antarctic Treaty System as a Legal Regime," *The Polar Journal* 9:2 (2019): 286–299.

42 Waldemar Fontes, "Uruguay en la Antártida. Una Visión Estratégica," *Revista Estrategia* 3 (2011): 124–137.

43 Hernán Rodrigo Moreano Andrade, "La Investigación Científica del Ecuador en la Antártida y su Consolidación 2005–2008," *Revista Científica y Tecnológica, Universidad Estatal Península de Santa Elena* 1:1 (2013): 1–11, available at https://repositorio.upse.edu.ec/handle/46000/7235 accessed 4 September 2024.

44 H. Moreano, "Ecuador Antártico—Pasado y Futuro," *Instituto Antártico Ecuatoriano* 2:1 (1990): 83–86, available at https://aquadocs.org/handle/1834/3731 accessed 4 September 2024.

45 Jimmy Florez Bejar and Daniel De la Cruz Maravi, "La Antártida: Presencia Latinoamericana en la Era del Cambio Climático," *Revista Científica de la Escuela Superior de Guerra del Ejército* 3:1 (2024): 97–103.

46 Jorge E. Núñez, *Territorial Disputes and State Sovereignty: International Law and Politics* (London and New York, NY: Routledge, Taylor & Francis Group, 2020), Chapter 6.

47 Adrian Howkins, "Latin America and Antarctica," in Ángela Vergara, ed., *Oxford Research Encyclopedia of Latin American History* (Oxford: Oxford University Press, 2017).

relation to the claimed territory, internal financial and political situations, level of development and generally democratic regimes, give the Latin American states a potentially robust standing in relation to any other claiming or interested party should they decide to act in cooperation and with a common goal in regard to Antarctica.

Central, strong or advantaged states and Antarctica

British scientific expeditions to Antarctica started in the nineteenth century.[48] Importantly, by two different Patents in 1908 and 1917, Britain unilaterally declared its dominion over the area overlapping almost entirely the sectors of Antarctica claimed by Argentina and Chile.[49] More precisely, by the British Letter Patent of 1908:[50]

> the group of islands known as South Georgia, the South Orkneys, the South Shetlands, and the Sandwich Islands, and the territory known as Graham's Land, situated in the South Atlantic Ocean to the south of the 50th parallel of south latitude, and lying between the 20th and the 80th degrees of west longitude, are part of our Dominions, and it is expedient that provision should be made for their government as Dependencies of our Colony of the Falklands

Because of its ambiguity (the British Letter Patent might have implied territories in continental Argentina and Chile to be part of the British dominions), this document was modified by the British Letter Patent of 1917:

> Our Colony of the Falkland Islands, the Dependencies of Our said Colony shall be deemed to include and to have included all islands and territories whatsoever between the 20th degree of West longitude and the 50th degree of West longitude which are situated south of the 50th parallel of South latitude; and all islands and territories whatsoever between the 50th degree of West longitude and the 80th degree of West longitude which are situated south of the 58th parallel of South latitude.

48 See, for example, John Murray, "The Exploration of the Antarctic Regions," *Scottish Geographical Magazine* 2:9 (1886): 527–548; John Murray, "The Scientific Advantages of an Antarctic Expedition," *Proceedings of the Royal Society of London* 62:379–387 (1898): 424–451, available at https://royalsocietypublishing.org/doi/abs/10.1098/rspl.1897.0131 accessed 5 September 2024.

49 A Patent or Letter Patent is a legal document by which the British Crown granted a variety of privileges. See Klaus Boehm and Aubrey Silberston, *British Patent System: Volume 1, Administration* (Cambridge: Cambridge University Press, 1967).

50 "British Letters Patent of 1908 and 1917 constituting the Falkland Islands Dependencies," *Polar Record* 5:35–36 (1948): 241–243. Complete texts of the British Letters Patent of 1908 and 1917 available at https://www.cambridge.org/core/journals/polar-record/all-issues accessed 19 February 2025.

Therefore, by the Letters Patent of 1908 and 1917, Britain constituted the Falkland Islands Dependencies. The Letter Patent of 1908 made provision for the government of certain land areas lying between specified latitudes and longitudes, while no claim was made to jurisdiction over the high seas within these boundaries; and arguably there was still less of a claim being made to that part of South America which lies to the south of latitude 50 degrees south. The Letter Patent of 1917 defined the area more precisely in order to avoid this ambiguity. All subsequent British legislation for the administration of these Dependencies is based on the authority of these two documents. Interestingly, the United Kingdom distinguished later between the titles to the territories concerning the Falkland/Malvinas Islands and Antarctica.[51]

The United States' territorial ambition over Antarctica[52] has been present for decades. Technically, the United States has no territorial claim to Antarctica, does not recognize the territorial claims made by Argentina, Australia, Chile, France, New Zealand, Norway and the United Kingdom and maintains the right to make future claims.[53] For several reasons, including geostrategic location and natural resources, the importance of an American Antarctic is unquestionable to the northern state.[54] Therein, their position related to the sovereignty freeze can be explained when the situation is assessed multidimensionally. Early claims from Argentina and Chile[55] were against the United States' intention to internationalize the area.[56] Despite the renewal of the Antarctic Treaty,[57] in recent times the situation is still characterized by

51 See paragraph 2 and its note 2 in ICJ Pleadings, Oral Arguments, Documents Antarctica Cases (United Kingdom v. Argentina; United Kingdom v. Chile) [1956] where it says "It will be understood that although, for reasons of convenience, the territories to which the present Application relates were constituted part of the Falkland Islands Dependencies for administrative purposes, the British *title* to these territories is a separate and independent one which in no way derives from or depends on the title to the Falkland Islands themselves." Complete text available at https://www.icj-cij.org/sites/default/files/case-related/27/027-19550504-APP-1-00-EN.pdf accessed 16 January 2024.

52 For a comprehensive view on the different positions of those involved, including the United States, see Peter J. Beck, *The International Politics of Antarctica* (London and New York, NY: Routledge, Taylor & Francis, 2014).

53 See the United States Department of State official website for further details available at https://www.state.gov/key-topics-office-of-ocean-and-polar-affairs/antarctic/ accessed 22 February 2024.

54 Robert D. Hayton, "The 'American' Antarctic," *American Journal of International Law* 50:3 (1956): 583–610.

55 "Argentine and Chilean Territorial Claims in the Antarctic," *Polar Record* 4:32 (1946): 412–417.

56 Jason Kendall Moore, "Tethered to an Iceberg: United States Policy toward the Antarctic, 1939–1949," *Polar Record* 35:193 (1999): 125–134.

57 For the Antarctic Treaty full text and the latest news concerning Antarctica and the Antarctic system see the Secretariat of the Antarctic Treaty website available at https://www.ats.aq/index_e.html accessed 22 February 2024.

tensions and divergent views.[58] Indeed, the need for an Antarctic Law that is comprehensive enough to deal with these and future challenges—such as non-militarization[59] and resource management[60]—with a view that encompasses all agents including individuals, communities and states is of utmost importance.[61]

Russia is one of the states with sovereignty claims over Antarctica.[62] The maritime legal framework created by the United Nations Convention on the Law of the Sea (UNCLOS) may foster conflicts with the ATS[63] including issues pertaining to the territorial sea, the exclusive economic zone and the continental shelf.[64] Russia's increasing securitization understanding of Antarctica seems to be reflected in their national interest to both protect the area from territorial claims and to reserve their right to make a territorial claim.[65]

Like other central, strong or advantaged states, China has a multi-level approach toward Antarctica.[66] Starting in the 1980s by joining the Antarctic Treaty and by being accepted as a consultative party,[67] China's presence and influence in both Antarctica and the ATS have grown over the years and have become part of Chinese national strategy.[68] Therein, by making use of their non-territorial claimant state capacity, China has been able to exercise several rights including the right to conduct scientific research, information exchange, exploitation and utilization of natural resources and overall freedom of access for peaceful purposes.[69]

58 Marcus Haward and Andrew Jackson, "Antarctica: Geopolitical Challenges and Institutional Resilience," *The Polar Journal* 13:1 (2023): 1–18.
59 Jeffrey McGee, David Edmiston and Marcus Haward, "Militarisation of Antarctica," in Jeffrey McGee, David Edmiston, and Marcus Haward, eds., *The Future of Antarctica: Scenarios from Classical Geopolitics* (Singapore: Springer, 2022), 105–124.
60 Claudia Sosin, "Continental Shelves in the Antarctic Region: Implications for Resource Management," *The Polar Journal* 12:1 (2022): 122–147.
61 Bruno Arpi and Jeffrey McGee, "Rediscovering the Importance of Antarctic Law for the Early Twenty-First Century," *Australian Journal of International Affairs* 76:3 (2022): 248–265.
62 For a comprehensive view on the different positions of those involved, including Russia, see Peter J. Beck, *The International Politics of Antarctica* (London and New York, NY: Routledge, Taylor & Francis, 2014).
63 Jeffrey D. Myhre, *The Antarctic Treaty System: Politics, Law, and Diplomacy* (London and New York, NY: Routledge, 2019).
64 Liu Weizhe, "UNCLOS' Impact on and Implications for Antarctic Maritime Disputes," *China Oceans Law Review* 16:3 (2020): 64–82.
65 M. Boulègue, "The Militarization of Russian Polar Politics," *Chatham House Research Paper* (2022) available at https://www.chathamhouse.org/sites/default/files/2022-06/2022-06-06-militarization-russian-polar-politics-boulegue_0.pdf accessed 29 February 2024.
66 Nengye Liu, "The Rise of China and the Antarctic Treaty System?" *Australian Journal of Maritime & Ocean Affairs* 11:2 (2019): 120–131.
67 Madhu Rajan, "China in Antarctica," *China Report* 23:1 (1987): 57–64.
68 Nong Hong, "China and the Antarctic: Presence, Policy, Perception, and Public Diplomacy," *Marine Policy* 134 (2021): 1–10.
69 Liu He, "Legal Challenges to the Antarctic Treaty System and the Protection of China's Basic Rights and Interests in Antarctica," *China Oceans Law Review* 3 (2021): 51–76.

India does not formally recognize territorial claims in Antarctica. India's engagement with the Antarctic region started soon after its independence with the "Question of Antarctica" at the UN about whether there was a need for its internationalization.[70] Becoming a signatory to the Antarctic Treaty in 1983, India's approach toward the area has been characterized by scientific cooperation. However, research shows that India may diversify its activities depending on the national interest in the region.[71]

Antarctica and the Antarctic Treaty System

The territorial dispute relating to Antarctica encompasses several unique issues: legally, sovereignty is frozen; no indigenous or permanent population lives in the area; the region is a demilitarized zone; there are a number of original claimants and, post-Treaty, there are further interested parties; the territory itself includes land, water and the exclusive economic zone,[72] and natural resources are present.[73]

It is important to provide historical context for the signing of the Antarctic Treaty[74] that brought together already existing territorial disputes between Argentina, Chile and Britain, and the geopolitical ambitions of agents such as the United States and the former USSR. Together with the seven original claiming states—Argentina, Australia, Chile, France, New Zealand, Norway and the United Kingdom—Belgium, Japan, South Africa, the United States and the former USSR were the 12 original signatories to the Antarctic Treaty, signed in 1959, and effective since 1961.[75] These 12 states had scientists working on issues pertaining to Antarctica during the International Geophysical Year (1957–1958).

70 Sanjay Chaturvedi, "Rise and Decline of Antarctica in Nehru's Geopolitical Vision: Challenges and Opportunities of the 1950s," *The Polar Journal* 3:2 (2013): 301–315.

71 Bipandeep Sharma, "India and the Emerging Geopolitics of Antarctic," *Strategic Analysis* 47:6 (2023): 520–533.

72 Christopher C. Joyner, "The Exclusive Economic Zone and Antarctica: The Dilemmas of Non-Sovereign Jurisdiction," *Ocean Development and International Law* 19:6 (1988): 469–491.

73 While this chapter and, in particular, this section focus on the ATS, it is important to note that there may be other international agreements directly and indirectly relevant to Antarctica. For further details see Patrizia Vigni, "The Interaction between the Antarctic Treaty System and the Other Relevant Conventions Applicable to the Antarctic Area," in J. A. Frowein and R. Wolfrum, eds., *Max Planck Yearbook of United Nations Law* (Alphen aan den Rijn: Kluwer Law International, 2000), 481–542.

74 Klaus Dodds, "La Administración del Continente Polar: Los Orígenes Geopolíticos del Tratado Antártico de 1959," *Istor Revista de Historia Internacional* 10:39 (2009): 27–49.

75 Kurt M. Shusterich, "The Antarctic Treaty System: History, Substance, and Speculation," *International Journal* 39:4 (1984): 800–827. For the current and complete list of parties, including original claimants, signatories, consultative and non-consultative, refer to the Secretariat of the Antarctic Treaty, Parties, available at https://www.ats.aq/devAS/Parties?lang=e accessed 27 August 2024.

The Treaty prioritizes cooperation by ensuring that Antarctica is used for peaceful purposes and prohibits, *inter alia*, any military measure (Art. I); by promoting freedom of scientific investigation and cooperation (Art. II); and encouraging the exchange of plans for scientific programs and scientific personnel and the exchange and free availability of scientific observations and results (Art. III).[76]

In what is central to this monograph, issues regarding sovereignty are included in Art. IV of the Antarctic Treaty, which establishes a *status quo ante*:[77]

1. Nothing contained in the present Treaty shall be interpreted as:
   (a) a renunciation by any Contracting Party of previously asserted rights of or claims to territorial sovereignty in Antarctica;
   (b) a renunciation or diminution by any Contracting Party of any basis of claim to territorial sovereignty in Antarctica which it may have whether as a result of its activities or those of its nationals in Antarctica, or otherwise;
   (c) prejudicing the position of any Contracting Party as regards its recognition or non-recognition of any other State's right of or claim or basis of claim to territorial sovereignty in Antarctica.
2. No acts or activities taking place while the present Treaty is in force shall constitute a basis for asserting, supporting or denying a claim to territorial sovereignty in Antarctica or create any rights of sovereignty in Antarctica. No new claim, or enlargement of an existing claim, to territorial sovereignty shall be asserted while the present Treaty is in force.

By determining sovereign neutrality over Antarctica, Art. IV sidesteps potential disputes and conflicts over territorial claims.[78] Nevertheless, claimants and non-claimants are protected because the Treaty (a) should not be interpreted as renunciation of previously asserted rights or basis of claim; (b) does not prejudice the position of any party in relation to its recognition or non-recognition of any other state's right of claim or basis of a claim. Interestingly, the clause "or those of its nationals" opens the possibility to have claims made on behalf of, but not ratified by, the state concerned.[79] It must be stressed that

76 Complete Antarctic Treaty text available at https://documents.ats.aq/keydocs/vol_1/vol1_2_AT_Antarctic_Treaty_e.pdf accessed 5 September 2024.

77 J. Peter A. Bernhardt, "Sovereignty in Antarctica," *California Western International Journal* 5 (1975): 297–349.

78 Gillian Triggs, "The Antarctic Treaty System: A Model of Legal Creativity and Cooperation," in Paul Arthur Berkman, Michael A. Lang, David W. H. Walton and Oran R. Young, eds., *Science Diplomacy: Antarctica, Science, and the Governance of International Spaces* (Washington, DC: Smithsonian Institution Scholarly Press, 2011), 39–49.

79 Gillian Triggs, "The Antarctic Treaty System: A Model of Legal Creativity and Cooperation," in Paul Arthur Berkman, Michael A. Lang, David W. H. Walton and Oran R. Young, eds.,

Art. IV has "frozen" the issue regarding sovereignty over Antarctica, but the provision does not solve any actual or potential problem in that regard.

In 1991, the Protocol on Environmental Protection to the Antarctic Treaty was signed, entering into force in 1998.[80] According to Art. 2 "The Parties commit themselves to the comprehensive protection of the Antarctic environment and dependent and associated ecosystems and hereby designate Antarctica as a natural reserve, devoted to peace and science." Art. 3 states a series of environmental principles. Importantly, Art. 4 states that the Protocol supplements the Antarctic Treaty—i.e. it does not modify or amend it.[81]

Neither the Treaty nor the Protocol have a termination date. More precisely, the Antarctic Treaty and/or the Protocol may be modified or amended at any time by unanimous agreement of the Contracting Parties (Art. XII, a and b of the Antarctic Treaty; Art. 25.1 of the Protocol). Moreover, Art. 25.2 of the Protocol states that after 50 years from the Protocol's entry into force (i.e. from 2048), any of the Antarctic Treaty Consultative Parties can call for a conference to review the Protocol's operation.

In addition to the original Treaty itself and the Protocol, the ATS encompasses "Recommendations" adopted at Consultative Meetings (ATCM) and several other documents including two Conventions for the Conservation of Antarctic Seals (London 1972)[82] and the Conservation of Antarctic Marine Living Resources (Canberra 1980).[83] The ATCM is held annually and consists of the Consultative Parties, the Non-Consultative Parties and Observers (Art. IX, Antarctic Treaty). Measures, Decisions and Resolutions are adopted by consensus at the ATCM.[84] During each ATCM, the Committee for Environmental Protection (CEP) also meets.[85] Providing independent and objective scientific advice on various issues, the Scientific Committee on Antarctic Research (SCAR) is an Observer at both the ATCMs and CEPs.

Science Diplomacy: Antarctica, Science, and the Governance of International Spaces (Washington, DC: Smithsonian Institution Scholarly Press, 2011), 43.

80 Duncan French, "Sustainable Development and the 1991 Madrid Protocol to the 1959 Antarctic Treaty: The Primacy of Protection in a Particularly Sensitive Environment," *Journal of International Wildlife Law and Policy* 2:3 (1999): 291–317.

81 For the complete 1991 Protocol on Environmental Protection to the Antarctic Treaty see https://www.ats.aq/e/protocol.html accessed 9 September 2024.

82 Complete text of the 1972 Conventions for the Conservation of Antarctic Seals available at https://treaties.un.org/doc/Publication/UNTS/Volume%201080/volume-1080-I-16529-English.pdf accessed 10 September 2024.

83 Complete text of the Convention on the Conservation of Antarctic Marine Living Resources available at https://documents.ats.aq/keydocs/vol_1/vol1_12_CCAMLR_CCAMLR_e.pdf accessed 10 September 2024.

84 For further details about the ATCM and Other Meetings refer to the official Secretariat of the Antarctic Treaty website available at https://www.ats.aq/e/atcm.html accessed 10 September 2024.

85 For further details about the CEP see the official Secretariat of the Antarctic Treaty website available at https://www.ats.aq/e/committee.html accessed 10 September 2024.

Finally, the Commission for the Conservation of Antarctic Marine Living Resources (CCAMLR) and SCAR's Standing Committee on the Antarctic Treaty System (SCATS) complete the ATS.[86]

Questions about the effectiveness and legitimacy of the ATS have been raised.[87] Yet, others maintain the ATS has enabled collaboration and peaceful governance.[88] Regardless of the different opinions about its performance and its own internal and external challenges, it is a fact that the ATS has been instrumental in building and maintaining a conflict-free area. However, it is also a fact that questions about sovereignty and relevant territorial disputes have been simply postponed. Therefore, in an attempt to answer such questions, the next section will explore some guidelines proposed by the author.

Multidimensionality and Antarctica

By accepting the intricacy of the Antarctica case, it is possible to argue that a unidimensional approach—e.g. one that is only legal, only political or only focused on past or current issues—will not help attain a fair arrangement for the whole of humanity. *Brevitatis causa*, while unidimensional approaches seek to explore and understand a fragment of the object or subject of study in question—here, Antarctica and relevant guidelines—and the way a scholarly discipline conceives it, the author's proposed multidimensional approach is more interested in the object or subject of study itself, its elements, features and interrelations within and without the sphere of reference.[89]

A complex situation in fact and in law, such as in the case of Antarctica, requires a multidimensional approach, for example, by incorporating a multidisciplinary vision;[90] this approach is needed if the various governments representing each claiming and interested agent are actually going to prioritize the common global interest of all humanity. This section will explore the issue pertaining to sovereignty over Antarctica under the ideal circumstances

86 For further details about the ATS see SCAR's official website available at https://scar.org/policy/antarctic-treaty-system accessed 10 September 2024.

87 Patrick Flamm, "Legitimating the Antarctic Treaty System: From Rich Nations Club to Planetary Ecological Democracy?" *Australian Journal of International Affairs* 76:3 (2022): 266–285; Yelena Yermakova, "Legitimacy of the Antarctic Treaty System: Is It Time for a Reform?" *The Polar Journal* 11:2 (2021): 342–359; and several others.

88 Alejandra Mansilla and Julia Ann Jabour, "Turned 60, Is the Antarctic Treaty System in Good Health?," *The Geographical Journal* 189:1 (2023): 2–6; Thomas Lord, "The Antarctic Treaty System and the Peaceful Governance of Antarctica: The Role of the ATS in Promoting Peace at the Margins of the World," *The Polar Journal* 10:1 (2020): 3–21; and several others.

89 For details about dimensional understanding including uni- and multidimensionality see Jorge E. Núñez, *Cosmopolitanism, State Sovereignty, International Law and Politics: A Theory* (London and New York, NY: Routledge, Taylor & Francis Group, 2023).

90 Luis Valentín Ferrada, "Five Factors that Will Decide the Future of Antarctica," *The Polar Journal* 8:1 (2018): 84–109.

designed in Núñez (2017).[91] *Brevitatis causa*, it is assumed all the involved agents are part of a hypothetical situation. As a result, the only requirement is that all parties are motivated to reach a reasonable solution. Therefore, there is an assumption that all parties have appointed free and equal negotiators to achieve this goal. Within this ideal environment, the negotiators will examine the guidelines outlined below and arrive at an agreement that could not be reasonably rejected by free and rational beings.

Paraphrasing Núñez (2017), these agents have selected representatives who will participate in negotiations to allocate the sovereignty over Antarctica. These representatives act in the negotiations as if they do not know which of these populations they represent and without knowledge of certain characteristics about themselves (such as gender, ethnicity or social status); they know of the existence of the territory to which sovereignty has to be allocated, that the populations they represent have somehow a right to claim it or what the author labels as a colorable claim,[92] and they are aware of the nature of the negotiations they are involved in. Then, in order to allocate the sovereignty over Antarctica, they know they have to decide which principles are applicable.

Núñez (2020)[93] suggested some basic guidelines for a permanent and peaceful understanding in Antarctica. Considering the ideal situation just described, the territorial disputes reviewed in this monograph, and the many dispute settlement procedures and remedies previously reviewed and assessed by the author,[94] it is now possible to explore in more detail these basic guidelines for a permanent and peaceful understanding about Antarctica. Therein, these guidelines are listed below and, thereafter, addressed individually.

1. States are equal according to public international law.
2. Sovereignty can be shared.

91 Jorge E. Núñez, *Sovereignty Conflicts and International Law and Politics: A Distributive Justice Issue* (London and New York, NY: Routledge, Taylor & Francis Group, 2017), Chapter 7.

92 A colorable claim is strong enough to have a reasonable chance of winning but does not assert that the claim is certain or even likely to win. It is a non-frivolous argument either supported by reference to law or facts that may be proven in court. The distinction between the "colorability" of a claim and a winning claim has to do with two different steps in a judicial procedure. The colorability of the claim is related to admissibility. For more details see Jorge E. Núñez, *Cosmopolitanism, State Sovereignty, International Law and Politics: A Theory* (London and New York, NY: Routledge, Taylor & Francis Group, 2023), Chapter 7; Jorge E. Núñez, *Territorial Disputes and State Sovereignty: International Law and Politics* (London and New York, NY: Routledge, Taylor & Francis Group, 2020), Chapter 4; Jorge E. Núñez, *Sovereignty Conflicts and International Law and Politics: A Distributive Justice Issue* (London and New York, NY: Routledge, Taylor & Francis Group, 2017), Chapter 6.

93 Jorge E. Núñez, *Territorial Disputes and State Sovereignty: International Law and Politics* (London and New York, NY: Routledge, Taylor & Francis Group, 2020), Chapter 6.

94 Jorge E. Núñez, *Territorial Disputes and State Sovereignty: International Law and Politics* (London and New York, NY: Routledge, Taylor & Francis Group, 2020), Chapter 5; and Jorge E. Núñez, *Sovereignty Conflicts and International Law and Politics: A Distributive Justice Issue* (London and New York, NY: Routledge, Taylor & Francis Group, 2017), Chapter 5.

3. Claiming exclusive sovereignty over a territory where there can be no claim is as legally and logically absurd as it is morally questionable.
4. To secure a peaceful and definitive arrangement, the final agreement must somehow benefit all interested parties, must recognize (in whole or in part) their claims, and the result must not be detrimental to any of the agents. Consequently, sovereignty of the disputed territories should not be totally in the hands of only one or a few of the claiming parties.
5. If existing conditions in terms of sovereignty continue, they will only perpetuate a *status quo* and, therefore, a legal and political limbo securing only one result: a volatile area that can only benefit those agents with the means to explore and exploit the area.
6. Any arrangements in relation to Antarctica should avoid any form of domination and, therefore, guarantee to all interested parties equal footing in the decision-making process related to any Antarctic issue.
7. To neutralize self-centered interests that could only benefit one or more of the agents instead of all, the arrangements should be independent from the UN system legally and politically.

1. States are equal according to public international law.

It is a fact that some states are more equal than others in realpolitik despite public international law granting legal sovereign equality.[95] Yet, the UN Charter art. 2.1 states: "The Organization is based on the principle of the sovereign equality of all its Members." Therefore, this guideline distinguishes between the world of the rule and the world of the facts.[96] Therefore, while this law may recognize sovereign equality, that recognition does not mean empirical equality.

2. Sovereignty can be shared.

If such an agreement is reached, it must be one that agents could not reasonably reject later on, and so to achieve this bias must be eliminated.[97] Many scholars in legal and political theory and international relations use the

95 R. P. Anand, "Sovereign Equality of States in International Law," *International Studies* 8:3 (1966): 213–224; Hans Kelsen, "The Principle of Sovereign Equality of States as a Basis for International Organization," *Yale Law Journal* 53:2 (1944): 207–220; R. Hjorth, "Equality in the Theory of International Society: Kelsen, Rawls and the English School," *Review of International Studies* 37:5 (2011): 2585–2602.

96 For details about the distinction between the world of the rule and the world of the facts see Jorge E. Núñez, *Sovereignty Conflicts and International Law and Politics: A Distributive Justice Issue* (London and New York, NY: Routledge, Taylor & Francis Group, 2017), Chapter 4.

97 For details about the distinction between the world of the rule and the world of the facts see Jorge E. Núñez, *Sovereignty Conflicts and International Law and Politics: A Distributive Justice Issue* (London and New York, NY: Routledge, Taylor & Francis Group, 2017), Chapter 6.

expression "shared sovereignty" and similar terminology to refer to various different realities.[98] The author has argued elsewhere that shared sovereignty should (a) guarantee all claiming sovereign states do genuinely share their rights and obligations over the third territory, and that they do so on an equal footing basis; (b) respect the classical non-intervention[99] approach related to sovereignty; (c) assume that sovereign states are internationally equal;[100] (d) make no distinction between weak and strong states in what is referred to as the decision-making process since their representatives are considered to be free and equal agents. The author calls this conception "egalitarian shared sovereignty."[101]

3. Claiming exclusive sovereignty over a territory where there can be no claim is as legally and logically absurd as it is morally questionable.

Broadly, sovereignty disputes are under an umbrella of incertitude since all of the agents start with a *status quo* and any decision in the negotiations may imply actions on either side that may result in gains but also losses for any of them. Furthermore, their representatives in any negotiation would also consider in their decisions that sovereign rights imply obligations. Thus, these representatives would have to bear in mind that, although they may have current information about Antarctica, they would not know its factual features in the future. The author has argued elsewhere that *maximin* is not a general rule in cases of uncertainty.[102] However, it is the desirable one in situations

98 Jorge E. Núñez, *Sovereignty Conflicts and International Law and Politics: A Distributive Justice Issue* (London and New York, NY: Routledge, Taylor & Francis Group, 2017), Chapter 3.

99 This refers to the non-intervention principle in international public law. In brief, a state should not interfere in any way in the internal affairs of any other sovereign state. See UN Charter, art. 2.7: "Nothing contained in the present Charter shall author the United Nations to intervene in matters which are essentially within the domestic jurisdiction of any state or shall require the Members to submit such matters to settlement under the present Charter; but this principle shall not prejudice the application of enforcement measures under Chapter VII." Also stated in the UN General Assembly Resolution 2625 (XXV): "(a) The principle that States shall refrain in their international relations from the threat or use of force against the territorial integrity or political independence of any State, or in any other manner inconsistent with the purposes of the United Nations" and "(c) The duty not to intervene in matters within the domestic jurisdiction of any State."

100 See previous guideline: "States are equal according to public international law."

101 Jorge E. Núñez, *Sovereignty Conflicts and International Law and Politics: A Distributive Justice Issue* (London and New York, NY: Routledge, Taylor & Francis Group, 2017), Chapter 6.

102 Jorge E. Núñez, *Sovereignty Conflicts and International Law and Politics: A Distributive Justice Issue* (London and New York, NY: Routledge, Taylor & Francis Group, 2017), Chapter 6.

of high indeterminacy,[103] when the stakes are high and the worst position is tolerable.[104]

4. To secure a peaceful and definitive arrangement, the final agreement must somehow benefit all interested parties, must recognize (in whole or in part) their claims, and the result must not be detrimental to any of the agents. Consequently, sovereignty of the disputed territories should not be totally in the hands of only one or a few of the claiming parties.

While the *status quo* or the exclusive sovereignty of Antarctica by one of the agents are both valid options, they could literally result in either a loss of claimed rights for one or several claimants or permanent interference when deciding issues with consequences to all of them. If they wanted to have actual use of their claimed rights over the area they would have to make mutual concessions; in essence, they would have to "slice" their rights into different portions or shares.[105] In that respect, the author has previously argued that claiming and interested agents would agree that they would have "equal" shares of sovereignty over Antarctica, which means that these parties would have equal standing or status. Therein, all parties would have a right to participate and the decision-making process in each case would be subject to egalitarian consensus—i.e. all the parties should be granted an equal input into the decision-making process.[106]

5. If existing conditions in terms of sovereignty continue, they will only perpetuate a *status quo* and therefore, a legal and political limbo securing only one result: a volatile area that can only benefit those agents with the means to explore and exploit the area.

103 Decision theory principles under conditions of risk are as follows: expected value (the individuals discount the maximum payoff of each option depending on its probability and then they choose the highest one); *maximax* or "wishful thinking" (the individuals choose among options depending on which one offers the best of all possible results); *maximin* (the individuals choose under a pessimistic or conservative approach so they opt for the best worst outcome). For a more detailed view about *maximin* and its application in conditions under uncertainty see John Rawls, *A Theory of Justice*, Revised Edition (Oxford: Oxford University Press, 1999), 130 and ff.

104 For further analysis on this point see Ingo Heidbrink, "Claiming Sovereignty Where There Can Be No Sovereignty: Antarctica," *Environment, Space, Place* 8:2 (2016): 99–121.

105 Jorge E. Núñez, *Sovereignty Conflicts and International Law and Politics: A Distributive Justice Issue* (London and New York, NY: Routledge, Taylor & Francis Group, 2017), Chapter 6.

106 When discussing territorial disputes and sovereignty conflicts, the author argued that representatives of relevant parties in any negotiations over the sovereignty of a disputed territory would reject the just acquisition, the best interest of the child, the difference principle and equal shares. For further details see Jorge E. Núñez, *Sovereignty Conflicts and International Law and Politics: A Distributive Justice Issue* (London and New York, NY: Routledge, Taylor & Francis Group, 2017), Chapter 6.

Assuming that claiming and interested agents decided to leave behind the *status quo* and the exclusive sovereignty and, instead, decided to somehow distribute Antarctica, this would not solve the controversy either. That is because, even though the parties agreed to distribute, for example, natural resources, other highly controversial issues remain. This is not only a matter of distribution because the resources have to be mined, or piped, and someone has to do the work, and someone, whether a private individual or the state, has to own the mines, pipes, etc. The author has argued before[107] that equality *stricto sensu* and the difference principle do not work in relation to the distribution of natural resources because the question here is not just of a distributive nature. Natural resources have to be owned, explored and then exploited. But that exploitation must also be efficient if a solution is going to be reached and respected. Indeed, natural resources imply several different aspects—e.g. means for the exploration and exploitation, geographical location, relevant knowledge, etc. It is for that reason that the shares should be represented as bundles of rights and obligations, benefits and burdens.[108] In terms of property rights, all the agents could come to different arrangements—e.g. co-ownership of the natural resources, involving both rights and obligations—in what the author labels the "egalitarian consensus principle" or equal right to participate.[109]

6. Any arrangements in relation to Antarctica should avoid any form of domination and, therefore, guarantee to all interested parties equal footing in the decision-making process related to any Antarctic issue.

The author has previously maintained that domination[110] means the ability or capacity[111] somebody has to arbitrarily[112] exercise power over others for their

107 When discussing territorial disputes and sovereignty conflicts, the author argued that representatives of relevant parties in any negotiations over the sovereignty of a disputed territory would reject the just acquisition, the best interest of the child, the difference principle and equal shares. For further details see Jorge E. Núñez, *Sovereignty Conflicts and International Law and Politics: A Distributive Justice Issue* (London and New York, NY: Routledge, Taylor & Francis Group, 2017), Chapter 7.

108 Two points must be made clear: because the model aims to safeguard the interests of all the parties, the different combinations of natural resources in the bundle is in terms of their exploration and exploitation—not their ownership or the distribution of consequent benefits; and as this requirement is defined by bundles, each bundle may be constituted of diverse elements that taken together offer the same outcome: an efficient exploitation.

109 Jorge E. Núñez, *Sovereignty Conflicts and International Law and Politics: A Distributive Justice Issue* (London and New York, NY: Routledge, Taylor & Francis Group, 2017), Chapter 6.

110 Jorge E. Núñez, *Territorial Disputes and State Sovereignty: International Law and Politics* (London and New York, NY: Routledge, Taylor & Francis Group, 2020), Chapter 3.

111 The author distinguishes between ability and capacity only in the sense they may have been naturally in the subject, acquired or developed.

112 By arbitrary the author means as and when the subject wishes or without any other control than the subject himself. The term discretionary is the more general notion, i.e. that an

own benefit regardless of the consequences brought to the others.[113] Therein, non-domination implies the ability or capacity for someone's affairs not to be arbitrarily interfered with by someone else. When a sovereign state is dominating another sovereign state, there is arbitrary power. Conversely, when a sovereign state willingly accepts externally imposed limitations by another sovereign state, there is non-domination.

7. To neutralize self-centered interests that could only benefit one or more of the agents instead of all, the arrangements should be independent from the UN system legally and politically.

The author has argued that although the UN aims to grant sovereign equality among states, its members do not have a real equal footing.[114] Social and political relations between UN members have a direct impact in dispute settlements. The UN agenda for peace is largely dependent on whether states are willing to relinquish the use of their power to control disputes. Nevertheless, its own system reveals a contradiction: veto power in the Security Council is only granted to certain sovereign states. Moreover, the Security Council does not reflect the current global power distribution. Similarly, the UN General Assembly, at first glance a fair environment for sovereign states to participate in, has been regarded as ineffective or irredeemably biased because of the different bargaining powers of its members.[115]

Conclusion

The chapter focused on Antarctica and the ATS, considering past events, the current situation and a potential future. The first two sections introduced factual and legal issues. In doing so, the first part sketched historical and current

---

arbitrary decision presupposes discretion, but that not every discretionary decision is taken arbitrarily (for there can be very good reasons that motivate this decision).

113 For the purpose of this monograph, the fact that the consequences may be positive or negative to the recipient does not change the arbitrary nature of the original interference. There is no teleological justification to an arbitrary choice. The original interference is defined as arbitrary or not by its own merits.

114 For an analysis of these pitfalls in relation to the United Nations system and its application to dealing with territorial disputes and sovereignty conflicts, see Jorge E. Núñez, *Territorial Disputes and State Sovereignty: International Law and Politics* (London and New York, NY: Routledge, Taylor & Francis Group, 2020), Chapter 5; and Jorge E. Núñez, *Sovereignty Conflicts and International Law and Politics: A Distributive Justice Issue* (London and New York, NY: Routledge, Taylor & Francis Group, 2017), Chapter 5.

115 Jack E. Vincent, "Predicting Voting Patterns in the General Assembly," *The American Political Science Review* 65 (1971): 471–498; Axel Dreher, Peter Nunnenkamp and Rainer Thiele, "Does US Aid Buy UN General Assembly Votes?" *Public Choice* 136 (2008): 139–164; T. Y. Wang, "U.S. Foreign Aid and UN Voting: An Analysis of Important Issues," *International Studies Quarterly* 43 (1999): 199–210; and many others.

claims; and the second part included references to Antarctica and the ATS. The objective of the first two sections was to explain what the situation is in law and in fact and to highlight that questions about sovereignty remain unanswered. Both these sections showed that although there is an international legal acknowledgment of the principle of equality of states, realpolitik seems to challenge this view—i.e. some states are "more equal" than others—and therefore, any future arrangements concerning Antarctica should accommodate in fact and in law a form of fairness. In that vein, it is possible to argue that a regional approach in the form of a bloc or a continental (or sub-continental) alliance could strengthen the position of continental players, in particular Latin American agents, against external interests in the region by bettering the bargaining power of what may be individually weak international actors. Thereafter, the final section presented and explored guidelines to offer a permanent and peaceful solution.

Assuming these guidelines were of academic and/or actual use, there would still be several other pending questions. For example, the chapter only considered some sovereign states. Therefore, the role that other agents such as individuals, communities and other states might play should be investigated further. Importantly, questions about "who counts"[116] as having the right to claim sovereignty and "on what grounds" or according to what category of claim[117] require dedicated analyses.

Regardless of the many questions that remain unanswered, the chapter demonstrated that both in fact and in law the ATS sidesteps issues pertaining to sovereignty. Therefore, if the aim were to answer the question about sovereignty over Antarctica in a peaceful and permanent way, the intricacy of such a task must be firstly acknowledged. Indeed, it is because of the multi-agent, multi-contextual, multi-realm and multi-existence nature of issues pertaining to Antarctica that a multidimensional understanding may help reimagine in theory, and hopefully, in practice, a way of resolving an otherwise "frozen" dispute.

The next chapter will bring together the main points of this monograph, highlight their explanatory importance in law, political science and international relations, and point to possible further implications. The value of these implications is twofold: first, in highlighting the hermeneutical and methodological tools at the theoretical level that concern different territorial disputes in

116 For the author's view on "who counts" in negotiations about territorial disputes and sovereignty conflicts see Jorge E. Núñez, *Territorial Disputes and State Sovereignty: International Law and Politics* (London and New York, NY: Routledge, Taylor & Francis Group, 2020), Chapter 4; and Jorge E. Núñez, *Sovereignty Conflicts and International Law and Politics: A Distributive Justice Issue* (London and New York, NY: Routledge, Taylor & Francis Group, 2017), Chapter 6.

117 For details about different categories of claims relevant to territorial disputes see Jorge E. Núñez, *Territorial Disputes and State Sovereignty: International Law and Politics* (London and New York, NY: Routledge, Taylor & Francis Group, 2020), Chapter 4.

the Americas and second, in establishing some guidelines for future scholarly research, law and policymaking to deal with them peacefully and permanently.

Bibliography

Abdenur, Adriana Erthal and Danilo Marcondes Neto. "Rising Powers and Antarctica: Brazil's Changing Interests." *The Polar Journal* 4:1 (2014): 12–27.

Anand, R. P. "Sovereign Equality of States in International Law." *International Studies* 8:3 (1966): 213–224.

Andrade, Israel de Oliveira, Leonardo Faria de Mattos, Andrea Cancela da Cruz-Kaled and Giovanni Roriz Lyra Hillebrand. *Brazil in Antarctica: The Scientific and Geopolitical Importance of PROANTAR in the Brazilian Strategic Surrounding Area*. Brasilia: IPEA, Institute for Applied Economic Research, 2020.

"Argentine and Chilean Territorial Claims in the Antarctic." *Polar Record* 4:32 (1946): 412–417.

Arpi, Bruno and Jeffrey McGee, "Rediscovering the Importance of Antarctic Law for the Early Twenty-First Century." *Australian Journal of International Affairs* 76:3 (2022): 248–265.

Beck, Peter J. *The International Politics of Antarctica*. London and New York, NY: Routledge, Taylor & Francis, 2014.

Bejar, Jimmy Florez and Daniel De la Cruz Maravi. "La Antártida: Presencia Latinoamericana en la Era del Cambio Climático." *Revista Científica de la Escuela Superior de Guerra del Ejército* 3:1 (2024): 97–103.

Bernhardt, J. Peter A. "Sovereignty in Antarctica." *California Western International Journal* 5 (1975): 297–349.

Bertone, Martín, Pablo Melara and Tamara Culleton. "Territorio, Conciencia Nacional y Educación. Las Islas Malvinas y la Antártida Argentina en las Políticas de Estado Peronistas (1946–1955)." *Centro Educativo de las Fuerzas Armadas Argentinas* (2023) available at https://cefadigital.edu.ar/handle/1847939/2403 accessed 28 August 2024.

Boehm, Klaus and Aubrey Silberston. *British Patent System: Volume 1, Administration*. Cambridge: Cambridge University Press, 1967.

Boulègue, M. "The Militarization of Russian Polar Politics." *Chatham House Research Paper* (2022) available at https://www.chathamhouse.org/sites/default/files/2022-06/2022-06-06-militarization-russian-polar-politics-boulegue_0.pdf accessed 29 February 2024.

Brady, Anne-Marie. *China as a Polar Great Power*. Cambridge: Cambridge University Press, 2017.

Brady, Anne-Marie. "China's Rise in Antarctica?" *Asian Survey* 50:4 (2010): 759–785.

Brady, Anne-Marie, ed. *The Emerging Politics of Antarctica*. Oxford and New York, NY: Routledge, 2013.

Bugueño, Carolina and Pablo Mancilla. "Una Aproximación a las Controversias Diplomáticas entre Chile, Argentina y Gran Bretaña en el Continente Antártico, 1906–1961." *Revista de Historia de América* 136 (2005): 9–20.

Caillet-Bois, Ricardo R. "Las Malvinas y la Antártida Argentina." (1956) available at https://cefadigital.edu.ar/bitstream/1847939/798/1/Revista%20ESG%20no.%20322-1956_Caillet-Bois_84.pdf accessed 28 August 2024.

Câmara, Paulo E. A. S., Ana F. Barros-Platiau, Israel De Oliveira Andrade and Giovanni R. L. Hillebrand. "Brazil in Antarctica: 40 Years of Science." *Antarctic Science* 33:1 (2021): 30–38.

Caplan, Sergio G. and Sergio Eissa. "Análisis Estratégico del Sistema Malvinas, Antártida y Atlántico Sur." *Centro Educativo de las Fuerzas Armadas Argentinas* (2015) available at https://cefadigital.edu.ar/handle/1847939/1588 accessed 28 August 2024.

Cardone, Javier Ignacio. *Antarctic Politics of Brazil: Where the Tropic meets the Pole.* Cham: Palgrave Macmillan, 2022.

Chaturvedi, Sanjay. "Rise and Decline of Antarctica in Nehru's Geopolitical Vision: Challenges and Opportunities of the 1950s." *The Polar Journal* 3:2 (2013): 301–315.

Conforti, Benedetto. "Territorial Claims in Antarctica: A Modern Way to Deal with an Old Problem." *Cornell International Law Journal* 19:2 (1986): 249–258.

Dodds, Klaus. "Antarctic Geopolitics." In *Handbook on the Politics of Antarctica*, Dodds, Klaus, Hemmings, Alan D. and Roberts, Peder, eds. 199–214. Cheltenham: Edward Elgar Publishing, 2017.

Dodds, Klaus. "La Administración del Continente Polar: Los Orígenes Geopolíticos del Tratado Antártico de 1959." *Istor Revista de Historia Internacional* 10:39 (2009): 27–49.

Dodds, Klaus, Alan D. Hemmings and Peder Roberts, eds. *Handbook on the Politics of Antarctica.* Cheltenham: Edward Elgar Publishing, 2017.

Dreher, Axel, Peter Nunnenkamp and Rainer Thiele. "Does US Aid Buy UN General Assembly Votes?" *Public Choice* 136 (2008): 139–164.

Ferrada, Luis Valentín. "Five Factors that Will Decide the Future of Antarctica." *The Polar Journal* 8:1 (2018): 84–109.

Ferrada, Luis Valentín. "Latin America and the Antarctic Treaty System as a Legal Regime." *The Polar Journal* 9:2 (2019): 286–299.

Flamm, Patrick. "Legitimating the Antarctic Treaty System: From Rich Nations Club to Planetary Ecological Democracy?" *Australian Journal of International Affairs* 76:3 (2022): 266–285.

Fontes, Waldemar. "Uruguayan Antarctic links during the 1950s Decade." In *Antarctica in the 1950s: Perspectives from the Southern Cone*, León, Consuelo, Jara, Mauricio and Llanos, Nelson, eds. 141–156. Chile: LW Editorial, 2021, available at https://www.lweditorial.cl/ANTARTIC-book-PDF.pdf#page=141 accessed 4 September 2024.

Fontes, Waldemar. "Uruguay en la Antártida. Una Visión Estratégica." *Revista Estrategia* 3 (2011): 124–137.

French, Duncan. "Sustainable Development and the 1991 Madrid Protocol to the 1959 Antarctic Treaty: The Primacy of Protection in a Particularly Sensitive Environment." *Journal of International Wildlife Law and Policy* 2:3 (1999): 291–317.

González, Pablo Mancilla. "Chile, Argentina y Gran Bretaña en el Continente Antártico, 1906–1961. Una Aproximación a las Controversias Diplomáticas." *Revista de Estudios Históricos* 3:1 (2006): 1–20.

Graber, D. A. "Struggle for a Continent: Who Will Rule Antarctica?" *World Affairs* 113:1 (1950): 12–16.

Harrington, Jonathan. "China in Antarctica: A History." *Southeast Review of Asian Studies* 37 (2015): 1–19.

Haward, Marcus and Andrew Jackson, "Antarctica: Geopolitical Challenges and Institutional Resilience." *The Polar Journal* 13:1 (2023): 1–18.

Hayton, Robert D. "The 'American' Antarctic." *American Journal of International Law* 50:3 (1956): 583–610.

He, Liu. "Legal Challenges to the Antarctic Treaty System and the Protection of China's Basic Rights and Interests in Antarctica." *China Oceans Law Review* 3 (2021): 51–76.

Heidbrink, Ingo. "Claiming Sovereignty Where There Can Be No Sovereignty: Antarctica." *Environment, Space, Place* 8:2 (2016): 99–121.

Hemmings, Alan D. "Antarctic Politics in a Transforming Global Geopolitics." In *Handbook on the Politics of Antarctica*, Dodds, Klaus, Hemmings, Alan D. and Roberts, Peder, eds. 507–522. Cheltenham: Edward Elgar Publishing, 2017.

Heron, David Winston. "Antarctic Claims." *Foreign Affairs* 32:4 (1954): 661–667.

Hjorth, R. "Equality in the Theory of International Society: Kelsen, Rawls and the English School." *Review of International Studies* 37:5 (2011): 2585–2602.

Hong, Nong. "China and the Antarctic: Presence, Policy, Perception, and Public Diplomacy." *Marine Policy* 134 (2021): 1–10.

Howkins, Adrian. "Latin America and Antarctica." In *Oxford Research Encyclopedia of Latin American History* (2017) available at https://oxfordre.com/latinamericanhistory/display/10.1093/acrefore/9780199366439.001.0001/acrefore-9780199366439-e-434 accessed 9 May 2024.

Iturra, Karen Manzano. "La Competencia por los Derechos Antárticos: Chile y Argentina en la Zona Austral (1890–1910)." *Revista Política y Estrategia* 131 (2018): 41–55, available at https://www.politicayestrategia.cl/index.php/rpye/article/view/205 accessed 29 August 2024.

Iturra, Karen Manazno and Diego Jiménez Cabrera. "Antártica Chilena. Discusiones en torno a la Plataforma Continental y la Geopolítica Austral." *Revista Política y Estrategia* 139 (2022): 21–37, available at https://www.politicayestrategia.cl/index.php/rpye/article/view/992 accessed 29 August 2024.

Jara, Mauricio. "Una Disputa Doblemente Pospuesta: Chile y el Territorio Antártico: 1906–1948." *Revista Notas Históricas y Geográficas* (2021): 131–138, available at https://revistanotashistoricasygeograficas.cl/carga/wp-content/uploads/2021/01/n9-10-10.pdf accessed 29 August 2024.

Joyner, Christopher C. "Antarctica and the Indian Ocean States: The Interplay of Law, Interests, and Geopolitics." *Ocean Development and International Law* 21:1 (1990): 41–70.

Joyner, Christopher C. "Nonmilitarization of the Antarctic: The Interplay of Law and Geopolitics." *Naval War College Review* 42:4 (1989): 83–104.

Joyner, Christopher C. "The Exclusive Economic Zone and Antarctica: The Dilemmas of Non-Sovereign Jurisdiction." *Ocean Development and International Law* 19:6 (1988): 469–491.

Kelsen, Hans. "The Principle of Sovereign Equality of States as a Basis for International Organization." *Yale Law Journal* 53:2 (1944): 207–220.

Lee, Wei-chin. "China and Antarctica: So Far and Yet So Near." *Asian Survey* 30:6 (1990): 576–586.

Liu, Nengye. "The Rise of China and the Antarctic Treaty System?" *Australian Journal of Maritime & Ocean Affairs* 11:2 (2019): 120–131.

Lord, Thomas. "The Antarctic Treaty System and the Peaceful Governance of Antarctica: The Role of the ATS in Promoting Peace at the Margins of the World." *The Polar Journal* 10:1 (2020): 3–21.

Lozada Maldonado, Wolker Helmer. "Implicancias Geopolíticas de la Presencia del Perú en la Antártida." *Fuerza Aérea del Perú* (2021) available at http://209.45.53.131/handle/fap/381 accessed 2 September 2024.

MacKechnie Jr., Russell W. "Sovereignty in Antarctica: The Anglo-Argentine Dispute." *Syracuse Journal of International Law and Commerce* 5:1 (1977): 119–148.

Mancilla, Alejandra. "The Moral Limits of Territorial Claims in Antarctica." *Ethics & International Affairs* 32:3 (2018): 339–360.

Mancilla, Alejandra and Julia Ann Jabour. "Turned 60, Is the Antarctic Treaty System in Good Health?" *The Geographical Journal* 189:1 (2023): 2–6.

McGee, Jeffrey, David Edmiston, and Marcus Haward. "Militarisation of Antarctica." In *The Future of Antarctica: Scenarios from Classical Geopolitics*, McGee, Jeffrey, Edmiston, David and Haward, Marcus, eds. 105–124. Singapore: Springer, 2022.

McLean, Lydia and Jenny Rock, "The Importance of Antarctica: Assessing the Values Ascribed to Antarctica by Its Researchers to Aid Effective Climate Change Communication." *The Polar Journal* 6:2 (2016): 291–306.

Moore, Jason Kendall. "Tethered to an Iceberg: United States Policy toward the Antarctic, 1939–1949." *Polar Record* 35:193 (1999): 125–134.

Moreano Andrade, Hernán Rodrigo. "La Investigación Científica del Ecuador en la Antártida y su Consolidación 2005–2008." *Revista Científica y Tecnológica, Universidad Estatal Península de Santa Elena* 1:1 (2013): 1–11, available at https://repositorio.upse.edu.ec/handle/46000/7235 accessed 4 September 2024.

Moreano, H. "Ecuador Antártico—Pasado y Futuro." *Instituto Antártico Ecuatoriano* 2:1 (1990): 83–86, available at https://aquadocs.org/handle/1834/3731 accessed 4 September 2024.

Murray, John. "The Exploration of the Antarctic Regions." *Scottish Geographical Magazine* 2:9 (1886): 527–548.

Murray, John. "The Scientific Advantages of an Antarctic Expedition." *Proceedings of the Royal Society of London* 62:379–387 (1898): 424–451, available at https://royalsocietypublishing.org/doi/abs/10.1098/rspl.1897.0131 accessed 5 September 2024.

Myhre, Jeffrey D. *The Antarctic Treaty System: Politics, Law, and Diplomacy.* London and New York, NY: Routledge, 2019.

Núñez, Jorge E. *Cosmopolitanism, State Sovereignty, International Law and Politics: A Theory.* London and New York, NY: Routledge, Taylor & Francis Group, 2023.

Núñez, Jorge E. *Sovereignty Conflicts and International Law and Politics: A Distributive Justice Issue.* London and New York, NY: Routledge, Taylor & Francis Group, 2017.

Núñez, Jorge E. *Territorial Disputes and State Sovereignty: International Law and Politics.* London and New York, NY: Routledge, Taylor & Francis Group, 2020.

Rajan, Madhu. "China in Antarctica." *China Report* 23:1 (1987): 57–64.

Rawls, John. *A Theory of Justice.* Revised Edition. Oxford: Oxford University Press, 1999.

Roberts, Peder and Alejandra Mancilla, eds. *Colonialism and Antarctica: Attitudes, Logics, and Practices.* Manchester: Manchester University Press, 2024.

Ruidías Villalaz, Manuel. "La Antártida y la Importancia de las Actividades Científicas Desarrolladas por el Perú." *Revista de la Escuela Superior de Guerra Naval* 18:1 (2021): 65–78.

Sánchez, Wilder Alejandro and Otto Raul Tielemans Jr. "Reinvigorating Peru's Role in Antarctic Geopolitics." *The Polar Journal* 5:1 (2015): 101–112.

Sharma, Bipandeep. "India and the Emerging Geopolitics of Antarctic." *Strategic Analysis* 47:6 (2024): 1–14.

Shusterich, Kurt M. "The Antarctic Treaty System: History, Substance, and Speculation." *International Journal* 39:4 (1984): 800–827.

Sosin, Claudia. "Continental Shelves in the Antarctic Region: Implications for Resource Management." *The Polar Journal* 12:1 (2022): 122–147.

Sullivan, Walter. "Antarctica in a Two-Power World." *Foreign Affairs* 36:1 (1957): 154–166.

Triggs, Gillian. "The Antarctic Treaty System: A Model of Legal Creativity and Cooperation." In *Science Diplomacy: Antarctica, Science, and the Governance of International Spaces*, Berkman, Paul Arthur, Lang, Michael A., Walton, David W. H. and Young, Oran R., eds. 39–49. Washington, DC: Smithsonian Institution Scholarly Press, 2011.

Vidal, Florian. "The Antarctic Peninsula: Argentina and Chile in the Era of Global Change." *The Polar Journal* 13:1 (2023): 13–30.

Vigni, Patrizia. "The Interaction between the Antarctic Treaty System and the Other Relevant Conventions Applicable to the Antarctic Area." In *Max Planck Yearbook of United Nations Law*, Frowein, J. A. and Wolfrum, R., eds. 481–542. Alphen aan den Rijn: Kluwer Law International, 2000.

Vincent, Jack E. "Predicting Voting Patterns in the General Assembly." *The American Political Science Review* 65 (1971): 471–498.

Wang, T. Y. "U.S. Foreign Aid and UN Voting: An Analysis of Important Issues." *International Studies Quarterly* 43 (1999): 199–210.

Weizhe, Liu. "UNCLOS' Impact on and Implications for Antarctic Maritime Disputes." *China Oceans Law Review* 16:3 (2020): 64–82.

Wilson, Robert E. "National Interests and Claims in the Antarctic." *Arctic* 17:1 (1964): 15–31.

Yermakova, Yelena. "Legitimacy of the Antarctic Treaty System: Is It Time for a Reform?" *The Polar Journal* 11:2 (2021): 342–359.

10 Conclusive remarks, limitations and future implications

Introduction

This final chapter brings together the main points of this monograph, highlights its explanatory importance in legal and political sciences and international relations and shows possible further application of the conceptual and hermeneutical tools and multidimensional approach to other disputes.

The monograph aimed to apply the author's multidimensional approach to assess and explain territorial disputes in the Americas. In that sense, this book is another step toward more comprehensively exploring and, hopefully, finding potentially viable ways to solve territorial disputes. The path began with Núñez (2017),[1] which presented sovereignty conflicts as a matter of ideal theory and, therefore, did not consider real implications in territorial disputes. By bringing together historical and conceptual analyses, Núñez (2017) focused on disputes between two sovereign states (*de jure* and *de facto*) over the sovereignty of a populated non-sovereign third territory (e.g. Falkland/Malvinas Islands, Gibraltar, Kashmir) and argued for a hypothetical agreement to deal with them by suggesting principles that cannot be reasonably refused. Thereafter, Núñez (2020)[2] explored factual and logical, ideal and non-ideal features in ongoing territorial disputes around the world. Together with conceptual elements, many current territorial disputes were introduced to compare and contrast some differences and find some common, arguably constant, features. Therein, while Núñez (2020) offered an understanding of the dynamics of territorial disputes, it also contributed to the literature on international law and politics by developing a more integrated approach to theory building. Having determined in theory and in fact the intricate nature of territorial disputes in Núñez (2017) and Núñez (2020), it was obvious that current disciplinary understandings in legal and political sciences and international relations were inadequate to comprehend and assess their complex

1 Jorge E. Núñez, *Sovereignty Conflicts and International Law and Politics: A Distributive Justice Issue* (London and New York, NY: Routledge, Taylor & Francis Group, 2017).
2 Jorge E. Núñez, *Territorial Disputes and State Sovereignty: International Law and Politics* (London and New York, NY: Routledge, Taylor & Francis Group, 2020).

DOI: 10.4324/9781003350828-13

nature. Therein, Núñez (2023)[3] introduced a novel theory and methodology. In contrast to the traditional unidimensional understandings applied by the legal and political sciences and international relations, Núñez (2023) proposed what the author calls the multidimensional approach. Multidimensionality acknowledges the complexities present in issues concerning sovereignty and cosmopolitanism and their dynamics, e.g. territorial disputes. In order to gain a better understanding of this complexity and show how the multidimensional approach could work, a set of elements, features and variables labeled as the pluralism of pluralisms were advanced and characterized—i.e. agents and players; contexts, realms and modes of existence; dimensions; and time and space.

By accepting that territorial disputes in the Americas are intricate, this monograph challenged the existing fragmentation in the study of this issue. Indeed, existing research either lacks interdisciplinarity on territorial disputes, or, despite some attempts to conduct interdisciplinary studies, they are circumscribed to an element or a feature of a particular dispute—e.g. they are only a legal or a political study. The pluralisms explored in the preceding chapters included several agents such as sovereign states, communities and individuals playing different roles in different territorial disputes; the international, regional and domestic contexts that are intertwined in these differences; and the many factual, normative and axiological elements and features present in them.

In doing so, the first part—i.e. Chapters 1, 2 and 3—presented the overall aim of this work, its methodology and potential relevance; key concepts such as sovereignty and territorial disputes; and the notions of pluralism of pluralisms and multidimensionality. In turn, the second part introduced and reviewed ongoing territorial disputes in the Americas. Chapter 4 established the base for the rest of the second part by highlighting common roots to disputes despite their individual particularities. Chapters 5 and 6 presented a series of cases and notions—i.e. colonialism, neo-colonialism and colonial mindset—to explain how different agents and contexts still play a central role in the origin, continuation and potential escalation into conflict of these disputes. Chapter 7 focused on disputes between continental agents with similar bargaining power and brought to light that regional guarantors are likely to be key in attaining a peaceful and permanent understanding between otherwise challenged and challenger agents. Chapter 8 referred to a particular kind of agent—i.e. communities—and the role they may play in territorial disputes that goes beyond traditional actors such as sovereign states; therein, notions such as right-peopling of the territory, indigenous self-determination and black self-determination were advanced. In the third and final part, Chapters 9 and 10 bring together some guidelines for policymaking in regard to dealing with crisis, with focus on territorial disputes and a blueprint on how to deal

3 Jorge E. Núñez, *Cosmopolitanism, State Sovereignty, International Law and Politics: A Theory* (London and New York, NY: Routledge, Taylor & Francis Group, 2023).

with the still open question of sovereignty over Antarctica. The following sections will, first, explain how the multidimensional approach integrates different findings concerning territorial disputes. Thereafter, the final sections will acknowledge the limitations of this work and suggest some recommendations, along with policy and research guidelines.

Applying the multidimensional approach

As argued in Núñez (2020),[4] there is a need to understand and assess territorial disputes more comprehensively. First, the assumptions, concepts and consequences one discipline may take as self-evident, logically coherent and scientifically binding may be exclusive to that community of experts and not necessarily shared by the broader scientific society or the entities in a territorial dispute or sovereignty conflict. Hence, many disputes and conflicts remain unresolved and in a legal and political limbo. Second, studies in relation to these disputes and conflicts and possible remedies for them are limited because they center only on a particular conflict or region. With these fragmented analyses (fragmented because of the methodology of the science of reference, and the object of study) outcomes are inevitably of limited significance in theory and in practice.

In addition to the author's own work, to date, Huth[5] offers the most extensive view on territorial disputes and sovereignty conflicts by bringing together a series of assumptions and hypotheses. Although not multidimensional in nature, Huth includes in these assumptions and hypotheses some of the pluralisms the author advances and explains how they might interplay in the origin, continuation and potential escalation into conflict of these disputes as well as their possible peaceful and permanent settlement. A summary of Huth's assumptions and hypotheses about territorial disputes at large follows below. Interestingly, they concur with this monograph's findings about territorial disputes in the Americas.

4 Jorge E. Núñez, *Territorial Disputes and State Sovereignty: International Law and Politics* (London and New York, NY: Routledge, Taylor & Francis Group, 2020).

5 The bibliography in legal and political sciences on territorial disputes is either outdated or fragmented. As an example, see Paul K. Huth, *Standing Your Ground: Territorial Disputes and International Conflict* (Ann Arbor, MI: University of Michigan Press, 2001). Huth offers in Chapter 1 a comprehensive list of academic literature, but all entries were published before 2000 and are fragmented by discipline and geographical location. For a more up-to-date list of resources refer to Jorge E. Núñez, *Territorial Disputes and State Sovereignty: International Law and Politics* (London and New York, NY: Routledge, Taylor & Francis Group, 2020), Chapter 9.

Assumption 1. Due to the anarchical nature of the international system, state leaders cannot depend upon a recognized supranational authority to settle disputes with other countries.[6]

Assumption 2. A central concern of state leaders is to retain their position of domestic political power.[7]

Assumption 3. The ability of state leaders to remain in office is strongly related to generating support among various domestic political constituencies.[8]

Assumption 4. Domestic political groups consistently seek to shape the domestic and foreign policy of state leaders… These groups are able to exert pressure and influence on political leaders through a variety of channels.[9]

Assumption 5. State leaders believe that a foreign policy setback… will impose high domestic costs to them.[10]

Assumption 6. Domestic political institutions structure and induce political elites to resolve conflict in particular ways… promote the use or threat of violence…where other systems…delegitimize violence and favor compromise.[11]

Assumption 7. The development of norms and practices by state leaders for resolving domestic political conflict, in turn, affect their approach to the resolution of international conflict.[12]

Assumption 8. The threat or use of military power is the ultimate recourse for state leaders to resolve disputes.[13]

Assumption 9. State leaders seek to maintain diplomatic and military flexibility in their foreign relations with other states.[14]

Departing from these assumptions, Huth presents a series of hypotheses pertaining to territorial disputes. For instance, hypotheses based on assumption 1:

6 Paul K. Huth, *Standing Your Ground: Territorial Disputes and International Conflict* (Ann Arbor, MI: University of Michigan Press, 2001), 41.
7 Paul K. Huth, *Standing Your Ground: Territorial Disputes and International Conflict* (Ann Arbor, MI: University of Michigan Press, 2001), 41.
8 Paul K. Huth, *Standing Your Ground: Territorial Disputes and International Conflict* (Ann Arbor, MI: University of Michigan Press, 2001), 41.
9 Paul K. Huth, *Standing Your Ground: Territorial Disputes and International Conflict* (Ann Arbor, MI: University of Michigan Press, 2001), 43.
10 Paul K. Huth, *Standing Your Ground: Territorial Disputes and International Conflict* (Ann Arbor, MI: University of Michigan Press, 2001), 44.
11 Paul K. Huth, *Standing Your Ground: Territorial Disputes and International Conflict* (Ann Arbor, MI: University of Michigan Press, 2001), 45.
12 Paul K. Huth, *Standing Your Ground: Territorial Disputes and International Conflict* (Ann Arbor, MI: University of Michigan Press, 2001), 46.
13 Paul K. Huth, *Standing Your Ground: Territorial Disputes and International Conflict* (Ann Arbor, MI: University of Michigan Press, 2001), 47.
14 Paul K. Huth, *Standing Your Ground: Territorial Disputes and International Conflict* (Ann Arbor, MI: University of Michigan Press, 2001), 47.

there is a relationship[15] between the strategic location of bordering territory and the possibility of a territorial dispute and/or its resolution.[16] Hypotheses based on assumptions 2 and 3: there is a relationship between (a) the location of ethnic minorities in the target territory who share common ethnic ties with the predominant group in the challenger agent and (b) the possibility of a territorial dispute and/or its resolution.[17] Hypotheses based on assumptions 1, 2 and 3: there is a relationship between the location of natural resources of economic value in the bordering territory and the possibility of a territorial dispute and/or its resolution.[18] Hypotheses about the international context based on assumptions 5 and 8: there is a relationship between the balance of conventional military forces between challenged and challenger agents and the possibility of a territorial dispute and/or its resolution.[19] This includes involvement in political–military disputes with other states, stalemate in negotiations, previous defeats, military alliances, common adversaries and previous settlements. And, finally, hypotheses about the domestic context based on assumptions 1 to 5: there is a relationship between a previous challenger's domestic situation and the possibility of a territorial dispute and/or its resolution.[20] This includes unsettled territorial disputes with the target, prior militarized disputes between the same agents, prior loss of territory, prior status as a colony or overseas dependency and having a democratic political regime.

Huth's assumptions and hypotheses based on real case territorial disputes around the world, including those in the Americas, plainly encompass a pluralism of pluralisms—i.e. agents, players, contexts, realms and modes of existence.[21] Clearly, the many relationships Huth presents in these assumptions and hypotheses stress the importance of moving beyond unidimensionality toward multidimensionality, an essential requirement if the aim is to understand and assess territorial disputes in their intricacy. This is because, by application of the multidimensional approach, the scholar in question is able to use linear and nonlinear dimensional views simultaneously and consider how these pluralisms may interact. More precisely, Huth includes in these assumptions and

15 Note that in these and the following hypotheses the relationship may be positive or inverse. For further details, refer to the relevant pages in Paul K. Huth, *Standing Your Ground: Territorial Disputes and International Conflict* (Ann Arbor, MI: University of Michigan Press, 2001).

16 Paul K. Huth, *Standing Your Ground: Territorial Disputes and International Conflict* (Ann Arbor, MI: University of Michigan Press, 2001), 49–50.

17 Paul K. Huth, *Standing Your Ground: Territorial Disputes and International Conflict* (Ann Arbor, MI: University of Michigan Press, 2001), 50–51.

18 Paul K. Huth, *Standing Your Ground: Territorial Disputes and International Conflict* (Ann Arbor, MI: University of Michigan Press, 2001), 52–53.

19 Paul K. Huth, *Standing Your Ground: Territorial Disputes and International Conflict* (Ann Arbor, MI: University of Michigan Press, 2001), 53–59.

20 Paul K. Huth, *Standing Your Ground: Territorial Disputes and International Conflict* (Ann Arbor, MI: University of Michigan Press, 2001), 59–64.

21 See Chapter 3.

hypotheses a number of elements and features such as supranational authorities, state leaders, political power, political groups, norms and practices, military power, diplomacy and natural resources. Arguably, an approach that is disciplinary—e.g. only legal or only political—is not sufficient to fully capture the complexity present in territorial disputes. There is a pressing need for a multidimensional approach that moves away from disciplinary unidimensionality and embraces rationality, emotion, nationalism, prejudice and multiple perspectives. Ergo, a multidimensional approach that includes interdisciplinary as well as non-disciplinary understandings is needed because of the multifaceted and multi-layered nature of global issues such as territorial disputes.

In order to better understand how both rational and non-rational factors influence positions across these geopolitical divisions, this monograph brought together various disciplines to explore, for example, how representations in popular culture have colored opinion, and highlighted the lack of historical knowledge, with misunderstandings caused by inappropriate use of the languages of law and politics remaining disassociated from the contexts of cultural and human geography. Therein, by applying the linear vertical approach it is possible to understand why central, strong or advantaged states like the United States and the United Kingdom might not be open to question their own claims to sovereignty and explore avenues to solve the dispute peacefully and permanently in benefit of other involved agents—e.g. because they understand "sovereignty" in law and politics as supreme, indivisible, not shareable, defined by "territory" in terms of space and eternal in terms of time; furthermore, a leader's prestige depends on the existence of an alien foe (Chapters 5 and 6). Additionally, by application of the linear horizontal approach, it is possible to compare and contrast the different legal and political systems that the agents involved in a dispute may have and find out ways in which a compromise could be attained without blurring their respective spheres of sovereignty, i.e. options other than exclusive singular sovereignty (Chapter 7).

Two further approaches—linear diagonal or transversal, and curved or spiral—can help in different ways to understand why it would be important to: (1) neutralize the influence of international context agents such as China, India, Russia and the United Kingdom; (2) discard the United Nations and its institutions as a potential means to solve the dispute; (3) consider whether the inclusion of regional guarantors might improve the viability of a successful and permanent peaceful solution; and (4) include in analyses a potentially controversial issue, that is the defining role played by the different type of normative orders involved—i.e. Chapter 7 clearly indicates that the Judeo-Christian tradition and its institutions, in comparison to others, foster peacebuilding by several means dedicated to that effect.

In turn, nonlinear approaches could enable the distinction between the many different other agents, realms and modes of existence at play. For instance, depending on the potential remedies applicable to territories in which sovereignty is in question, nonlinear approaches such as self-referred, regressive, chaotic and random, could incorporate (a) the interests of communities such as indigenous peoples and implanted populations and explore whether notions such as native self-determination and black self-determination are relevant (Chapter 8); (b) the role individuals and normative systems other than law may play in fostering peacebuilding (Chapter 7); (c) the role different kinds of agents including individuals, communities and sovereign states might play in the origin, continuation and potential escalation into conflict of these disputes when considering if they stem from or are fueled by colonialism, neocolonialism or colonial mindset or syndrome (Chapter 8).

Clearly, the territorial disputes in the Americas encompass several agents at play in different contexts. Although these disputes have common roots (Chapter 4), they all have their own particularities. For instance, there are evidently several sovereign states involved. However, the monograph showed that within these sovereign states, their populations might not be uniform in their positioning concerning a dispute and, consequently, there might be different groups and individual interests. Moreover, notions such as "territory" and "borders" are open to discussion—e.g. as in the direct and indirect interference in maritime exclusive economic zones, geostrategic locations and the exploration and exploitation of natural resources.

Importantly, the monograph has exposed a myriad of elements and features that influence the dynamics of territorial disputes. Although in theory they may have clearly demarcated spheres, several cases in the Americas highlight that, undoubtedly, law and politics are intertwined. Realpolitik shows emerging economies are often indebted. The previous chapters demonstrated that there has been (and still is) direct and indirect interference of agents that might appear to be alien to disputes in the Americas (Chapters 4, 5 and 6). Unsurprisingly, the least advantaged agents face challenges in relation to the strength of legal and political principles such as sovereign equality, generating different relative positions in any actual bargaining situation; for example, the choice could be between their financial stability or their human rights. Importantly, more central, stronger or advantaged agents, seemingly alien to these disputes, might foster the *status quo*, fuel these disputes or promote peacebuilding depending on their own domestic, regional and international situations and consequent agendas.

Indeed, like the previous chapter, these closing lines offer an outline sketch of how to apply a multidimensional understanding to territorial disputes. Evidently, there is much more detailed work to be done on how the pluralisms that are advanced here interact and how others might interplay. Furthermore, in each case, different linear and nonlinear views should be tested to allow different outcomes and, therefore, potential new avenues to understand these disputes more comprehensively and, potentially, resolve them.

Limitations

Like its predecessors, this monograph brings together a proposal on how to understand and assess territorial disputes more comprehensively. Núñez

(2017) accepted some limitations including the lack of exploration of non-ideal issues that could undermine the actual applicability of the methodology introduced and its outcome. To deal with these limitations, Núñez (2020) explored a sample of ongoing territorial disputes around the world, including a dedicated chapter on cases pertaining to the Americas. However, these cases were very succinctly introduced at the time because the monograph aimed to provide a global and interdisciplinary study to develop general guidelines for dispute settlement and conflict resolution that current remedies fail to offer. In turn, Núñez (2023) brought together a new way to understand and assess territorial disputes and suggested the next move should aim to review real case scenarios in more detail by incorporating the multidimensional approach and, therefore, gain a more accurate understanding about them.

The review of ongoing real cases in this monograph has enabled the testing of arguments and hermeneutical tools presented and developed in its predecessors. Consequently, the preceding chapters enable the advancement of some partial conclusions that may foster future theoretical and empirical research. However, in addition to this step forward that continues on the path of Núñez (2017), Núñez (2020) and Núñez (2023), the review also included several cases and the setting up of basic conceptual, theoretical and methodological elements and features. On the one hand, it is because of this approach that it is possible to apply the author's theory and methodology, integrate findings and bring to light, for example, common roots to actual disputes and conflicts. On the other hand, it is true that such an approach prioritizes integration over the particular characteristics of individual cases across the Americas. As a result, attributes of a somewhat more specific nature have not been included this time. For example, although different agents such as individuals and communities were taken into account, an in-depth exploration of individual cases should consider military governments, political parties and/or ideologically distinct factions such as those mentioned in Chapter 7—i.e. *guerrilleros*, the Sandinista National Liberation Front in Nicaragua (FSLN), the Zapatista Army of National Liberation (EZLN) in Mexico and the Revolutionary Armed Forces of Colombia (FARC). As stated in Núñez (2023), inclusion of these agents allows an understanding of how and why an individual or a community may play different roles within and without their sphere of interrelation with others, ranging from a two-people, egalitarian relationship to a dictatorship (with or without political parties). Furthermore, the role of political parties and political leaders may or may not operate in favor of their community.[22]

The next step should aim to review individual real case scenarios by incorporating the multidimensional approach. In doing so, future research and

22 Empirical research supports the claim that in territorial disputes a leader's prestige may work against a community's wishes. See Jorge E. Núñez, *Territorial Disputes and State Sovereignty: International Law and Politics* (London and New York, NY: Routledge, Taylor & Francis Group, 2020).

analyses should incorporate the different pluralisms relevant to a single territorial dispute. Furthermore, any future research and analyses should be open to accept that there may be other pluralisms, elements and features, and other ways in which they may interrelate when particular real case scenarios are examined—e.g. as suggested in this monograph, new notions such as colonial syndrome and different ways to define what a community means and how notions such as self-determination may apply to them.

In addition to the review of individual real case scenarios and the incorporation of those pluralisms already considered and any others that may emerge, it is not only appropriate to acknowledge that this work may be original, significant and rigorous in developing a more integrated approach to theory building, but it is also important to accept that further research and analyses should test these findings and recommendations. Indeed, as with any other scholarly work, the conceptual and hermeneutical means, methodology and theory, and their application to real territorial dispute cases in the Americas advanced here will only be useful once these ideas are applied empirically. For example, real-world observation and experimentation by means of bringing together otherwise challenged and challenger agents might enable parties to think differently since all views and claims would be considered through a lens of neutrality and context.

A further point that deserves a mention is the fact that the findings included in this monograph should be compared and contrasted with cases in other areas of the world. The testing of these findings may enable existing methods to be used to understand other territorial disputes more comprehensively and, hopefully, advance permanent and peaceful arrangements. For instance, although it may be a controversial issue, it would be of utmost importance to study if some religions favor peacebuilding in theory and in practice (Chapter 7).

Ultimately, the methodology and theory underlying these pages and, more broadly, the author's work, will be as limited or as thorough as the different agents at play allow for reciprocal effective communication. The author maintains that the multidimensional approach and methodology are key in regarding conflict as a mechanism for positive change. For instance, they enable effective communication because they offer all agents an equal standing regardless of the background of origin and the shifting of traditional role-playing within the dispute. They also foster the development of tools for dialogue and neutralize preconceived views about conflict; promote the inclusion of emotional intelligence by means of self-awareness of positioning in relation to the dispute arguably based on emotional (non-rational) factors that in time have found or created rationale in law and politics; and support the "art of questioning" without preconceptions or assumptions. In sum, like any other work by the author, the multidimensional approach and methodology applied to cases reviewed in this monograph promote cooperation and exchange based on procedural justice rather than competition and ego-nationalistic placement centered on outcome.

Some final remarks: partial conclusions and guidelines

Regardless of their limitations, these chapters show that it is in the multidimensional understanding of issues concerning territorial disputes that a path can be built toward a more comprehensive explanation of their intricacy. From the previous pages, which include a series of theoretical elements and features as well as the review of several territorial disputes in the Americas, it is possible to summarize some points that are present in real case scenarios:

- Sovereignty and territorial disputes are intertwined (Chapter 2).
- Sovereignty and territorial disputes encompass several pluralisms—e.g. agents, contexts, realms (Chapter 2).
- The role of regional organizations and guarantors suggests a higher likelihood for peacemaking and peacekeeping (Chapter 2).
- Traditional scholarly approaches used in disciplines such as the legal and political sciences and international relations are limited because of their tunnel vision. The argument favors the move from these unidimensional views toward multidimensionality (Chapter 3).
- Differences in the Americas have common roots (Chapter 4).
- Differences in the Americas are multi-faceted and multi-layered (Chapter 4).
- Any population in a disputed territory, whether implanted for "right-peopling" reasons or indigenous, may present a different interest to the ones represented by the claimant sovereign states (Chapter 5).
- Differences are influenced by the domestic, regional and international contexts (Chapter 5).
- Central, strong or advantaged states use hard and/or soft power to influence individuals, communities and states in Latin America and the Caribbean and, therefore, do interfere with issues pertaining to law and politics, including territorial disputes (Chapter 6).
- Population and government may but not necessarily have the same interest in relation to a dispute (Chapter 7).
- Domestic, regional and international contexts influence each other (Chapter 7).
- Elements and factors that influence territorial disputes include identification; type of regime; leaders' prestige; regional involvement in the form of institutions, arbitrators and guarantors and non-interventionism; the distinction between domestic crises and international peacebuilding (Chapter 7).
- Any research on territorial disputes should include other normative systems in addition to law such as religion. Importantly, some religions seem to favor peacebuilding in theory and in practice (Chapter 7).
- Territorial disputes may include agents other than sovereign states such as internal groups like indigenous peoples and implanted populations arguing for their right to self-determination (Chapter 8).

- Self-determination may imply secession, but it does not need to. More precisely, the ways in which self-determination and secession are characterized and applied are fundamental in the resolution of territorial disputes (Chapter 8).
- Although there is an international legal acknowledgment of the principle of equality of states, realpolitik seems to challenge this view—i.e. some states are "more equal" than others (Chapter 9).
- If the aim were to answer the question about sovereignty over Antarctica in a peaceful and permanent way, the intricacy of such a task must be firstly acknowledged (Chapter 9).

In short, these partial conclusions support the premise that territorial disputes are intricate and there is a need to capture more fully the reciprocal influence of the many pluralisms at play; therefore, a unidimensional view that solely focuses on a particular element or feature and/or does so from a particular disciplinary standpoint is insufficient. Multidimensionality allows these disputes to be comprehended in a more refined way and upholds the aspiration of peaceful and permanent settlement.

The subsections below incorporate some connections to the author's previous work, reflecting on the way in which both research and policy could be sharpened in terms of their analyses and comprehension of territorial disputes.

Research guidelines

- Multidisciplinary studies are important to understand the complex nature of these disputes, but they are not enough. Any study that aims to fully comprehend territorial disputes (or any other intricate phenomena) should incorporate interdisciplinary and transdisciplinary research[23]

While multidisciplinary research allows the involvement of different disciplines, it does not guarantee integration and can result in a variety of outcomes. In turn, interdisciplinary research permits the interaction between disciplines and enables the researcher to move beyond *a priori* established and/or disciplinary domains. This interaction fosters co-creation—e.g. of a project framework or methodology. Transdisciplinary research may be part of interdisciplinary research but in all cases moves beyond *a priori* established

23 For up-to-date information about interdisciplinary and transdisciplinary research see SHAPE-ID available at https://www.shapeidtoolkit.eu/ accessed 15 October 2024. See also Julie Thompson Klein, "Discourses of Transdisciplinarity: Looking Back to the Future," *Futures* 63 (2014): 68–74; Bianca Vienni-Baptista, Isabel Fletcher and Catherine Lyall, eds., *Foundations of Interdisciplinary and Transdisciplinary Research: A Reader* (Bristol: University of Bristol Press, 2023); Bianca Vienni-Baptista, Isabel Fletcher, Catherine Lyall and Christian Pohl, "Embracing Heterogeneity: Why Plural Understandings Strengthen Interdisciplinarity and Transdisciplinarity," *Science and Public Policy* 49:6 (2022): 865–877.

and/or disciplinary domains and permits the collaboration—e.g. co-design, co-creation—between academic disciplines and other agents such as society at large, non-governmental organizations, policymakers and activists.

- "Art of questioning" without preconceptions or assumptions

Arguably, scientific disciplines have become "narrow minded" because of their specific spheres—e.g. concepts, conceptions, bodies of theory and methodologies.[24] A corollary of such a degree of specialism is the current fragmentation of disciplinary studies. Indeed, scholars from different disciplines like legal and political sciences and international relations would explore the same territorial dispute but from different realms of reference—i.e. either factual, normative or axiological—or assess the issue according to different modes of existence—i.e. they would understand and explore the relevant object or subject of study as either ideal, natural, cultural or metaphysical.[25] Obviously, their results would be determined (or at least influenced and, arguably, biased) by *a priori* concepts, assumptions and beliefs. The multidimensional approach the author suggests incorporates these disciplinary concepts, assumptions and beliefs without being determined by them. In particular, a nonlinear dimensional understanding allows for reflection that cuts across disciplinary divisions and predetermined outcomes—i.e. the nonlinear dimensional model accepts pluralities that may have unconventional interrelations within and without their respective spheres. Consequently, multidimensionality allows the questioning of *a priori* concepts, assumptions and beliefs.

- Self-awareness of positioning in relation to the dispute arguably based on emotional (non-rational) factors

Agents such as individuals and states may have supreme authority over themselves. The former is labeled self-ownership while the latter is called sovereignty.[26] Whether the statement is accepted or not, it is a truism that agents have relationships of different kinds with other self-owners and sovereigns that may

24 The author distinguishes intentionally between concepts and conceptions. While concepts are public and intersubjective with a certain normative aspect, a conception is associated with the concept which one—e.g. agents such as individuals, communities and states and scholarly disciplines like legal and political sciences and international relations—takes to be analytic to or constitutive of the concept. For further detail see Jorge E. Núñez, "State Sovereignty: Concept and Conceptions," *International Journal for the Semiotics of Law-Revue internationale de Sémiotique juridique* 37 (2024): 1–20.

25 For an understanding of realms and modes of existence see Jorge E. Núñez, *Cosmopolitanism, State Sovereignty, International Law and Politics: A Theory* (London and New York, NY: Routledge, Taylor & Francis Group, 2023), Chapter 5.

26 For a detailed discussion see Jorge E. Núñez, *Sovereignty Conflicts and International Law and Politics: A Distributive Justice Issue* (London and New York, NY: Routledge, Taylor & Francis Group, 2017).

imply enmity, neutrality or some form of allegiance. Ideal theory allows for the assumption that, for example, agents with self-ownership or sovereignty may be mutually disinterested.[27] However, realpolitik shows that territorial disputes are often highly emotional, with the participants taking the view that "victory for us is to see you suffer."[28] Unsurprisingly, opposed agents in disputes, including scientific scholarly agents working as individuals and in communities, may maintain statements such as "this is the truth, everything else is false."[29] Therefore, it is of utmost importance that any research on a territorial dispute has an *a priori* epistemological and methodological acknowledgment. Therein, explanations and analyses should take into account the presence of presupposition, recognizing that there is an intentional act of discernment and consequent choice of features that, for whatever scholarly reason, are more relevant than others.[30]

- Consciousness-raising

By breaking academic disciplinary isolation, consciousness-raising[31] can be broadly characterized as the acknowledging of one's place in a system while taking action and feeling inspired to do something about that system. The notion is intertwined with the previous points about multi-, intra- and transdisciplinary studies, the art of questioning and self-awareness. By accepting to learn about oneself as an individual and accounting for one's particular characteristics—e.g. gender, religion, disciplinary background, country of origin—it is possible to have self-awareness about the role being played and positions taken in relation to systems such as societal structures and territorial disputes. In turn, building connections by means of multi-, intra- and transdisciplinary studies with others' experiences including concepts, assumptions and beliefs fosters the art of questioning and enables isolation to be broken, ultimately fostering a critical position that transcends actual and potential biases.

Policy guidelines

- Domestic and regional preventive means

27 John Rawls, *Justice as Fairness* (Cambridge, MA: Harvard University Press, 2003), 12 and 131.

28 Philip C. Winslow, *Victory for Us Is to See You Suffer: In the West Bank with the Palestinians and the Israelis* (Boston, MA: Beacon Press, 2007).

29 Jorge E. Núñez, *Cosmopolitanism, State Sovereignty, International Law and Politics: A Theory* (London and New York, NY: Routledge, Taylor & Francis Group, 2023), Chapter 7.

30 Jorge E. Núñez, *Cosmopolitanism, State Sovereignty, International Law and Politics: A Theory* (London and New York, NY: Routledge, Taylor & Francis Group, 2023), Chapter 4.

31 Lauren McCarthy and Kate Grosser, "Breaking Isolation: Consciousness-Raising as a Methodology for Academic Activism," *Organization* 30:5 (2023): 1152–1167.

Territorial disputes and domestic situations can spill across borders. For instance, several cases reviewed in this monograph and situations like the ongoing socioeconomic and political crisis in Venezuela put pressure on neighboring individuals, communities and states. Leaders in the Americas should understand these crises as a regional problem and come together to explore ways of protecting involved agents and dealing with the issue regionally, without the interference of non-continental players. Indeed, there are already clear "menus" of regional organizations, procedures for peaceful and permanent settlement of disputes and resultant remedies. But, in order for these procedures to be both effective and efficient, regional organizations should count on the necessary legal, political and financial domestic support. Therein, there should be clearly defined and dedicated domestic legislation, bodies or organizations and means to trigger their regional counterparts' involvement.

- Non-intervention

This regional, multi-level and multilateral approach has its basis in the Monroe, Calvo and Drago doctrines, a policy position that is also known as "America for the Americans" which is embodied in the legal framework of the Rio Treaty and the Organization of American States (OAS).[32] It is true, however, that since their inception, and especially during the Cold War, these doctrines have been interpreted differently (arguably, manipulated) to support interventions in Latin America under the pretense to protect regional interests, ranging from unilateral interventions by the United States to multi-lateral interventions supported by the OAS. In situations like the current climate in Venezuela and any territorial dispute, these doctrines should be invoked in a way that reflect the principles stipulated in their original form: the political and territorial inviolability of Latin American nations and non-intervention by powers outside the Latin American hemisphere. Invoking the doctrine in this way would, perhaps, be better understood as "America for the Americans" and/or "Latin America for the Latin Americans" when appropriate.

- Regional guarantors

Traditional public international law regards states as equal legal entities. The United Nations Charter (article 2.4) and the OAS Charter (articles 17 and 20) expressly inform that the territory of a state is inviolable and that states shall refrain from resorting to threats or the use of force between them. However, the most recent principles of public international law—the responsibility to protect and humanitarian intervention—allow the use of force, under certain requirements, against sovereign states to protect civilians from violations of their human rights. Despite the good intentions of the new institutions of

32 See Chapters 2 and 4.

international law, there are several cases in which classical powers have used force with seemingly justifiable ends, but which resulted in the legitimization of neo-colonial actions on less powerful states. Examples such as Syria, Iraq and Afghanistan clearly show that, despite human rights-based justifications, interventions by states outside the region, far from achieving peace and international and local security, aggravated the situation both internally and regionally. Conversely, several peaceful settlements that followed territorial disputes and sovereignty conflicts in the Americas demonstrate that regional guarantors were key.[33] Moreover, in tune with the previous policy guidelines, regional involvement—in the form of institutions, arbitrators and guarantors and non-interventionism—brings a balance between the principles of territorial integrity, equality among sovereign states and the responsibility to protect without legitimizing dubious interventions.

- Define and characterize self-determination

The right to self-determination is complex. There are people around the globe intending to use the institution of public international law to achieve different degrees of autonomy. Indeed, in several territorial disputes in the Americas there are notions such as indigenous self-determination and black self-determination that are gaining more central roles.[34] However, public international law does not offer a precise characterization of the right to self-determination or its key defining elements. The lack of legal precision brings several hermeneutical problems. Among them, the ones that are relevant to territorial disputes are: dismemberment of territory, the right to determine political status and the concept of "people."[35] Controversially, self-determination may threaten the constitutive elements of a sovereign state by the division of its population and dismemberment of its territory, so it goes against a principle of public international law—i.e. territorial integrity. Ultimately, hermeneutical problems and the consequent controversies around the application of the notion of self-determination are to be expected unless there is a clearly defined and widely accepted global and/or regional legal concept that determines the necessary requisites for its application.

- Encourage cooperation

The previous guidelines foster cooperation between otherwise challenger and challenged parties in territorial disputes. The author has consistently

33 See Chapters 4 and 7.
34 See Chapter 8.
35 For a detailed account of self-determination see Jorge E. Núñez, *Territorial Disputes and State Sovereignty: International Law and Politics* (London and New York, NY: Routledge, Taylor & Francis Group, 2020), Chapter 3.

maintained that these kinds of situations may evolve into cooperation as well as domination.[36] The Americas offer several successful examples where challenger and challenged agents had the option to cooperate or dominate and they chose the former, which resulted in peaceful, efficient and successful outcomes at a domestic and regional level. For example, early in 2017, the Peruvian government created the Temporary Permit of Permanence (PTP, in Spanish) to protect the rights of Venezuelans who have been forced to migrate because of the political and humanitarian crisis in their country.[37] The PTP allowed Venezuelans who entered Peru legally to legitimize their stay in the country, enabling them to work and access services such as health and education, and even to revalidate university degrees. It also allowed them to obtain a Unique Taxpayer Registry Number (RUC, in Spanish) to carry out economic activities and make tax contributions. The PTP was consistent with the Inter-American Commission on Human Rights' (IACHR) recommendations, which urged American states to implement measures to protect Venezuelan migrants. Therefore, the PTP upholds the principle of equality and non-discrimination in its protection of the rights of Venezuelan migrants in Peru. Several Latin American states followed the Peruvian example. Importantly, and in tune with the guidelines proposed here, the PTP is an intermediate solution which respects Venezuela's territorial integrity and national sovereignty while ensuring both the protection of human rights and non-interference of agents from outside the Latin American region. In addition to the PTP, this monograph has referred to several examples of territorial disputes in the Americas in which other agents, in addition to sovereign states, are taking part in cooperative solutions—e.g. the arrangements for the co-management of the Nahuel Huapi National Park between Argentina and the Mapuche, and the proposal by organizations like Proceso de Comunidades Negras (Black Communities' Process, PCN) to grant the Raizal people the right to political-organizational autonomy.[38] Finally, a regional cooperative approach would enable non-central agents to generate consensus and act as a bloc against more central, stronger or advantaged powers in resolving peacefully and permanently situations like

36 For the author's views on domination see Jorge E. Núñez, *Cosmopolitanism, State Sovereignty, International Law and Politics: A Theory* (London and New York, NY: Routledge, Taylor & Francis Group, 2023); Jorge E. Núñez, *Territorial Disputes and State Sovereignty: International Law and Politics* (London and New York, NY: Routledge, Taylor & Francis Group, 2020); and Jorge E. Núñez, *Sovereignty Conflicts and International Law and Politics: A Distributive Justice Issue* (London and New York, NY: Routledge, Taylor & Francis Group, 2017).

37 Denny Piña García and Anabella Rivera Parra, "Migración Venezolana en el Perú: El Régimen del Permiso Temporal de Permanencia (PTP)," *Ley y Gobierno* 2:2 (2023): 47–66; Jonathan Palatz Cedeño, "Possibilities of Building Regional Migration Governance due to the Venezuelan Diaspora in Ibero-America (2015–2018)," *International Journal of Humanities and Social Sciences* 13:7 (2019): 1043–1047; and many others.

38 See Chapters 4 and 8.

the Falklands/Malvinas sovereignty question, the Mexico–United States border controversy and Antarctica's future.

Conclusion

Having completed its aim, this monograph constitutes a step forward in the understanding and exploration of territorial disputes in the Americas. Indeed, as the previous sections acknowledge, there may be theoretical and empirical limitations to this work. Conversely, its worth in exposing the intricacy present in the cases explored is unquestionable.

By exposing the intricate nature of these disputes, it is possible to understand why current assessments in scholarly disciplines like law, political science and international relations are insufficient in fully comprehending them. Unsurprisingly, this is also true in terms of the adequacy of current domestic, regional and international organizations and the procedures and remedies that are meant to solve them peacefully and permanently.

The monograph's original contribution by means of the theory of multidimensionality enabled the finding of common roots to disputes as well as several other intertwined issues that may work in positive and negative synergy. In contrast to traditional scholarly unidimensional understandings that guarantee hypotheses, assumptions, methods, tests and results in isolation, multidimensionality enabled the discernment of elements and features that could contribute toward peacebuilding by observing how different pluralisms interrelate—i.e. positive synergy. Moreover, with multidimensionality it is possible to anticipate when and how these pluralisms may trigger a dispute, its continuation and its potential escalation into conflict—i.e. negative synergy.

In the same respect as Núñez (2017), Núñez (2020) and Núñez (2023), the monograph's significance lies in its contribution to legal and political sciences and international relations by continuing the development of a more integrated approach to theory building. Scholarly disagreements in their respective evaluations of the same phenomena—e.g. territorial disputes—are to be expected. However, by providing a set of theoretical and hermeneutical tools common to multiple scientific disciplines and applying them to several different case studies, this monograph and its predecessors provide solid ground for furthering scholarly research integration while avoiding tangential reasoning.

Lastly, originality and significance are defining characteristics in terms of the quality of this monograph. Of equal importance is the rigor adopted to conduct the relevant research and find the compelling evidence that enabled the testing of both the theory and the methodology proposed by the author. The depth and breadth of the sources included in these pages, which encompass different time periods, locations, scholarly disciplines and languages, are a testament of such diligence.

Indeed, as the preceding pages show, it is clear that some elements and features may be more relevant in a certain territorial dispute than others. Moreover, there may be territorial disputes that deserve further exploration.

Obviously, the assessment and explanation of every issue pertaining to every territorial dispute in the Americas goes beyond the scope of this monograph. Therein, the recommendations, conclusions and overall learning outcomes are partial and aim to provide evidence of how it is possible to apply the theory and methodology the author proposes in advancing a more comprehensive understanding of territorial disputes. Ultimately, the hope remains that in the future the author's suggestions will find their place among those who believe in cooperation that transcends individualistic interests for the sake of global peace and growth by tackling crises such as territorial disputes multidimensionally.

Bibliography

García, Denny Piña and Anabella Rivera Parra. "Migración Venezolana en el Perú: El Régimen del Permiso Temporal de Permanencia (PTP)." *Ley y Gobierno* 2:2 (2023): 47–66.

Huth, Paul K. *Standing Your Ground: Territorial Disputes and International Conflict.* Ann Arbor, MI: University of Michigan Press, 2001.

Klein, Julie Thompson. "Discourses of Transdisciplinarity: Looking Back to the Future." *Futures* 63 (2014): 68–74.

McCarthy, Lauren and Kate Grosser. "Breaking Isolation: Consciousness-Raising as a Methodology for Academic Activism." *Organization* 30:5 (2023): 1152–1167.

Núñez, Jorge E. *Cosmopolitanism, State Sovereignty, International Law and Politics: A Theory.* London and New York, NY: Routledge, Taylor & Francis Group, 2023.

Núñez, Jorge E. *Sovereignty Conflicts and International Law and Politics: A Distributive Justice Issue.* London and New York, NY: Routledge, Taylor & Francis Group, 2017.

Núñez, Jorge E. "State Sovereignty: Concept and Conceptions." *International Journal for the Semiotics of Law-Revue internationale de Sémiotique juridique* 37 (2024): 1–20.

Núñez, Jorge E. *Territorial Disputes and State Sovereignty: International Law and Politics.* London and New York, NY: Routledge, Taylor & Francis Group, 2020.

Palatz Cedeño, Jonathan. "Possibilities of Building Regional Migration Governance due to the Venezuelan Diaspora in Ibero-America (2015–2018)." *International Journal of Humanities and Social Sciences* 13:7 (2019): 1043–1047.

Rawls, John. *Justice as Fairness.* Cambridge, MA: Harvard University Press, 2003.

Vienni-Baptista, Bianca, Isabel Fletcher and Catherine Lyall, eds. *Foundations of Interdisciplinary and Transdisciplinary Research: A Reader.* Bristol: University of Bristol Press, 2023.

Vienni-Baptista, Bianca, Isabel Fletcher, Catherine Lyall and Christian Pohl. "Embracing Heterogeneity: Why Plural Understandings Strengthen Interdisciplinarity and Transdisciplinarity." *Science and Public Policy* 49:6 (2022): 865–877.

Winslow, Philip C. *Victory for Us Is to See You Suffer: In the West Bank with the Palestinians and the Israelis.* Boston, MA: Beacon Press, 2007.

Index

Note: Page numbers are in bold; italics refer to reference tables and figures, respectively; and 'n' refers to footnote numbers.

FSC
www.fsc.org
MIX
Papier | Fördert
gute Waldnutzung
FSC® C083411

Kolibri 360 GmbH
Ferdinand-Jühlke-Straße 7
99095 Erfurt, Deutschland
produktsicherheit@kolibri360.de